Praise for
DILIP HIRO

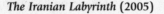

The Iranian Labyrinth (2005)

"Hiro has covered Iran extensively, and [as] the author of books on the Iranian revolution and the Iran-Iraq war, he guides us through Iran's intricacies by focusing on key institutions, leaders and social groups . . . Women, youth and the intelligentsia frustrate attempts to wrap Iran in a social and political straitjacket tailored to a strict interpretation of Islam."
—Shaul Bakhash, *Washington Post*

"One of the . . . finest books I've read about Iran . . . A precious compendium of dates and facts, a compact reference work that will be invaluable on future reporting trips to Iran . . . Hiro's prose is workmanly; the gems in his book carefully gleaned bits of knowledge."
—Lara Marlowe, *Irish Times* (Dublin)

"Dilip Hiro's book is a good primer about Iran, and it filled in several gaps in my knowledge about the country, especially its history . . . He is also very good at talking to people on the ground and uses his several trips to the country well."
—Amitabh Pal, *The Progressive*

"Once again, he does not disappoint . . . He gives a sense of emotion to the characters inside this Labyrinth. He does not just talk about women's issues; he tells the reader about a precise woman and her specific journey . . . [Hiro] succeeds at taking the reader inside and out of the Iranian Labyrinth, while encouraging the reader to venture back."
—John W. Sutherlin, *Middle East Policy*

"Punctuated by people-on-the-street interviews that reveal a breadth of popular opinion in Iran, Hiro's portrait makes for provocative reading."
—*Kirkus Reviews*

Secrets and Lies: Operation "Iraqi Freedom" and After (2004)
Longlisted for the George Orwell Prize for Political Writing

"Dilip Hiro coolly dismantles the political lies, distortions and obfuscations that allowed the United States and Britain to launch an illegal invasion of Iraq . . . Hiro is painstaking . . . Masterly."
—Roy Greenslade, *Guardian*

"Middle East commentator Dilip Hiro recounts the misuse of intelligence that led to war."

—Donald Morrison, *Financial Times*
(Best books on Politics and Religion in 2005)

"An extraordinary account of confusing events. Hiro has fashioned a well-rounded, thought-provoking story about the Bush administration's bellicose preparations, the invasion and the postwar headaches."

—Stanley Meisler, *Los Angeles Times*

"Often riveting . . . Hiro also offers some superb insights into the political divisions within post-Saddam Iraq and the chances for the emergence of genuine pluralistic, democratic society there."

—Jay Freeman, *Booklist*

"Dilip Hiro has added another formidable chapter to the invaluable record he has been compiling of developments in the critically important Middle East region. His review of the invasion of Iraq, its background, conduct, and aftermath, is once again deeply informed, meticulously documented, and perceptively analyzed . . . A major contribution."

—Noam Chomsky

The Essential Middle East: A Comprehensive Guide (2003)

"Entries on subjects as diverse as the Kharijis, the original Muslim 'fundamentalists,' and Israel's invasion of Lebanon are models of informed compression. Mr. Hiro can see both sides of an argument, applying the same stringent scrutiny to the Zionists' Irgun and the Arabs' Islamic Jihad."

—*Economist*

"A much needed reference work on this volatile region."

—*Booklist*

"Huge encyclopedic dictionary . . . covering everything from aal ('Arab families or clans of distinction') to 'Zawahiri, Ayman' and 'Zionist Congresses'."

—*Publishers Weekly*

Iraq: In the Eye of the Storm (2003)

"For a rigorous and non-partisan analysis of Iraq's recent history, you could hardly do better than pick up Dilip Hiro's *Iraq* which traces the path of its relationship with the West and its neighbors. The book ends with a prophecy that has since been proved correct: we should not expect Iraq's soldiers or civilians to welcome invading forces as 'liberators', let alone allies."

—Nicholas Lezard, *Guardian*

"I had dutifully tossed a handful of paperbacks into my duffel before coming to Iraq in 2003 . . . including Dilip Hiro's *Iraq: In the Eye of the Storm.*"

—Robert F. Worth, *New York Times*

"In describing daily life in Iraq, Hiro convincingly describes the devastating effect of sanctions upon ordinary Iraqis . . . Those who blithely approach war with Iraq and see only positive effects would do well to read this book."

—Jay Freeman, *Booklist* [Boxed Review]

"Highly readable and provocative book . . . offers a critical analysis of both the Iraqi regime and the West's duplicitous role in buttressing Saddem Hussein when was useful for advancing Washington's regional interests . . . Highly recommended for informed citizenry and all public libraries."

—Nader Entessar, *Library Journal*

"A clear account of recent developments in Iraq by a writer renowned for his scholarship on Iraq and Islamic fundamentalism."

—Peter Beaumont, *Observer*

"A compact history that delves into the strengths and failures of sanctions, life on the street in Iraq and the cult of personality surrounding Saddam. Accurate and very readable."

—Noam Chomsky, MSNBC.COM

Neighbors, Not Friends: Iraq and Iran After the Gulf Wars (2001)

"Exceedingly thorough, scrupulously balanced and dispassionate . . . electrifying and enlightening."

—Cal McCrystal, *Financial Times*

"Engaging, readable, jargon-free book . . . "

—Nader Entessar, *Library Journal*

"Hiro is a model political analyst. His approach is as incorrigibly nonpartisan at it is methodical."

—Justin Wintle, *Sunday Times*

BLOOD
OF THE
EARTH

THE BATTLE FOR THE WORLD'S VANISHING OIL RESOURCES

DILIP HIRO

NATION
BOOKS

BLOOD OF THE EARTH
The Battle for the World's Vanishing Oil Resources

Published by
Nation Books
An Imprint of Avalon Publishing Group, Inc.
245 West 17th Street, 11th Floor
New York, NY 10011

AVALON
publishing group incorporated

Nation Books is a copublishing venture of the Nation Institute and Avalon Publishing Group.

Library of Congress Cataloging-in-Publication Data is available.

ISBN-10: 1-56025-544-7
ISBN-13: 978-1-56025-544-4

9 8 7 6 5 4 3 2 1

Book design by Maria E. Torres

Printed in Canada on recycled paper
Distributed by Publishers Group West

Contents

List of Maps, Charts, and Illustrations

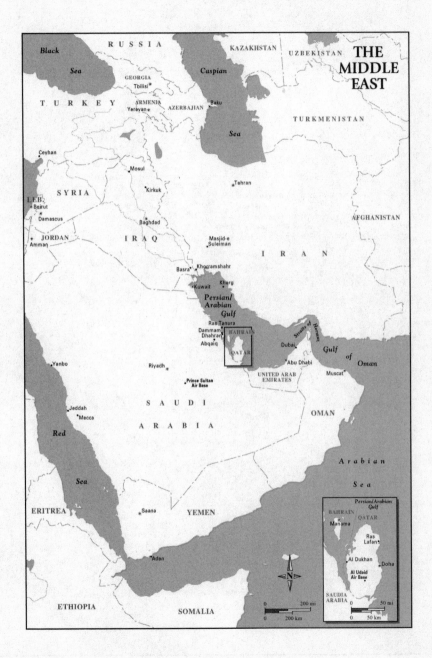

THE
MIDDLE
EAST

RUSSIA

Black
Sea

Caspian

KAZAKHSTAN

UZBEKISTAN

GEORGIA
Tbilisi

ARMENIA
Yerevan

Baku

AZERBAIJAN

Sea

TURKEY

TURKMENISTAN

Ceyhan

Mosul

Kirkuk

Tehran

SYRIA

LEB.

Beirut

Damascus

Baghdad

AFGHANISTAN

JORDAN

Amman

IRAQ

Masjid-e
Suleiman

I R A N

Basra

Khorramshahr

Kharg

Kuwait

Persian/
Arabian
Gulf

Ras Tanura

Straits of Hormuz

Dammam
Dhahran

BAHRAIN

Dubai

Abqaiq

QATAR

Abu Dhabi

Gulf
of
Oman

Yanbo

Riyadh

Prince Sultan
Air Base

UNITED ARAB
EMIRATES

Muscat

S A U D I

A R A B I A

OMAN

Jeddah

Mecca

Red

Arabian

Sea

Sea

Sea

ERITREA

Saana

YEMEN

ETHIOPIA

Adan

SOMALIA

Persian/Arabian
Gulf

BAHRAIN

QATAR

Manama

Ras
Lafan

Al Dukhan

Doha

Al Udaid
Air Base

SAUDIA
ARABIA

N

0   200 mi

0   200 km

0   50 mi

0   50 km

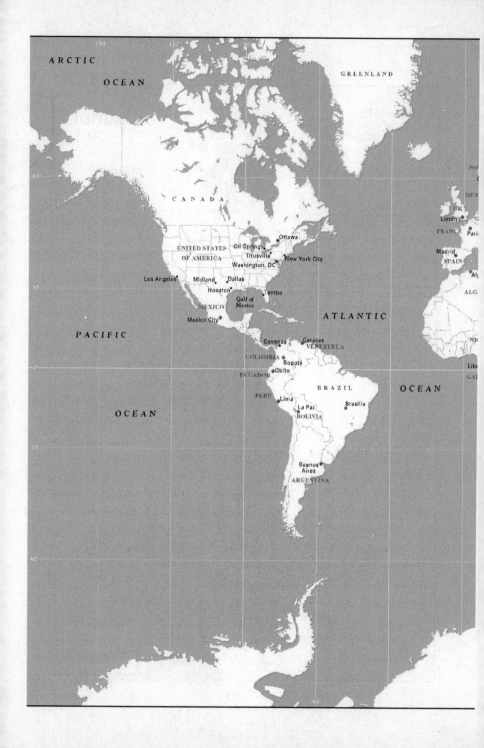

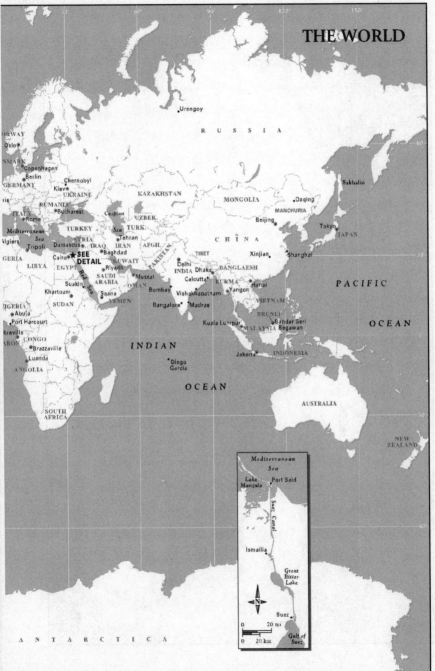

THE WORLD

Urengoy

RUSSIA

ORWAY
Oslo
NMARK
Copenhagen
Berlin
GERMANY
Kiev
Chernobyl
iis
UKRAINE
RUMANIA
Bucharest
ITALY
Rome
Caspian
UZBEK.
KAZAKHSTAN
MONGOLIA
Daqing
MANCHURIA
Sakhalin
Beijing
Tokyo
JAPAN
Algiers
Mediterranean
Sea
Tripoli
TURKEY
Sea
TURK.
SYRIA
Damascus
Tehran
IRAN
AFGH.
CHINA
Xinjian
Shanghai
Baghdad
GERIA
Cairo
SEE
DETAIL
EGYPT
IRAQ
KUWAIT
Riyadh
TIBET
Delhi
INDIA
Dhaka
BANGLAESH
LIBYA
SAUDI
ARABIA
Muscat
PAKISTAN
Calcutta
BURMA
Hanoi
PACIFIC
Red Sea
OMAN
Bombay
Yangon
Khartoum
Suakin
Saana
YEMEN
Vishakhapatnam
VIETNAM
OCEAN
IGERIA
SUDAN
Bangalore
Madras
Abuja
Port Harcourt
Kuala Lumpur
BRUNEI
Bandar Seri
Begawan
bieville
MALAYSIA
ABON
CONGO
Brazzaville
INDIAN
Jakarta
INDONESIA
Luanda
ANGOLA
Diego
Garcia
OCEAN
AUSTRALIA
SOUTH
AFRICA
NEW
ZEALAND

ANTARCTICA

Mediterranean
Sea
Lake
Manzala
Port Said
Suez Canal
Ismailia
Great
Bitter
Lake
N
Suez
0   20 mi
0   20 km
Gulf of
Suez

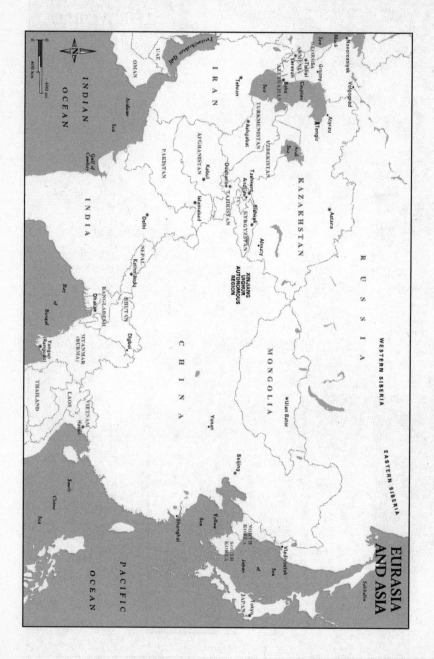

Preface

This book is about oil—its birth, life, and approaching death—and its rivals and successors, present and potential.

As oil seepages, and as bitumen, petroleum has been known to us since antiquity. It appears in Zoroastrian literature and the Bible. But it was only in 1846, when wells were drilled and petroleum extracted in commercial quantities, that it became an object of everyday utility in the form of kerosene used as an illuminant. In a little over a century it would come to dominate human life like no other commodity before or since.

It replaced coal as fuel to power steamships in 1877 when the Nobel brothers built the world's first oil-fueled steamship, named *Zoroaster*. And once it was married to the internal combustion engine in 1882, its status was destined to rise higher. In 1908 it started elbowing out coal to move the cargo ships of the United States across oceans. It was not long before it was embraced by the navies of the rival European powers. The adoption of the internal combustion engine, fueled by gasoline or diesel, changed the nature of armed conflict in World War I. As the world's top producer of oil, the United States led the way both in war and in peace. Its citizens began witnessing the rise of an egregious lobby in its domestic politics, a nexus of petroleum and political power that continues today, and that operates abroad to a slightly lesser effect in the geopolitics of oil.

Ultimately it was oil-less Japan's acute need for the commodity that led it to bomb Pearl Harbor in Hawaii in 1941, which inducted the United States into World War II on the Allied side and doomed the Axis Powers to eventual defeat in 1945. The memorable words uttered by Senator Henry G. Berenger, director of Comité Generale du Pétrole of France, about World War I— that "the blood of the earth" had proved to be "the blood of victory"—could equally be applied to World War II.

Cheap and abundant oil became the engine that drove post–World War II capitalism to higher levels of prosperity. Oil and political power became interlinked in the West. Petroleum products penetrated every facet of Western life. The Persian Gulf region became the prime source of this vital commodity, with the links between the largest producer, Saudi Arabia, and the United States, the leader of the Western world and Japan, becoming unbreakable. While the oil wells of the United States grew old and tired, those of the Arabian Peninsula and the Persian Gulf— the heartland of Islam—were young and prolific, and gushed.

After providing a brief sketch in the introduction of the evolution of energy sources, I focus on the oil state of Texas and the two Bushes (father and son), who have strong roots in the Texan petroleum industry, and were installed in the White House within twelve years of each other. The current average yield of the onshore oil wells of Texas, however, is a fraction of what oil wells in Qatar are yielding. My narrative of the visits to these two contrasting territories and my descriptions of the workings of an oil rig and a donkey pump—images universally associated with petroleum—provide a striking diptych and an entrée into the current debate raging over oil.

Chapter 1 narrates the birth pangs of commercially extracted oil with tales of high drama and colorful characters from the shores of the Caspian Sea to the mountains of Pennsylvania to the deserts of Iran and the Arabian Peninsula.

After illustrating, dramatically, the ubiquity of petroleum and petroleum products in Western life, in chapter 2, I describe how oil and gas came to be formed over tens of millions of years and got trapped in underground reservoirs, and how oil, a complex chemical amalgam, is refined in stages to give us a dazzling variety of products for everyday use.

This marvelous boon of nature, however, is not limitless. It was the genius of M. King Hubbert, an American geophysicist, to quantify the tapped and untapped deposits of petroleum and predict when its extraction would reach its apogee and then decline terminally, as had happened with earlier minerals. Those who scoffed at his scientific conclusions fell silent when his forecast that the reserves of the Lower 48 would peak in the early 1970s proved right. This, in short, is the thrust of chapter 3, which ends part I of the book.

The succeeding part focuses on the geopolitics of oil and provides a chronological account. While chapter 4 covers the events up to and including the Arab-Israeli War of October 1973, the following chapter takes the narrative to the present. The numerous case studies related in these two chapters illustrate time and again the vital role played by petroleum and petroleum products in war and peace. The wide-ranging survey covers not just the United States, western Europe, the Soviet Union, and the oil-producing countries of the Middle East, but also Mexico and Venezuela, which at different times inspired the oil-rich states in the Persian Gulf region to assert their national rights over the commodity at the expense of avaricious Western oil giants. Out of this communal thinking grew the Organization of the Petroleum Exporting Countries (OPEC) in 1960.

The increasing assertiveness of OPEC members, with abundant reserves of oil and gas, has worried policy makers in the

United States, the most profligate consumer of petroleum, whose politicians are loath to urge their voters to curb their wasteful habits. But instead of legislating to save energy and develop renewable sources, they have been mollycoddling their fellow citizens that beyond the perennially unstable and unpredictable Middle East exists a cornucopia of oil in the Caspian Basin. Chapter 6 examines in detail claims made by the George W. Bush administration in its policy document issued in May 2001, and demolishes the dream not only in the Caspian region but also in Latin America and West Africa.

In a world of aging oil wells, two giant nations—China and India, accounting for nearly two-fifths of humanity—have embarked upon fast industrialization and urbanization, thereby making unprecedented demands on the supplies of oil and natural gas. Chapter 7 outlines the history of China's domestic oil industry and its failure to meet the burgeoning demand for hydrocarbons, resulting in an aggressive campaign to acquire equity oil and gas abroad that has seen the Chinese petroleum companies taking stakes in more than forty countries. Chapter 8 deals with India along the lines of the previous chapter.

Collectively, the first two parts of the book convey a stark message: The finite oil sources are running out at an alarming rate.

The final part examines both finite and infinite alternatives to petroleum. Chapter 9 focuses on finite resources: natural gas, uranium, and coal. Though natural gas is being talked about as the fuel of the twenty-first century, a virtual exhaustion of this energy source is predicted only a generation after that of oil, around 2050. The same applies to uranium, the fuel for nuclear power plants. In both cases I conduct a wide-ranging survey of the countries where these fuels are used and examine their merits and demerits. Given the relatively short lives of both these comparatively new fuels, the world will be forced to return to coal, which was the leading source of energy in the nineteenth century.

But, as a dirty fuel that pollutes the air to an unacceptable level, its wide-scale use in the future could only be guaranteed if it were turned into "clean coal" through a process called Integrated Gasification Combined Cycle (IGCC), which converts coal oil into a synthetic gas—syngas—which is subjected to extreme heat and pressure, resulting in the separation of hydrogen ready to be used as fuel and liquid carbon dioxide (CO_2) to be stored underground or under the seabed.

Since vehicles are huge consumers of hydrocarbons, chapter 10 examines the virtues of hybrid cars, which combine an internal combustion engine with an electrical system, each to be used in different circumstances. Equally importantly, it examines the prospects of hydrogen cells powering cars of the future.

All of the above alternatives are acquiring urgency in view of the warming of the Earth's atmosphere, caused by a rising level of greenhouse gases produced by the burning of fossil fuels. Chapter 11 marshals the ever-increasing evidence of the rising temperature and contrasts the seriousness with which European nations and China and India are treating this problem, which knows no boundaries, with the laxity displayed by the present administration in the United States, whose Senate refuses to ratify the 1997 Kyoto Protocol on climate change. It highlights the progress that European countries and Japan have made in developing renewable sources of wind, sun, and biofuels and in using them to an increasing degree and compares that to the tardiness shown by the U.S. federal government in this sphere.

The final chapter offers a summary and concludes with a warning that, since the energy crisis already exists in giant nations like China and India, there should be no debate about whether or not the Western nations should build more wind turbines or opt for nuclear power stations, but every option must be pursued at once, making sure that emissions are limited to a minimum for the sake of future generations.

The chronology is not indexed.

Since the twenty-six-nation European Union now uniformly uses the metric system of weights and measurements, and the United States is still on the traditional British system of inches and pounds, it has become necessary for authors and journalists to provide two sets of figures. I have done so. A tonne, meaning a metric ton, weighs 2,200 pounds, whereas a ton equals 2,240 pounds. And 1 cubic meter equals 35.3 cubic feet.

I am particularly indebted to the following (in alphabetical order) for assisting me with my research: Talmiz Ahmad, Mani Shankar Aiyar, Bruce Brady, Juma Ali al Buainain, Ron Smith, and Peter Stewart. My friend and fellow author Paul Kriwaczek very kindly drew the sketches and charts. My profuse thanks to Carl Bromley, my editor, for going beyond the call of duty to help me improve the text.

Dilip Hiro
London
June 2006

Introduction:

Midland to Al Dukhan; Emptying Texan Oil Wells to Gushing Persian Gulf Oil Fields

Oil has proven to be more than a fuel. In conjunction with the internal combustion engine, it has revolutionized warfare and engendered a civilization centered around automobiles. It has emerged as a prize that petroleum-poor countries covet and petroleum-rich states thrive on. It has shaped the course of wars and proved to be a primary engine of peacetime prosperity. Its reach has gone beyond mechanical power and into the realm of political power.

Anyone looking for a nexus between oil and political-economic power in the United States would end up in Texas, a state with two petroleum centers—one dealing with the overseas world, Houston; and the other focused on the United States, Midland. The latter is a town associated not only with two presidents but also with the commander of Central Command (Centcom), General Tommy Franks, who conducted both post-9/11 wars led by the United States—the second of which was, in the final analysis, about oil.

As the petroleum world's capital city, Houston draws oil barons and sheikhs from all over the globe. Since the 1973–74 oil price explosion, however, oil sheikhs have become the rule rather than the exception in Houston. Of the eight countries of the Persian Gulf region possessing two-thirds of the globe's proved petroleum and two-fifths of natural gas reserves, six are monarchies. In all cases the hereditary ruler is the supreme authority. As such, he and his courtiers hold the keys to hydrocarbon riches. It is not accidental that Saudi king Abdullah ibn Abdul Aziz, worth $21 billion, is one of the richest persons on the planet. It is these oil sheikhs, overflowing with petro-dollars, who have forged links with the oil interests in Houston and, through them, with influential American politicians.

Say the word *oil*, and two images crop up: one static (an oil rig), and the other dynamic (a donkey pump in motion). An iconic emblem of petroleum is a tall steel rig with a rotating drill in the midst of a desert or atop a robust platform in the middle of a sea. How exactly does that device reach a source of oil underground and how is the precious liquid then lifted to the surface are the questions that arise immediately in the mind of the curious. So too does the rocking of a donkey pump in the oil regions of the United States.

I set out to inquire—in the vicinity of Midland, Texas.

WELCOME TO MIDLAND
HOME OF PRESIDENTS AND FIRST LADIES
VISITOR CENTER
EXIT 136

So reads a vast billboard on Interstate 20 at the entrance to Midland, west Texas, bearing two supersize photographs, captioned "Sponsored by Friends of George W. and Laura Bush."

The one in the left hand corner shows a smiling George Herbert Walker Bush in an open-necked shirt, red sweater, and black jacket, with his blonde wife, Barbara, donning a white shirt with collars protruding out of a blue polo-neck sweater, resting her left forearm on George's shoulder in a comradely fashion, both gazing into the middle distance. The other photograph, placed just below the first, carries an image of George Walker Bush in a white shirt, gray tie, and black jacket, with a distant look in his narrow, hooded eyes, hogging most of the space, standing well apart from his smiling wife, Laura—in a red polo-neck sweater with a gaze into the middle distance—squeezed into a corner.

Long before Midland became famous due to its association with the forty-first and forty-third presidents of the United States, it was the financial and administrative hub of the petroleum industry in west Texas—part of the Permian Basin, named after the sea that covered much of Texas many millions of years ago. And its nearby twin town of Odessa was the engineering and servicing center of the oil industry.[1] To highlight their town's financial muscle, Midland city council members boastingly named the main east-west thoroughfare Wall Avenue, after Wall Street in New York.

It was the lure of oil that enticed patrician George H. W. Bush in 1948 to migrate from Connecticut to the twin towns of Midland-Odessa in the sun-baked, rain-starved scrubland of west Texas, with its unforgiving skies and perpetual winds, its stark, wide open plains frequently disturbed by dust storms—known to outsiders as the region of catfish, barbecues, and Lone Star beer.

George H. W. Bush was born in Milton, Massachusetts, to Prescott Bush—an investment banker who was director of Dresser Industries, the largest oil-services corporation in the United States, for over two decades—and brought up in the affluent, leafy suburb of Greenwich, Connecticut. In 1942, when he was eighteen, he enrolled in the military and served as a navy pilot in the Pacific. Three years later he married Barbara McCall, a daughter of a publishing mogul. Their son, George Walker, arrived in 1946. Bush Sr. graduated from Yale University two years later, majoring in economics.

He was offered a job in the family's banking firm. He turned it down. Instead, as one version would have it, he, Barbara, and their infant son George W. put their meager worldly possessions into an old automobile and drove to the oil wells of Texas. The place they rented in a slum of Odessa offered a bathroom shared with a local prostitute.

Another, more credible version has it that George Bush Sr. went to Odessa to work for International Derrick & Equipment Company, owned by Dresser Industries.

He started as a humble clerk in the supply store of the company. Soon, backed discreetly by his banker father and his contacts, Bush Sr. focused on Midland, then a town of twenty thousand souls (a fifth of its present size). The social and business hub of Midland was the Petroleum Club, established in 1947 to facilitate meetings between those who aspired to forge ahead in the petroleum industry as "oilmen," meaning investors in the oil industry. His first move was to form an oil-development company specializing in royalty rights for those on whose land petroleum and gas were struck.

In 1951 he moved to Midland. He bought a three-bedroom detached house, measuring 1,655 square feet, with a lawn and porch at the front and a shed at the back, at 1412 West Ohio Avenue, and went on to furnish it with a swimming pool, then a rarity.[2]

It was within walking distance of the Petroleum Club, at the corner of Marienfeld Street and West Wall Avenue. Today the club is a grandiose place, with Italian marble and oak paneling surrounding a two-story atrium with a waterfall and green plants, and half a dozen private dining rooms—including the one called the Wildcatters' Room—on the ground floor. The lounge, ballroom, and dining room on the second floor overlook the artificial waterfall and greenery. At $500, the initiation fee is modest, but the annual dues are a whopping $2,000.

George Bush Sr. proved to be an energetic, gregarious, and

popular Midlander and a devout Episcopalian, the favored church of the upper- and upper-middle-class white Protestants. In 1953, in partnership with Hugh Liedtke and another friend, he formed Zapata Petroleum. The name was inspired by the Hollywood movie *Viva Zapata*, released a year before, with Marlon Brando playing the Mexican revolutionary Emiliano Zapata (1879–1919), which proved a box office hit with Midlanders, especially those from Southside, the other side of the railroad tracks splicing Midland—i.e., the Hispanics and blacks. But, in stark contrast to the penniless Zapata of real life, the company named after him was flush with lucre, with the private bank of Bush Sr.'s uncle, Herbert Walker, investing $350,000, and his father another $50,000.

During its first year of operation, Zapata Petroleum drilled 128 wells in the Permian Basin without hitting a dry hole. Such an unbroken run of good luck is rare. Bulging with cash, Bush Sr. moved to a bigger, better house in 1955.

Half a century later, on a dry sunny day in June, when I arrived at 1412 West Ohio Avenue, I found it fenced and bearing a tricolor sign:

GEORGE W. BUSH CHILDHOOD HOME INC.
A TOTAL RESTORATION
PROJECT OF THE COMMUNITY
AND
PERMIAN BASIN BOARD OF REALTORS

The realtors' plan to transform it into a tourist attraction once it had been restored to its 1951–55 condition, with the same wallpaper, carpeting, and appliances—at the cost of $1.8 million— would be realized in April 2006, and capped by the opening of THE GEORGE W. BUSH CHILDHOOD HOME to the public.

Just across the street, a much smaller sign announced, THE

EPISCOPALIAN CHURCH OF THE HOLY TRINITY, next to the church's logo of a yellow shield with a cross in red.

When I mentioned the Episcopalian Church to Ron Smith the next day, he said curtly: "I belong to the Church of Christ." (The advertisements of the numerous churches in Midland fill ten pages of the local Yellow Pages directory.) Ron Smith is a pleasant-looking man of sixty-seven, well scrubbed, his stout upper frame supported by thin legs. A Midlander, he works in Odessa as the marketing and contracts manager of Alariat Services, which services the oil industry. "Odessa is a blue-collar town, Midland a white-collar," he said. "In Midland you get geologists and engineers; in Odessa, drillers and semiskilled workers." What about Houston? I inquired. "It's the international oil center of America; it deals with the foreigners."

Unusually for late June in west Texas, the day was mild, with clouds blocking the sun. A soft breeze kept Ron Smith and me comfortable in our long-sleeved shirts. Smith had graciously volunteered to drive me to an oil well being drilled by his company. Luckily for me, he chose a site in the Pegasus oil field, about fifteen miles (twenty-five kilometers) southwest of Midland, which, I was to learn later, is typical of the Permian Basin.

Once we left the urban environment of Midland, the sight of donkey pumps, invariably painted black and often nodding, became a bizarre feature of the landscape. The famed red earth of Texas was carpeted with grassy foliage peppered with cactus—a reminder to the visitor that the area was once in essence a desert. Yet, without exception, the plots of land were securely fenced. This, I presumed, had to do with the subterranean riches of oil and natural gas, a discovery that was made in the mid-1920s. To find suddenly that your patch of land held petroleum reserves in its bowels was tantamount to winning the lottery. "The early landowners possessed mineral rights and they got royalties on oil," Smith told me. How much, I asked. "Twelve to 20 percent of the price of oil. The families who got rich on oil leases are the Scarboroughs, the Parkers, and the Mabees. However, the new land sales exclude mineral rights."

At our destination, I stood next to Smith. As I turned my head, he pointed out the living quarters of the rig supervisors and drillers to my left—and then, in succession, a cylindrical diesel storage tank, a robustly built changing room, an electric generator, a cylindrical water tank, and finally, a pair of mud pumps powered by orange-painted diesel engines.

The function of the muddy water puzzled me. "As a hole is drilled with a rotating drilling bit, mud is circulated down the hollow drill pipe and back up between the pipe and the surrounding subsurface," Smith explained. "The mud cools the drilling bit, pushes up to the surface the chipped subterranean material produced by the toothed bit, while holding back any water, gas, or oil in the surrounding rock. It's crucial to see that the mud has the correct density, viscosity, and filtering properties and it's pumped at the right pressure."

Smith pointed to a steel cabin—painted navy blue and posted with a sign saying LARIAT RIG 12, next to the raised floor of the 150-foot-high derrick of the rig, topped by a fluttering Stars and Stripes unaccompanied, for a change, by the single-starred flag of the Lone Star State—and said, "That's the control cabin. That's where the rig supervisor sits surrounded by instruments which monitor the progress of drilling and the contents of the various subsurface layers. They instantly detect any traces of oil or gas. As the drilling goes on around the clock, the rig supervisor shares his tasks with a relief supervisor."

Altogether, the site had a crew of fourteen men, Smith continued. Besides the rig supervisor, a relief supervisor, and three drilling engineers, there were nine roughnecks. Roughnecks! I repeated, surprised. "Yes. That is the term for skilled helpers who help the drillers by lifting pipes and connecting them, and handling the massive rotating drilling bits made up of intermeshing teeth that rotate along different axes."

Any semiskilled helpers? "We don't have them," Smith replied. "But they're called roustabouts. They get $12 an hour, and roughnecks $18. They all live nearby and go home after their shifts. Others live on the site." And are there any on fixed salaries? "Only the rig supervisors. They get about $80,000 a year. And a driller is paid by the hour, $25."

What about maintenance? "We have our maintenance engineers in Odessa. If there's a broken hole, or if there's a loss of circulation of the mud water, then the rig supervisor calls the maintenance in Odessa."

Finally, the average duration of a drilling project: "Barring a major hiccup, we finish the job in fifteen to twenty days," Smith concluded. "We drill between five thousand and ten thousand feet and charge about $500,000 to $700,000."

Who decides where to drill and how, I asked Smith as we returned to his silvery car, which, despite the cloudy sky, gleamed.

"The corporations like Schlumberger offer three-dimensional seismic images to clients," Smith explained. "That helps the oil explorer to choose a site. In west Texas, if you are in a tried and tested area, one out of two drilled holes will end up productive. But if you are in a previously unexplored area, then nine out of ten wells will be dry. So nowadays when it comes to tackling unexplored areas, only major vertically integrated oil companies with a lot of working capital get involved."

Suppose the well being drilled by LARIAT RIG 12 showed oil; what would follow? "Cementing the hole and casing it with steel piping," Smith replied. "That's the sort of job Halliburton does well, turning a hole into a productive oil well."

When does a donkey pump get installed? "If the underground

pressure is high, it makes the oil rise to the surface naturally. That is what we call a flowing well—a rarity in our area these days. Anyway, in time the pressure at the bottom of the hole is no longer enough to lift the oil to the surface. That's when a pumping unit is installed. It consists of a motor-driven walking beam, which is connected to a pump at the bottom of the well by a string of steel rods running through the tubing. The rocking motion of the walking beam activates the underground pump and lifts the oil up the tubing to the surface."

Soon Smith and I faced a walking beam—or donkey pump— having left his car to walk gingerly over steel rollers built into a ramp to keep the cattle and goats and sheep away from it. So here is a pumping well, I remarked. "Precisely," Smith said. "And those steel rods being moved by the rocking beam, they're called sucker rods." He then showed me a small pipeline issuing from the site which was connected to a storage tank several miles away. "That's where another company collects the oil from a storage tank and transports it to a refinery."

With some donkey pumps nodding and others not, did an idle pump mean an exhausted well? "Not at all. The pumps are on a timing device; they only run eight to twelve hours a day," Smith replied. "Anyway, most of these are stripper wells." Stripper?! "Yes, that's the term we use for wells which are almost exhausted. It's like squeezing the last droplet from a lemon. They yield a maximum of fifteen barrels per day [bpd], more often only one or two barrels. It costs $16 to get a barrel out of the ground. So it's not worth bothering unless the oil price is $20-plus." I was to discover later that four-fifths of the 704,000 operating wells in the United States are stripper wells—a deeply worrying sign of the advanced age and declining volume of U.S. onshore oil reserves—and that the total national output is 7.24 million bpd. That is, an American oil well produces a measly 10 bpd.[3]

• • •

The next day I found myself standing in front of a vast geological wall map of Texas, with rocks of different formations and ages shown in different colors—green, red, orange, brown, and gray. My host was Bruce Brady, president of the Great Western Drilling Company in Midland, established in 1936, when there were 2,000 producing wells and 1,300 dry holes in the Permian Basin. A tall, lean man of about sixty, tanned, with an ascetic face, he was a trained geologist.

"Approximately 20 percent of America's oil and gas reserves are located here in the Permian Basin, 250 miles [400 kilometers] wide and 350 miles [560 kilometers] long," he said.

Referring to my visit to the Pegasus oil field, where I saw scores of donkey pumps lifting oil, I asked why more wells were being drilled. "The first oil well was found in the Permian Basin in 1926—without the benefit of modern technology," Brady explained. "So we ended up bypassing much oil due to our insufficient knowledge of the exact locations of the oil and gas deposits, and also because of the artificial stimulation we caused by shooting the wells with nitroglycerine [as an explosive]. In those days, the rule of thumb was one well for every forty acres. That applied to all oil reservoirs, homogeneous or not. Then we found that for inhomogeneous oil fields we needed a closer spacing of wells. That gave a spurt to fresh drilling—which is continuing. Also we have to remember that reservoir pockets keep shifting."

What about improvements in oil exploration and drilling technologies? "That too," he said. "In our drilling, sometimes we drill further into an already existing productive well. One well was drilled 7,000 feet half a century ago. Recently, when we went to 8,000 feet, we penetrated a new reservoir. Overall, drilling deeper gives us more oil. There was a time when drilling 15,000 feet was the limit. Then twenty years ago we reached 20,000 feet. Now we are going even further down."

How would he rate west Texas as an oil basin? "What we have here are low-volume oil wells with a long life, maybe as long as fifty years. The downside is that you get a maximum of 100 barrels a day from a well. The lifting cost is high, more than $15 a barrel. As oil fields mature, grow old, oil becomes more expensive to produce. "

What were the chances of finding a productive well in the region? "Fifty-fifty," Brady replied. "Still, my company drills only 30 percent of wells on its own. In 70 percent of the cases we go into partnership with others to reduce the risk. Before exploration, the interested persons set up a syndicate. You may get as many as two hundred investors, individuals and companies, for a single venture."

That is where the Petroleum Club of Midland comes in. It is here that investors meet and form syndicates to fund oil exploration and drilling—just one well, or many.

Unsurprisingly, over the past several years the Petroleum Club had developed links with the Midland Country Club, which owns an eighteen-hole golf course on the outskirts seven miles north of the Petroleum Club. Some weeks after my Midland trip, I would learn later, it held its sixth annual golf tournament at the Country Club.

Gushing Oil Wells of the Persian Gulf

That reminded me of my visit earlier in the year to the headquarters of the Al Dukhan oil field of Qatar Petroleum (QP) on the western shoreline of the Persian Gulf. The sprawling, fifty-four-building complex contained not just the administrative and operational offices, but also such recreational facilities as sailing and surfing—and golfing.

A striking feature of the golf course was that it lacked grass. Instead, it was saturated with seeping petroleum. That made it worth an entry in the *Guinness Book of Records*. "It started with nine holes," Fadi Al Yousfi told me. "Then they expanded it to an eighteen-hole. The additional holes were located outside the walled compound. To reach them, the perimeter wall had to be broken to install locked gates."

A tall, robust, fair-skinned man with a raven black mustache and crew cut, Fadi Al Yousfi, wearing shirt and trousers, stood out from his colleagues in the Public Relations Department of Qatar Petroleum, all of whom were dressed in long white shirts and *dishdashas*, the traditional Arab head covering secured by a black rounded rope. Yet he had not ever wielded a golf club.

By "they," he meant the British, who had owned the oil company that operated in Qatar from 1925 to 1976 under different names—the Anglo-Persian Oil Company (APOC), followed in 1935 by Petroleum Development (Qatar), later renamed Qatar National Petroleum Company (QNPC).

It started drilling in the Al Dukhan area in the autumn of 1938 and found oil there near the sea. Astonishingly, I found that the first well is *still* productive, with its oil flow controlled by a complicated valve known as "Christmas tree," painted a sandy brown. It is located inside the compound of the company's headquarters next to an ochre-colored mound.

A large sign bearing the company's logo and white letters in Arabic (at the top) and English against a deep blue background read:

AL DUKHAN NO. 1 WELL
SPUDDED—6TH OCT 1938
COMPLETED—8TH JAN 1940
TOTAL DEPTH—5686 FEET

Further work in the oil industry was interrupted by World War II and did not resume properly until 1947. A boost came in 1951 when the nationalization of the Anglo-Iranian Oil Company created an urgent need to increase production outside Iran. Al Dukhan's output rose sharply from 32,000 bpd in 1950. That is when the administrative-operational-residential complex was built by the QNPC by the seaside in Al Dukhan.

On my arrival there in February 2005, I found that the site's low, whitewashed buildings, manicured lawns, and neatly cut hedges gave off a lingering aura of the British rule in tropical or subtropical colonies like India.

Qatar, a protectorate of Britain since 1916, became independent in 1971. The dramatic increase in its oil revenue due to a steep price rise in 1973–74 had enabled its government to buy the QNPC and rename it Qatar General Petroleum Company (QGPC). In the new millennium the Qatar General Petroleum Company became simply Qatar Petroleum.

What intrigued me most was that more than six decades on, Al Dukhan No. 1 Well was still flowing, and that it did not need a donkey pump to lift its petroleum.

I mentioned this to Juma Ali al Buainain, head of production operations, as he plied me with black cardamom coffee served in dainty cups in his well-appointed office. A dark, plump man of middle age sporting a well-trimmed mustache and dressed in a starched white long shirt and *dishdasha*, he was apologetic about his smoking.

"The Al Dukhan oil field consists of three oil reservoirs and one gas reservoir—at Khuff, found in 1959," Al Buainain explained. "We began using the gas from Khuff to boost the underground pressure in the nearby oil reservoirs to raise the oil to the surface. Natural gas is highly compressible and can be reduced by a factor of 300. So it is an efficient mechanism for expelling oil from its reservoir." Hence, no donkey pumps, rocking up and down, I said. "Precisely. We also have water-injection facility to boost the subsurface pressure. That was installed in 1989."

How large is the Al Dukhan oil field? "Eighty kilometers [50 miles] long and eight kilometers [five miles] wide, with recoverable petroleum reserves of 2.2 billion barrels." And the cost of lifting a barrel of oil? "Just a dollar."[4] And the average output per well? "About 150 wells producing 990,000 barrels per day last year [2004] . . . that's 6,600 bpd per well." *That was 660 times the American average*, I gasped. "Well, the oil in the Arab Gulf is like water gushing out from a tap the moment you open it," al Buainain said with undisguised pride. "The oil in America is like water trickling drop by drop when you open the tap and shake the pipe. Their oil fields are old. Ours are young and prolific.[5] Also, our labor costs are low as our drilling crew are mainly from India, Pakistan, and Bangladesh."

How low? "The unskilled worker gets $500 a month, which is a week's wage in America."

Being the first and the largest petroleum find in Qatar, Al Dukhan continues to be a success story. It has attracted a motley mix of nationalities. During my lunch at the well-stocked self-service restaurant, I noticed Europeans, Americans, Chinese, Indians, and foreign Arabs.

Qatar is a flat, arid, and windswept limestone peninsula of about 1,500 square kilometers (600 sqare miles), barely the size of a largish county in Texas, jutting out from the vast Arabian Peninsula. Traveling west from the capital, Doha, to Al Dukhan, fifty-two miles (eighty-four kilometers) away, I saw nothing more salubrious than clumps of date palms, coarse grass, and occasional stunted brushwood. Yet, thanks to its bountiful hydrocarbon treasure, Qatar has undergone a breathtaking transformation in less than three generations. Now, with a population of 800,000, its per capita income of $35,000 is on a par with that of the United States.

But income and wealth distribution are highly skewed. Even though only half of the hydrocarbon revenue is spent on administration and economic development, the sums are truly staggering. In 1999 Emir Hamad bin Khalifa al Thani appointed his first cousin Saud bin Muhammad al Thani chairman of the National Council for Culture, Arts, and Heritage, and authorized him to buy art for five museums, including a Museum of Islamic Art, a National Library and a Natural History Museum. Saud al Thani's reckless three-year buying spree established him as the world's biggest buyer of art at the staggering cost of $1.2 billion. His mere appearance at auctions put many serious bidders to flight.[6]

Such tales pertained to a principality whose population in 1926 (when oil was first discovered in western Texas) was less than 25,000, with two-fifths of them living in the fishing village of Doha. What sustained them, precariously, were year-round fishing and seasonal pearling from May to October. A section of the population was descended from the slaves that local Arabs had brought from East Africa and Zanzibar in the nineteenth century to work as divers in the arduous pearling trade. Pearling required the superhuman feat of deep diving, holding one's breath for several minutes, and resurfacing with a catch of pearl oysters.

I mentioned the pearling trade to Eisa Sultan al Sulaiti, my traveling companion from Doha to Al Dukhan and back. He was twenty-seven, black and bearded, and clothed in the traditional long Arab white shirt and *dishdasha*. "My grandfather was a pearl diver," he said. "During the season he would go to Doha from his village in the north near Bahrain."

All that changed, however, around 1930, with the arrival of cheap artificial pearls from Japan, I told Al Sulaiti at some length. He responded to this sad tale of history with a long sigh.

Al Sulaiti knew vaguely the fate of the pearl divers. I doubted, however, that he was aware that it had all had to do with a noodle seller in Japan named Kokichi Mikimoto, a bald, clean-shaven, stern-looking man. After many years of experimenting, he discovered that by inserting a bead in the mantle of a pearl oyster, he could produce artificial pearls. The discovery earned him many accolades in Japan and spawned a new industry, but caused widespread misery not only in Qatar but also in neighboring Bahrain and Kuwait, as their boats were laid off, merchants went bankrupt, and divers returned inland. The demise of the centuries-old natural pearl industry compelled the local rulers to strenuously examine oil exploration prospects to repair their shattered economies.

So what did your father do, I asked al Sulaiti. "He worked for the oil company," he replied, brightening up. "They paid well. And after every three weeks at the drilling site, he visited the family for a week."

Being the eldest son in the family, Eisa went to college. After graduation, he joined the Public Relations Department of Qatar Petroleum at its head office in Doha, and rose rapidly in the civil service hierarchy.

On our return journey, as we approached Doha—now an attractive modern city of 370,000—al Sulaiti asked, "What do you think of our new Corniche?" He was referring to the curving shoreline. "By night, a fairyland; and by day, an architect's fondest dream come true," I replied. He flashed a broad smile.

Following a report by an Italian company of architects, Doha municipality's planning department had adhered to its recommendations for the shape and size of the buildings along the Corniche and just behind—as well as colors and building materials. The result was a curvaceous seafront lined with spanking new buildings of assorted shapes and heights but so distanced and proportioned that they blended together like an imaginatively conceived and meticulously executed abstract painting.

As he drove along the Corniche, Eisa pointed out a succession of roundabouts, slowing down when he approached the one called

Port. Pointing to the moored boats, he said, "That was the old jetty for the dhows, our traditional boats, the place where my grandfather worked as a pearl diver. Here he took a boat north to go to his village—via Manama in Bahrain, where we have relatives."

Further on, he slowed again. Pointing toward a vast, solidly built structure in pastel gray, set away from the shoreline and surrounded by vast, manicured lawns, Eisa said, "This is the *diwan* [administrative office] of our emir." I threw a quick glance, wondering whether the *diwan* was built of real stone. "This is our White House," Eisa announced proudly.[7] Much bigger than the White House, I observed. He smiled.

George W. Bush, a Faltering Oilman

Bahrain and the real White House. The two names, I vaguely recalled, were interlinked.

During his career as an oilman, the present occupant of the White House, George Walker Bush, was saved from bankruptcy by a contract awarded to his company by Bahrain's prime minister, Sheikh Khalifa bin Salman al Khalifa.

So, a fast rewind—to the Midland of the 1950s. After attending Sam Houston Elementary School, George W. enrolled at San Jacinto Junior High School and continued until 1959, when his rapidly prospering father moved to Houston to make his first million, a hugely impressive sum in those days. There, with his rising political status, Bush Sr. would be courted by the superrich Saudis and others from the Arabian Peninsula. A key role would be played by Prince Bandar—son of Prince Sultan, Saudi defense minister, at the center of tens of billions of dollars' worth of purchases of U.S.-made weapons—after his being posted to Washington in 1982 as his country's ambassador, a job he would keep for a record twenty-three years. A pasty-faced man of medium height and plumpish build with a well-trimmed mustache and a goatee, with a kink in his crew-cut hair, he would become a friend of the Bush Sr. family to the point of being nick-named "Bandar Bush." He spent time at the Bush family vacation home in Kennebunkport, Maine, and went hunting with Bush Sr.

What George W. would share with his father were the elite Phillips Academy in Andover, Massachusetts, and Yale University, where he majored in history in 1968. And he would inherit, too, the cozy camaraderie that Bush Sr. had developed with Bandar. Indeed, many years later, "Bandar Bush" would drop by George W. Bush's White House and his ranch at Crawford, Texas, as frequently and informally as he used to with his father. What cemented the relationship between the two sides was the investment of over $1.4 billion by the members and allies of the House of Saud in the institutions and companies linked to the Bushes and their associates, primarily into the Carlyle Group, the globe's richest private equity firm; Halliburton, the world's largest oil-servicing corporation (which would be associated with Dick Cheney in the 1990s); and the ailing Harken Energy, linked to the hapless George W. Bush.[8]

Back in Houston after graduation, George W. joined the Air National Guard in Texas—thus avoiding military service in Vietnam—with a six-year commitment. His service record remains mired in controversy. What is undisputed, though, is that he was granted an early release—by a year—to enroll at Harvard University Business School.

After graduating with a Master's degree in business administration from Harvard, George W. decided to strike out on his own at the age of thirty-one. He returned to Midland to live in an apartment above a garage. He married a local librarian, Laura Welch, the only child of a builder, and switched to her church, United Methodist.

Aping his father, George W. set up Arbusto (Spanish for "bush") Energy Inc. with $20,000 of his own and $4.4 million from relatives in Houston and on the East Coast as well as local friends who belonged to the Petroleum Club. But the next year, he changed direction and contested a U.S. House of Representative seat in his district. He lost to Democrat Kent Hance, who scornfully portrayed him as "an Ivy League carpetbagger."

He then took a crash course in oil drilling, leasing, and other basics of the industry at Midland College. Arbusto Energy got going properly in March 1979. Most of its drilling ventures resulted in dry holes. Yet, thanks to tax loopholes, Arbusto Energy generated more than twice as much in tax deductions as in profits.

He spent most of his nights in bars, drinking with his buddies in the oil business.

In January 1982, facing a bleak future, George W. changed the name of Arbusto Energy to Bush Exploration, believing, rightly, that with his father installed as vice president in the White House, "Bush" in the title would attract more investors than "Arbusto." A family friend in New York invested $1 million in his firm—then worth only $400,000. But it continued to drill one dry hole after another. He became an alcoholic.

When George Bush Sr. was put in charge of deregulating the energy industry by President Ronald Reagan, he forged close contacts with Kenneth Lay, the chief executive officer of Enron Corporation, a Houston-based energy supplier. This relationship would prove beneficial to both Bushes.

In 1984, friendly investors arranged a deal in which Bush Exploration was acquired by a drilling company called Spectrum 7. George W. became its chairman and chief executive officer. When petroleum prices crashed to $14 a barrel in 1985 from a record high of $41 in 1981, investment in the industry dried up. Houston and Dallas witnessed bank failures and real estate meltdown, with oil giants shedding staff. The depressed petroleum price also lowered the value of productive wells. Bush went on drinking binges, including three-day, twenty-four-hour bar parties for golfers at the Midland Country Club, where he was fondly called Dubya.

In 1985 Spectrum 7 lost $1.6 million and faced bankruptcy. It was not alone. Financial ruin stared many in the face. This led some Midlanders to rediscover their Christian faith. A group of them, including George W., started a community Bible study program, meeting weekly to study the Bible and pray. Church attendance, always high, rose further.

As oil prices crashed to a record low of $10 in the spring of 1986, gloom and despondency enveloped Midland and western Texas. Local church elders invited evangelist Arthur Blessitt to Midland. He had acquired a high profile and secured a place in the *Guinness Book of Records* by carrying a ninety-six-pound cross of Jesus into sixty countries.[9] His sermons drew large crowds. George W. asked friends to arrange a meeting with him in a hotel coffee shop. It was Blessitt, and not the renowned Billy Graham, who turned George W. into a born-again Christian, which in turn helped him kick the drinking habit where previous attempts had failed.

While George W. battled valiantly against the demon of drink, his father rushed to Riyadh to complain to King Fahd that the oil glut created by his government had made it too cheap and was driving U.S. petroleum companies to the wall. Fahd promised to help.

Around that time Harken Energy Inc., a Dallas-based company aggressively buying up troubled petroleum firms, noticed the Bush name at Spectrum 7. A deal, finalized in September 1986, brought George W. $500,000 worth of Harken Energy stock, a seat on the board of directors, and a consulting contract worth $60,000 to $120,000 a year.

Though oil prices moved upward and Bush Sr. became president in January 1989, the fortunes of Harken did not rise. During that year, the renamed Harken Oil & Gas lost more than $12 million. It was then that superaffluent citizens and royals of the Gulf states began appearing as fairly godmothers for the Bushes: they had cultivated the habit of investing in U.S. companies linked to influential public figures.

Abdullah Taha Baksh, a property tycoon in Jiddah, bought nearly one-fifth of the ailing company's equity. He was also involved with the shady Bank of Credit and Commerce International (BCCI), whose leading stockholders included Sheikh Khalifa bin Salman al Khalifa, the prime minister of Bahrain.[10]

Even though Harken lacked experience in offshore drilling inside or outside the United States, it acquired "exclusive offshore drilling rights" in Bahrain in the face of competition from the long-established Amoco Corporation thanks to the direct intervention of Bahraini premier Sheikh al Khalifa.

This contract aroused enough suspicion to spur the *Wall Street Journal* editor to assign three reporters to investigate. While absolving George W. Bush or anyone else from Harken of any "wrongdoing or influence peddling," the investigators said, "yet what does emerge is a complex pattern of personal and financial relationship behind Harken's sudden good fortune. The mosaic of BCCI connections surrounding Harken Energy may prove nothing more than how ubiquitous the rogue bank's ties were. But the number of BBCI-connected people who had dealings with Harken—all since George W. Bush came on board—likewise raises the question of whether they mask an effort to cozy up to a presidential son."[11]

Throughout his business, and then political, career, George W. Bush was rescued from a succession of failures by his rich, powerful father and his influential associates and friends with money and valuable contacts, both at home and in the oil-rich Arab Gulf states. A blatant example was how Enron's Lay picked up George W. Bush in Texas after Bush Sr.'s defeat in 1992 and helped him become governor of Texas, and then went on to become a top contributor to his presidential campaign.[12]

Yet, following his nomination as the presidential candidate at the Republican Party Convention on August 3, 2000, George W. Bush had the audacity to say, "In Midland, Texas, where I grew up, the town motto was, 'The sky's the limit,' and we believed it. There was a restless energy, a basic conviction that with hard work, anybody could succeed and everybody deserves a chance."

Denying unpalatable reality and a tendency to concoct favorable "facts" emerged as leading features of Bush's character under the limelight of the presidency.

The Penny Drops

In the aftermath of the terrorist attacks on the United States in September 2001, Bush's habit of making things up and staying in denial in the face of bleak reality got a free ride.

It was only after his hasty, ill-planned invasion of Iraq in March 2003—which created more problems than it solved—and its disastrous consequences that the American public woke up to the major flaws in Bush's character.

Yet, as columnist Andrew Sullivan, his onetime admirer, noted in June 2006, "Bush cannot acknowledge that his war policy— just enough troops to lose—has created a war of attrition in which soldiers are often overwhelmed and demoralized and stretched to the limit." When presented with embarrassing or gloomy evidence, he just shunts it aside. "His view is that of a former addict whose life was transformed by a rigid form of Christianity," explained Sullivan.[13]

But reality has a way of penetrating even the most insular mind. In this case it was the nosedive in his approval ratings to a dismal 31 percent in the spring of 2006 that led Bush to concede for the first time in public that some of his statements about the Iraq War and its consequences were wrong.

There was another vital policy area where reality finally broke in: energy. For five years of his presidency, Bush had reassured

BLOOD OF THE EARTH

Americans—consuming 25 percent of the world's oil while producing only a third of it—that there was plenty of oil in the international market. Then, suddenly, in his State of the Union speech in January 2006, he talked of "energy independence" and announced that his Advanced Energy Initiative would increase federal funds for research into clean fuels that would include zero-emission coal-fired plants and "revolutionary" wind and solar technologies.

True, the next day, his energy secretary, Samuel Bodman, would explain that Bush's target of a 75 percent reduction in Middle Eastern imports by 2025 was "purely an example." Yet, it had to be said that it had finally dawned on Bush and his team, with their roots deep in the oil and auto industries, that petroleum—an end product of natural processes at work for tens of millions of years—was entering a declining cycle of its finite life, and that there was an urgent need to develop rapidly such finite, bridging fuels as natural gas and uranium, as well as renewable sources like wind, sun, tide, and biofuel.

As it was, finding and extracting mineral oil in commercial quantities had been an uphill task for humans. The early pioneers of the petroleum industry had struggled hard and long in atrocious working conditions against heavy odds in their search for oil.

Part I
Oil: A Biography

ONE

The Search
for Oil

If you journey to the suburban town of Surakhani, north of Baku,
the capital of Azerbaijan—meaning "Land of Fire"[1]—past a virtual forest of rusting rigs, each one surrounded by puddles of oil,
across the flat Absheron Peninsula, and stop by an outdoor tea
shop on the outskirts of Surakhani, you will witness a miracle.
You will see the nearby rocky hillock burning bright at its base,
orange flames leaping out of the rocks. The sight will likely
remind you of a passage by the historian Plutarch (46–120 AD)
in which he describes how the villagers of Babylonia set a street
with oil seepages on fire to impress Alexander of Macedonia
(356–323 BC).

And, if you befriend a local who is past their sixtieth year, he
or she would tell you that before World War II, known in the
Caucasus as the Great Patriotic War, bright orange flames used to
emanate from the far side of the hillock. Since the blaze provided
an easy marker for the Nazi warplanes seeking to bomb the
nearby oil facilities, the government extinguished it by dumping
tens of tons of earth on it. Soon after the war, though, an accidental flame of a match set alight the opposite side of the hillock.
Hence the eternal flame, its source the natural gas seeping
through the fissures of the rocks.

Not far from this site is a fire temple called Atishgah (Persian
for "place of fire")—a square building enclosed by a walled

compound—where an eternal flame once flickered inside the cloisters of stone. And it was in this area that in 1870 an oil field containing over one billion barrels of petroleum was discovered. It was named Surakhaniskoye.

The origins of a fire temple and worship of "the eternal flame" date back to a much earlier period, when the prophet Zoroaster (c. 628–551 BC) propagated his Manichean doctrine, and the inhabitants of the region, known as Aryans, worshipped fire and paid homage to it in their early scriptures. But the building of the Atishgah and the surrounding complex containing rooms for the pilgrims and a restaurant started in the seventeenth century and continued until the mid-1850s, funded chiefly by Hindu merchants from Punjab and Gujarat, who worshipped their goddess of fire, Agni (a derivative of "ignite"), and who were aware of its location along the famed Silk Route. The temple acquired a reputation for bringing happiness and welfare to its devotees as well as visitors, who included both Hindus and Zoroastrians from Iran and India.[2]

The "pillars of fire" mentioned in the Judeo-Christian scriptures resulted from the flammable gas, associated with oil deposits, escaping from the fissures in porous limestone. In his book *Babylon to Baku*, Z. Bilkadi listed allusions to oil in ancient times, some of them in the Bible. "The reeds of Moses caulked with tar" is one example. Another is in the Book of Daniel, which mentions "a bush that was burning but was not consumed, a pillar of cloud by day and of fire by night, the fiery furnace" as well as the "burning fiery furnace" of the Babylonian king Nebuchadrezzar.[3] Archaeological excavations in Iraq and Iran indicate that oil in its heavy form of bitumen was used for building roads and for coating walls and hulls of ships.

In its geological context, "oil" is a shortened version of crude oil, or more appropriately petroleum (Latin, *petra* = stone + *oleum* = oil). Strictly speaking, given the organic origin of petroleum/oil, this word meaning rock oil is incorrect, but is a convenient generic term used for oil, gas, and related substances.

A mixture of hydrocarbons found underground in a gaseous or liquid state, the term *oil* is applied to the liquid form. It is often greenish or dark brown, and sometimes black. Chemically, it is an organic compound of carbon and hydrogen, the basis of all life on Earth. Carbon accounts for 82 to 87 percent of the weight of crude oil, and hydrogen 12 to 15 percent, the rest being oxygen, nitrogen, and sulfur.

Starting with scooping oil from seepages, humans graduated to digging shallow pits to extract it more efficiently. The inhabitants of Burma (now Myanmar) used bamboo pipes to case shallow wells and transport the commodity. The Chinese were the first to deploy mechanical means. Their rig for drilling wells consisted of a large stone tied to a hefty rope that was repeatedly lifted and dropped gradually to penetrate the earth. Out of this evolved, many centuries later, the cable tool in which a heavy steel chisel attached to a cable was raised and lowered to pierce the subsurface dirt, sand, and rock as a jackhammer, its task eased by the pouring of water. A bailer was periodically lowered into the hole to bring up the subsurface chips. As oil or gas, being lighter than water, came out to the top of the bore, the discovery of the prized hydrocarbons was fairly straightforward. The only problem was that when subsoil water was struck, its flow was so copious that the bailer could not remove it rapidly enough. That led to casing the bore with a steel pipe and then drilling with a smaller chisel that would fit inside the pipe. Each major water source that was encountered needed a string of pipes that was smaller than the previous one. Later the cable tool would be replaced by a steel pipe with a toothed bit attached to it, and the pipe would be rotated by steam power to make the bit cut into the subsoil.

Ahmad al Belazuri (died ca. 892), an Arab traveler in the ninth century, noted that the economic life of the Absheron Peninsula had traditionally been linked to oil. Later, Arab historian Masoudi Abdul Hussein (d. 957) referred to two main sources of oil on Absheron—black and white. After his visit to the peninsula in the thirteenth century, another Arab chronicler, Muhammad Bekran, described how petroleum was extracted from shafts in Balakhani, a suburb of contemporary Baku.

In his *Travels*, Venetian merchant Marco Polo (1254–1324) referred to a black spring near Baku that provided oil, which was used for heating, cleaning the skin diseases of camels, and preparing an ointment for human sores and burns. In 1636, Adam Oleari (1603–1671), a German traveler and diplomat, noted that Baku had thirty wells of oil, both brown and white, and that the mineral gushed out of the holes.

"In the seventeenth century, white oil, used for lacquer, was scooped up from the ground by the bucketful," Sara Ashorebely, a ninety-two-year-old local historian, told Daniel Williams of the *Washington Post*. "Ornate labeled clay cubes were used to transport lamp oil to Persia. Silkworm breeders used it because its smoke seemed to energize the worms."[4]

Once Baku had been occupied by Russian general Mikhail Matyushkin, Czar Peter the Great (1672–1725) issued decrees concerning oil extraction in 1723 and demanded 16,000 kilograms (35,000 pounds) of white oil from the area. In 1803, Qasimbey Mansurbeyov of Baku pioneered the offshore oil industry by extracting oil from two wells in the Bibi Heybat Bay at a distance of eighteen meters (fifty-nine feet) and thirty meters (ninety-eight feet) from the shore.

After the czar had consolidated his control of the region by turning the several khanates into Russian protectorates in 1805, oil exploration accelerated. During the next quarter century, the number of manually dug oil wells, some of them 35 meters (115 feet) deep, rose to 116. But their total yield at 720 bpd was puny.

In 1834 Nikolai Voskoboynikov, director of the Baku oil fields, invented a special distilling machine that could produce kerosene from black or white oil. Until then, white oil had been the only source of kerosene.

In 1846 Fyodor N. Semyonov, a Russian mining engineer working for Caucasus Head Management, successfully used a cable rig to drill a well in Bibi Heybat, northeast of Baku, and struck oil at a depth of twenty-one meters (sixty-five feet). But the wheels of czarist bureaucracy moved so slowly that it was not until July 14, 1848 that the documentary proof of drilling for oil was included in a report to Czar Nicholas I by the Russian governor-general of Caucasus, Count Vorontsov.

Thus 1848, and not 1846, became a landmark in the annals of the petroleum industry. It was ten years later that the first commercial oil well was drilled in North America—in Oil Springs, Ontario, Canada, by James Miller Williams.

The oil industry in the Baku region, however, did not take off until after 1871, when the czar abolished the state monopoly. Those Azeri peasants whose lands were found to contain petroleum suddenly became as rich as Croesus. Others benefited by trading in the commodity. One such was Zain al Abidin Taghiyev (1823–1924), a pious Shia Muslim who sported a trimmed black beard and a long walrus mustache over his well-fleshed lips and under his long nose and thick eyebrows. The son of a shoemaker, he apprenticed as a bricklayer at age six and never went to school. He became a stonemason, then a freight handler and contractor. He set up an oil-trading company in his name. By 1878 he would become an oil baron, and he lived to the ripe old age of 101. Though illiterate, he left behind a valuable collection of books in his library, most of which were preserved in a museum after the Bolshevik Revolution of 1917. What gave the Baku petroleum industry a big push was the discovery in July 1873 of the first major oil gusher—named Vermishevsky—in Balakhani. Within three months, it yielded 1.5 billion kilograms (3.3 billion pounds) of oil.

The American Scene

By 1873, the first successful oil well drilled in the down-at-the-heels hamlet of Titusville, Pennsylvania, was fourteen years old.

Today, very little of that historic place remains. What has survived is Oil City, a small town originally called Cornplanter after a Seneca Indian chief, fifteen miles (twenty-four kilometers) south of Titusville, proud of its remarkable nineteenth-century houses and shops of stone. To get there from New York City, you need to abandon Interstate 80 and drive north through an enchantingly rugged landscape. Ambling along the almost deserted streets of Oil City, it requires a great leap of imagination to visualize it as the heart of a thriving industry that extracted oil from almost two thousand wells.

It all started in 1857, several hundred miles from Oil City, in New Haven, Connecticut, where a group of investors established Pennsylvania Rock Oil Company (PROC) to mine a flammable substance that rose to the surface in this hilly northwestern region of Pennsylvania. This mineral, called "rock oil," was used by the local people as medicine to relieve headaches and toothaches.

The East Coast investors knew that in the Caspian region as well as in Galicia and Rumania, this rock oil was being distilled to produce kerosene, used as an illuminant. Supplies of the traditional illuminant, whale oil, were in free fall as sperm whales had been hunted to the point of near extinction. PROC owners decided not to dig for the mineral but to drill for it as the Chinese had done for salt for many centuries.

They settled on one Edwin L. Drake (1819–1880), a thirty-eight-year-old former railway conductor who had tried his hand at several other jobs to undertake the operation, partly because he was lodged in the same Tontine Hotel in New Haven as James Townsend, a local banker and the leading PROC investor, and partly because of his can-do attitude to life. A well-built man with a thick beard and longish hair, his determined look inspired confidence, bolstered by his habit of dressing in a three-piece suit and a top hat, and by the title of colonel that PROC investors misleadingly conferred on him.

During his first trip to northwestern Pennsylvania in December 1857, Drake tied up a lease on a farm near Titusville (population 125) whose owner had been manually collecting three to six gallons of oil daily from a seeping spring.

When he returned to Titusville the next spring, Drake had to make do with manual digging as he lacked the equipment and funds for a drill. After many months of futile effort, he managed to get $1,000 from Townsend in New Haven. But his drillers—experienced only in drilling for salt—proved unreliable. Drake focused on building a steam engine to power the drill.

It was not until the spring of 1859 that Drake finally found William Smith—a blacksmith who forged tools for salt drillers—and his two sons, who proved equal to the task. Together they fabricated a derrick and assembled the necessary equipment. By early summer, however, the PROC directors had tired of the project. Then the venture capital ran out. Resolved to continue, Townsend stepped in and paid the invoices with his own money.

Toward the end of August, even Townsend was at the end of his tether. He sent Drake the last installment of cash by money order and instructed him to cease the operation forthwith and return. It would be some days before the money and the letter would reach Drake.

On the afternoon of August 27, 1859, a Saturday, when the drill had punched through sixty-nine feet (twenty-one meters) of subsoil, it suddenly dropped into a crevice. The crew stopped working. The following day, when William Smith arrived to inspect the well, he noticed a dark fluid which, on close examination, turned out to be petroleum. On Monday, a surprised Drake found William Smith and his sons surrounded by barrels, tubs, and washbasins filled with oil. He installed a hand pump over the hole and began extracting oil manually.

Later that day came the cash and closure orders for Drake from Townsend. "Too late," muttered Drake as he read the letter. For once delay had resulted in a positive outcome. Almost half a century later, history would repeat itself in the midst of the Zagros Mountains in Iran, inaugurating the first petroleum well in the region, which would prove to be a cornucopia of oil and natural gas.

Today, at the lightly guarded Drake Well State Park outside Titusville, you see a likeness of the original wooden structure that housed Drake's rig, surrounded by replicas of the equipment and tools actually used. Just across the road stands the Oil Museum, which displays the myriad aspects of petroleum and natural gas in three dimensions as well as with sepia-colored pictures, including tough-looking drillers carrying weapons, a common practice.[5] It was in that ambience that Titusville opened a new era in the United States—the era of hydrocarbons.

Competing Oil Centers

Powered by private entrepreneurs, both Azeri and foreign, including the Nobel brothers—Robert, Ludwig, and Alfred—from Sweden, who had settled in the Russian capital of Saint Petersburg, and the Paris-based banking family of the Rothschilds, headed by Baron Alphonse Rothschild, the booming oil industry in the Baku region scored many firsts.

The Nobels were the first to create an integrated oil corporation that engaged in exploration, production, and transportation. The practice of replacing coal with oil as fuel for steamships originated here. The Nobel brothers built the world's first oil-fueled steamship, *Zoroaster*, in 1877. That year witnessed the transport of oil by a pipeline, another pioneering step by the Nobels but financed by the Rothschilds, from Baku to the Black Sea coast of Georgia. Then came oil transport by railway, another first. In 1898 the Rothschild brothers founded the Mazut Transportation Society and launched the first oil tanker, which plied the Caspian Sea. In 1915 the process of lifting oil with injected gas was tested successfully when deep pumps were submerged in the Romani oil fields on the Absheron Peninsula.

The foreign oil barons functioned alongside the Azeris. Besides Taghiyev, who would be the first to import a car into Azerbaijan, there were the shepherd grandfather of Sara Ashorebely—who discovered oil seeping from his pastures and went into partnership with the Rothschilds to build a refinery to produce kerosene and gasoline—and Musa Naghiyev (1849–1919), the richest Azeri of them all.

Born into a poor peasant family and already working at age eleven, Musa Naghiyev was apprenticed as a cargo handler. He was a lean man with a luxuriant black beard and a drooping mustache, an aquiline nose and sad eyes, who wore stiff-collar shirts and ties and a round black cap. His financial rise was meteoric. Afraid that he would lose his riches as fast as he had gained them, he invested in real estate. He constructed ninety-eight buildings, including four hospitals and a technical college, and became the largest landlord ever in Baku. He is remembered both for being the most miserly of the oil barons as well as for leaving behind magnificent architectural landmarks that now glitter like jewels amid monolithic, factory-produced Soviet-style apartment blocks in the Azeri capital.

By 1901, Azerbaijan had outpaced the United States in oil output with 11.5 million tons a year to 9.1 million tons, and was producing more than half of the global supply, with Baku becoming one of Russia's major industrial centers. Azerbaijan maintained its prime position in the oil industry until the 1905 revolution in Russia, when sabotage in the Baku region resulted in many oil wells being set ablaze.

Despite this brief setback, Baku remained a leading oil center, crammed with investors, geologists, engineers, technicians, brokers, industrialists, and tens of thousands of badly organized workers. It was full of elaborate, ornate mansions, one of them built by the Nobels just up the road from the slums of the workers, mostly Russian peasants. They were like indentured laborers tied to their employers, who paid them irregularly and banned them from marrying. Their working conditions were abominable. The oil derricks were so close to one another that they engendered a high risk of fire, and the noise level was horrendous. The oil-refining district dominated by the Rothschild refinery was so polluted that it was called Black City. (Later, after the 1917 Bolshevik Revolution, the Soviet regime would preserve the hideous Nobels' and Rothschilds' plants as museums to illustrate, tellingly, the horrors of unbridled capitalism.)

It was in such an environment that a Georgian born in Gori named Joseph Stalin (born Jugashvili) arrived in Baku. In his mid-twenties, the young Stalin, with a neatly trimmed black beard, a rich thatch of hair, a sharp slim nose, and fleshy lips with intent eyes, cut a dashing figure. He combined his considerable organizational skills to band oil workers into a union with the Robin Hood tactics of extracting cash from the local rich and robbing banks. His daredevil acts attracted the wife of a leading oil executive. He went on to blackmail the husband successfully and use the money to shore up the workers' union.

Thus it was in Baku that Stalin had his first taste of grassroots agitation by masterminding strikes, and it was here that he sharpened the organizational talent that would ultimately lead him to the supreme office in the Soviet Union. His activities in Baku ended when he was thrown in jail. The prison cell where he was incarcerated is maintained to this day as a historic site, but only a tiny, insistent minority of visitors to the city is furnished with this information.

The Texan Boom

It was the first month of the first year of the twentieth century when the discovery of a gusher at Spindletop near Beaumont in southeast Texas, nineteen miles from Port Arthur, placed the Lone Star State firmly in the world of oil.[6] And it was at Spindletop that the drilling-industry terminology was spawned—with a well-borer becoming a driller, a skilled helper a roughneck and a semiskilled helper a roustabout—which became common currency throughout the United States and later spread overseas.

In Texas, petroleum was first discovered in the small town of Corsicana in 1893, when local city council members set up a company to find water. The credit went to the three robustly built, strong-jawed brother-drillers called the Hamills—Al, Jim, and Curt. They used a rotary drill that was then deployed only by water-well contractors. But the Corsicana oil well's yield peaked at 2,300 bpd, and by 1900 the initial enthusiasm in the area had subsided.

Once more it was the dogged persistence of an eccentric that brought about the Spindletop bonanza. He was Patillo Higgins, a lumber merchant and mechanic who applied his skills using only the single arm he possessed, and who nurtured an unshake-able belief that the seepage of natural gas around a salt dome south of Beaumont signaled the presence of petroleum. His con-viction was so staunch that several local moneyed men financed his drilling attempt in 1893. It failed. His second try met with the same fate. So also did his next fling.

Higgins then contacted Captain Anthony Lucas, a former naval engineer of the Austro-Hungarian Empire, well versed in drilling salt domes for salt in Louisiana. After investigating the Spindletop area, he organized drilling as an investor—without Higgins.

Lucas's endeavor proved futile, but only after he had discovered subsurface sand streaked with petroleum.

That, however, proved an insufficient incentive for prospective investors. So he turned to Pennsylvania-based John Galey, a big man with a bushy mustache who had the reputation of "smelling oil." In turn, Galey approached Andrew Mellon, a Pittsburgh capitalist, to finance three more tests in the Beaumont area. This time Lucas resolved to drill up to 1,200 feet (366 meters), double the previous record. And, following Galey's advice, he contacted the Hamill brothers.

They started drilling on October 27, 1900, with a twelve-inch bit. When they ran into sand at 160 feet (49 meters), they improvised by hammering an eight-inch pipe through the quicksand, a solution that later came to be known as "casing the hole." Then they ran a four-inch bit through the pipe. Later, when they encountered gas, they came up with another innovation. They mixed clay with the water they encountered and produced a mud that blocked the gas and allowed them to continue drilling. The circulating mud tackled the gas problem and brought up to the surface any evidence of oil.

By the time the Hamill brothers had pierced 900 feet (274 meters) after nearly ninety days of drilling, they encountered nothing more promising than sand streaked with petroleum. Galey proposed closure. But Al Hamill, the chief driller, insisted on sticking to the original plan of 1,200 feet. He got his way. The Hamill brothers drilled another 50 feet (15 meters), until Christmas Eve, celebrated the festive season at home, and reported for work on January 1, 1901.

After chipping through 140 feet (43 meters) of limestone, acting as a huge stopper over a dark, viscous treasure for millions of years, the Hamills encountered a harder layer. Their drilling pipe jammed and the bit wore out. After repairing the damage and replacing the bit, they resumed drilling on January 10.

At 10:30 A.M., at a depth of some 1,100 feet (335 meters), suddenly the derrick whimpered and shuddered. The muddy water swelled out of the bore and flooded the rig platform. Just as a torrent of greenish brown petroleum along with rocks, water, and mud gushed out of the well, thick clouds of methane gas emanating from the hole mixed with the wintry air.

Scared out of their wits, the Hamills ran for their lives. Once the violent outburst of the underground world was seemingly over, they picked up the courage to walk slowly back to the center of the ground-shattering event. Just then there was another mighty roar, followed by mud, rock, oil, and gas springing from the bowels of Mother Earth. Then silence. Next came the gurgling of more petroleum rising and flowing slowly—as a preamble to a dark rain covering a large area of the countryside, where the land value would soar within a few years from $10 to $900,000 an acre.

Over the next three days the Spindletop gusher disgorged 250,000 barrels of crude oil. The well, named Lucas 1, would settle down to yielding 75,000 bpd in a state where the normal range was 50 to 100 bpd.

Soon the discovery at Spindletop morphed into poems, melodramas, novels, and songs. A marching song, "Lucas Geyser," went:

You talk about your Klondike rush,
    and gold in frozen soil;
But it don't compare with Beaumont rush,
    When Lucas he struck oil.[7]

Sadly, almost all those who celebrated the Spindletop saga ignored Patillo Higgins, whose dogged vision had made the dream of black gold come true.

Spindletop created a new social phenomenon of petroleum boomtowns, which attracted a perennially floating oil-field population of drifters, including roughnecks, roustabouts, pipeliners, cart drivers, gamblers, rum runners, and prostitutes. The pattern continued unabated. Half a century later, when the family of the newly arrived George Bush Sr. rented a house in Odessa, they found themselves sharing the bathroom with a local whore.

This was in dramatic contrast to what would happen in Iran at just about the same time, when geologist and petroleum engineer George Reynolds, an India-born Scotsman, led a crew of Azeris, Canadians, and Poles into the Zagros Mountains in search of oil. He made it crystal clear to his men that sex with Iranian women was strictly forbidden.

Iran Strikes First

George Reynolds' prohibitions extended beyond whoring to drunkenness, and were laced with an exhortation to his men to act like "reasonable human beings." It meant that his hard-working crew had to traverse 150 miles (250 kilometers) to the Iraqi port city of Basra for a night with a local prostitute.

Traveling in the opposite direction in 2004, I headed for the place where Reynolds met with success—Masjid-e Suleiman (literally, "Mosque of Suleiman"), the ancient site of a Zoroastrian fire temple built around a permanent gas escape—from Shuster, a historic settlement, toward the Zagros Mountain range, with strips of its rugged exterior fashioned into asphalted hairpin bends and steep slopes hugging stomach-churning sheers.

A tall, robust figure with a fleshy face, Reynolds was often seen in public either with his pipe and solar hat or his little dog. He contrived to transport equipment weighing forty tons from Chia Surkh, near the Iran-Iraq border, where his oil-finding venture had failed in 1904, to this mountainous region of Maiden-e Naft (literally, "Field of Oil"), some 330 miles (540 kilometers) apart. He did so by shipping it first to Baghdad by road, deploying nine hundred mules, then to Basra by boat, next to Khorramshahr in Iran, and on to the penultimate leg of the journey to Shardin. It took his men a whole year to fashion a road to Maiden-e Naft, which he had visited earlier to discover that its rocks were "saturated with petroleum."

A man of many talents, Reynolds had explored for oil earlier in Sumatra. Now he started out with generous funding by London-based William Knox D'Arcy; he had won a sixty-year oil concession covering most of Iran in 1901 from Muzaffar al Din Shah for $20,000 (£4,000) and an equal amount in the shares of his company and 16 percent of the profit. Over time, D'Arcy, a prematurely bald, heavily built and puffy-faced Englishman with long sideburns, would win the epithet of a "capitalist of the highest order." He had a knack for betting on the right horse at racecourses. In another context, he chose Reynolds, who turned out, after long, nerve-racking months, to be a winner.

A graduate of the Royal Indian Engineering College, Reynolds started his career with the Indian Public Works Department. He had a gift for rigging machines and picking up foreign languages. He was as demanding of himself as of others. Above all else, Reynolds was a tower of tenacity. He had started on his latest venture in 1902 in the Chia Surkh sector by having all machine parts shipped to Basra, then transported upstream to Baghdad, and finally transported by mules and porters over the Iraq-Iran border, which ran through a rocky desert. There, assisted by his motley crew, he assembled the machinery and got to work in abominable conditions, frequently hobbled by lack of spare parts, edible food, and potable water.

The surrounding terrain was desolate, bereft of life or trees, all dun-colored hills and valleys and a jumble of twisted rock produced by a series of cataclysms over thousands of millennia, relieved here and there by patches of scrub. The pitiless landscape offered Reynolds's men extremes of temperature, sizzling heat during the day and freezing, teeth-chattering cold at night. Their bedroom and dining tents crawled with scorpions and snakes in summer, when the furnace heat of the season forced these creatures out of their holes and crevices.

Reynolds's success came in January 1904 when he struck oil. The discovery raised the spirits of D'Arcy, an equally colorful character albeit in a different mold. Born in 1848 in Newton Abbot, England, to a lawyer, he went to a private school in London. At seventeen, he migrated along with his father to Rockhampton in Queensland, Australia. He became a successful lawyer and an addict of horse racing. His gambling instinct led him to organize a syndicate to revive the old Mount Morgan gold mine. It yielded far more of the much-coveted metal than anybody had dreamed. He returned to England in 1889 as a very affluent businessman and established himself in London as a speculator and an organizer of syndicates.

When Edouard Cotte, an agent of the recently deceased Baron Julius de Reuter, approached D'Arcy in 1900 to invest in petroleum exploration in Iran, which had experienced oil seepage for centuries and whose inhabitants used it for binding bricks and caulking boats, D'Arcy evinced instant interest. He dispatched two geologists to visit the areas around Chia Surkh and Shustar. Their favorable reports led to an agreement between D'Arcy and Muzaffar al Din Shah.

D'Arcy's high hopes, aroused by the discovery of oil in the Chia Surkh region, crashed when the two successful wells ran dry after a few months. Having sunk more than £300,000 (today's £120 million) into the venture, he was unwilling to invest any more.

Just then, out of the blue, the Burmah Oil Company (BOC) turned into a fairy godmother for D'Arcy. It expressed keen interest in his oil concessions. Out of this emerged the Concession Syndicate in 1905.

It was the newly born Concession Syndicate that funded Reynolds's move to the Maidan-e Naft region, the last throw of the dice by the venture capitalists in Britain. Reynolds arrived there with his equipment in 1906. So rough was the terrain that it took many months to build a road to the sites in and around Masjid-e Suleiman. It was not until January 1908 that drilling started. Working conditions were grueling. Procuring drinking water was a Herculean task. Another major problem was security.

Yet these problems were dwarfed by the fast-deteriorating financial situation. The project had so far cost D'Arcy and BOC £500,000, a monumental sum (today's £200 million/$368 million). Nervous BOC directors called on D'Arcy to cough up £20,000/$37,000 cash by April 30, 1908. An equally distraught D'Arcy ignored the deadline. On May 14, the directors sent a short cable to Reynolds telling him to expect a letter of instructions. In it they ordered him to go no deeper than 1,600 feet (488 meters) for the two wells being drilled. If he failed to strike oil by then, he should stop work, shut down the operation, and take as much of the machinery as possible to Khorramshahr.

While the BOC letter meandered its way eastward across Europe, hopeful smells began rising from one of the two wells. Then disaster struck. A drill bit got unscrewed and got lost in the borehole. It took several days to recover the bit and resume drilling—through the hardest stratum yet encountered. Now vapors of the released natural gas began rising so abundantly that the crew could not only smell them but also see them.

It was so hot that Reynolds slept outside his tent at the base camp, some distance away from the noisy round-the-clock work sites. On May 25 he went to bed at the usual hour. Around 4 A.M. on May 26, a sudden, dramatic outburst of human shouting mixed with earthy rumbles and the sprouting of gushing oil—

rising fifty feet (fifteen meters) above the top of one of the derricks—woke him up. He jumped up, saw the sight, dressed, and
rushed to the scene to savor every moment. The drill hole was
less than 1,200 feet (366 meters) deep, barely three-quarters of
the depth mandated by BOC directors.

Unbeknownst to him, Reynolds had tapped into a 100-square-
mile (259-square-kilometer) field, the largest discovered so far in
the world, containing nearly two billion barrels. (In 1922, as
Shell Oil Company's local manager, George Reynolds would
strike it lucky again, at the La Rosa field in the Maracaibo Basin
in Venezuela, with a gusher.[8])

In any event, following the copious find at Masjid-e Suleiman,
the Concession Syndicate morphed into the Anglo-Persian Oil
Company (APOC) in 1909, a corporation that would dominate
the economic and political life of Iran for more than four decades.

Today, both the oil well and the original seventy-five-foot
drilling rig, along with its accompanying steam engine and
boiler, all painted in navy blue and resting on a raised platform,
surrounded by a high fenced wall—with a signpost above the
entrance in Persian and English reading MASJID-I SULAIMAN WELL
NUMBER 1 THE FIRST OIL WELL IN THE MIDDLE EAST—remain the
prized possession of the National Iranian Oil Company's subsidiary National Iranian South Oil Company.

The company's public relations director, Mirza Javad Ahmadi, a
broad-shouldered man of medium height sporting a few days' dark
stubble, took me to the historic site, a short drive from the company's spacious headquarters. Past a low steel gate, a large signboard
by the steps to the drilling rig's platform provided the essential
information in blue and red lettering in Persian and English:

WELL NO. 1 MASJID-I-SULAIMAN
COMMENCED JANUARY 23TH [SIC] 1908
STRUCK OIL AND WELL COMPLETED MAY 26TH 1908

DEPTH 1179 FEET/360 METERS
PRODUCTION 36,000 LITRES/8,000 GALLONS PER DAY

Lucky Strike in Kirkuk

Across the Iran-Iraq border, the Kirkuk area in Mosul province was widely known since antiquity as a site of "eternal fires" caused by the leaking of natural gas through countless holes in the hilly terrain. In modern times, Mosul became part of the sprawling Ottoman Empire. During World War I, when the Ottomans were allies of Germany, the Germans drilled four productive shallow wells near the famed site, found oil, refined it, and transported the products by road tankers to military units. However, the output was very small.

It was not until the night of October 14, 1927, that Kirkuk entered the colorful chronicle of oil. At Baba Gurgur, six miles northwest of Kirkuk, a greenish brown column of oil burst forth from a depth of 1,500 feet (457 meters) with a thunderous roar that reached Kirkuk, to a height of over 100 feet (30 meters) and drenched the countryside while clouds of the associated methane gas filled the air. More than seven hundred laborers toiled nonstop for nine days to erect dykes and walls to contain nature's bountiful outpouring. Baba Gurgur No. 1 well went on to yield an unmatched 60,000 bpd.

The latest oil field was estimated to have the reserves of seventeen billion barrels, a colossal figure that dwarfed all others. These subterranean riches belonged to a consortium called Turkish Petroleum Company (TPC)—consisting of APOC (50 percent), Compagnie Française des Pétroles, (22.5 percent), Royal Dutch Shell (22.5 percent) and Calouste Gulbenkian, a Portuguese Armenian who had worked for the family's oil business in Baku (5 percent).[9]

So far the geologists of APOC—headed by John Cadman, an obstinate, opinionated Englishman—and other companies had focused on the folded structure of the foothills of the Zagros Mountains in Iran and Iraq: their visible surface promised petroleum reservoirs trapped underground. With a dismissive wave of their hands, they flatly ruled out any possibility of the even terrain of the Arabian Peninsula, covered largely with sand and occasionally with gravel, holding oil deposits. It lacked the specific subterranean structure to trap large volumes of petroleum, they confidently announced.

Their unanimous chorus was rudely interrupted by Major Frank Holmes (1874–1950).

Holmes, "Abu al Naft"

Born and raised on a sheep farm in Otago, New Zealand, Frank Holmes started his professional life at seventeen at a gold mine in South Africa. He spent the next twenty-three years in the gold, tin, and coal mines of Australia, Malaya, Mexico, Nigeria, and Russia. A sturdy, robust man, blue-eyed and sunburned, he was always immaculately dressed in his three-piece suit, with a hat resting jauntily on his head. A born raconteur, he entertained his audiences with anecdotes of his adventures and mishaps in exotic places. He effortlessly allied his assertiveness and willfulness with considerable charm, breezy bluster, and presence of mind. At the start of World War I in 1914 he presented himself to Winston Churchill, then first lord of the admiralty, to enlist in the military. The small, flabby-faced British politician with a snub nose was famed for his gruff, outgoing style.

"How old are you?" he asked Holmes.

"Just forty, sir."

"That's a bit old," Churchill grumbled, aware that the recruitment age limit was thirty-five.

"It's exactly your age, sir."

"In that case, you're in the prime of life. We'll see what can be done."[10]

Holmes became a quartermaster in the army with the rank of major. In 1918, his ears pricked up when, in the course of procuring beef for the British military in Addis Ababa, Ethiopia, an Arab merchant mentioned oil seepages along the Arabian side of the Persian Gulf. From that moment, he became obsessed with exploring for oil on the Arabian Peninsula—a quest he followed doggedly for fourteen tortuous years.

In 1919 he established Eastern and General Syndicate Ltd. in London to develop business opportunities in the Middle East. His start was modest, a drugstore in Aden. From that British colony, he set out to cultivate various rulers in the peninsula by traveling to their principalities and sultanates.

Having obtained confirmed reports of oil seepages in Bahrain, he arrived there in 1922, describing himself as a butterfly collector on a mission from Eastern and General Syndicate Ltd. Armed with a vast white parasol bordered in green, the color of Islam; a green gauze veil over his khaki pith helmet to protect his face from flies; and more than fifty bags, boxes, and crates containing presents for Abdul Aziz ibn Saud, the sultan of Najd and its Dependencies—popularly known as Ibn Saud—he flaunted a letter of invitation from the Najdi sultan on the flimsiest of pretexts.

His sunny disposition, breezy charm, and lavish presents yielded him glowing success in 1923. Ibn Saud awarded him an oil concession for the eastern Al Hasa region covering 40,000 square miles (10,360 square kilometers) for an annual rent of £2,000 ($10,000), a very substantial sum in those days.

Back in Bahrain, the ruler, Sheikh Hamad al Khalifa, was more interested in water, which was scarce, than in petroleum. Holmes drilled for water in 1925. It sprouted. What delighted him even more was that the water contained traces of oil. True to his royal word, the ruler gave him an oil concession covering 320 square miles (830 square kilometers).

In contrast, the neighboring Al Hasa province of Najd yielded him neither water nor oil. By 1926 the funds of the Eastern and General Syndicate had dried up, even though it failed to pay Ibn Saud the annual rent for two years. Holmes grew desperate. Setting aside his pride, he offered to sell his concessions to APOC, his powerful rival and adversary. It rejected the overture summarily.

As a last resort, Holmes traveled to the United States. Luck smiled on him there. He got San Francisco–based Standard Oil Company of California (Socal) interested in his Bahrain concession. But when it founded a Canadian subsidiary, Bahrain Petroleum Co. (Bapco), to handle the concession, it discovered to its chagrin that the Anglo-Bahraini Agreement of 1914 barred Bahrain from giving petroleum concession to non-British companies without London's prior agreement.

Pressured by the U.S. administration in 1929, London yielded on the strict condition that all communications between Bapco and the ruler would pass through the British political agent in Bahrain.

By 1930, the Bahraini ruler was desperately keen on oil exploration. The region's pearling industry, of which Bahrain was the nucleus—engaging eighteen thousand Bahrainis, a fifth of the population, and one thousand boats—was in the doldrums due to the cheap, artificial pearls from Japan flooding the international market.

Bapco commenced drilling in October 1931. The next year, on May 31, the ruler's fervent prayers were answered. The drillers struck oil just short of 2,000 feet (610 meters). Though the well's yield of 500 bpd was modest, the discovery of petroleum in the shadow of the Arabian Peninsula was a landmark in the history of oil.

It opened a new chapter. Overnight all major British and American oil corporations revised their policies on the Arabian Peninsula.

"Over the course of a decade, Major Holmes, with his obsession about oil, had become a figure of condescension and ridicule," noted Daniel Yergin in his book *Prize*. "But now his instinct, and his vision, had been vindicated. . . . After all, the tiny island of Bahrain was only twenty miles from the mainland Arabian Peninsula where, to all outward appearances, the geology was exactly the same."[11]

The discovery earned Holmes the sobriquet of Abu al Naft, "Father of Oil," among Arabs. He richly deserved it. Asked, many years later, what had made him so confident of the Arabian petroleum prospects contrary to the almost unanimously negative verdict of the leading geophysicists, Holmes tapped his nose with his finger. "This was my geologist," he quipped.[12]

While working conditions on Bahrain's drilling sites were not as abominable as the ones that George Reynolds and his crew had endured in Iran a generation previously, there was a disgraceful gap between the lifestyles of the Americans and their subordinates. The Americans lived in portable Nissan cabins furnished with electric light, refrigerators, running cold and hot water, and bathtubs. Their 350 underlings—Bahrainis, Indians, and Iraqis—sheltered not in tents but in fragile huts made of local palm leaves, which leaked copiously when it rained. They worked a seven-day week, with the Bahrainis allowed to go home once every seven weeks for seven days. Most of the Indians and Iraqis had no families on the island to return to.

Burgan, the Richest Treasure So Far

Bahrain's grand fortune put the normally jovial, thickset ruler of Kuwait, Sheikh Ahmad al Sabah, in a foul mood. He described the oil find in Bahrain as "a stab to my heart," plunging an imaginary sword into his ribcage, during his meeting with Holmes, whom he had earlier awarded an oil concession for 3,600 square miles (9,300 square kilometers). But, instead of making use of the rights, Eastern and General Syndicate had sold them to Gulf Oil Company, owned by the Mellon family of Pittsburgh, in the United States.

By 1930 the pearling industry, the number-one foreign earner in Kuwait, had collapsed. And due to the Great Depression, the number of pilgrims going to Mecca through Basra and Kuwait had plummeted.

But when, moved by the urgent pleas of the Kuwaiti ruler, Gulf Oil and Eastern and General Syndicate prepared to explore for oil, they found their hands tied by the Anglo-Kuwaiti Agreement of 1913. It barred any non-British company from oil exploration in Kuwait without London's prior permission.

The story did not end there, however.

Once more, in this epic saga of oil, a totally unexpected twist in the tale shored up the sagging fortunes of the petroleum prospectors in Kuwait. In early 1932 His Majesty's Government in London welcomed as U.S. ambassador Andrew Mellon, who three decades earlier had funded the Spindletop venture in Texas and whose Gulf Oil Company had prospered since then. Now, naturally, he pressed the right levers. And, pronto! The British government relented on its nationality requirement on the condition that it be able to review all the bids and recommend one to the Kuwaiti ruler.

Gulf Oil faced stiff competition from APOC, a London-based company with a majority of its shares held by His Majesty's Government, whose chairman, Cadman, had lately become eager to gain a foothold on the Arabian Peninsula. In the end, instead of getting embroiled in a ruinous bidding war, they decided to cooperate. The result was a joint-venture company formed in December 1933, with its ownership divided equally between the hitherto rivals, named Kuwait Oil Company (KOC).

It obtained petroleum concessions for seventy-four years. It began exploring in 1935. The locals pointed to the asphalt pit in southeast Kuwait at Burgan. But KOC executives refused to look. We must do our seismic investigation first, they announced haughtily to the bemused Kuwaitis.

KOC's scientific exercise got going in 1936. For almost two years, the company's test drilling yielded a depressing succession of dry holes. It was not until late 1937 that KOC got around to exploring a site near the asphalt pit favored by the local inhabitants.

It yielded the much-cherished treasure. On February 23, 1938, KOC drillers struck oil at Burgan No. 1 well. It overflowed with the thick, greenish brown liquid. Sheikh Ahmad al Sabah was ecstatic, and so was Holmes. His vindication was now total and unqualified.

Measuring thirty miles (forty-eight kilometers) by fifteen miles (twenty-four kilometers), the Burgan oil field held fifty billion barrels of petroleum, a virtual underground sea of oil. Its contents amounted to a third of all the known oil deposits of the planet Earth. The cumulative oil deposits of the United States, then the world's largest producer, were barely two-thirds of the treasure found at Burgan with a single successful strike. The collective reserves of Burgan along with the associated Maqwa, and Ahmadi fields—forming the Great Burgan complex—would later add up to a staggering seventy billion barrels.

The petroleum that sprang forth from Burgan No. 1 well was the end product of a process dating back fifty million years, to when Kuwait lay buried beneath a much larger Persian Gulf.

Now, within weeks, further evidence of Holmes's prescience would follow—with another prolific find in the kingdom of Saudi Arabia, the country founded in September 1932 by Ibn Saud by the amalgamation of Hijaz and Najd and its Dependencies.

Ghawar Beats Them All

The Saudi kingdom covers four-fifths of the vast Arabian Peninsula, which has been associated since antiquity with mirages; sand dunes, soft and steep—their different layers a riot of colors and shades like a painter's palette, mixing brick red with white, honey brown with pink, orange with cream, and yellow with gray—rising haphazardly from the gravelly desert floor; caravans of camels held together by cords tying the tail of a front animal to the penetrated nostrils of his follower, lumbering along with their loads; and Bedouin, desert nomads, who instinctively wrap their faces with their head cloths at the first hint of a sandstorm, and often know most of the countless dunes of Arabia individually since each of them basically retains its own particular shape despite periodic avalanches. The survival skills of these hardy Bedouin are legendary: they eat sand-filled unleavened bread, drink scarce bitter water drawn from wells, and endure the extreme heat and chill as well as the blinding daytime glare that generates optical illusions.

Ibn Saud, a tall, robust man, sad-eyed, wearing a neatly trimmed mustache and a goatee and possessing a great presence, was one such hardy inhabitant of the Arabian Desert. Having regained his ancestral Riyadh region from the rival Rashid clan in 1902, he captured the eastern Al Hasa province in 1913. After the collapse of the Ottoman Empire five years later, he conquered the Asir region along the Red Sea in 1920. The following year he added the northern Shammar region to his realm, and styled himself the sultan of Najd and its Dependencies. In 1924 he captured the Hijaz province, home to the holy Islamic shrines in Mecca and Medina.

When he sought international recognition as king of Hijaz and Najd and its Dependencies in 1926, the Soviet Union was the first major power to oblige. Britain followed in 1927. Two years later, when Ibn Saud fell out with his more militant

Islamist supporters, Britain assisted him militarily to crush their rebellion.

The Great Depression of 1929 resulted in a steep decline in the number of Muslim visitors to Mecca for their annual hajj pilgrimage, and left Ibn Saud in financial straits. Moscow lent him a helping hand by giving him credit, part of which he used to buy Soviet wheat. He actively sought fresh bids for an oil concession in Al Hasa, which Frank Holmes had forfeited in 1925 due to his failure to pay him the £4,000 ($20,000) rent. When he tried to interest APOC in oil rights, its chairman, Cadman, rebuffed him—a slight he never forgot or forgave.

His fate brightened with the discovery of oil in Bahrain in 1932. The interest of U.S. oil companies mounted sharply; they were eager to capitalize on his deep aversion toward APOC.

What crucially helped APOC's American competitors was the defection of Harry St. John Bridger Philby—a small, stocky man, balding and bearded, with tiny, hooded eyes. He came from the ranks of the upper echelons of the British civil service. Privy to his government's betrayal of the Arabs after the dissolution of the Ottoman Empire, he resigned from his prestigious job, converted to Islam, and took up residence in Jiddah. He soon became a close adviser to Ibn Saud.

It was Philby who eased the path of Standard Oil Company of California to Ibn Saud. They inked a contract on May 29, 1933. Ibn Saud awarded Socal the Al Hasa concession, covering 360,000 square kilometers (140,000 square miles), for sixty years. The contract provided for a lump sum up front of $175,000—$150,000, payable in gold sovereigns worth £30,000, and the first-year rent of $25,000, paid in gold sovereigns worth £5,000.[13] However, $150,000 was a loan to be repaid by Ibn Saud from future royalties. After eighteen months, Socal would advance a further loan of $100,000 to Ibn Saud. The contract specifically banned the transfer of rights and obligations to any other entity without the written permission of the Saudi government.

Socal set up a subsidiary, California-Arabian Standard Oil Company (Casoc). In 1936 Texas Oil acquired a half share in Casoc, with their joint venture bearing the name of Caltex. Simultaneous drilling started at several locations in the Dammam area near the coast, some sixty kilometers (thirty-eight miles) from the Bahraini capital of Manama—with Dammam Number 7 initiated in early 1937. The results were so repeatedly and depressingly poor that Socal's directors in San Francisco instructed the Saudi office that no further project was to be undertaken without their approval of a detailed plan.

Dammam Number 7 proved singularly inauspicious. It suffered blockages. Then the walls of the borehole caved in. Additional drill pipes were late to arrive. On top of that, there were assorted accidents. At the end of a year of drilling, the crew had managed to pierce only 4,200 feet (1,280 meters). And they encountered no trace of oil.

Then, as if to add one more nail-biting episode to the overly exciting drama of oil strikes, on March 4, 1938, Socal headquarters received a cable from their Saudi office: "Dammam No. 7 blew in at 4,274 feet with a flow of 1,585 bpd." Within the next three days, the output more than doubled. Unable to handle such an outpouring of the black gold, the crew channeled the flow back into Dammam No. 1, where the drilling had commenced two years earlier!

Astonishingly, at the site it was not the success at finding petroleum that excited the Americans. Instead, they were mesmerized by the arrival at the well of a minor, middle-aged member of British royalty—Princess Alice, Countess of Athlone, a granddaughter of Queen Victoria. A year earlier, during his visit to Britain, Crown Prince Saud had been entertained by fifty-two-year-old Princess Alice at the horse races at Ascot. He invited her to his kingdom.[14] Thus she became the first member of the British royal family to visit the Saudi kingdom and the first European woman to cross it from the Red Sea to the Persian Gulf. "Alice was tremendous," said a company official later, referring to her visit, in the *Aramco World Magazine*. "She was a greater success than Dammam No. 7."

Commercial production started in 1939. During World War II, work came to a virtual standstill, with the total output at 20,000 bpd.

Production picked up after the war. In 1947 Caltex expanded into a consortium of four U.S. companies—Socal (later Chevron) 30 percent, Texaco 30 percent, Standard Oil of New Jersey (later Esso, then Exxon, finally ExxonMobil) 30 percent, and Standard Oil of New York (Socony) 10 percent—called Arabian American Oil Company (Aramco).

Saudi Arabia's big break came in 1948—exactly a century after the first successful oil-well drilling in Azerbaijan was officially recorded by the Russian czar. That year witnessed the discovery of the Ghawar oil field at its north end, Ein Dar. The full extent of this gargantuan field was only fully determined in 1950, with the drilling of a well 200 kilometers (125 miles) to the south of Ein Dar, at Haradh. Its simple anticlinal structure was 250 kilometers (150 miles) long and 90 kilometers (58 miles) wide. With an ultimate estimate of eighty-seven billion barrels of crude oil, Ghawar became the unchallenged world leader, leaving the Burgan of Kuwait trailing behind.

What is it that has made the Persian Gulf region so superabundant in petroleum? Explains Colin J. Campbell in his book, *The Coming Oil Crisis*: "It has to do with the fact that the Persian Gulf area was uniquely endowed with both oil source-rocks laid down in the warm Jurassic seas and with tight seals from the salt deposited when the seas subsequently dried up."[15]

The full discovery of the Ghawar field in 1950 coincided with the inauguration of the oil age, displacing the era of coal, which, since the turn of the century, had been the prime mover in the industrial West. Cars became ubiquitous, giving rise to an automobile civilization; and petroleum products invaded every facet of Western life.

TWO

In Every Pore of Western Life

Petroleum and its products are indispensable to modern life in the West. But to what degree?

A novel way to illustrate its sheer indispensability would be to compile a petroleum alphabet. Here is my attempt. A for aspirin; B for benzene; C for cellulose; D for diesel; E for ethanol; F for fertilizer; G for gasoline; H for heating oil; I for ion exchange resin; J for jet fuel; K for kerosene; L for lubricants; M for methane; N for nylon; O for oxy-acetylene gas; P for plastics; R for resin; S for solvents; T for tar; U for urea; V for Vaseline; W for wax; X for xylene; Y for yarn; and Z for . . .

Or one could plainly state that oil industry's annual turnover is $2,400,000,000,000; or that the top four of the ten richest hereditary rulers—King Abdullah of Saudi Arabia, worth $21 billion; Sultan Hassanal Bolkiah Muizzaddin Waddaullah of Brunei, $20 billion; Sheikh Khalifa bin Zayed al Nahyan of Abu Dhabi, $19 billion; and Sheikh Muhammad bin Rashid al Mukatam of Dubai, $14 billion—are based in oil-rich territories; or that, of the globe's seven most profitable companies, four are oil corporations: Exxon Mobil, Royal Dutch Shell, BP, and Chevron. In 2005, the profits of Exxon Mobil, the uncontested leader in the business and, with a revenue of $340 billion, number-one corporation in the United States, amounted to a staggering $25.3 billion, higher than the gross domestic products of many of the Afro–Asian–Latin American countries.[1]

A more dramatic way to grasp the critical importance of oil in our lives, however, would be to start discarding objects or systems either made from oil or petrochemicals or fueled by them. The above alphabet should come in handy in conducting the exercise.

The first, much-loved object to be towed away would be the family car, followed by the elaborate house-heating mechanism. Next to go would be the telephone system, since the phones, landline or mobile, are made of plastics, with the same fate befalling the television set and its remote control mechanism, and radios, as well as still and video cameras, and films, and DVD players.

House walls would be stripped bare of fireproof wallpaper and paint. The bedroom would be deprived of the mattresses, filled with polyurethane foam, the sheets and pillowcases made of polystyrene fabric, and anything else containing a shred of human-made fiber—and hot-water bottles made of synthetic rubber.

The study room or home office would be cleared of personal computers, printers, toners, printing ink, and all floppy discs—as well as CD-ROMs, with their jewel cases made from petrochemicals. All pens would be removed, since they are all encased in plastic—and so would the Scotch tape, paper adhesives, and the wastepaper baskets. The kitchen would lose not just the refrigerator, the vinyl-coated table covering and plastic dish-holder, but also all plastic bottles, polyethylene bags, kitchen countertops, grocery bags, food containers, waxed paper and packaging, artificial sweeteners, dishwashing liquid and detergents, grease solvents, floor wax, and plastic garbage cans.

Wardrobes would be stripped of all clothing containing human-made textile fibers—shirts, underwear, blouses, and skirts—and shoes with synthetic rubber soles and waterproof boots. Bathrooms would lose all their soap containers and synthetic skin scrubbers, as well as bath plugs. And bathroom cabinets would be emptied of all pharmaceuticals, Vaseline jars, shaving creams, and toothpaste and toothbrushes.

Outside the residential area, the garage would be denuded of car tires, brake fluids, lubricant oils, grease, air bags, weed killers, plant holders, gasoline containers, sweeping brushes, wheelbarrows, footballs, basketballs, water hoses, and toys. And in case there is a patio, its plastic chairs would be forfeited.

Finally, the strictly personal belongings: women's handbags would lose all cosmetics as well as spectacle frames. Men would find their wallets confiscated unless they are made of genuine leather.

What explains the all-pervasive presence of oil and its products in our daily lives is their chemical composition. They are compounds of hydrogen and carbon, the essential elements of living organisms, called hydrocarbons—as are the above-listed items. The ultimate source of carbon and hydrogen lies in the materials that formed the primordial Earth. Yet all these petrochemicals combined consume only 7 percent of the global oil output. The term *petrochemicals* came into vogue in the 1930s, when there was a gradual switch-over from coal tar—whose by-product was until then the feedstock for synthesizing organic chemicals—to petroleum for producing synthetic organic products.

Most of the petroleum is used for transportation and electric power generation. Nine-tenths of the world's transportation system depends on oil, the rest on steam. In the most advanced economy, that of the United States, three-fifths of the petroleum is burned to power transport, civilian and military, personal—cars and motorcycles—and commercial, vans, trucks, and aircraft. Booming tourist, holiday, and recreation industries are totally dependent on affordable car, bus, and air travel.

Oil-Powered Transport, Civilian and Military

Life without cars is unimaginable in North America, Europe, or Japan. An automobile is as much a part of Western existence today as central heating or asphalt roads. Whether it is going to work or a shop or a restaurant, to call on friends or family members, to see a physician or a lawyer, to go on vacation or move, it is the family car that does the transporting. This is especially true of the United States, where an average car owner travels 1,000 miles a month and there is a gasoline service station for every 400 households. In addition, millions of tons of assorted materials—from tiny sewing needles to giant bulldozers—are shipped weekly by truck along the United States' endless highways and byways. Little wonder that in the United States, home to fewer than 300 million in 2003, there were 231,290,000 vehicles and 191 million drivers.[2] That means 5 percent of humanity owning 30 percent of the world's vehicles.

Small wonder that the automobile and related industries are at the core of the manufacturing sector of the U.S. economy, creating a very substantial percentage of its wealth and jobs. One can either flaunt a wide array of statistics to hammer home the primacy of autos in the United States—or cite an economic fact or two of the post–World War II era illustrating the negative impact of a hefty jump in petroleum prices on the economy.

Each of the half-dozen major hikes in crude oil prices during that period caused a decline in the American GDP within six to nine months.[3] As a rule of thumb, a $5 rise in the price of an oil barrel slices off one half of 1 percent of the U.S. gross domestic product. (The 2005–06 price rise has yet to work its way through the transportation and manufacturing systems, and may not be as adversarial as before due to the abundant supply of cheap Chinese-made products, covering the gamut from clothes and shoes to electrical and electronic durables to computers.)

Yet one can sometimes reach similar conclusions through simple personal observations. Such was the case with me during my weeklong stay in Midland, Texas, in mid-2005. In the course of my ten-minute walk along West Wall Avenue, a main thoroughfare, from Ramada Inn to Blue Moon Chinese Restaurant, I noticed that of the thirty-three commercial establishments, all but nine were related to automobiles—gasoline service stations, car insurance, automobiles for sale, tires, batteries, brakes, upholstery, air conditioning, silencers, window tinting, and U-haul trailers. The exceptions were: tiles, real estate, life insurance, pawning, tattoos ("Drunks and Minors under 18 Not Allowed")—and of course the Chinese eatery, my destination.

The above narrative applies to civilian life. But the military is equally, if not more, dependent on oil. Since all its hardware and transport systems—tanks, planes, armored personnel carriers, warships, submarines, and armored Humvees (a distorted acronym of High Mobility Multipurpose Wheeled Vehicle)—are powered by the internal combustion engine, it cannot function without petroleum.

It was as early as 1912 that Winston Churchill, then first lord of the British admiralty, ordered the construction of five oil-fired battleships instead of coal-fired vessels, thus inaugurating the entry of petroleum into military strategy. The introduction of the tank in combat followed four years later, during World War I. By the time that armed conflict ended in 1918, the Allies had 150,000 motorcycles, cars, and trucks to transport soldiers and supplies. Since then, oil and oil products have become central to military planning and combat.

Then there is electricity, without which it is impossible to visualize the modern world. Generating plants, fueled by oil and natural gas, provide nearly two-thirds of electric power in the Unites States as well as other Western nations.[4] "Petroleum is a determinant of well-being, of national security, and international power for those who possess this vital resources and the converse for those who do not," says Robert Ebel of the Center for Strategic and International Studies in Washington.[5]

Oil Haves and Have-Nots

The gap between the oil haves and have-nots is related purely to geography. Petroleum and natural gas are hydrocarbons derived primarily from the microscopic plankton—the passively floating or weakly swimming animal or plant life in water—in seas and lakes, and from the plants whose dead remains got drained into lakes and seas by rivers. Only the right temperature of the sea or lake, available mostly in tropical conditions, combined with a steady supply of nutrients—iron, nitrate, phosphate, and silica—already dissolved into the water, could create blooms of plankton and other microscopic life forms. (The reason why today there are petroleum systems far away from the tropics is the displacements of the tectonic plates, mostly northward, during the past millions of years, which explains why the southern hemisphere is poor in oil.) On their demise, these dead organisms, as well as the excrement of their predators, began sinking slowly into the water. On their way to the bottom, almost all of them got oxidized due to the presence of oxygen in the water. The lower the oxygen content of the water—as in deep lakes, lagoons, stagnant marine troughs, or sinkholes—the greater the chance of the dead mass rich in carbon and hydrogen reaching the bottom.

In practice, only between 0.2 and 2 percent of the original mass fell on the water bed. And this material could build up slowly only if it did not get mixed up with the sediment discharged by rivers. Over millions of years, this concentrated mat hardened into a layer of nutrient-rich source rock to be buried gradually under sandy sediment pouring in from the rivers, with the sediment turning into sandstone over time. Given such heavy odds, the creation of oil and gas reservoirs over millions of years was rare indeed.

In the summer of 2005, an unusual occurrence near the offshore Swedish island of Landsort in the Baltic Sea re-created the ancient phenomenon. When the seventy-year-old hotelier Ingrid Sjoblom first noticed the streaks of bluish green algae in the water off Landsort, near Stockholm, she got excited and climbed a watchtower to take snapshots. Two days later the algae was transformed into a thick, stinking slush. "In one place you could throw a big rock into the water and it wouldn't sink, that is how thick it was," she said. The algae thrived because of the unusually warm weather, lack of wind, and prolific nutrients in the water. "The Baltic, one of the only two brackish, or low salinity, seas in the world [the Black Sea is the other], has a very simple ecosystem," explained Ivar Ekman of the *International Herald Tribune*. "It is also unusually shallow and has a very slow water exchange with the adjacent seas."[6]

Origins of Oil and Gas

To comprehend the existence of subterranean reservoirs of oil and gas, one has to think in terms of rocks and a time frame extending over hundreds of millions of years. The Phosphoria source rock in Wyoming in the United States, for instance, is 280 million years old, and the underlying sandstone is 20 million years older. With a 200-million-year history, the Jurassic era source rocks in the Texan and Persian Gulf regions are comparatively young.

Petroleum is formed in two stages: the creation of kerogen shale and its subsequent cooking at the right temperatures. Kerogen is a fatty but fine-grained organic material that is insoluble in water and is lighter than it.

In the first phase, the dead organic material—originating in microorganisms, including bacteria and single-cell, fat-rich marine algae that uses water-repelling hydrocarbon molecules to create a stable cell wall consisting of carbohydrates, protein and fat, and the excrement of their predators—undergoes transformation as it sinks to the bottoms of ancient lakes and seas to form a carpet on the floor. Over millions of years, this carpet is hardened into a layer of nutrient-rich rock, called kerogen shale or kergonites—a mixture of compounds with large molecules containing chiefly hydrogen and carbon but also traces of nitrogen, oxygen, and sulfur.

During the subsequent phase, the kerogen shale gets cooked at temperatures varying between 180 degrees Fahrenheit and 280 degrees Fahrenheit (100 degrees Celsius to 135 degrees Celsius)—existing between the depths of 7,500 feet (2,300 meters) and 15,000 feet (4,600 meters). The cooking results in heavy kerogen molecules breaking down into smaller molecules of oil and gas. The 7,500–15,000 feet subsoil range is known as the oil-gas window, and the cooked kerogen—chocolate brown or black in color, emanating petroliferous odor, and contained in clays and muddy limestone—is called petroleum, mature or hydro-carbon source rock.

This window is subdivided into two sections: the depth of 7,500–10,500 feet (2,300–3,200 meters), ideal for oil; and below 10,500 feet (3,200 meters), when kerogen gets cracked into gas, thus producing a mixture of oil and associated gas. On average, three-quarters of a gas accumulation in oil or oil-and-gas traps consists of combustible gases, with methane constituting more than four-fifths.

If kerogen gets depressed below the oil-gas window, then it gets too hot and is either transformed into gas or is progressively destroyed. If it lies above this window, it does not turn into oil-gas source rock and is called an immature rock.

The cooking leads to expansion of volume, especially in gas bubbles, which weakens the source rock and causes a rise in pressure. Because of this, the oil and associated gas mixture, being lighter than water, migrates upward through the vertical pores and fractures of the overlying sedimentary sandstone without mixing with the water that fills the microscopic pores in the sandstone, seeps through fissures and cracks, and rises to the ground. During this process the oil and gas split and travel to the surface at different speeds. On reaching the exposed surface, the gas disappears in the atmosphere and the oil deteriorates over time. This has been the fate of most of the liquid, semi-liquid, and gaseous hydrocarbons over the past countless millennia. Overall, only a minuscule fraction of the generated oil and gas finally ends up in exploitable oil fields.

Only in rare instances do the rising petroleum and gas run into an obstacle. Such an obstacle could be in the shape of rock folds or faults, reefs or sand lenses. If the rocks in the area have become folded and faulted for geological reasons, then petroleum and gas amass at the peak of the trap.

In some instances, the trap may exist above the source rock, as is the case with the Ekofisk field in Norway, which requires deep drilling to reach it. In other cases, the trap may exist at the margin of a geological depression, as it does in eastern Venezuela. In the latter case, crude oil is found at a shallow depth far removed from its original location. Also, surface erosion can bring the whole petroleum system near the surface. This was the case with the wells drilled near Baku and Titusville, Pennsylvania.

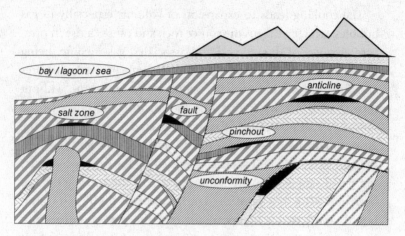

Different Oil and Gas Traps

The efficiency of a trap depends as much on the sealing power of the cap rock as on the difference between the underlying and overlying rocks. Salt and anhydrous calcium sulfate act as effective seals. Eastern Texas and the Persian Gulf region abound in such seals. That is the main reason for the existence of supergiant oil fields in Saudi Arabia and Kuwait. Since clay and shale lack the sealing qualities of salt rock, the seals in their cases get fractured and let the escaping petroleum either amass in a shallower trap or migrate to the surface.

At Spindletop in eastern Texas, the cap consisted of a 200-foot-thick (61 meters) stratum of sea salt, formed due to the recession of the Gulf of Mexico during the Jurassic era, which cannot be permeated by oil. A similar process was at work in the Persian Gulf region, where chocolate brown or black oil source rocks were created over scores of millions of years in the warm Jurassic seas and tight seals were provided by the dried salt left behind by the progressive drying up of the seas.

The combination of an oil source, a reservoir, and a trap is called a petroleum system. There are some six hundred such known systems in the world, containing recoverable commercial quantities of petroleum and gas, two-thirds of which are in accessible regions and the rest in remote inland areas or in deep offshore waters. Only one in twenty petroleum systems is considered gigantic, with reserves of one billion barrels of oil or more.

There is a tremendous variation in the size of the oil systems, the smallest producing only a few hundred barrels per day and the largest, mainly in the Middle East, such as the Ghawar in the Saudi kingdom, the Burgan in Kuwait, and the Safaniya off the Saudi coast, at thirty-eight billion barrels being the world's largest offshore field—yielding hundreds of thousands of barrels per day.

In chronological terms, the Persian Gulf region figures first— in the Jurassic Age (200 million–150 million years ago)—and the coast of West Africa last, during the Cretaceous Age of chalk and coal. The oil-bearing areas are generally called basins, a term used for a geological depression.

In the Persian Gulf area, the above-mentioned organic material was formed in warm Jurassic seas and amassed in stagnant lagoons and sinkholes, lacking oxygen in the water, within a platform of carbonate (salt of carbonate acid) which had received only a limited amount of sediment discharged by rivers, and the tight seals were provided by the salt deposited by the evaporating seas.

Other provinces conducive to the creation of oil source rocks were the Baltic Sea, Black Sea, and Caspian Sea, as well as the Gulf of California and Lake Maracaibo in Venezuela. In the North Sea, on the other hand, the organic matter gathered in stagnant rifts toward the end of the Jurassic Age, 150 million years ago. Finally, in West Africa, rift lakes opened up along the coast of the South Atlantic during the Cretaceous age, which fol- lowed the Jurassic period.

Shift from Coal to Oil

As described in chapter 1, the discovery of oil on the Arabian side of the Persian Gulf occurred in the 1930s. At that time, coal was an almost exclusive source of energy in western Europe and a predominant one in North America. The Middle Eastern oil output was a puny 5 percent of the global total. The outbreak of World War II stopped further exploration and production in the Arabian Peninsula, although not in Iran, which was occupied by British and the Soviet troops during the conflict. Due to the over-exploitation of the oil acreage to meet wartime demands, the United States consumed two-fifths of its total reserves, reducing them to twelve billion barrels. That in turn enhanced the preeminence of Kuwait's colossal Burgan oil field, then estimated to contain three times the American total.

However, Burgan ceded its prime place in 1948 to Ghawar in Saudi Arabia. The Saudi output rose so steeply that the earnings of the Arabian American Oil Company soared from $2.8 million in 1944 to $115 million in 1949.[7]

As the governments of war-ravaged Europe, buttressed by Washington's Marshall Plan aid, tried to rebuild their economies, they opted for oil instead of coal wherever they could, thus following the example of the United States. So there was a large-scale switch-over from coal to petroleum after World War II. In the western Europe of 1948, coal provided 80 percent of the energy and petroleum a mere 10 percent, the coal to oil ratio being 8:1. Remarkably, this ratio halved in a decade.

Nothing illustrated the dominance of coal in western Europe's daily life more than the chimneys of homes and factories belching black clouds of smoke. Every house in Britain and other western European countries contained a storage place for coal. When the air filled with fog in London or Rotterdam, the streets and roads turned into thick black smog, making breathing hazardous.

The rising demand for petroleum in western Europe in turn led to a jump in production in the Middle East, where the industry was dominated by a cartel called the "Seven Sisters." Five were American—Esso, Gulf, Socal, Socony, and Texaco—one British, British Petroleum, and one Anglo-Dutch, Royal Dutch Shell. All of them were furiously active in the Persian Gulf region.

An incredibly rapid growth in production lifted the business turnovers and profits of these companies to stratospheric heights. During the period of 1948–60, the average rate of return on capital of the oil corporations operating in the Persian Gulf region reached an astronomical 111 percent![8]

In western Europe, the pace of switch-over to oil accelerated when the authorities outlawed burning coal at home or in the workplace. They rationalized the move on health grounds. What they did not publicize, then or later, was the fact that a heat unit obtained from locally mined coal was two-and-a-half to three times more expensive than the one obtained from oil, then selling for less than $1 a barrel. The changeover from coal to oil in the 1950s and 1960s saved western Europe $3.5 billion a year,[9] or $100 billion in today's money.

By 1967, oil had become the source of half of western Europe's energy needs. Over the past two decades, the consumption of oil and oil products in western Europe registered an astonishing tenfold increase. Most of its oil imports originated in the Persian Gulf region, then producing almost a third of the global total. Two-thirds of the exports from the region were handled by five U.S. petroleum giants.

Across the Atlantic, Americans also took to petroleum and petroleum products with unabashed zeal. U.S. oil usage trebled in a quarter century following World War II.[10]

This happened for the following reasons: the massive highway construction undertaken during the presidency of Dwight Eisenhower (1953–61), which encouraged automobile travel; the emergence of vast suburbs throughout the United States, made possible by accelerating car ownership; and the rapid advancement of the petrochemical industry, which delivered an ever-lengthening catalogue of organic chemical compounds for popular use.

"After the war, petrochemical production expanded enormously in both the range of products and the tonnage produced," observes Kenneth Deffeyes, a former Princeton University professor of geophysics. "A major petroleum complex grew up around the Houston Ship Channel. Large petroleum refineries supplied hydrocarbons. Salt from the salt domes was turned into hydrochloric acid, chlorine, and sodium hydroxide. Sulfur, originally from the caps of salt domes, was a source of sulfuric acid. Bromine came from seawater. Portions of the complex were owned and operated by various companies."[11]

Petroleum Refining and Petrochemicals

Since crude oil is composed of liquids (kerosene and gasoline), semisolids (bitumen), and gases (butane, methane, and propane, present as minuscule bubbles), it is fairly fluid. Its density, measured by a scale set by the American Petroleum Institute (API), varies between 15 and 45 degrees, the higher figure signifying lightness. Heavier petroleum is green or dark brown, and the lighter variety, containing dissolved natural gas, can be as colorless as the refined product.

Given its complex composition, petroleum has to be put through a process that separates its constituents in stages. This is done by distillation, which separates molecules that boil at different temperatures and are then cooled. In other words, oil is refined by fractional distillation, which separates it into fractions of variable volatility. The task of the early refineries was to transform oil's stable molecules into saleable products. Their most marketable product was kerosene, then used primarily for generating light from hurricane lanterns.[12]

The arrival of the gasoline-powered automobile in 1905 created a vast demand for gasoline made up of smaller molecules than those of kerosene. By using traditional distillation, the amount of gasoline that refiners could separate from crude oil was 10 to 20 percent by volume.

This led to subsequent processing of the earlier (reaction) products achieved by means of catalytic reformers, thermal cracking units, or cokers (used to absorb unwanted material). Each of these more complex processing units also incorporated a fractional distillation tower to separate its own reaction products.

Thermal cracking is used as a follow-up on the primary distillation to make smaller molecules out of larger ones. In practice, refining or separation is done inside tall cylinders, called fractional distillation towers, by catalyst crackers, whereby heat and a catalyst accelerate the chemical reaction.

Thermal cracking, however, produces some unstable molecules prone to participating in further chemical reactions. Out of this phenomenon the petrochemical industry has arisen. The larger molecules are put through cracking and reforming to produce a variety of end products: asphalt, cleaning agents, explosives, fertilizers, fibers, gasoline/petrol, jellies (petroleum jelly, popularly known as Vaseline), jet fuel, kerosene, medicines, naphtha, paints, plastics, synthetic rubber, and waxes.

German and American corporations pioneered commercial petrochemical products before World War I. Initially the feedstock for these plants was a tar produced as a by-product from the chemical treatment of coal. The switch-over from coal to petroleum, initiated in the early 1930s, was completed by 1950.

In sum, refining of crude oil takes place in two phases: primary and advanced. In the first phase there is a separation of the basic components of crude oil—liquefied petroleum gases (LPG, butane and propane, used as cooking gas supplied in steel cylinders), followed by gasoline, naphtha (consumed as feedstock for petrochemicals), kerosene (used both domestically and as Avtur, jet fuel for aircraft), gas oil (consumed as diesel in vehicles and as heating oil), and finally, fuel oil (used to power ships and electricity and other industrial plants).

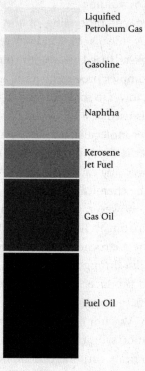

Liquified Petroleum Gas

Gasoline

Naphtha

Kerosene Jet Fuel

Gas Oil

Fuel Oil

In the subsequent phase, either gas oil or fuel oil is put through the thermal process or crackers to obtain diesel or gasoline.[13]

In practice, each refinery is built to process crude oils of certain API grades into specific end products. With that objective in mind, a process designer assembles a set of basic processing units that fall into three categories: primary, meaning those that separate oil's compendium of hydrocarbons into fractions of more closely related properties; advanced, meaning those that chemically convert the separated hydrocarbons into more popular products; and purifying (called cokers), meaning those that remove unwanted elements and compounds from the end products.[14]

In chemical terms, oil contains three series of carbon and hydrogen organic compounds: the paraffin, naphthalene, and aromatic series. The paraffin series, accounting for 50 to 60 percent of the oil by weight, is the most extensive, ranging from methane gas to gasoline to lubricating oil and waxes. The naphthalene series yields volatile liquids to tarry bitumen. Finally, the aromatics (so called because they smell) series gives mainly benzene but also parexylene and xylene.[15] The list of everyday products and items manufactured with an input from aromatics is overlong—ranging from aspirin, air bags, and easy-to-wear clothes, to recent high-tech developments such as the CD-ROM.

While refiners manufacture ultralong carbon chains to make plastic polyethylene and polyvinyl chloride (PVC), animals and plants produce hydrocarbon chains naturally: they are readily recognized by their water-repelling quality. Wax in the human ear is a case in point.

Petroleum is superior to all other sources of energy, but while its derivatives—used to run cars and generate electricity—can be replaced, those utilized for producing pharmaceuticals cannot. So, taking a long view of the future of our civilization, instead of consuming oil to fuel transport and power-generating stations, we should save it for the manufacture of most of our wonder drugs.

THREE

A Finite Resource

Anybody researching the petroleum industry is bound sooner or later to come across Marion King Hubbert (1903–89), an American geophysicist. His parents, William Bee and Cora Virginia Hubbert of San Saba, central Texas, named him after a teacher they admired, although the name can also be for girls. As an adult and a scientist, he resorted to calling himself M. King Hubbert to make plain his sex. He suffered from another handicap—a slightly asymmetrical face, the result of a boyhood accident in which a log rolled over him.

When he was five, his parents moved to Fort Stockton, where his father worked as a ranch foreman. Later they returned to San Saba County. After attending public schools in Fort Stockton and San Saba, Marion King enrolled at a private high school. Here he evinced keen interest in such fresh inventions as telephones and cars powered by steam engines.

After graduating from Weatherford Junior College in 1923, he enrolled at the University of Chicago—then regarded as the most innovative institution of higher education in the United States. Five years later he obtained a master's degree in geophysics. He then worked as an oil geologist in the southwestern states while also working toward his doctorate. In 1931, he was hired by Columbia University as an instructor in geophysics. During the summer vacation, he engaged in geological studies for Amerada

Petroleum Corporation in Oklahoma, the Illinois State Geological Survey, and the United States Geological Survey (USGS). He obtained his doctorate in geophysics in 1937, but failed to get promoted to assistant professor at Columbia. This might have been due to either his pugnacious nature or his Texan drawl. Anyway, he quit Columbia three years later to serve as a senior analyst at the Board of Economic Warfare in Washington, D.C. Later, he would often mention his shabby treatment by Columbia University, his chubby, big-eared, spectacled face contorted by undiminished bitterness.

In 1943 he returned to Texas, where he joined Shell Development Company as a research geophysicist in the Exploration and Production Research Division and rose to become first the chief consultant (general geology) and then an associate director in the division. As a trained scientist, he applied rigorous reasoning to the study of complex geological phenomena, and went on to publish seventy major scientific papers and several books on subsurface water, geological structures, and energy resources. He was fond of describing his contributions to geology and geophysics as "eminently theoretical." But the plain fact was that his findings ended up having a very practical impact on raising social consciousness to conserve mineral resources, especially petroleum and natural gas, and even on Washington's policies toward oil-producing countries.

In the early 1950s, he revised theories about the flow of subterranean fluids that showed that fluids get trapped under circumstances that until then had been considered impossible. His contribution had a major impact on the techniques used to pinpoint petroleum and gas deposits. He became a leading expert at judging the capacities of oil fields and natural gas reservoirs. He went on to forecast that the yield of a petroleum reserve over time would resemble a bell curve, peaking when half of the petroleum had been extracted, and then declining.

His big break, however, did not come until March 1956 at the spring meeting of the southern district of the American Petroleum Institute (API) at the Plaza Hotel in San Antonio, Texas. In his paper "Nuclear Energy and the Fossil Fuels," he forecast that oil production in the Lower 48 would reach its peak between the late 1960s and early 1970s, and then decline. Hubbert estimated the aggregate U.S. oil reserves that would be found and exploited by "conventional methods" then in vogue at 150 to 200 billion barrels. (Oil reserves or deposits are defined as future production from the existing wells with the use of current technology.) Next he guessed the most likely annual production rates for the minimum and maximum reserves. That led him to estimate when the maximum output would be achieved.

Hubbert presented his paper at a time when the mood in the petroleum industry in the United States in general, and in Texas in particular, was extremely bullish. This was aptly illustrated by the municipal council members in Midland adopting the credo "The Sky's the Limit"—a motto that, according to George W. Bush's acceptance speech at the 2000 Republican Convention, had inspired him as a boy growing up in Midland.

Hubbert's bosses at Shell Oil Company knew the content of his paper, and were deeply dismayed by its pessimistic conclusion. "He said later that Shell Oil head office was on the phone right to the last five minutes before the talk, asking Hubbert to withdraw his prediction," writes Kenneth S. Deffeyes—a heavyset geophysicist with a cheerful expression who worked alongside Hubbert for nine years—in his book *Hubbert's Peak*. But Hubbert was on sure ground, confident of the scientific model he had built and the differential equations he had applied. "Hubbert had an extremely combative personality, and he went through with his announcement," notes Deffeyes. "His belligerence during technical arguments gave rise to a saying around the lab, 'That Hubbert is a bastard, but at least he's *our* bastard.' "[1]

Hubbert's paper divided the oil and gas geologists into two camps: pro- and anti-Hubbert. Some of his critics dismissed his forecast since they had heard similar doomsday scenarios from other geophysicists before. Others were simply too addicted to the extremely lucrative business of petroleum and gas to envisage an end to the cornucopia in their lifetime.

By 1971, however, the scoffers were silenced, and the admirers were vindicated. In 1970 the conventional petroleum output in the Lower 48 reached its peak at 11.3 million bpd, and since then it has been declining, down to 6.83 million bpd (including shale oil, oil sands and natural gas liquids, and enhanced recovery) in 2005. By the early 1970s, Hubbert's standing had risen to such heights that the curve he used in his 1956 paper became known as Hubbert's curve, and the peak of the curve as Hubbert's peak.

In 1975, with the United States still reeling from the ill effects of the oil-price explosion caused in the wake of the Arab oil embargo from October 1973 to March 1974, the National Academy of Sciences (NSA) accepted Hubbert's calculations on oil and natural gas depletion while acknowledging that its own earlier high estimates had been wrong.

By then Hubbert had retired from Shell Oil and joined the United States Geological Survey as a senior research geophysicist. Once the NSA endorsed his realistic estimation of U.S. hydrocarbons, Hubbert became a media star. Still glowing in the limelight, he left the USGS in 1976. By the time he died thirteen years later, his acolytes had applied his methodology to the new finds in the North Sea, exploited chiefly by Britain and Norway, and predicted the peak production between the mid- and late-1990s. In reality, Britain's output peaked in 1999 and Norway's in 2000. It thus became evident that Hubbert's formula could be applied on a global scale.

The impressive, proven fact about a bell curve is that it represents not just the pattern of the mass scale extraction of a fairly recently discovered mineral such as crude oil, but also the pattern of its discovery. In his book *The Coming Oil Crisis*, Colin J. Campbell—a heavily built, chubby-faced Briton with a penetrating gaze, who worked as a geologist with Amoco for many years—shows how petroleum discoveries made in each decade follow a bell curve. Starting with 125 billion barrels in the period up to 1930, the finds reached a peak in the 1960s at 370 billion barrels, declining steadily thereon down to 50 billion barrels in the first half of the 1990s, when his research ended.[2]

Discoveries Lagging Behind Consumption

"In any region," writes petroleum geologist Joseph Riva, a former oil analyst with U.S. Congressional Research, in his report *World Oil Production After Year 2000: Business As Usual or Crises?*, "the large fields are the biggest targets and are usually found first. As exploration proceeds, the average size of the fields discovered decreases, as does the amount of oil found per unit of exploratory drilling."[3]

In the case of the United States, by 1950 all the anticlines visible from a helicopter had been drilled.

Later, more sophisticated methods of geological mapping were devised and used. As with other minerals, explorers investigated the large and easy prospects first, and then turned to exploiting small and obscure ones in established oil-bearing basins while also simultaneously attempting to raise the recovery rate from the already discovered oil fields through improved technology.

Current statistics illustrate how skewed the global distribution of petroleum is. Of the approximately 50,000 oil fields in the world today, the largest 40 account for nearly half of the total output.[4]

Increasingly, oil companies have found themselves exploring and developing remote hydrocarbon reserves, both inland and offshore. This requires deploying expensive, advanced technology and investing large sums of cash to build an infrastructure to extract and transport the commodity over long distances to maritime terminals. The cost of drilling one ultradeep offshore oil well can reach the astronomical sum of $100 million. It therefore takes several years to transform newly found oil fields into sources of commercial oil supplies. This is as true of the fields of Alaska in the 1980s as it is of the Caspian Basin today.

Worldwide, the average annual new discoveries of 13.5 billion barrels during the 1980s and 1990s compares poorly with the current annual consumption of 30 billion barrels. Since then, disregarding the big discoveries in the late 1990s in the Caspian Basin, the Gulf of Mexico, and off the coast of West Africa, petroleum corporations have consistently discovered decreasing amounts of oil.[5]

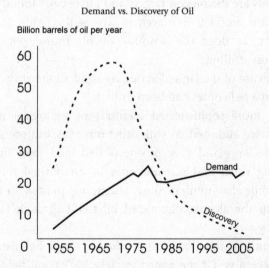

Demand vs. Discovery of Oil

Billion barrels of oil per year

"As demand increases while our existing production base declines, we come squarely to the magnitude of the task before us," remarked Lee Raymond, chief executive officer of Exxon Mobil, in 2003. The following year, oil companies worldwide spent $8 billion on exploration but discovered only $4 billion of commercially useful oil. Some companies have tried to meet the challenge by falsely overstating the reserves they possess. In early 2005, Royal Dutch Shell chief executive officer Jeroen van der Veer announced that his corporation had overstated its oil and gas reserves by a third.[6]

Today, four out of five barrels in the world are coming from the pre-1973 fields, which include Hassi Massoud field (discovered in 1956) in Algeria, with more than 1 billion barrels, and Ekofisk (found in 1969) in Norway with over 1 billion barrels— and a majority of them (called mature, meaning old) are yielding declining quantities. To keep the old oil acreage productive entails more expense than the freshly discovered ones.

Alarmingly, the overabundant Burgan oil field in Kuwait, which has accounted for four-fifths of the national oil output, has been showing signs of fatigue. More alarmingly, the king of kings in the oil hierarchy, the Ghawar oil field in Saudi Arabia, struck in 1948–50, which, since its discovery, has yielded a mammoth quantity of 55 billion barrels, is on its way to "maturity"—at least in its northern sector, where its most productive wells are located. Its southern sector, geologically less favorable to oil extraction, is filled with high-viscosity petroleum, which costs more to extract.[7]

Predicting the Peak

To be able to judge when the peak output will be reached, a follower of Hubbert's methodology should have some idea of the ultimate recoverable size of a natural resource. The ultimate figure consists of (a) what has been extracted so far, (b) what remains of the discovered finds, and (c) what remains undiscovered.

In the case of oil, we know that by the end of 2005, about a trillion barrels of oil had been extracted worldwide, and $10 trillion had been invested in petroleum oil fields and tankers, refineries, and the vast network for distributing gasoline and diesel and supplying fuel oil to power-generating plants and electricity to consumers through transmission lines. There is no dispute about (a).

But disagreements arise on (b) and (c). These are centered mostly on the estimated or expected reserves in Siberia, West Africa, eastern South America, and the Caspian Basin. According to the *BP Statistical Review of World Energy June 2006*, the total proved world reserves at the end of 2005 stood at 1.20 trillion barrels—well below the USGS estimate of 1.64 trillion barrels.

The high USGS figure is the result of two factors, one technical and the other political. The USGS applied the same method to estimate the unrecovered oil reserves outside the United States as it had done inside. It divided the United States into small areas and invited oil estimates from geologists for each of them. It considered each area to be independent. This was a false assumption, since oil fields do not exist within artificially drawn lines. The geologists guessed the volumes of known oil fields as a whole even when they did not fall completely within their area of study. By totaling up these estimates, the USGS ended up with an inflated statistic—both inside the United States and outside. So, as before, in 2000 the USGS announced overly optimistic estimates of global oil.

As governmental bodies, the USGS and the U.S. Energy Information Administration (EIA) are susceptible to political pressure and prone to presenting rosy scenarios. For instance, in the mid-1990s U.S. Energy Department officials mentioned reserves of 100 billion barrels in the Caspian Basin, only to be upstaged by the EIA's figure of 292 billion barrels. Later, when all the hype (originating primarily in Washington) fizzled out, oil experts throughout the world put the Caspian Basin on a par with the North Sea with reserves of some 40 billion barrels.

"It would be a huge mistake to base U.S. energy policy on

what the USGS thinks about future oil supplies," one former high-ranking U.S. energy official told Paul Roberts, the author of *The End of Oil*. "And the Energy Information Administration has put out such overblown numbers, and done it with such arrogance, that it should be statutorily barred from answering questions about oil."[8]

According to Colin Campbell, even the figures published annually by BP are on the high side, as they are based on the information officially provided by the listed countries.

This is due to the rule change at OPEC. Since its inception in 1960, it had considered solely the member country's production capacity when assigning it a share of the world market. But in 1985 it decided to take into account also the petroleum reserves of the member state. Its six leading members—Iran, Iraq, Kuwait, Saudi Arabia, the United Arab Emirates, and Venezuela—started raising their respective reserves. Their aggregate oil deposits increased from 762 billion barrels in 1984 to 900 billion barrels three years later, a jump of 30 percent. Part of the rise could be rationalized as rectifying earlier underestimates; the rest was more wish fulfillment than reality.

The crest would be reached when half of the total oil had been extracted. So, if the ultimate recoverable oil is 2.1 trillion barrels, as estimated by Hubbert in 1982, then half of that amount would be mined by 2006. If we take the BP figure of 2.20 (1 trillion consumed + 1.20 trillion in proven reserves) trillion barrels, then half of that total volume would be extracted by 2010, given an average annual output of 33 billion barrels. If one accepts the USGS estimate, which is 440 billion higher than BP's, then one should add another seven years and get 2017. So the worldwide peak will be reached between 2006 and 2017.

Most likely, however, actual oil production will not follow the neat outline of a bell curve, and, after reaching a crest, it will fall steadily for a few years and then rise to another crest before finally going into a terminal decline. Assuming that the second peak will appear in 2017, we have only a decade ahead of us before the irreversible fall sets in.

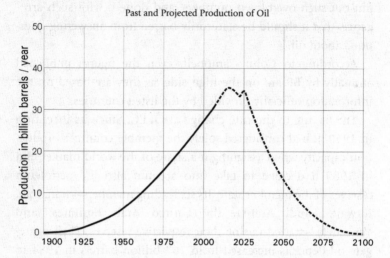

Past and Projected Production of Oil

However, since three-quarters of all known reserves lie in OPEC states, where most of the forty largest oil fields are located, one should divide the globe into OPEC and non-OPEC regions. Russia, the most endowed non-OPEC country, is expected to reach its peak output by 2015. But the crest of OPEC states will not appear until around 2025. That means the non-OPEC world will become increasingly dependent on oil imports from OPEC members during the next two decades.

Problems in Raising Output

The above scenario assumes that the projected output will materialize to meet the demand that is set to rise to two and a half times the current annual rate of 1.6 percent, to reach 102 million bpd in 2017 from the current 83 million bpd.

But there are several obstacles—economic, engineering, and political, among others—to pumping up production to that level.

Achieving the required output by 2017 will require an investment of $100 billion a year—to be continued beyond that date for the next two decades. In April 2001, U.S. Vice President Dick Cheney commissioned an independent task force of the Council on Foreign Relations and the James Baker III Institute for Public Policy at Rice University, Houston (chaired by Edward Morse and directed by Amy Myers Jaffe), to produce a report on new energy policy.

Their report, titled "Strategic Energy Policy Challenges for the 21st Century," pointed to "political difficulties and underinvestment in oil-producing countries as prime culprits in a crisis of energy production growth." Though the document did not name them, Iran and Iraq, possessing the second- and third-largest petroleum reserves, respectively, were apparently at the top of that list.[9] "[T]he U.S. government has operated under the assumption that the oil companies of these countries would make the investments needed to maintain enough surplus capacity to form a cushion against disruptions elsewhere," the report continued. "For several years these assumptions appeared justified. But recently, these things have changed. These Gulf allies are finding their domestic and foreign policy interests increasingly at odds with U.S. strategic considerations, especially as Arab-Israeli tensions flare. They have become less inclined to lower oil prices in exchange for security of markets, and evidence suggests that investment is not being made in a timely enough manner to increase production capacity in line with increasing global needs. A trend toward anti-Americanism could affect regional leaders' ability to cooperate with the United States in the energy area." The document concluded that the major problems were concentration of resources in the Middle East Gulf region and "the vulnerability of the global economy to domestic conditions in the key producer countries."[10]

There was no sign of an annual investment on the order of

$100 billion being planned, much less implemented. More than 90 percent of the planet's proven oil reserves are owned by countries, nationalized petroleum companies, and Russian oil companies, most of which are currently closed to direct foreign investment. Nothing illustrated the marginalization of the American corporations from the oil-rich Middle East Gulf region better than the statistic that in 2000, their investment in this area amounted to only 70 cents of every $100 spent by them for oil and gas exploration and development.[11]

In the oil industry's league table, the top nine positions are taken by the nationalized oil companies—with Saudi Aramco possessing 259 billion barrels of oil at the top, followed by the National Iranian Oil Company with 126 billion barrels, and Petroleus Mexicano with 16 billion barrels at the bottom. With oil reserves of 13 billion barrels, Exxon Mobil, the largest private oil corporation in the world, is only twelfth in rank. BP, the second-largest private oil major, ranks seventeenth; and ChevronTexaco, with 9 billion barrels, is the last but one in the top twenty.[12]

Of the nine largest oil companies, six are in the Persian Gulf region or North Africa—areas prone to political instability. Among the remaining corporations, based respectively in Nigeria, Venezuela, and Mexico, only the last functions in a relatively stable political environment.

In theory, the major Russian oil companies, owned largely or fully by the state—Lukoil possessing 16 billion barrels, Gazprom 14 billion barrels, and Yukos 12 billion barrels—are open to foreign investment. But in practice non-Russian investors face severe hurdles.

It was not investment alone. World demand is rising by 2 to 3 million bpd a year. And, to compensate for the oil extracted from aging fields, the companies need to cover the declines. "That's another 4 to 5 million bpd," Sadad al Husseini, the recently retired head of the exploration and production division of Saudi Aramco, told Peter Maas of the *New York Times Magazine* in August 2005. In other words, if the long-established demand and depletion patterns continue, every year the world will need to tap fields or wells to pump an additional 6 million bpd. "[Production] [c]apacity is not just a function of reserves," continued Husseini. "It is a function of reserves plus know-how plus a commercial system that is designed to increase the resources exploitation." Raising capacity required more engineers, drilling of more wells, and having more pipelines and processing facilities, and rigs and steel. "Currently, the global oil industry suffers a deficit of qualified engineers to oversee such projects and the equipment and the raw materials—for example, rigs and materials—to build them."[13]

Given these constraints, the EIA's forecast in 2004 that Saudi Arabia, then producing 10.6 million bpd, would raise its output to 18.2 million bpd by 2020 seemed preposterously optimistic. Referring to the claim of Saudi oil minister Ali Al Naimi that "we can maintain 12.5 or 15 million bpd for the next thirty to fifty years," Husseini remarked that 12.5 million bpd by 2009 was realistic, but "not 15 million bpd by 2015."

Much of the current hype by the EIA and the U.S. Department of Energy seems more like whistling in the dark to keep up spirits than applying rosy gloss to an increasingly alarming scenario. Contrary to their public posturing, the top officials of these governmental organizations seem to have registered the glaring fact that today, only one out of eight rigs in the United States is drilling for oil; all others are for gas.[14]

Little wonder that in 2004 the U.S. Energy Department's National Energy Technology Laboratory commissioned a report on trends in global oil output from Science Applications International Corporation (SAIC). In February 2005, the SAIC's team, led by energy analyst Robert Hirsch, released its report, titled

Peaking of World Oil Production: Impacts, Mitigation, and Risk Management. For some months, though, the only copy available to the public was posted on the Web site of Hilltop Public School, in Chula Vista, California!

"Because oil prices have been relatively high for the past decade, oil companies have conducted extensive exploration over that period, but their results have been disappointing," said the SAIC report. "If recent trends hold, there is little reason to expect that exploration success will dramatically improve in the future. . . . The image is of a world moving from a long period in which reserves additions were much greater than consumption to an era in which additions are falling increasingly short of annual consumption. This is but one of a number of trends that suggest that the world is fast approaching the inevitable peaking of conventional world oil production."[15]

Falling Output, Rising Demand

Worldwide, the predicted decline in oil output will occur against rising demand, which is expected to reach 102 million bpd in 2017. "As populations grow and economies take off, millions in the developing world are enjoying the benefits of a lifestyle that requires increasing amounts of energy," wrote David O'Reilly, chairman and chief executive officer of Chevron, in a two-page advertisement that appeared in many newspapers in the United States and Europe in September 2005. "In fact, some say that in twenty years the world will consume 40 percent more oil than it does today. At the same time, many of the world's oil and gas fields are maturing. And new energy discoveries are mainly occurring in places where resources are difficult to extract, physically, economically, and even politically."

As it is, at present a quarter of the human race—1.6 billion people—has no access to fossil fuels or electricity. Overall, oil consumption in developing nations is set to rise 2.5 times between now and 2020, from 27 million bpd to 67 million bpd. Petroleum usage in China is increasing at an incredible 15 percent a year, doubling every five years, and in India at 6 percent. By 2020, half of the oil output will be consumed by the developing world, up from its present share of a third of the total.

By then, worldwide demand for electricity will be 70 percent higher than it is today, to satisfy the needs of hundreds of millions of Chinese and Indians owning electrical appliances, television sets, microwave ovens, and personal computers.

Countervailing Factors

Optimists rightly point out the countervailing factors at work. Some of these are of long standing; others came into play as human innovation and expertise were applied to the oil industry.

In the former category are the secondary and tertiary means of recovering petroleum. While explaining how Al Dukhan Number 1 well in Qatar, drilled in 1940, continued to yield oil sixty-five years later, Juma Ali al Buainain told me that gas from the nearby gas field was used to boost the underground pressure in the nearby oil reservoirs to raise the petroleum to the surface. He thus described a secondary means of recovering oil.[16]

Yet despite the combined recovery gained by the primary and secondary means, on average about half of the petroleum in the reservoir is left untapped.

In 1980, when oil prices reached $41 a barrel, tertiary or enhanced recovery was introduced in the United States. It consisted chiefly of using steam injection to recover thick, viscous oil in California, or injecting carbon dioxide to increase the volume of oil and thus reduce its viscosity. During the next six years the number of such initiatives rose to 512, and then fell steadily, to 200 in 1998. Since then the yield from this method has stabilized at 700,000 bpd, roughly about a tenth of the total national output.[17]

In the 1990s, encouraged by negligible royalties and taxes, Western oil corporations deployed a largely untested technology to convert extra heavy crude available in the Orinoco river belt area of Venezuela into lighter synthetic oil for export. They succeeded. By 2005, their production soared to 600,000 bpd, a fifth of the national total.[18]

Then there is also water injection. "Nowadays we are using water injection to get the oil out," said Bruce Brady of the Great Western Drilling Company in Midland. "New types of chemicals are used in the water for injection, which increases the yield. They also give more exposure to the source rock and that yields more oil."[19]

There is a downside to secondary and tertiary methods of recovery. If the wrong method is used, or if too much petroleum is extracted too swiftly, it can damage the subterranean structure and severely cut the size of the recoverable oil. Overexploited fields in the past have collapsed suddenly and left behind large pools of trapped petroleum, which have remained inaccessible so far.

Elsewhere, there has been much advancement in seismic profiling of the underground. Nowadays oil-servicing corporations like Halliburton can provide amazing, computerized, three-dimensional seismic images of the subsoil, pinpointing where oil and gas source rocks are located and even indicating the most efficient routes to reach them.

The limit of the 15,000-foot (4,570-meter) depth was crossed in the mid-1980s. Now drillers can drill up to 20,000 feet (5,100 meters), about four miles, and beyond, using conventional equipment.

Moreover, specialized rigs penetrate the earth as far as 50,000 feet (15,240 meters). Modern technology allows the drills to rotate at an angle, even perpendicularly, and detect oil and gas electronically.

Equipped with such advanced technology, oil corporations can now operate in almost any environment or climate—a floating platform anchored 10,000 feet (3,050 meters) above the seabed in the Caspian Sea or on permanently frozen tundra in Russia's northern Siberia, sites that were earlier considered economically or technically infeasible.

Already, the new seismic techniques have resulted in the discovery of oil and gas in the deep sea off the West African coast. And the prospect of finding hydrocarbon deposits has improved in the deltaic areas of the Gulf of Mexico and off the coast of Brazil, as well as in the Arctic provinces of Canada, Greenland, Norway, and Siberia.

Furthermore, the amount of recoverable oil has been rising steadily. Until the 1970s, drillers considered themselves fortunate to extract 30 percent of the oil deposit from a field. But, equipped with the latest mapping and drilling technology, operators can see where the remnant lies within an oil reservoir, and this enables them to drill a precisely targeted hole to access it. They can thereby raise the recovery rate to as much as 50 percent or even higher. According to Bruce Brady, this has encouraged oil companies to try reviving declining fields or even examining the abandoned ones.

Taking the above into account, the USGS has estimated the gain afforded by the new technology at 700 billion barrels, an add-on of a whopping one-third to the most reliable ultimate reserves of 2 trillion barrels.

The main flaw in the USGS's sunny estimate is that it totally overlooks the possibility of overexploitation of prolific fields and their sudden collapse. Some experts are predicting such a scenario for the superabundant fields of Ghawar and Burgan after several decades of intense exploitation of these underground seas of oil.

None of the countervailing factors singly or collectively can alter the plain fact that like all minerals, petroleum is finite, and will be exhausted.

On the other hand, humans have yet to discover a commodity that comes anywhere near oil with its various uses. It is a mineral that has shaped history and civilization like no other since it was first extracted on a commercial scale in 1846.

Part II
Geopolitics of Oil

FOUR

Speed, Oil, and Wars– Up to 1973

Ultimately, it all boils down to speed—the human race's unending quest for it on land and water and in the air. The pursuit of speed on land resulted in an automobile powered by an internal combustion engine, which would revolutionize civilian life like no other invention before or since. The search for speed on water led to an oil-fueled ship with an internal combustion engine at its heart, which strongly impacted military affairs and revolutionized the way war is waged.

It was during the first decade of the twentieth century that disparate developments in the United States, Britain, and the Middle East converged to make the above possible. The main actors in this drama were Muzaffar al Din Qajar, the shah of Iran; William Knox D'Arcy, a British entrepreneur; Antoine Kitabji, an Armenian Iranian serving as Iran's director general of customs; Kaiser Wilhelm II of Germany; Henry Ford, an American industrialist; Admiral John Arbuthnot Fisher of the British Navy; and Winston Churchill, the first lord of the (British) admiralty.

Each of these players—some strong-willed, others merely venal—pursued his interest ardently. The sickly yet profligate Muzaffar al Din Shah was perennially short of funds, ready to raise cash on anything of value—present or potential—he could sell. As a middleman, expecting a handsome kickback, Kitabji was intent on enticing a moneybags in Europe to gamble on the potential oil riches of Iran. D'Arcy was by temperament and experience a gambling man, addicted to horse racing since his late teens. An engineer by training, Henry Ford (1863–1947), a slim, mustached man, given to wearing bow ties and Trilby hats, left Edison Illuminating Company in Detroit to work with George Selden, who acquired a patent for a gasoline car in the United States in 1885, to design and manufacture one. In 1887, Wilhelm II became the kaiser of Germany. A robustly built man with muttonchop whiskers, he was in the habit of enhancing his commanding presence by appearing in his medaled military uniform topped with a spiked helmet. Plainspoken and petulant by turns, he was determined to raise Germany to the status of Great Power by building a navy more powerful than Britain's—an aim that Admiral Fisher, later backed by Churchill, was equally resolved to frustrate.

Since his father, Nasser al Din Shah, ruled for nearly half a century, Muzaffar al Din Shah—a big hulk of a man with florid cheeks and a luxuriant mustache running across his face, seldom seen without his fez—was well advanced in age when he ascended the throne in Tehran in 1896. He inherited from his father physical ailments—including gout, which caused him much excruciating arthritic pain—and reckless prodigality. He continued his father's routine of undertaking lavish trips to Europe by raising fresh loans, which only worsened Iran's fiscal state, perennially lacking foreign currencies to pay for foreign imports and travel.

With Iran placed strategically between two expanding empires—the czarist from the north and the British from the east, in the Indian subcontinent—both keen to influence Iran through diplomacy and other means, its rulers tried to exploit the situation to their material advantage. By the end of the nineteenth century, however, czarist Russia had the upper hand, with the Iranian economy tied to Russia's, and Saint Petersburg seriously contemplating naval presence in the warm waters of the Persian Gulf as a means to establish political hegemony over Iran and shut out other Great Powers.

The British government feared the prospect. It saw salvation in the shah's periodic forays into Europe to raise further funds. It was for this purpose that Kitabji arrived in Paris in the winter of 1900–01, ostensibly to open an Iranian exhibition. With the assistance of a retired British diplomat, Kitabji aroused D'Arcy's interest to bid for an oil concession in Iran.

In mid-April 1901, a representative of D'Arcy's arrived in Tehran with the authority to sign a deal. He worked closely not only with Kitabji but also with Sir Arthur Hardinge, the British minister in Tehran, who, aware of the degenerate ways of the shah, described him as "an elderly child."

Between them, they won the backing of all the leading ministers and courtiers. Alerted about the negotiations on an oil concession, the Russian minister in Tehran did his best to derail them. The shah began to demur. So D'Arcy's envoy raised his offer by a further £5,000 ($25,000), taking the immediate cash payment to £20,000 ($100,000). Muzaffar al Din Shah signed the historic document on May 28, 1901.

For an oil concession in all of Iran, except the five northern provinces adjoining Russia, covering a quarter of the country, for sixty years, the shah received £20,000, along with another £20,000 worth of shares as well as 16 percent of annual net profits.

Among those who were keeping a watchful eye on the oil deliberations was Admiral Fisher, a small, rotund dynamo of a man with a well-clipped salt-and-pepper mustache, who advocated switching from coal to oil—thus from steam engines to internal combustion engines—in the Royal Navy. He had noted that by carrying out this change-over, American cargo ships were cutting their fuel costs by three-quarters and gaining a third in cargo volume while saving more money by shedding engineers and coal stokers. But he was opposed by most other admirals. They argued that Britain had enormous coal reserves but no petroleum of its own.

By then, the British Navy was being challenged by its fast-expanding German counterpart, since Kaiser Wilhelm had realized, rightly, that the British might arose from the supremacy of its navy.

As described earlier (in chapter 1), the oil exploration near the Iran-Iraq border by D'Arcy's company ended in a fiasco in 1904—the year Admiral Fisher became the first sea lord. Already, listening to his pleas, the British government had begun expanding and modernizing its navy. The intensified naval race between London and Berlin manifested itself in the size and speed of the warships, the range and accuracy of their guns, and in forging such new weapons as the submarine and the torpedo. They both aimed to "rule the waves," meaning "control sea lanes."

However, to clinch his argument for oil at the expense of coal—faster acceleration and cruising speed—which would enable warships to sail ahead of the enemy's vessels and encircle the head of the enemy's fleet—higher efficiency, lower running costs, more space for the fighting forces and lethal weapons, and greater maneuverability—Fisher needed to come up with a prolific source of petroleum to which Britain had reliable access.

So when D'Arcy could no longer afford to fund oil exploration in Iran, it was the intervention of the admiralty that resulted in Burmah Oil Company rescuing D'Arcy's firm and creating Concession Syndicate. In the words of T. A. B. Corley, a Burmah Oil Company historian, D'Arcy's financial needs "coincided exactly with those of the foreign office, anxious about the route to India, and of the admiralty, seeking reliable fuel-oil supplies."[1]

By 1905, the gasoline-fueled car had soundly defeated its

rivals powered by steam or electricity, and Henry Ford had introduced his Model A automobile. This would prove to be a har-
binger of unprecedented change in civilian life.

In Britain, a debate raged among the cabinet ministers of the
Liberal government between "navalists," who favored additional
funds for the Royal Navy, and "economists," who wanted to
channel funds into social welfare to pacify public protest at
home. Among the debaters was Winston Churchill, president of
the Board of Trade, who backed the idea favored by the "economists" of fashioning an Anglo-German naval agreement.

There was political turmoil in Iran as well. Yielding to popular
pressure, the seriously ailing Muzaffar al Din Shah issued a
decree in August 1906 authorizing the establishment of a parliament and signed the constitution drafted by the parliament in
December. He died a few days later.

It was during the reign of his son, Muhammad Ali Shah, that
George Reynolds, working for Concession Syndicate, struck oil at
Masjid-e Suleiman. That field, containing more than one billion
barrels, became the fourth field of such magnitude in the world.

So the Royal Navy acquired an abundant supply of petroleum
from a source virtually under British control. Thus began a link
between oil and military that with time would become both
more intimate and more fraught.

Naval Race with Germany

Buoyed by his expanded naval force, Kaiser Wilhelm II decided
to flex his military muscle in Morocco—the only major North
African territory not properly colonized by any European
nation—thus coming into conflict with France, the dominant
power in North Africa. In July 1911 he ordered the German bat-
tleship *Panther* to sail into the Moroccan port of Agadir to "protect German citizens from hostile tribesmen." This aroused
anti-German sentiment not only in France but also in Britain.

The incident changed the mind of Churchill, then home secretary, and led to his defection to the "navalist" camp in the cabinet. Though the Agadir crisis ended two months later with Germany accepting a French protectorate in Morocco in exchange for a French colony elsewhere in Africa, Churchill jumped at Prime Minister Herbert Asquith's offer of the first lord of the admiralty.

Churchill adopted the policy of switch-over to oil advocated by Admiral Fisher. With oil, he wrote, "we should be able to raise the whole power and efficiency of the navy to a definitely higher level; better ships, better crews, higher economies, more intense forms of war power." As he put it, "mastery itself was the prize of the venture."[2]

Churchill ordered the construction of five oil-fueled warships in April 1912, thus making the security of Britain, then a superpower, reliant on foreign petroleum. The next year, to assist the cash-strapped Anglo-Persian Oil Company (APOC)— the renamed Concession Syndicate—Churchill announced that the British government would buy 51 percent of APOC's equity for £2.2 million, in exchange for APOC's legal commitment to supply oil to the Royal Navy for the next twenty years.[3] (The law to this effect would be passed in June 1914, on the eve of World War I.) In order to safeguard its interest in APOC, Britain immediately enhanced its military presence in Iran and the Persian Gulf.

By so doing, Britain inaugurated the geopolitics[4] of oil, which continues with ever more players and ever higher stakes. Its lead would soon be followed by other Western countries, especially the United States. And four decades later, it would be Iran whose decision to nationalize oil would create an international crisis, with Britain and the United States ganging up to defeat the nationalist and democratic aspirations of most Iranians.

World War I (1914–18)

With the outbreak of World War I in mid-1914, in which the internal combustion engine appeared at the heart of a tank—introduced in the battlefield in 1916—the importance of oil rose sharply. Equally vital were warplanes. By the time the conflict ended in November 1918, Britain had fifty-five thousand and France sixty-eight thousand warplanes—two-thirds as many as the motorized vehicles deployed by the Allies to transport fighting men and materials. Germany produced forty-eight thousand warplanes.[5]

The troops, equipped with the latest oil-fueled weapons, easily overpowered the best-trained cavalry and infantry of the enemy. The speed and ease of mechanized movement allowed the planners to conduct warfare over a much larger area than ever before. Equally unprecedented were the figures of the war dead: thirteen million.

The sharp rise in demand for petroleum products led to a tenfold increase in the output of APOC between 1912 (when the decision to switch to oil was made by the British Navy) and 1918. But this proved inadequate to meet the Anglo-French needs. The United States stepped in as soon as it joined the war in April 1917. It could afford to do so. Its output of 920,000 bpd amounted to two-thirds of the global total. For the last year and a half of the armed conflict, it supplied four-fifths of the Allies' petroleum needs.

On the other side, the naval blockade shut off oil supplies to Germany by sea. Before it could conquer the oil fields of Rumania, the local saboteurs put oil wells out of action for five months. The amounts its engineers were able to extract near Kirkuk, under Ottoman control, were too small to make any difference. Indeed, the acute scarcity of oil products that it faced in the approaching winter was a major factor forcing Germany to surrender on November 11, 1918.

Referring to "the tremendous army of motor lorries" in France and Flanders that he had witnessed during the hostilities, Lord Curzon, a leading member of the British wartime government, said, "The Allied cause had floated to victory on a wave of oil."[6]

Senator Henry G. Berenger, director of Comité Generale du Pétrole of France, declared that oil—"the blood of the earth"— had proved to be "the blood of victory . . . Germany had boasted too much of its superiority in iron and coal, but had not taken sufficient account of our superiority in oil."[7]

Interwar Period

Following the dissolution of the Ottoman Empire in November 1918 in the wake of its defeat in World War I, the League of Nations gave Britain mandate over Mesopotamia, consisting of the Baghdad and Basra provinces, in April 1920.

A bitter dispute arose over the future of the Kurdish-majority province of Mosul in southeastern Turkey. Arguing that their armistice agreement with the Allies required them to surrender those parts of their empire that had an Arab majority, they refused to give up their sovereignty over Mosul. It was in this province that the Germans, allied with the Ottomans, had extracted oil near Kirkuk, albeit on a small scale.

So the British were determined to gain legal control of Mosul, which they had captured during the war. The dispute rumbled on while the British government installed Emir Faisal as king of Mesopotamia in August 1921 and then signed a treaty with him that placed military and economic control of his kingdom in its hands. Finally, the issue was referred to the League of Nations arbitration committee, chosen by the leading lights of the League—Britain and France.

Unsurprisingly, in 1925 the committee decided in favor of seceding Mosul from Turkey and awarding it to King Faisal I. It was thus that the kingdom of Iraq came to consist of the historical

Baghdad and Basra provinces, inhabited by ethnic Arabs, and the Kurdish-majority province of Mosul.

In October 1927, the Turkish Petroleum Company (TPC), owned largely by the Anglo-Persian Oil Company after World War I, struck a gusher near Kirkuk, thus unveiling a chapter in the regional history in which Iraq became a strategic prize for the victors of the war to control. Working in conjunction with the French, the British tried to exclude the American oil corporations from Iraq. Washington argued that it was entitled to a share because it had supplied the bulk of the oil needs of the Allies after it entered the war. Years of complicated and protracted negotiations followed.

The result was the transformation of the TPC into Iraq Petroleum Company (IPC) in 1931. Its ownership was divided between British, French, and Dutch government-owned companies—respectively, APOC, Compagnie Française des Pétroles, and Royal Dutch Shell—with 23.5 percent of the equity each, and two U.S. corporations (Standard Oil of New Jersey and Standard Oil of New York), with 11.75 percent each, and the remaining 6 percent held by Partex, owned by Calouste Gulbenkian, a Portuguese-Armenian oilman.[8]

The following year, APOC found itself at loggerheads with Reza Shah of Iran. He faulted the company on several counts: its refusal to pay the corporation tax introduced in 1930; its failure to submit detailed accounts of its expenditures to his government; and its denial of access to the Iranian auditors to inspect company accounts in order to safeguard the 16 percent of the net profit that Iran was entitled to. He therefore unilaterally cancelled APOC's petroleum concession. Iranians greeted the shah's decision with rejoicing in the streets.

APOC took the case to the League of Nations. Following its mediation, the shah signed a new agreement with APOC in 1933 that stipulated an 80 percent reduction in APOC's concession—

from 500,000 square miles (1,295,000 square kilometers) to 100,000 square miles (259,000 square kilometers)—in two stages. The shah's growing ties with Nazi Germany in the mid-1930s worried the British government, which attempted to expand its oil-exploration activities to Kuwait. There the Kuwait Oil Company met with success in 1938.

Mexico Leads the Way

It was in 1938 that the Mexican government of General Lazaro Cardenas nationalized foreign oil companies—in line with Article 27 of its 1917 reform constitution—the most important of which was Mexican Eagle, owned chiefly by the British and managed by Royal Dutch Shell, producing two-thirds of Mexican oil.

Industrial-political trouble started in late 1934 in the wake of the election of General Cardenas, a plump, puffy-faced former war minister, as president. A radical, he introduced land redistribution along with social, educational, and industrial reform, and combined these with a program of public works. He thus widened his popular base. In May 1937 oil employees went on strike, and other industrial workers planned a supportive general strike. Cardenas appointed an official committee to examine the accounts and activities of the oil firms. When the committee recommended higher wages and improvement in working conditions, it won the support of the president. After initial resistance, the companies accepted the wages as part of the committee's recommendation but refused to let unions have a say in management's decisions.

To the thrill of Mexicans, Cardenas nationalized the oil companies on the night of March 18, 1938. An instant celebratory march by jubilant crowds in Mexico City lasted into the early hours of the next day. They uproariously welcomed the historic decision as an end to alien control of their most precious resource. The oil companies denounced the move as illegal and asserted that any oil produced by the nationalized Mexican corporation was "stolen goods." When Britain protested, Cardenas severed diplomatic ties with the country. "If the expropriation is seen as succeeding," said one Shell director, "a precedent is established throughout the world, particularly in Latin America."[9] These would prove to be prophetic words—except that the country to nationalize the assets of another major British oil corporation would be Iran.

During the run-up to World War II, which broke out in September 1939, all the contending powers regarded petroleum supplies as a crucial element in their military planning. Britain was the leader in the Persian Gulf region, followed by France and the United States. It was an American corporation, Caltex (California-Texas Company, formed by Socal and Texaco Oil in 1936), that struck oil in Saudi Arabia in 1938. The following year, Saudi king Ibn Saud added further area to the original Al Hasa concession to Caltex.

Immediately, the State Department accredited the U.S. minister to Egypt to Saudi Arabia, thus formally establishing diplomatic relations with the kingdom founded seven years earlier.

Germany had been actively developing coal hydrogenation to produce synthetic fuels since the end of World War I. By the late 1930s, fourteen such plants were running, and six more were under construction. As for its oil imports, they came from the Soviet Union and Rumania. When, in the wake of Cadenas's oil nationalization in March 1938, Britain led a petroleum embargo and attempted to shut off Mexico's traditional customers, Nazi Germany stepped in and became the top buyer of Mexican oil. Fascist Italy followed suit. And so did Japan.

Encouraged by its military leaders and local oil companies, the Japanese government had started controlling crude oil imports, refining facilities, and petroleum fields in its Chinese colony of Manchuria as a vital means to safeguard national security since the early 1930s. This hurt the American and European corporations, which then owned a majority of Japan's petroleum business. They protested. In August 1934, Henri Deterding of Royal Dutch Shell and Walter Teagle of Standard Oil lobbied the State Department to scare Tokyo into moderating its nationalist stance by hinting at a severance of American petroleum exports to Japan. The State Department was equivocal. Nonetheless, the mutual Japanese-American tension over oil supplies escalated and contributed to the buildup to World War II.

Lacking substantial oil resources at home or in its Chinese colonies, Japan coveted the rich oil fields of the Dutch East Indies (now Indonesia). Judging, rightly, that its move to grab these oil fields would lead to a robust response from Washington, Japan mounted a preemptive strike on the U.S. Pacific Fleet at Pearl Harbor in Hawaii in December 1941—thereby prompting the United States' entry into the conflict.

World War II (1939–45)

Whereas in World War I cavalry continued to play a role on battlefronts until the end, it was nonexistent by the time World War II erupted. Both the transport of troops and their fighting machines were dependent on petroleum products. Their degree of dependence could be judged by the fact that an armored battalion needed 17,000 gallons of oil products to cover 100 miles (160 kilometers).

By the spring of 1940, Nazi Germany had captured France, Norway, the Netherlands, and Denmark, and seized their oil stocks. These were in excess of what Germany had consumed in invading its neighbors. Its domestic output of 72,000 bpd of synthetic fuels amounted to nearly half of its total oil supply, providing almost all of its aviation fuel.[10]

Unlike in World War I, Rumania was this time allied with Germany, and accounted for nearly three-fifths of Nazi Germany's oil imports in 1940. It was partly to retake the Rumanian oil fields from the Soviet Union, which had occupied northeastern Rumania in June 1940, that Hitler decided to invade the Soviet Union. His other, more compelling reason for that invasion was to capture the vast oil fields of Baku, Grozny, and Maikop in the Soviet Caucasus. The Baku area was the cradle of the Soviet petroleum industry, supplying three-quarters of the union's oil output of 640,000 bpd in 1940. During the war, it supplied nine-tenths of aircraft fuel to the Soviet military.[11]

Germany launched its multipronged Operation Barbarossa, involving three million troops, against the Soviet Union on June 22, 1941. Its leader, Hitler, diverted his forces southward from Moscow in 1941–42 to capture the Baku oil fields to secure fuel for his military, which lacked petroleum products. Field Marshal Erich von Manstein appealed to Hitler for more soldiers for his embattled Sixth Army at Stalingrad (now Volvograd). "It's a question of the possession of Baku, field marshal," Hitler replied. "Unless we get the Baku oil, the war is lost."[12] The Germans came within a few hundred miles of Baku, but failed to overcome the Soviet resistance, and this in turn compelled the German generals to limit the deployment of mechanized vehicles, thus severely handicapping them in their combat operations.

Seemingly, Hitler's overall plan was to personally direct the capture of the Caucasus and for his marshal Erwin Rommel to conquer North Africa and Egypt, thus forming a pincer to grab Iraq and Iran, then ruled by pro-German Reza Shah.

Moscow and London lost little time in frustrating such an outcome. On August 25, 1941, Soviet and British troops invaded Iran at five points. Iranian resistance collapsed after two days, and a cease-fire was signed. The Soviet forces occupied the northern part of Iran and the British the southern. On September 16, fearing that the Soviet troops were marching down to Tehran, Reza Shah abdicated in favor of his eldest son, Muhammad Reza, a diffident, inexperienced man of twenty-two. Moscow and London would control Iran, including its oil output, for the duration of the war.

Once the United States entered the conflict, in December 1941, the oil consumption of the sharply increased Allied forces rocketed to 1.23 billion barrels a year, or 3.37 million bpd. With the United States providing most of the Allies' needs, its petroleum companies extracted 1.45 billion barrels a year at a time when its total proven reserves were less than 20 billion barrels.[13]

Such a high rate of extraction raised worries in Washington, and made its policy makers look more closely at foreign sources of oil outside of Latin America, where escalating nationalist feelings had resulted in the nationalization of foreign oil corporations in Mexico. This was the backdrop against which an increasingly close relationship developed between the United States and King Ibn Saud of Saudi Arabia, who became more dependent on foreign loans as his income from Muslim pilgrims to Mecca collapsed due to the war.

In 1940, Ibn Saud requested financial assistance from Caltex and the British government. Caltex made an advance payment against future royalties after winning an extension of two more years for their concession. But that was not enough. In January 1941, Caltex promised Ibn Saud a loan of $6 million.

Two months later came the U.S. Lend-Lease Act of 1941, which authorized the president to sell, exchange, lend, lease, or otherwise transfer military equipment to friendly nations under attack by the Axis Powers.

Saudi Arabia did not fall into this category. And President Franklin D. Roosevelt, a handsome, wheelchair-bound, patrician politician with a populist touch, was well aware that Ibn Saud was not a constitutional monarch.

Yet his chance to aid Ibn Saud came after the U.S. Congress approved a $425 million loan to Britain in July 1941. Roosevelt instructed the administrator of the Federal Loan Agency to "tell the British [that] I hope they can take care of the king of Saudi Arabia. This is a little far afield for us."[14] Since London was already providing subsidies to Ibn Saud, it had no problem complying with Roosevelt's request.

The following month, Reza Shah of Iran was forced to abdicate by the Soviet and British governments, whose forces occupied the country, and his son Muhammad Reza ascended the Peacock Throne. To neutralize the traditional influence of Moscow and London, the new shah courted the United States. It obliged. In March 1942, Roosevelt ruled that Iran was eligible for the lend-lease aid.

In the case of Saudi Arabia, however, Roosevelt had to rationalize how helping the kingdom was crucial to the security of the United States. It took awhile for his advisers, especially Harold Ickes, the interior secretary, briefed by Socal and Texaco presidents, to convince him that preserving the petroleum concession in Saudi Arabia was vital to the national security. The first sign of progress came in May 1942 when, as a preliminary step toward making Saudi Arabia eligible for aid under the Lend-Lease Act, the United States opened a one-man legation in Jiddah under James Moose, who spoke halting Arabic, as chargé d'affaires.

This did not assuage the fears of the Socal, Texaco, and Caltex presidents, who were paranoid about the influence of the British in Saudi Arabia and the nightmare of losing their concession in the kingdom.

They had noticed that the British government had no compunction in overthrowing the government of Rashid Ali Gailani, the nationalist prime minister of Iraq, in April 1941 when he refused to kowtow to the diktats of London. The only way to block such a development, they figured, was to persuade the Roosevelt administration to provide financial aid directly to Ibn Saud.

In mid-February 1943, they visited Washington for talks with the Committee on International Petroleum Policy, sponsored by the State Department, to discuss ways of excluding the British interests from the Saudi kingdom and ensuring the maintenance of exclusive American involvement in exploiting Saudi oil resources. They also met Ickes, who favored governmental involvement. They succeeded.

Over lunch on February 16, 1943, Ickes convinced Roosevelt. Two days later he signed a document saying, "I hereby find the defense of Saudi Arabia is vital to the defense of the United States," and authorizing lend-lease aid to the Saudi government. Soon afterward, the U.S. mission in Jiddah was upgraded, and Colonel William Eddy was appointed U.S. minister. Son of an American missionary who had grown up in Sidon, Lebanon, Eddy was fluent in Arabic. Roosevelt also accepted Ickes's recommendation to establish the Petroleum Reserves Corporation (PRC) to acquire and participate in the development of foreign oil reserves.

Though Roosevelt made his decision in wartime, Washington's declaration that the Saudi Kingdom's security is in the national interest of the United States has been reasserted in peacetime by presidents both Democrat (such as Jimmy Carter) and Republican (such as Ronald Reagan).

A month later, the Committee on International Petroleum Policy recommended that the PRC acquire options on Caltex's future production, to be used exclusively for military purposes. Ickes went one step further, recommending that the PRC buy the Caltex concession in the Saudi kingdom for the U.S. administration. He was backed by the Secretaries of War and Navy.

On June 26, Roosevelt approved the PRC plan and instructed Ickes to negotiate with Caltex the purchase of all its equity. This came as a shock to the presidents of Socal, Texaco, and Caltex.

But the stakes were high. On the eve of the talks between the administration and the concerned oil corporations, U.S. Secretary of State Cordell Hull said, "It is in our interest that no great power be established on the Persian Gulf opposite the important American petroleum development in Saudi Arabia."[15]

During the subsequent two-month-long negotiations, the administration lowered its proposal for 100 percent ownership to 70 percent, and finally settled for 33 percent, while securing the option to purchase Caltex's total output in war and half of it during peacetime.[16]

For diverse reasons this agreement was opposed by other petroleum corporations, the U.S. Congress, and the British government. By now, on the battlefields, the tide had turned decisively in favor of the Allies, especially in North Africa. Taking all these factors into account, Ickes abandoned the effort—while placing the blame on the oil companies' avarice.

In the Middle East, the rivalry between Britain and the United States continued, albeit in a low key, even though the income of Caltex was a modest $2.8 million in 1944.

Ickes recommended bilateral talks to reach an understanding with London on petroleum. But Lord Halifax, the British ambassador in Washington, found his discussions with the State Department so frustrating that he sought a meeting with Roosevelt. During their conversation on February 18, 1944, the president drew a rough sketch of the Middle East. "Persian oil is yours," he said. "We share the oil in Iraq and Kuwait. As for Saudi Arabian oil, it's ours."[17]

But that was not the end of the matter. While American oil companies had monopolized oil exploration in Saudi Arabia, its king, Ibn Saud, had a long history of political and military ties with London.

That was why Roosevelt kept secret his planned meeting with Ibn Saud at his meeting with Churchill and Joseph Stalin at the Soviet sea resort of Yalta in early February 1945. His aircraft *Sacred Cow* carried him and his entourage to the Suez Canal Zone in Egypt, where an American cruiser, USS *Quincy*, was anchored in the Great Bitter Lake in the canal, halfway between the Mediterranean and Red seas. Soon after King Ibn Saud and his entourage arrived from Jiddah aboard the American destroyer USS *Murphy*.

The two leaders got along famously when they met on February 14. They spent five hours together, interspersed by lunch, with Colonel Eddy, much trusted by Ibn Saud, acting as the translator. Later, Eddy would publish an account of the historic meeting as *F.D.R. Meets Ibn Saud*.

Ibn Saud, walking with difficulty and carrying a cane, remarked that the two of them were the same age and were both afflicted with physical disabilities, his stemming from battle wounds to his legs, which stopped him from climbing stairs, and Roosevelt's from polio, which confined him to a wheelchair.

Roosevelt said: "You are luckier than I because you can still walk on your legs and I have to be wheeled wherever I go."

Ibn Saud said: "No, my friend, you are more fortunate. Your chair will take you wherever you want to go, and you know you will get there. My legs are less reliable and are getting weaker every day."

Roosevelt said: "If you think so highly of this chair, I will give you the twin of this chair as I have two on board."

Ibn Saud accepted the offer, even though he saw that the wheelchair was much too small for his large frame.[18]

They discussed oil, a Jewish homeland in Palestine, the postwar scene in the region, and the establishment of a U.S. military base in Dhahran amid the oil fields of Al Hasa.

When the memorandum of the five-hour conversation was later put on record, it showed that Roosevelt promised that he would do "nothing which might prove hostile to Arabs," and that he would not alter the United States' basic policy in Palestine without "full and proper consultation with both Jews and Arabs."[19]

On his part, Ibn Saud was sufficiently moved by the Nazi atrocities against the Jews that soon after his return home he declared war against Germany. He thus secured a seat for Saudi Arabia at the founding convention of the United Nations in San Francisco. As for Roosevelt's promises on U.S. policy, they fell by the wayside with his sudden death on April 12, 1945.

Overall, though, this meeting seemed to have laid the foundation for a Saudi-American alliance whereby, in return for Washington's protection of Saudi Arabia, its regime would guarantee continued domination of its oil industry by U.S. corporations.

Once Churchill had learned about Roosevelt's meeting with the Saudi king, he set in motion a diplomatic blitz to confer with Ibn Saud. They met three days after the Ibn Saud–Roosevelt confabulation at a hotel in Fayoyum on the banks of Lake Karoun fifty miles (eighty kilometers) southwest of Cairo.

In contrast to the behavior of the chain-smoking Roosevelt, who, respecting the religious injunctions of Wahhabi Islam, refrained from smoking or drinking in the king's presence, Churchill showed no such sensitivity. When informed of the injunctions of Wahhabi Islam against drinking and smoking, he noted, "I was the host and I said if it was his religion that made him say such things, my religion prescribed as an absolute sacred rite smoking cigars and drinking alcohol before, after, and if need be during, all meals and the intervals in between."[20]

Among the factors that determined the final outcome of the war in Europe and Asia in August 1945, oil was at the top of the list. Washington's unchallenged supremacy in the petroleum industry ensured victory for the Allies.

Summing up the situation, a top State Department official wrote in August 1945: "A review of the diplomatic history of the past thirty-five years will show that petroleum has historically played a larger part in the external relations of the United States than any other commodity."[21]

After World War II

Exports of Saudi oil resumed in 1946. An American military advisory delegation arrived in Riyadh to reorganize Ibn Saud's regular army just as he granted the Pentagon a three-year lease on the military airfield at Dhahran.

In order to invest further into drilling for petroleum and erecting a pipeline to transport oil to the Mediterranean, Caltex, encouraged by the State and Defense departments, took in Standard Oil Company of New Jersey (later Esso, then Exxon) and Standard Oil Company of New York as partners in 1947 and renamed the new consortium the Arabian American Oil Company (Aramco).

The next year Aramco hit the jackpot with the Ghawar oil field at its northern end. By 1950, the estimate of the reserves of this mammoth field—more than eighty-five billion barrels—had surpassed the wildest dreams of oilmen.

With this, the petroleum deposits of the Persian Gulf region became twice as large as those of the United States and matched the rest of the world. Unsurprisingly, Aramco's profits catapulted to $115 million a year.

By now the United States was fully engaged in the geopolitics of oil. Though Moscow withdrew its troops from the Iranian Azerbaijan in May 1946, U.S. Joint Chiefs of Staff declared five months later that it was "to the strategic interests of the United States to keep Soviet influence and Soviet armed forces as far as possible from the oil resources in Iran, Iraq, and the Near and Middle East."[22]

This strategic aim was contained in a speech by U.S. president Harry Truman in March 1947, when he pledged assistance to any nation "threatened with communist subjugation." Ostensibly aimed at Greece, Iran, and Turkey, its true target was the oil-rich area of western Asia. Within a year American arms and other military aid started flowing into the Persian Gulf region, with the U.S. Navy establishing a permanent naval presence in Bahrain from 1949 onward.[23] The overall objective was to safeguard petroleum supplies in the area.

In 1950, the first U.S. Air Force mission was posted at the Dhahran military base. The next year, Washington signed a limited five-year military cooperation agreement whereby the Pentagon leased the Dhahran air base. Sensitive to the rising Arab nationalist tide in the region and in his kingdom, King Saud (r. 1953–64), friendly with nationalist Egyptian president Gamal Abdul Nasser, let the agreement expire in 1956 and took to renewing it on a monthly basis.

Summarizing the relations with the Middle Eastern rulers, a Socal executive told the company's historian that the trouble with oil-rich countries began "about a year after the UN was formed in 1945 . . . delegates from various countries tend to gravitate toward others with common interests and this leads to a pooling of information as to how much each is receiving in the way of royalties and other income."[24]

These rulers became aware that Mexico had nationalized its oil industry in 1938 and that Venezuela had passed a law in 1947 requiring the oil companies to pay half of their profits as tax. As the Socal executive observed, "All the Middle East countries wanted the same increased share. They all got it, too, except Iran, where the British held out—and lost."[25] When the oil companies protested, in 1951 the U.S. assistant secretary of state helped to negotiate the 50/50 arrangement that he said was necessary to avert the threat of "the loss of the concession."

Kuwait and Saudi Arabia achieved Venezuela's 50/50 income-sharing formula. This was done by subjecting the oil company's earnings to a local corporation tax in such a way that the total of the royalty payments and the corporation tax amounted to half of the company's profits before the deduction of foreign taxes.

As a consequence, Kuwait's receipts leaped from $30 to $140 million a year and Saudi Arabia's from $39 million to $110 million.

By contrast, Iran's earning from oil exports in 1951 fell by half, from $45 million in the previous year, when they had accounted for seven-tenths of its total exports revenue. This was due to the nationalization of the Anglo Iranian Oil Company (AIOC).

Oil Nationalization in Iran

Reflecting the national mood, Iran's sixteenth Majlis (1950–52)—the Persian word for assembly—passed a motion on March 15, 1951, for the principle of oil nationalization, and then on April 28 spelled out the steps for the takeover of the AIOC. By seventy-nine votes to twelve, it also recommended that Muhammad Mussadiq, leader of the National Front, be appointed premier. Tall, with slumped shoulders and sad, droopy eyes and a very long nose in a thin, oval face with a high forehead, Mussadiq had an aristocratic pedigree but was a committed constitutional democrat. The Senate, too, supported the nationalization legislation. Muhammad Reza Shah Pahlavi gave his assent to the oil nationalization, creating the National Iranian Oil Company (NIOC), and appointed Mussadiq premier on May 1.

Having failed to thwart Iran's oil nationalization plan, the British government, aided by Western petroleum companies, spearheaded a boycott of the Iranian oil. It succeeded. The Iranian oil industry declined sharply. This provided an incentive to the Western oil companies in the Arabian Peninsula and Iraq to increase their output. Production in Saudi Arabia and Kuwait rose sharply.

Faced with a deteriorating economy, Mussadiq sought emergency economic powers from the seventeenth Majlis on July 13. Three days later, using his constitutional prerogative, Mussadiq appointed a minister of war. The shah, a small, slight figure with sharp features and a haughty expression, refused to accept Mussadiq's nominee and thus relinquish his active command of the military. Mussadiq resigned in protest. The shah nominated Qavam al Saltane as premier. This led to five days of strikes, rioting, and demonstrations. Relenting, the shah recalled Mussadiq.

On August 3, the Majlis gave Mussadiq emergency powers for six months and elected Ayatollah Abol Qasim Kashani speaker for a year. The Mussadiq–Kashani combine represented an alliance of the modern and traditional middle classes, both of whom wanted to rid Iran of foreign domination, whether political or economic.

Britain initiated moves to undermine Mussadiq by deploying the extensive intelligence network it had built up before and during World War II, when it occupied most of Iran. This was masterminded by Christopher Montague Woodhouse, a middle-aged senior official of the British secret intelligence service MI6, who arrived overland from Iraq armed with weapons and gold sovereigns worth millions of Iranian rials. He handed over most of the cash at secret locations to the Rashidian brothers—Assadollah, Qodratollah, and Saifollah—rich businessmen who had earlier worked for London to undermine German influence. Woodhouse also liaised with his U.S. CIA counterpart, Roger Goiran, in Tehran.

During the next few months, however, as the Western boycott of Iranian oil began hurting Iran further, and Mussadiq's appeals for aid to U.S. president Truman fell on deaf ears, his standing among the middle classes waned. As a result, his government became increasingly dependent on the following that the (Communist) Tudeh Party could muster in the street, the oil industry, and the civil service. This alienated clerical leaders from his government.

The British embassy's subversive activities increased. On October 13, 1952, the Iranian authorities arrested a general and a few businessmen for plotting against it with "a foreign embassy." Nine days later Mussadiq cut off diplomatic ties with

Britain. Woodhouse left behind a working group under dapper Assadollah Rashidian, the plump, chubby-faced, organizing genius among the Rashidian brothers, with extensive contacts among the strongmen of the Tehran bazaar. He was also in touch with Senator General Fazlollah Zahedi, who, under the aegis of the clandestine Committee to Save the Fatherland, had recruited many of the two hundred officers retired or dismissed by the Mussadiq government.

Faced with a paltry income from oil exports and failure to get loans from the World Bank due to Washington's opposition, Mussadiq returned to the seventeenth Majlis (1952–54) in January 1953 with a request for a yearlong extension of his emergency powers. He got it.

Using his emergency authority, Mussadiq ordered the shah's illegally acquired lands to be returned to the state, cut the court budget, and forbade communication between the shah and foreign diplomats. He appointed himself acting minister of war. To dramatize his disapproval, the shah threatened in early February to leave Iran. Through this tactic he meant to galvanize all his forces and confront Mussadiq. Unwilling to engage in such an exercise just then, Mussadiq persuaded the shah to change his mind.

To resolve the dispute between the shah and the prime minister, the Majlis appointed a committee. It ruled that since the constitution put the military under the government's jurisdiction, the shah should cede his active command of the military. He refused. So on May 24, 1953, all but three of the fifty-seven deputies present voted to implement the committee's recommendation.

By then the British government had convinced the newly installed administration of U.S. president Dwight Eisenhower that Iran was slipping into the Soviet orbit while masking its pique at having lost its oil monopoly in the country. Allen Dulles, the CIA chief, a vehement anti-Communist, eagerly accepted the British interpretation of the events in Iran. Thus, the naked economic interest of the Anglo-American camp was wrapped into the high-minded ideological garb of freedom "from Communist subjugation."

In April 1953, having embraced the CIA's Operation Ajax, to be implemented by Kermit Roosevelt, the CIA's area chief for the Middle East, MI6 advised its agents to work for the American agency. On June 14 Eisenhower gave his approval to Operation Ajax. The CIA's psychological campaign against Mussadiq took off, with covertly funded Iranian opinion makers, journalists, and politicians denigrating him. Being an ardent liberal and constitutionalist who believed in freedom of expression, Mussadiq refrained from muzzling the press.

In July, Kashani failed to get reelected speaker of the Majlis. This gave Mussadiq more room for maneuver. He asked his Majlis supporters to resign so that he could order fresh elections without the shah's concurrence. Fifty-six deputies did so, thus causing de facto dissolution due to lack of quorum. On July 27 he ordered a referendum on the dissolving of the Majlis, to be held from August 3 to 10. Since the opposition boycotted it, Mussadiq won practically all the votes.

On the night of August 1, Roosevelt met the shah clandestinely at the royal palace. Together they worked out a four-point plan: an alliance with clerics; organizing publications, crowds, and monitoring of the opposition through paid agents; consolidating the support of royalist military officers; and an overall coordination of the operations with Zahedi and his friends. Their last meeting was on August 8.

Four days later, when Mussadiq declared that he would order fresh elections, the shah and his wife, Soraya Isfandiari, flew to their holiday villa on the Caspian Sea. From there, the shah sent two orders: one dismissed Mussadiq, and the other appointed Zahedi (who had gone underground to avoid arrest) as prime minister.

Colonel Nematollah Nasseri, the commander of the Imperial Guards, tried to serve the shah's decree on Mussadiq at the prime minister's residence on the night of August 15. But he found his soldiers surrounded by the troops commanded by General Taqi Riahi, the chief of staff, who had been tipped off earlier by a royalist officer. Nasseri was arrested and his forces disarmed. This signaled the failure of the royalist-CIA coup.

But that was not the end of the drama.

On the morning of August 16 the shah and his wife fled in their private plane first to Baghdad and then to Rome. Jubilant Mussadiq partisans took to the streets in Tehran. One section of Mussadiq's National Front demanded proclamation of a republic, while the other proposed a referendum on transforming the monarch into the constitutional head of state. Three days of rioting and demonstrations, coupled with increasingly radical demands by the demonstrators, unnerved Mussadiq.

On August 18 the U.S. ambassador, Loy Henderson, met Mussadiq to complain of the harassment being meted out to the Americans, and to promise American aid if law and order were restored. Mussadiq ordered police and army into the streets the next day to break up the demonstrations. This was his undoing.

It provided a cover to the royalist officers and Zahedi's Committee to Save the Fatherland to mount a coup against the government. It also gave an opportunity to the American and British agents, financed generously by CIA cash, to collect pro-shah crowds from south Tehran to provide a veneer of populism to what was essentially a military operation by the anti-Mussadiq forces.

The pro-shah demonstrators in south Tehran, where the vast bazaar is situated, materialized with the assistance of clerical leaders as well as pro-Western merchants and their allies. They marched to central Tehran, where they met up with pro-shah troops who had arrived from the Hamadan garrison 200 miles (320 kilometers) to the west.

They captured the radio station building. Just then, Zahedi was engaged in a battle to capture the prime minister and his residence, being defended by loyalist troops. It took thirty-five Sherman tanks and nine hours to overpower the pro-Mussadiq forces. All told, 164 soldiers and demonstrators died on August 19.[26]

Three days later the shah and his wife returned to Tehran to much public acclaim.

The CIA-MI6-engineered coup of August 19, 1953, which left three hundred people dead and a few thousand injured, gave a new lease on life to the shah's reign. It extinguished any chance of Iran evolving into a multiparty democracy and laid the foundation for royal dictatorship that lasted a quarter century. It was not accidental: it was the scramble for oil that led the CIA to mount its first-ever coup against a democratically elected government with a nationalist agenda; it became the template for many such coups over the next twenty years, culminating in the overthrow of President Salvatore Allende in Chile in September 1973.

Accepting Washington's advice, the shah did not abrogate the oil nationalization law. Instead, in 1954 the NIOC leased the rights to, and management of, Iranian oil for the next twenty-five years to a Western consortium with the following share-out: AIOC, 40 percent; Royal Dutch Shell, 14 percent; five major U.S. oil corporations (Esso, Gulf, Mobil, Socal, and Texaco) 8 percent each; and Compagnie Française des Pétroles, 6 percent.

As the leading shareholder in the new consortium, Britain, with its centuries-old imperialist history, could claim to have regained a foothold in Iran.

But on a long-term basis, it was on a losing wicket. The days of political and/or economic imperialism were numbered. This became evident in the autumn of 1956, when Britain conspired with France and Israel to invade Egypt—then ruled by the charismatic Nasser, an ardent exponent of Arab nationalism, who nationalized the Anglo-French-owned Universal Suez Canal Maritime Company in April 1956, at a time when two-thirds of Western Europe's oil imports from the Persian Gulf region passed through the Suez Canal.

The Suez War and Its Impact on Arab Oil

When the troika of Britain-France-Israel invaded Egypt on October 29–30, 1956, the Egyptians blocked the Suez with sunken ships. The Western Europeans appealed to Washington to meet their oil needs. Since the U.S. petroleum corporations at home had a spare capacity of 4 million bpd, they were in a position to help. But freshly reelected President Eisenhower refused to oblige partly because he feared an oil embargo by all of the Arab Middle East. He regarded the United Nations–brokered cease-fire, which came into effect on November 6–7, as inadequate and urged the occupying forces to withdraw. In the face of crippling oil shortages as winter advanced, London and Paris conceded a quick evacuation in late November.

Eisenhower's stance went down well with Saudi king Saud. During his visit to the United States in February 1957, he signed a new military cooperation agreement. He renewed the U.S. lease on Dhahran for five years and in return got the Pentagon's commitment to help double the Saudi army to fifteen thousand— and add a navy and air force to the kingdom's defense establishment. Also the Pentagon began supplying arms to the Saudi National Guard, mandated to curb domestic dissent.

In the region, Nasser emerged from this episode with enhanced prestige. This led to a dramatic rise in Arab nationalism.

In the spring of 1957, Nasser convened a conclave of Arab oil experts in Cairo. Among the prominent attendees was thirty-seven-year-old Abdullah Tariki, head of Saudi Arabia's Directorate of Oil and Mining Affairs (DOMA), a mustached man with a hooked nose and a ready smile. Educated in Kuwait, Cairo, and at the University of Texas to study geology and chemistry, he worked as a trainee geologist with Texaco before returning to Saudi Arabia in 1948. As the boss of DOMA in 1955, his first move was to raise the kingdom's income by wrenching control of refining and marketing from Aramco. Then he turned his attention to controlling output and prices. At the Cairo conference, he was the one to declare that petroleum was "the strongest of weapons that the Arabs wield."[27]

The move to bring together oil-rich countries of the Arab world gained momentum when the cartel of the leading Western oil majors—nicknamed Seven Sisters—tried to meet the challenge of the entry of cheap Soviet oil into the international market by slashing prices in late 1958 to early 1959. The situation worsened when, on March 10, 1959, Eisenhower, invoking national security, implemented the Mandatory Oil Import Program and limited imports to 9 percent of total consumption to protect domestic producers who, subject to the high cost of production, found it hard to compete with the imports.[28]

Further price reductions by the Seven Sisters pushed the total cuts to a third of the original price. This lowered the oil revenue of the host Arab states. They protested, and then acted.

They convened the Arab Petroleum Congress in Cairo in April 1959. It was attended by four hundred delegates. The foreign observers included Venezuela's development minister, Juan Pablo Perez-Alfonso, a bald, puffy-faced man with hooded eyes, who was angered by both BP's price cuts and the U.S. restrictions on Venezuelan oil imports.

He and Abdullah Tariki found themselves on the same wavelength. Together they helped to forge a common platform for themselves and the representatives of Kuwait, Iran, and Iraq. They all agreed to recommend that their governments establish an Oil Consultative Commission, defend the price structure, set up national oil companies, and replace the 50/50 principle with a 60/40 split in their favor.

What finally goaded the Arab states and Venezuela into action was a further 7 percent price reduction by Standard Oil of New Jersey in August 1960. The Arab leader to upstage Nasser was Abdul Karim Qasim of Iraq, which, unlike Egypt, was an oil-producing state. A long-faced army officer with a well-trimmed pencil mustache who led a coup against pro-British King Faisal II in 1958, Qasim saw himself as a rival to Nasser.

He rushed invitations to the Cairo signatories for a meeting in Baghdad on September 10. Besides the delegates of the host country, representatives from Iran, Kuwait, Saudi Arabia, and Venezuela attended the meeting, with Qatar sending an observer.

Four days later, the delegates set up OPEC, with the immediate task of restoring the price to its pre-cut level of $1.89 a barrel. They also called for a system of regulation of production and urged oil companies to consult the producing countries' governments. Accounting for four-fifths of the world's oil exports, OPEC had considerable clout.

It was formally inaugurated in January 1961 in Geneva (it moved its headquarters to Vienna in 1965). Later that year, Iraq took over all but 0.5 percent of the concession area originally allocated to the Iraq Petroleum Corporation. OPEC's membership expanded steadily, with Qatar joining in 1961, Libya and Indonesia in 1962, and Abu Dhabi in 1967.

The oil majors were opposed to OPEC's aims and policies, outlined at length in June 1962. The OPEC document stated that until the final goal of nationalization was achieved, the government of a member state should ensure that the contracted arrangements with the concessionaires specify maximum governmental participation and control over all aspects of their operations. It called on the member states to set a tax reference price and gradually reduce the area of existing concessions. The oil majors were particularly opposed to OPEC's demand that they maintain accounts as stipulated by the local government and make them available at all times for official inspection.[29]

Western governments ignored OPEC. In a classified report titled "Middle East Oil," the CIA dismissed OPEC in a short paragraph of four lines.

In Saudi Arabia, now a leading OPEC member, a power struggle developed between King Saud and Crown Prince Faisal. Abdullah Tariki backed Saud, who, for all practical purposes, lost out in 1962.[30] Tariki fell as well. The following year, feeling exhausted, Perez-Alfonso retired. Thus OPEC lost its two stalwarts in quick succession.

Tariki was succeeded by Sheikh Ahmad Zaki Yamani, a protégé of Faisal, as minister for petroleum and mineral resources. A plump, bespectacled man with a flabby, square face and well-trimmed goatee, Yamani, born in 1930, studied law first at Cairo University and then at New York and Harvard universities. On his return home, Crown Prince Faisal appointed him as advisor to his cabinet in 1958. Two years later he was promoted to minister of state. He became a director of Aramco in 1965. He was not too keen on strengthening OPEC. Nor was King Faisal, who had inherited the American lease of Dhahran from his predecessor.

But their attitude changed after the Six-Day Arab-Israeli War in June 1967, when Israel inflicted a quick and humiliating defeat on its Arab enemies.

1967 Arab-Israeli War

Against the background of rising tension between Israel and Egypt, early in the morning of June 5, 1967, Israel mounted preemptive air and ground assaults on Egypt, Syria, and Jordan. It destroyed three-fifths of Egypt's warplanes and more than two-thirds of the combat aircraft of Syria and Jordan. Israel went on to capture the Sinai Peninsula and the Gaza Strip on the Egyptian front, the West Bank and East Jerusalem on the Jordanian front, and the Golan Heights of Syria before accepting a cease-fire on June 10.

Arab oil ministers meeting in Baghdad decided to cut off oil supplies to the United States, Britain, and West Germany for their support of Israel. But, as the United States had a spare capacity of about 2 million bpd, it, Britain, and West Germany were unaffected by the Arab oil embargo, which lasted until the end of August 1967 and which set the scene for the formation of the Organization of Arab Petroleum Exporting Countries (OAPEC).

An angry Saudi king Faisal went on to terminate the Pentagon's lease of the Dhahran air base. (The Saudi kingdom remained free of any Western military presence until the fall of the shah of Iran in February 1979—except for a period in March 1973, when the Pentagon agreed to help organize and train four mechanized infantry battalions of the National Guard.)

The debacle of the war virtually destroyed Nasser and severely damaged the ideology of Arab nationalism he represented. He reached a compromise with his Arab rival, King Faisal, by withdrawing his troops from the North Yemeni civil war in December 1967.

It was against this backdrop of introspection and reconciliation that the emir of Kuwait, Sabah III ibn Salim I al Sabah, convened a conference of the rulers of Algeria, Iraq, Libya, and Saudi Arabia in January 1968 to form OAPEC. With its Great Burgan area containing the second-largest reserves in the world, Kuwait was well suited to be the convener. Membership in the new organization required that oil be the main source of national income, and its objective was to safeguard the interests of its constituents.

In 1970 Qatar joined OAPEC. The following year, when the requirement about petroleum being the chief source of income was removed, OAPEC grew by four—Bahrain, Egypt, Syria, and the United Arab Emirates—raising its total membership to ten.

Meanwhile, Saudi Arabia became actively interested in OPEC, and Yamani served as its secretary-general in 1968–69.

Prelude to Oil-Price Explosion

In 1950, the United States accounted for a staggering 56 percent of the total world oil output of 10 million bpd. Little wonder that the West Texas Intermediate (WTI)—between light and heavy oil—became the accepted international benchmark for pricing. During the next two decades the situation changed as oil consumption rose sharply in Western Europe. With its consumption of 10.7 million bpd out of the global total of 45 million bpd in 1970, the U.S. percentage came down to 24, where it has stayed since then.

Between 1950 and 1970, the world at large experienced a staggering 50 percent growth per decade. In the 1960s, as environmental restrictions on coal burning came into effect in the United States and Western Europe, forcing utility companies to switch over from coal to fuel oil, the American petroleum companies could not cope with the fast-growing market for oil. It was the hike in the oil production in the Persian Gulf region and North Africa that covered two-thirds of the increased demand of 21 million bpd.[31]

In short, the West became increasingly dependent on the Arab world and Iran for its oil. The power of OPEC members grew—as did that of the oil majors, the Seven Sisters. In 1968, they controlled 78 percent of the world's oil production, 61 percent of refining, and 56 percent of marketing facilities.[32]

Following the antiroyalist coup in Libya in September 1969, Libya curtailed oil production. And, in 1971, Venezuela upped the royalty from 60 to 70 percent of each oil barrel lifted.

The winter of 1969–70 was the coldest in the United States in three decades. In the 1960s domestic oil drilling encountered more and more dry holes.

Pressure mounted on the federal government to relax the import quota requirements as the spare capacity in the oil industry dwindled to 1 million bpd in 1970. In response, President Richard Nixon eased the quota system. In 1971, to control inflation caused by the Vietnam War, Nixon imposed price controls on oil, which in turn reduced money for exploration. From then on petroleum output began falling, thus making the United States vulnerable to an Arab oil boycott.

With petroleum demand growing in early 1973, Nixon delivered the first-ever presidential speech on energy. He abrogated import quotas altogether, since domestic output had started declining from 1971. He introduced a Voluntary Allocation System to ensure supplies to independent refiners. By the end of the year, total imports jumped to 6 million bpd from 3.2 million bpd in 1970, amounting to over one-third of the total consumption. A fifth of the imports came from the Middle East and North Africa.

In September 1973, aware of the energy crisis facing their main Western consumer countries and intent on securing compensation for the latest devaluation of the U.S. dollar—the currency used in petroleum transactions—OPEC members decided to double the price, from $2.55 to $5.09 a barrel. Talks with the oil majors on the subject scheduled for October were postponed due to the outbreak of the Arab-Israeli War, which lasted from October 6 to 25.

1973 Arab-Israeli War and Arab Oil Embargo

During the October 1973 Arab-Israeli War, OAPEC members reacted instantly to Nixon's order to airlift weapons to Israel on a massive scale. (It was OAPEC, *not* OPEC, members that imposed the oil embargo, with the non-Arab members of OPEC, Iran, and Venezuela conducting business as usual.) On October 17, they decided to cut output by 5 percent of the September figure and to maintain the same rate of reduction each month until the Israeli forces had withdrawn from all Arab territories occupied during the 1967 war, and the Palestinians' legitimate rights had been restored. Consumer countries were categorized as friendly, neutral, or hostile to the Arab cause, with the United States and the Netherlands in the last category. Friendly nations would be supplied at the September level, neutrals at a reduced level, and hostile none at all. OAPEC also confirmed the steep price rise decided earlier by OPEC.

While Saudi Arabia slashed its output, then running at 8 million bpd, by a whopping 25 percent, Iraq, ruled by the Baath Party, which had seized power in 1968, ignored the OAPEC decision.

In late November 1973, Algeria raised the price of its crude from $4.80 to $9.25 a barrel; three weeks later the oil ministers of the eight Persian Gulf countries, including Iran under the shah, pushed the figure to $11.65 a barrel ($43 in terms of 2003 cash). In turn this became the official price of OPEC, with the member countries' average taking rising fivefold, from $1.38 to $7 a barrel, in a year.

Since then, the OPEC price has become just one factor among several to determine the market price of the most precious commodity of all, which has come to be fixed by the daily movement of demand and supply on petroleum exchanges.

FIVE

Oil in War and Peace–
1974 to Present

It was a balmy morning in New York in late June 2005. In the vicinity of the World Financial Center in lower Manhattan, the small, immaculately maintained park drew its regular quota of au-pair women chaperoning their young charges in the soft breeze of the Hudson River. Local residents wearing a wide variety of clothing sat on sculpted marble benches next to short black lampposts in the park plaza, with its distinctive, but fake, gas lights. Here and there the Stars and Stripes fluttered in the breeze. Red banners carrying company names and signs reading SAILING LESSONS flew in the wind from boats named *Vanity Fair* and *Wired*. Arriving here, you felt there was no need to leave the confines of Manhattan to get all the greenery you wished.

Across the vast span of the quietly flowing Hudson, where sailboats cruised at dignified speed, a giant clock with huge hands showed 9:15, with the word COLGATE at its base against the background of reddish and gray skyscrapers. Some distance from the river, men and women sipped coffee at metallic tables under the shade of young trees.

Near the dun-colored twenty-one-story New York Mercantile Building, traders and brokers sat on benches smoking furtively, sipping coffee from paper cups and gossiping, as joggers in shorts and trainers and helmeted cyclists whistled past.

As the Colgate clock neared 9:40 on June 29, 2005—the day

after oil had closed at the record price of $60.54—the seats near the Mercantile Building emptied swiftly.[1] I joined the exodus.

Inside the Mercantile Building, I was received by Jenifer Semenza, an energetic young director of creative services of the New York Mercantile Exchange (Nymex).

Semenza and I stood behind the thick glass walls of Nymex's viewing gallery. The vast auction floor below us was divided into half a dozen sections, each with a circular area at its center—called a pit—with the crude oil section, the largest of all, nearest to the gallery. Specifically, the commodity to be traded was WTI crude oil, the standard in the United States since the mid-1950s.

Next to the walls of the huge hall were banks of computers—displaying not only the latest prices but also the latest news by CNN, Fox News, BBC, and MSNBC—next to a bank of telephones. An incoming phone call was notified not by rings but by flashing red lights. Traders flitted between the auction ring and the telephones and computers. They were all wearing waist-length jackets of different colors, with the symbols of their brokerage houses—MERC, EGO, DEAL, CASH, LOUD (Lou Daniels), BTU, YME, and so on—emblazoned on the back. "The colors are crucial," explained Semenza. "The last thing you want is to have traders making deals with their own company. But those wearing yellow jackets on the floor are Nymex employees, called reporters. They report to the man sitting on a raised platform. He is the floor supervisor, acting as an editor does with his reporters."

At 10 A.M. the bell rang. Instantly, the floor became a beehive of frantic activity. When Semenza slid open a windowpane of the gallery wall, the raucous sounds from the floor hit my eardrums like fusillades fired by a multiple rocket. In the crude oil pit, traders screamed and gesticulated like madmen (there were next to no women) as they competed to purchase and sell crude oil futures contracts.

But there was a method to this madness. "It sounds chaotic, but once you're in the ring itself or in the pit, and you know what you have to do and what you want to do, you concentrate on that activity, and you're not distracted by the other things around you," explains John Conheeney, retired chief executive officer of Merrill Lynch Futures, in *The eXchange of change, 1872–2002*. "Your ear picks up the sound; your eye picks up the hand signals. It's not as difficult as it first appears."[2]

Traders communicate by using their arms and hands. "Throwing out your arms means 'I am selling,' and pulling your arms inward means 'I am buying,' said Semenza. "The pit is just a mechanism to get the trades done.[3] Traders are in the business of executing orders for the major hedgers of the markets or for speculators. Those who trade for their own account, for their own profit or loss—they are the market makers. They lend breadth to the market." Traders rely on a team of runners—called clerks—who carry information back and forth from other brokers, who sit on the fringe of the action next to a bank of computers and telephones.

Once a deal is done, the traders write it on a paper card and throw the card into the center of the trading ring, the recording area. Here it is the task of the four seated men—wearing goggles to protect their eyes from the cards directed at them—to record each trade as each card reaches them. If the paper card does not reach the recording area of the pit, it becomes redundant. This can make a difference of millions of dollars.

Little wonder that traders endeavor hard and long to master the art of "the perfect throw" achieved by the perfect flick of the wrist. "These guys take classes to make sure they hit the recording area of the floor," said Semenza. "Some of them practice throwing cards from the porches of their houses." The extraordinary effort is well worth it. The average salary and bonus for experienced traders nears $1 million a year, with the best among them earning ten times as much.[4]

All those guys were dealing with buying and selling in the future. "So in the first half an hour of the opening of the floor, you establish the high, low, and settled price for each of the six months in the future," explained Semenza. "Today the first five minutes are given to the futures for July, then the next five minutes for August, and so on until January."

What exactly is a futures contract? I asked. "It's a promise to deliver a given quantity of a standardized commodity at a specified place, price, and time in the future," replied Semenza. "Futures contracts are derivatives, not the real thing. No oil physically changes hands. There are thousands of oil transactions daily, but few of these shipments are delivered. Instead, they are constantly retraded based on the current market price. You can say that the rights to a single barrel of oil are bought and sold many times over, with the profits going to the traders and speculators."

What then is the value of this exercise? I inquired. "The hourly and daily patterns of supply and demand help establish a realistic market price for oil. That in turn enables companies to negotiate a realistic price for oil contracts on current market conditions. It also helps them hedge against price fluctuations caused by variations in demand and supply and unexpected world events at a later date by locking in the current market price for future crude deliveries." Airline companies, eager to ensure stable prices for their fuel, are particularly active in the futures market.

The basic role of this market is to enable the buyer and the seller to minimize risk by reducing their exposure to volatility. The cash for the market comes chiefly from speculators who hope to make gains by placing themselves on the profitable side of the changes in supply and demand as well as the imponderable market psychology.

History of Pricing and Impact of Oil-Price Explosion

In the early days of the petroleum industry, when Standard Oil had the monopoly, it fixed the price. After its breakup in 1911 by the antitrust law, something like a free market emerged, in which the Texas Railroad Commission had the prime position. After World War II, seven oil majors set up a cartel, which exercised a stranglehold on the oil industry, from exploration to retailing, and which fixed prices to suit the interests of its members. Being vertically integrated—containing both upstream (extraction of oil) and downstream (refining and retailing) activities—these companies manipulated the prices the way they wanted. They ignored OPEC and its prices and got away with it. Yet, in 1972 the price of Arabian Light oil began to matter.[5]

The Arab oil embargo imposed by OAPEC during the October 1973 Arab-Israeli War, resulting in the quadrupling of prices, opened a new chapter. OPEC, which contained several OAPEC members, was able to make its prices stick. From then on, oil majors started taking OPEC seriously.

Among oil importers, the 1973–74 Arab embargo particularly hurt the United States, for several reasons: a substantial part of the American imports originated in the Middle East; the embargo was applied during autumn and winter, when demand for heating oil was high; it was accompanied by a steep price hike; and it came into effect at a time of declining oil output in the United States, which had no spare capacity to fall back on. The OAPEC move reduced the annual U.S. gross domestic product by $20 billion, and President Richard Nixon announced a national program to make the United States self-sufficient in oil by 1979.[6]

However, OAPEC members' resolve began to falter. Aware of the staunchly anti-communist views of Saudi king Faisal, British prime minister Edward Heath dispatched a special envoy to Faisal in late December 1973 to explain that any prolonged oil squeeze would weaken the West and thereby strengthen communism. It did not take long for pro-Washington president Anwar Sadat of Egypt, working in tandem with U.S. secretary of state Henry Kissinger—who had warned that the use of force by the United States to secure oil supplies from the Persian Gulf region could not be ruled out—to convince Faisal to discontinue the boycott. Faisal and Sadat then prevailed upon other OAPEC members to end the five-month embargo on March 18, 1974, "as a token of goodwill" to the West—even though the Israelis had not withdrawn from anywhere in the Arab-occupied territories and the legitimate rights of the Palestinians had not been restored.

Despite OAPEC states' unilateral concession, members of the Organization for Economic Cooperation and Development (OECD), a group of the richest nations, suffered an economic recession, which followed the oil-price explosion and lasted until late 1976.

In the intervening period, the United States led Western countries in conserving energy. The focus was as much on lowering heating levels in winter and better insulation for homes and business establishments as it was on saving gasoline by making automotive vehicles more efficient.

In the United States, the Energy Policy and Conservation Act of 1975 set the Corporate Average Fuel Economy (CAFE) standards. They mandated that car and truck producers meet the efficiency requirements as measured by miles per gallon (mpg) and averaged for the entire fleet of a particular model they manufacture. The law differentiated between conventional family cars and "light trucks," a category that included pickup trucks and (later) sport-utility vehicles (SUVs).

The subsequent improvements in engine, transmission, and chassis aerodynamics led to an average 1985 American automobile doing 25 mpg instead of 15 mpg before the enactment of CAFE standards. As a cumulative effect of other energy-saving efforts, the amount of energy needed to produce one U.S. dollar worth of wealth in the United States declined by a quarter.[7] Western Europe and Japan outdid the United States in this field.

In the oil-producing countries, the burgeoning petroleum revenues enabled the governments to start nationalizing Western oil companies, thus following the lead given by Iran, where the National Iranian Oil Company had taken over all the operations and ownership of the Western oil consortium in July 1973. Kuwait nationalized Kuwait Oil Company between October 1973 and March 1975. Saudi Arabia nationalized Aramco in stages from 1976 to 1980, after guaranteeing oil supplies to the constituent companies of Aramco, with the new entity renamed Saudi Aramco.

This enabled the ruling House of Saud and its hangers-on to exploit Saudi Aramco for their personal benefit. The most lucrative way was to secure kickbacks on oil sales. For instance, the Saudi government ordered one of the former constituents of Aramco to sell oil at $32 a barrel to "Petromonde," a Japanese company which then sold it to a Japanese refinery at $34.63, with $2.63 a barrel going to Petromonde as commission. On investigation, Petromonde turned out to be a London-based company with the same phone and telex numbers as Al Bilad, owned by Prince Muhammad ibn Fahd, son of the then crown prince.[8]

Amassing undreamed-of fortunes, these royalists would invest huge sums in U.S. equities and real estate, especially in Texas and California, thereby acquiring a personal stake in the American economy. Superrich Saudis would make a point of investing in companies associated with prominent politicians. Arriving as the Saudi ambassador to the United States in 1982, Prince Bandar, son of Saudi defense minister Prince Sultan, would become a linchpin in forging ties between affluent Saudi royals and commoners and leading Republican Party figures. He himself would become a family friend of George Herbert Walker Bush and James Baker III, who would end up as officials of the Carlyle Group, a private merchant bank awash with funds.

Contrary was the case in Iraq, which had severed its diplomatic relations with the United States and the UK during the June 1967 War, and where the ruling Arab Baath Socialist Party—commonly known as the Baath Party—was committed to reducing disparities between rich and poor. The oil-price explosion led to the unprecedented prosperity of Iraqis during the mid- to late 1970s, which enabled the Baath Party to consolidate its grip on the power it had seized in 1968. Investment in all economic sectors trebled or quadrupled, and grew steadily during the rest of the decade. The government raised the salaries of its civil servants and military personnel dramatically. Its ambitious five-year plan for 1976–80 promised a prosperous future for all. Unlike in the Gulf monarchies, and in Iran under the shah, petroleum revenue filtered down to ordinary citizens in Iraq, which had a strong public sector, extensive free public services, and a large body of small landholders.

Overall, through the nationalized oil companies, the governments came to control the prospecting and extracting activities. This in turn led to a new type of oil transaction—spot market—in which petroleum was offered for sale based on the rate of the day by the state-owned companies to Western corporations for refining and retailing.

The spot market grew up in Rotterdam. Oil tankers from producing countries arrived at Rotterdam to deliver the commodity to northwest Europe. Rotterdam had huge storage tanks. There were also several large refineries in the Rotterdam–Antwerp area. Thus the area became a way station. Since the Antwerp–Rotterdam–Amsterdam (ARA) conurbation is at the confluence of the Rhine, Waal, and Scheldt rivers, it is an ideal place to send oil and its products to destinations in northwest Europe. In

Rotterdam some oil traders began buying and selling by phone and telex. Out of that emerged the Rotterdam spot market.

From 1976, the price of the oil extracted from the Forties field in the North Sea was quoted in the exchange markets. Then it acquired the name Brent, the largest oil field in the North Sea. It is traded at the International Petroleum Exchange, London, and its major refining centers are in northwest Europe.[9]

The oil-price explosion in the mid-1970s made the global economy more volatile than before. Then gradual deregulation in the Western nations followed. As a result, futures contracts arose for currencies and gold. Nymex, then housed on the eighth floor of the World Trade Center, added heating oil in 1979, followed by gasoline two years later.

On March 30, 1983, Nymex introduced futures in crude oil. That meant the oil price being fixed daily on the open market would be determined by the give-and-take of Nymex traders, with buyers and sellers monitoring their computer screens worldwide. This undermined OPEC's price-setting powers. Yet major oil and financial companies were initially hostile to petroleum futures. On the other hand, given the overarching importance of oil, its daily closing price joined the illustrious list of the Dow Jones Industrial Average index, the gold price, and the U.S. Federal Reserve interest rate as the salient indicators of the state of the global economy.

Today the walls of Nymex blink with the latest information on the transactions on the vast floor, which, besides crude oil and its products, includes platinum. All of these are instantly available on the Internet.

Rising Star of OPEC and Saudi Arabia

The importance of OPEC rose sharply in the mid-1970s. It produced more than half of the global output in 1976 and provided seven-eighths of the exports.

Within OPEC, Saudi Arabia, possessing a substantial spare

capacity at any given time, emerged as the "swing producer" to quickly raise or reduce its production to balance the market and to help maintain the price fixed by OPEC. This in turn enabled it to have the final say on prices. Such a role made Aramco's top officials overconfident. "We are headed for 16 million bpd capacity by 1982," declared its chief executive, Frank Junkers, in May 1977—a declaration that would turn out to be an empty boast.

In contrast, the position of the United States weakened as it became increasingly dependent on petroleum imports, a sixth of which came from the Saudi kingdom in 1978. Far from the self-sufficiency it should have acquired by 1979 as anticipated by Nixon, a mere shortfall of 2 percent in its consumption—400,000 bpd—in mid-1979 led to panic buying and long gasoline lines.[10]

Within the Persian Gulf region, oil continued to play a central role in Iran, which was ruled by Muhammad Reza Shah Pahlavi. Once the NIOC had terminated the Western oil consortium's management and operational activities in mid-1973, the shah pressured the NIOC to raise its output. It did so by overexploiting oil wells, and hit the magic figure of 6 million bpd in 1974. Three years later, Iran's oil income of $19.5 billion accounted for three-quarters of the government's annual budget. During the revolutionary turmoil in 1978, production declined to 5.3 million bpd, with 4.5 million bpd sold abroad.

It was the oil workers' indefinite strike in December 1978 that dramatically dried up the government's coffers and paved the way for the shah's final departure from Iran in February 1979. The loss of Iran's supplies to the international market pushed up the price from $13 to $20 a barrel.

While the economic boom generated by the dramatic oil-price rise combined with the doubling of its output, followed by a recession, created a general environment for a revolutionary overthrow of the autocratic monarchy, thereby encouraging industrial workers to cripple the economy, the indefinite strike by oil workers, influenced by the underground (Communist) Tudeh Party, delivered the coup de grâce. This historic event, the last major revolution of the twentieth century, underscored the vital political-economic significance of petroleum.

By 1979, the high investment the Western petroleum corporations made in exploration after the oil-price explosion meant that the output in non-OPEC countries had begun rising. But it still lagged behind OPEC's total of 31 million bpd. Not for long, though. The outbreak of the Iran-Iraq War in September 1980 and OPEC's policy change would reverse the situation.

The 1980–88 Iran-Iraq War

The shah's overthrow by a revolutionary movement led by clerics caused a political earthquake in the region, leading to a spurt in oil prices to the extent that the period 1979–81 went down in history as the Second Oil Shock.

U.S. president Jimmy Carter—a Democratic leader with a leathery face, a Southern drawl, and an idiosyncratic syntax—dispatched a squadron of F-15 warplanes to Dhahran, Saudi Arabia. In a secret meeting between Hermann Eilts, the American ambassador to Saudi Arabia, and Crown Prince Fahd in Rome in May, it was agreed that the Pentagon would come to the kingdom's military aid in the event of a direct threat to it, and that in autumn the Carter administration would pressure Israel to make concessions on the Palestinian issue.[11]

A month earlier, the Congressional Research Service (CRS) of the U.S. Library of Congress published *Petroleum Imports from the Persian Gulf: Use of U.S. Armed Forces to Ensure Supplies* by John M. Collins and Clyde R. Mark, foreign and defense affairs specialists. It visualized two scenarios of Washington's military intervention in the region: the United States seizing selected oil fields if "embargoes or unbearable price-gouging" created "chaos . . . in the United States or elsewhere in the industrial world"; or the Pentagon assisting a government in the Gulf that faced the risk of losing oil resources following "internal turmoil or attacks by a hostile power." The authors concluded that it was doubtful that the United States would be able to seize and operate selected oil fields in the face of noncooperation by the local people and/or government. As for aiding a friendly government seeking assistance, Washington could help effectively only if it had a joint force—consisting of infantry, marine, navy, and air force personnel—either stationed in or around the region, or highly mobile.[12]

As it was, two months before the publication of the CRS report, and almost coinciding with the shah's downfall, the Carter administration had decided to establish a joint task force of fifty thousand—called the Rapid Deployment Joint Task Force (RDJTF, or RDF for short) at the MacDill Air Force Base in Tampa, Florida—for safeguarding Gulf oil supplies and to build up the American Fifth Fleet, operating from the British-controlled island of Diego Garcia, near Mauritius, in the Indian Ocean.

The second scenario in the report by Collins and Mark came to pass in Saudi Arabia on November 20, 1979—being Muharram 1, 1400 AH (After Hijra)[13]—the first day of the Islamic year. At 5:20 A.M., the dawn prayer time, some four hundred well-armed men, calling themselves Ikhwan (Brethren), seized the Grand Mosque in Mecca, the holiest shrine in Islam. They were led by Juhamian ibn Saif al Utaiba, a former military officer, and Muhammad ibn Abdullah al Qahtani, a religious figure. The insurgents had planned to take hostage King Khalid, who, they reckoned, would pray at the mosque on the first day of the fifteenth century of Islam. They were disappointed by his nonarrival (he was down with a severe cold, it was revealed later). But Utaiba and Qahtani went ahead with their plans. After their followers had closed all forty-eight gates of the mosque,

Utaiba gave a call for the overthrow of the Saudi rulers: they were deficient in Islamic attributes and had been forced upon the populace; and in any case in Islam there was no place for kings and the House of Saud lacked Islamic credentials.

The recapture of the Grand Mosque proved to be a torturous and bloody operation for the government. It had to deploy 10,000 security personnel of its own as well as thousands of Pakistani troops and a contingent of French antiterrorist experts (who had to be given special dispensation to enter Mecca, closed to non-Muslims), and wage a battle that lasted two weeks to restore order. In the process, 127 troops were killed, as were 25 worshippers and 117 Ikhwan members, including Qahtani. Of the 170 militants arrested, 67 were beheaded in public squares in different cities.[14]

The uprising in the Grand Mosque and its bloody end damaged the prestige of the House of Saud, the custodians of Islam's foremost holy shrine. Though King Khalid refrained from inviting American assistance in reclaiming the Grand Mosque, ties between Riyadh and Washington tightened further, with an accelerated construction of huge military complexes by San Francisco–based Bechtel Corporation at the strategic Hafar al Batin (near the Iraqi border), Khamis Mushayt (near the north Yemeni border) and Jubail, a port city on the Gulf, with many CIA and Defense Intelligence Agency (DIA) operatives working undercover as Bechtel employees.

Elsewhere, responding to the Soviet military intervention in Afghanistan in late December 1979, Carter, in his State of the Union address to the U.S. Congress on January 24, 1980, stated: "An attempt by any outside force to gain control of the Persian Gulf region will be regarded as an assault on the vital interests of the United States. It will be repelled by use of any means necessary, including military force."[15]

Soon afterward, Washington approached the six pro-Western Gulf monarchies for long-term access to their air and naval bases. Only Oman publicly agreed to grant it. However, the plans to expand the RDF to 300,000 personnel by the mid-1980s went ahead.

Regional tensions rose further when Iraq, ruled by President Saddam Hussein—a flabby-faced, beefy man with a thick black mustache, often seen in a military uniform with a beret—invaded Iran on September 22, 1980. Intense fighting broke out along the Iraq-Iran border and in the oil-rich Iranian province of Khuzistan. It resulted inter alia in the destruction of Iraq's two oil terminals in the Gulf. The world lost most of Iraq's petroleum output—running at a record 3.5 million bpd—as well as Iran's. Oil prices jumped to $40 a barrel—or $83 in today's money.

To cover the shortfall, Saudi Arabia raised its production to 10.3 million bpd, two-fifths of the OPEC total. It thus made itself even more indispensable to the United States, as well as to West Germany and France. The French ended up importing more than half of their oil needs from the Saudi kingdom.

Within ten days of the start of the Iran-Iraq War, the Pentagon rushed four radar surveillance aircraft (called AWACS, for Airborne Warning and Control System) to Saudi Arabia, along with four hundred military personnel to fly them and operate the ground control systems based in Dhahran. Within a month, the United States and Britain carried out (unpublicized) joint war exercises in the Persian Gulf. Washington and its allies—Britain, France, and Australia—sharply raised their naval strength around the mouth of the Gulf. By December, there were more than sixty Western warships in the area.

Record high oil prices boosted Saudi Aramco's income in 1981 to $119 billion, also a record. Flush with this money, Saudi Arabia, working in tandem with the CIA, bankrolled not just the fundamentalist Mujahideen in Afghanistan but also antileftist movements all over the world—from Renamo in Mozambique and Unita in Angola to the Contras in Nicaragua.

Once the threat of Iranian air strikes against Saudi oil fields or an Iraqi attack on the Iranian-occupied islands near the Strait of Hormuz had passed, and the U.S. presidential election in November 1980 had removed political uncertainty, Washington reiterated its intentions publicly. Kissinger was the first to speak up. As a potential adviser on the Middle East to the incoming Ronald Reagan administration, he said, "We must put a visible American presence into the perimeter of the facilities that have already been negotiated by the Carter administration."[16] The reference was to the military facilities secured by the Pentagon in Oman, Somalia, Kenya, and Egypt since early 1979.

In March 1981, when the Pentagon earmarked $418 million to develop RDF bases in Oman, Somalia, Kenya, and Egypt, the U.S. secretary of defense, Frank Carlucci, publicly called for permanent American military bases in Saudi Arabia. Riyadh reacted negatively. "The Gulf region is not in need of tutelage," said the Saudi minister of information, Sheikh Muhammed Abdo Yamani.

While Saudi leaders were reluctant to lease military facilities to the United States publicly, they were receptive to the informal advice given to them by Britain and France to create a supranational body of the Gulf states which could call on the West for military assistance in the event of serious internal or external threat to one or more of its members. The Islamic summit, held under the auspices of the Islamic Conference Organization (ICO) in Taif, Saudi Arabia in January 1981, provided an opportunity for leaders of the six Gulf states to meet. They decided to form the Gulf Cooperation Council (GCC). This was formally done four months later.

Aware of the strategic advantages that Bahrain offers—proximity to the oil fields of Saudi Arabia, Qatar, and the United Arab Emirates (UAE), and an ideal naval base from which to conduct reconnaissance missions in the Gulf—the Pentagon had maintained its interest in Bahrain going as far back as 1949. Since Bahrain was then a protectorate of Britain, the U.S. Navy had no problem having a presence there. On the eve of British military withdrawal from Bahrain in December 1971, the United States signed a secret agreement with the ruler, Sheikh Isa al Khalifa. It included leasing naval facilities, previously used by the British, to the United States for an annual fee of £300,000.[17] Bahrain now became the headquarters of the United States' Middle East Force.

Bahraini-American relations soured during the October 1973 war when, angered by Washington's support for Israel, the ruler stated that he had abrogated the agreement. But what he had really done was merely cancel the provision providing fueling facilities to the U.S. Navy and raise the annual rental to £2 million.[18]

Later, the Bahraini-American military agreement specifying naval and air facilities to the Pentagon was clandestinely renewed beyond the expiration date of June 1977.

Washington's commitment to safeguard the Saudi kingdom remained as solid as before. In October 1981, President Reagan said, "There is no way that we would stand by and see [Saudi Arabia] taken over by anyone who would shut off the oil."[19] A year later he declared: "An attack on Saudi Arabia would be considered an attack on the United States."

On January 1, 1983, Reagan renamed the Rapid Deployment Force the Central Command (Centcom), because its region of responsibility lay between Europe and Asia.[20] It became the fifth such command—others being the Southern Command (Southcom) based in Miami, the Northern Command (Northcom) in Colorado Springs, the Pacific Command (Pacom) in Honolulu, and the European Command (Eurcom) in Stuttgart, Germany.

As the Iran-Iraq War dragged on, oil became the key factor for the combatants. In 1982 it provided 98 percent of Iran's foreign earnings, showing a greater contribution to the national coffers than ever before. Tehran declared a maritime exclusion zone around its Kharg Island oil terminal, making any vessel entering it liable to attack. Iran's ally, Syria, shut off the pipeline carrying Iraqi oil to the Mediterranean and struck a heavy blow to Iraq's economy.

Due to the continued low oil production in Iraq and Iran, non-OPEC production outpaced OPEC's in March 1982. At 19 million bpd, OPEC contributed only about a third of the global production. Much of the non-OPEC new oil came from the North Sea and was sold on Rotterdam's spot market, where the price was determined by a variety of market factors. This made it hard for OPEC to maintain its reference price of $34 a barrel.

The year 1983 opened with the output of the British National Oil Company (BNOC) from the North Sea exceeding that of Algeria, Libya, and Nigeria combined. To maintain their market share, OPEC members resorted to giving unofficial discounts, the exception being Saudi Arabia. In February 1983 the BNOC cut its price from $34 to $31 a barrel.

At their fractious, two-week-long meeting in early March in London, OPEC members decided for the first time to slash prices by 15 percent—to $29 a barrel—*and* reduce output by 500,000 bpd. It officially named Saudi Arabia a "swing producer." For the new strategy to work, however, the remaining twelve members had to stop cheating on output and prices.

On March 30, OPEC received a blow when Nymex introduced crude oil futures. This weakened OPEC's price-setting clout further. Prices began sliding.

Riyadh lost patience. It declared that it would not tolerate its loss of market share, and warned fellow OPEC members not to cheat on their quotas. But nothing changed. At the June 1985 OPEC meeting in the Saudi city of Taif, Oil Minister Zaki Yamani revealed that his country's oil exports had dwindled to 2.2 million bpd, half of its OPEC quota, due to overproduction and price discounts by other OPEC members.[21]

Saudi Aramco attempted to regain ground from other OPEC members by offering a so-called netback deal to refiners: no matter the market price of petroleum products, they would get $2 a barrel profit, and only the remainder would go to Saudi Aramco. This accelerated the price slide. But what the Saudis lost on the price they gained on increased volume. Others followed the Saudi lead on netback deals, thus further undermining OPEC's power to set prices.

Finally, at their meeting in November 1985, OPEC members bit the bullet. Reversing what had been their policy since their inception, they decided to cease trying to protect price and instead secure and defend for OPEC "a fair share of the world oil market consistent with the necessary income of member countries' development."

With the removal of the hand of the regulating cartel, OPEC, and more specifically, Saudi Arabia, the supporting floor fell away at a time when more producers were seeking outlets for their oil than there were markets for it. The WTI oil price plunged from $32 to $10 a barrel in April 1986. OPEC became a house divided, with Algeria, Libya, and Iran favoring lowering the total output and restoring $29 a barrel, and Saudi Arabia and Kuwait—high-volume producers with small populations, committed to regaining market share at any price—flooding the market.

Aside from the economics of oil, Riyadh and Kuwait had another, specific political motive. In retaliation for Iraq's attacks on its oil tankers in the Gulf, Tehran had resorted to targeting the tankers of Saudi Arabia and Kuwait, openly allied with Baghdad. So Kuwait and Riyadh decided to get even with Tehran by severely curtailing its oil revenue.

The petroleum price collapse in the spring of 1986 slashed Iran's oil income by almost a half, reducing it to a mere $7.2 billion a year. This severely damaged the Islamic Republic's war effort. It never recovered from this crippling blow. Its failure to do so would lead to its acceptance of a United Nations–brokered cease-fire in 1988. Iraq also suffered financially, but it was cushioned by $12 billion in aid it received annually from its Gulf allies, the West, and the Soviet Union.

In sum, both in war and in peace, oil determined the main course of the recent history of Iran and Iraq.

Worldwide Impact of Oil-Price Collapse

The oil-price collapse had worldwide repercussions. The high cost of drilling in the North Sea and icebound Alaska became a loss-making activity, compelling the oil companies to curtail their operations and freeze future projects. The steep fall in the hard currency earnings of the Soviet Union—producing 12.5 million bpd, nearly 2 million bpd more than the United States, and exporting 4 million bpd—hurt its economy and oil industry badly. Western oil-exporting countries like Britain and Norway suffered, too.

The five U.S. oil giants sustained heavy losses in revenue and sacked tens of thousands of employees.

The skyscrapers in Houston and Dallas turned into empty shells as the real estate market shriveled. Bank failures became weekly news. Many small independent companies went bust as the value of their flowing wells plummeted and their production cost exceeded the sale price. The lucky few were bought up by those with a strong financial footing in a maelstrom of acquisitions and mergers. Among them was George W. Bush's Spectrum 7.

Oilmen from the Petroleum Club, Midland, and the Bayou Club in Houston made frantic calls to Vice President George Herbert Walker Bush at the White House for help to stanch the financial hemorrhage they were suffering. He in turn appealed to President Reagan. In response, Reagan dispatched Bush Senior to Riyadh to urge Saudi king Fahd to stop flooding the oil market and strive for $18 a barrel, widely regarded as equitable to producers and consumers.

Fahd pledged to help, as he was also under pressure from other OPEC members to act. He instructed Yamani to work toward the $18 goal as well as to acquire an increase in Saudi Arabia's OPEC quota. At the OPEC meeting in August 1986, Yamani agreed to an overall cut in OPEC output. This raised the price to $14–16 a barrel, still below what Fahd wanted. In October, when Yamani failed to endorse the king's aim, he lost his job. Hisham Nizar succeeded him.

The arrival of cheap oil after more than a decade caused other changes. It reversed the trend toward energy conservation in the United States, Western Europe, and Japan. Reflecting the popular mood in the United States, Reagan froze the CAFE standards in 1985. The American automakers made determined bids to reclaim the buyers who had opted for small, Japanese automobiles by designing bigger, more powerful machines with an ever wider choice of additional features. By so doing they threw away the gains made from improved technology. Their example was soon followed by car and truck manufacturers in Japan and Western Europe.

It was in this environment that the four-wheel-drive automobile called a sport- utility vehicle (SUV) appeared in car showrooms. Though it was really meant for workmen and inhabitants of the cold regions who needed to be able to steer their vehicles off the beaten track, it gradually became a status symbol in the United States—to the detriment of energy conservation.[22]

Such a vehicle would have been quite suitable in the oil-rich Persian Gulf, especially when, following the end of the 1980–88 Iran–Iraq War, oil production in the two countries picked up. Tehran's output rose by a quarter in four years, reaching 3.62 million bpd in 1993. In Iraq, possessing about one-tenth of the world's petroleum reserves, production surpassed 3 million bpd in the first half of 1990.

Soon, however, Baghdad's rising petroleum income came to a halt and reversed. Once again, oil-rich Arab states exploited the commodity to political ends, except that this time their target was a fellow Arab country.

Kuwaiti ruler Sheikh Jaber III al Sabah demanded that Iraq return the $12–14 billion it had received from Kuwait in the form of the oil it supplied to Baghdad's customers during the eight-year Iran-Iraq conflict. Saddam Hussein refused, arguing that he had waged war against Iran not just to safeguard his country but also to save the thrones of the Gulf monarchs, which were threatened by the rising tide of Islamic republicanism stemming from Tehran.

Sheikh al Sabah was not convinced. Backed by the UAE, he flooded the market in the spring of 1990, depressing the price from $18 to $11 a barrel. A drop of $1 a barrel reduced Baghdad's annual revenue by $1 billion—a loss that Saddam Hussein found intolerable in the face of the urgent demands for postwar reconstruction and jobs for the demobilized soldiers from a wartime army of one million, a staggering figure for a country with a population of sixteen million.

This was the precursor for Saddam's invasion of Kuwait, which resulted in the Third Oil Shock.

Iraq's Invasion of Kuwait and the 1991 Gulf War

Iraq invaded and occupied Kuwait on August 2, 1990. With this, Saddam Hussein's regime acquired another 9 percent of the world oil reserves. The United Nations Security Council passed a resolution condemning Iraq's aggression and demanding its immediate withdrawal. Iraq failed to comply. The Security Council imposed economic sanctions against Iraq and the occupied Kuwait on August 6, thus removing 4.8 million bpd of oil from the market. The price doubled, to $22 a barrel.

As a former oilman, President George H. W. Bush immediately

grasped the consequences of Saddam raising petroleum reserves under his control from 11 percent of the global total to 20 percent by incorporating Kuwait into Iraq, thus rivaling Saudi Arabia's 26 percent and challenging its role as the ultimate fixer of oil prices. Other Western nations and Japan shared his assessment, and backed him diplomatically and militarily in his confrontation with Iraq.[23]

Bolstered by Washington's financial, diplomatic, and intelligence assistance to his regime during his long war with Iran, Saddam had become overconfident about his links with it. He felt that by blocking the spread of republican Islamic revolution to the oil-rich Gulf monarchies, he had done the United States a great favor, and therefore it would overlook his invasion and incorporation of Kuwait. This was a gross miscalculation, and showed that Saddam had failed to comprehend fully the central role of oil in global geopolitics. Under no circumstances was an American president going to let an Iraqi leader bolster his oil reserves to the extent of challenging the Saudi monopoly as OPEC's swing producer.

Unsurprisingly, Bush focused on pushing the line that Saddam was on the verge of invading Saudi Arabia. When he telephoned King Fahd to warn him, the latter sent scouts into Kuwait. They reported that there was "no trace of the Iraqi troops heading toward the [Saudi] kingdom." Yet Dick Cheney, then U.S. secretary of defense, arrived in Jiddah, armed with satellite pictorial evidence that Iraqi warplanes were being loaded with chemical bombs and that Iraq had positioned surface-to-surface missiles in Kuwait aimed at Saudi targets.

In the past, such photographs were doctored to serve a political purpose. The satellite intelligence images supplied to Iraq during the Iran-Iraq War were often altered to make them misleading or incomplete. "We all recognized that the [satellite] information need not be accurate and that it is highly perishable given the dynamic nature of the conflict [between Iran and Iraq]," wrote Lieutenant-Colonel Oliver North, deputy director for political-military affairs at the National Security Council (NSC), to Vice-Admiral John Poindexter, the national security adviser, on February 10, 1986, in a memorandum. In any case, it is difficult for a layperson to read and interpret these images.[24]

However, Cheney's pictorial evidence gave Fahd a basis on which to invite U.S. troops to Saudi soil to help defend the kingdom. This was a momentous decision for the Saudi monarch to take. In the past, U.S. military personnel had worked inside the kingdom. But this time they were to be stationed in Arabia under their own flag. This was more than a military or political issue. It was a cardinal religious principle that non-Muslim troops were not to be posted on soil sanctified by the Prophet Muhammad—a principle that Saudi Arabia had enforced since its inception. This principle is the result of an Islamic concept which holds that all of the kingdom of Saudi Arabia is sacred.

Fahd's move would, in the coming years, lead to disaffection among his subjects and provide a platform for Osama bin Laden, a member of one of the wealthiest families in Saudi Arabia, to rail against the House of Saud as *munafiq* (i.e., deviant Muslim), and end up establishing Al Qaida, an extremist Islamist organization, which would destroy the World Trade Center in New York and damage the Pentagon in metropolitan Washington in September 2001.

During the seven-month-long crisis and the subsequent war in January–February 1991, Saudi Arabia was able to fill only two-thirds of the 4 million bpd gap left in oil exports following the UN sanctions on Iraq. The resulting economic recession in 1991–92 would be the third in less than two decades, and one of the main reasons for Bush's defeat by Democrat Bill Clinton.

By the end of 1990 the United States, leading a coalition of twenty-eight nations, assembled the most lethal fighting machine since World War II: 775,000 Western and 220,000 Arab and Muslim troops (most of them stationed in Saudi Arabia), equipped with 4,000 tanks and 2,900 warplanes and combat helicopters, and deploying 107 warships in the Persian Gulf, northern Arabian Sea and the Gulf of Oman, the Red Sea and the eastern Mediterranean. It faced 545,000 Iraqi troops in Kuwait and southern Iraq, equipped with 4,200 tanks and 150 combat helicopters, supported by 55 combat-ready warplanes.

During the forty-three-day war, the U.S.-led coalition mounted 106,000 air sorties, dropping 141,000 tons of explosives, and fired 315 cruise missiles. The Arab Monetary Fund estimated the damage to Iraq's infrastructure at $190 billion. The total estimated Iraqi dead were 57,600 to 62,600. Between 2,000 and 5,000 Kuwaitis, most of them civilian, died. The U.S.-led coalition lost 376 troops.[25]

While the Iran-Iraq War ended up as the longest conventional warfare of the twentieth century, the 1991 Gulf War, fought in essence for oil, proved to be that century's last major armed contest.

The retreating Iraqi troops set fire to all of Kuwait's 640 oil wells. And the U.S.-led coalition's bombing reduced Iraq's oil output by two-thirds. The end of the Iraqi occupation of Kuwait did not result in the UN sanctions on Iraq being lifted or even eased. They continued.

All of the foreign troops departed from Saudi Arabia—except for 37,000 U.S. troops, including air force personnel, and American warplanes based at the Prince Sultan air base in Al Kharj, 150 kilometers (94 miles) southeast of Riyadh. Their continued presence was justified by the Pentagon on the grounds that they were helping enforce the southern no-fly zone in Iraq below the 32nd parallel. This rationale convinced nobody in Saudi Arabia. The southern no-fly zone was imposed by President Bush Sr. in August 1992 as part of Operation "Southern Watch," mounted to punish Saddam Hussein for his lack of cooperation with the

UN inspectors charged with finding and destroying chemical, biological, and nuclear weapons, and the facilities to manufacture them. So what was the justification for the presence of American troops between February 28, 1991, when the Gulf War ended, and the launching of Operation "Southern Watch"? they rightly asked.

Oil in the Post–Cold War Era

The disintegration of the Soviet Union in December 1991 formally signaled the victory of the American bloc in the Cold War dating back to 1946.

Russia inherited the legacy of close and multifarious ties with Iraq, including an estimated $8 billion credit accorded to Baghdad during its war with Iran. With the Russian economy going into a tailspin, this sum acquired more importance than before. To placate Russia, Iraq offered oil exploration contracts to Russian oil companies, especially Lukoil in October 1994.[26]

France was another major creditor of Iraq, which owed it $4.5 billion.

Both Russia and France knew that the only way they would be able to recover their loans was to see that at least the oil embargo against Iraq was lifted. That partly guided their stance on the UN inspections to ensure that Iraq did not possess any weapons of mass destruction (WMD).

Considering itself the only (unofficial) representative of the Third World on the Security Council, China adopted a moderate stance on Iraq. It abstained on Resolution 678 (November 1990) authorizing UN members to use "all necessary means" to expel Iraq from Kuwait. With industrialization gaining dizzying momentum, China became a net importer of oil in 1993. This turned Beijing's attention increasingly to petroleum-rich countries like Iraq. The China National Petroleum Corporation (CNPC) began courting Iraq's oil ministry for development contracts. The chances of finding fresh oil reserves in Iraq are fairly high, but exploration has been frozen at the same stage that the western states in of the United States reached half a century ago.[27]

In short, the Chinese-French-Russian axis that emerged at the Security Council by early 1995 was underpinned as much by oil interests, present and potential, as by ideological and strategic factors.

Following the start of the oil-for-food scheme for Iraq in December 1996, the U.S. administration of Bill Clinton announced that American companies were free to buy Iraqi oil. They did—until Saddam Hussein, angered by the Pentagon's Operation "Desert Fox" against Iraq in mid-December 1998, banned direct sales to U.S. oil companies or traders. Saddam thus deprived the American firms of their trading profits, which were diverted to the middlemen from Russia, France, and China.

Yet, in 1999, according to the Washington-based Petroleum Industry Research Foundation, Iraq emerged as the fastest-growing source of U.S. petroleum imports, with American companies buying more than a third of the 2 million bpd exported by Baghdad.

Part of the reason for American companies to seek out Iraqi crude was the Clinton administration's 1996 Iran–Libya Sanctions Act (ILSA), which banned trade with Iran, the second-largest producer in OPEC, whose output was on a par with Iraq's. ILSA had a life of five years, and it required a presidential executive order each year for its renewal.

ILSA gave the president discretionary powers to impose sanctions against any individual or company anywhere in the world that invested more than $40 million in an Iranian or Libyan oil or gas project.[28]

Arguing that these sanctions violated international trading laws, the European Union (EU) threatened retaliatory action were the U.S. president to take action under ILSA. With its oil companies heavily engaged in Iran, France protested loudly. Germany expressed disapproval by renewing its export-credit guarantees to Iran. To Washington's dismay, Turkish prime minister Necmettin Erbakan signed a $20 billion natural gas deal with Iran within days of the promulgation of ILSA in August 1996.

In September 1997, an oil consortium led by Total of France, and including Gazprom of Russia and Petronas of Malaysia, signed a $2 billion contract with the NIOC to develop its vast South Pars gas field. The plan was to extract twenty billion cubic meters of natural gas annually by 2001, enough to satisfy two-thirds of France's demand. Total's president, Thierry Desmarest, told the Paris-based *Le Monde*, "The French law prohibits French companies submitting to U.S. extraterritorial legislation."

Washington declared that Total, Gazprom, and Petronas had violated ILSA and that it would penalize them. But this turned out to be empty rhetoric. Doing so would have meant applying American legislation extraterritorially, thus violating international law.[29]

The Clinton administration's failure to apply ILSA sanctions against Tehran helped Iran. Later Royal Dutch Shell, Agip of Italy, and Bow Valley of Canada signed big contracts with Iran. The discovery of the biggest oil field in thirty years at Azadegan, with an estimated six billion barrels, put Iran on the path to becoming the second-largest possessor of oil reserves.

The financial crisis in the "tiger economies" of Thailand, Indonesia, and South Korea in the summer of 1997, which spread to Hong Kong, Malaysia, and the Philippines, combined with OPEC's unwise decision to increase its output by a hefty 10 percent in November, caused a slump in oil prices, which collapsed to below $10 a barrel in early 1999.

In the United States and Europe, this led to megamergers. British Petroleum merged with Amoco (formerly Standard Oil of Indiana) in December 1998 to become BPAmoco, and then BP in 2002. Based in Courbevoie, France, Total bought Belgium-based PetroFina in 1999 to become TotalFina and then TotalFinaElf the following year.[30] In the United States, Exxon combined with Mobil and Chevron with Texaco to create, respectively, Exxon Mobil and ChevronTexaco.

In March 1999, at Iran's behest, OPEC cut its production by 1.7 million bpd and secured the cooperation of four non-OPEC producers—Mexico, Norway, Oman, and Russia—to reduce their collective output by nearly 500,000 bpd. Other, smaller cuts followed. These moves cumulatively lifted the price to $18 a barrel by the end of the year.

None of these reductions affected Iraq. Noting the suffering the Iraqi people were enduring due to the UN sanctions, OPEC exempted Iraq from quota restrictions. The subsequent flexibility gave Baghdad a role in oil-price fixing that it had not played before.

Iraqi Oil at the Center of a Geopolitical Game

In early 2000 it emerged that when it came to repairing the run-down oil industry of Iraq, the European subsidiaries of such U.S. oil-servicing corporations as Halliburton (chief executive officer Dick Cheney) were in the forefront. Placing bids through their foreign subsidiaries and affiliates, more than a dozen American companies signed up tens of millions of dollars' worth of contracts with Iraq for oil-related equipment between mid-1998 and the end of 1999.[31]

When 2000 opened with an increasingly tight hydrocarbon market, with oil selling at $28 a barrel, impacting positively on Baghdad's economic and diplomatic standing, Saddam Hussein grew more confident—as did China, France, and Russia at the UN Security Council. Indeed, the oil-price rise, which saw the commodity selling at $34 a barrel in March—a ten-year high—shaped Washington's stance on Iraq.

It reversed its past policy of insisting on UN inspectors conducting their task with utmost severity. Instead of greeting enthusiastically the announcement of Hans Blix—head of the newly created UN Monitoring, Verification, and Inspection Commission (UNMOVIC)—in August 2000 that its newly trained inspectors were ready to travel to Iraq, U.S. secretary of state Madeleine Albright appeared embarrassed by the announcement. She stressed that the United States would not use force to compel Iraq to accept UNMOVIC inspectors. She then lined up with the UN ambassadors of China, France, and Russia in urging Blix not to press the issue.

Thanks to the thriving world economy, the global demand for petroleum exceeded supply despite OPEC's decision to raise output twice within months. Any interruption in Iraq's output—running at 3.6 million bpd in August 2000, the highest ever, and freed from any OPEC-mandated limit—would spike up the prices even further; so calculated U.S. policy makers rightly.

During his tour of all OPEC members to invite each head of state to attend the organization's fortieth anniversary summit in Caracas, Venezuela, in September, President Hugo Chavez visited Baghdad in August. "The time has come for OPEC to show its power," Chavez said in Baghdad, the city where OPEC was founded. "The only way to counter international pressure is for OPEC to strengthen its political will." With OPEC's eleven members, including Iraq, pumping 32.5 million bpd, or 42 percent of the global total, Chavez's words carried weight. A puffy-faced, narrow-eyed, heavily built former military officer of mixed American Indian and African blood, Chavez is a leftist who has forged friendly relations with Cuba's Fidel Castro and China's Communist leaders. He had an additional reason to meet Saddam. Since Iraq was extracting oil outside the OPEC quota, he wanted to ensure that Saddam would cooperate with his overall policy of maintaining discipline within OPEC regarding sticking to allocated production levels.[32]

Clinton was dejectedly aware of growing American dependence on oil imports. The United States was importing 60 percent of the 19 million bpd it consumed—a twofold increase since 1983—and the trend was up. In the past decade, domestic oil output had fallen by 15 percent while consumption had grown by 11 percent.

At the OPEC summit in Caracas in September, the leaders resolved to maintain market stability by developing "remunerative, stable, and competitive" pricing policies, and settled for the price of an oil barrel in the $22–28 range. They decided to calm oil traders by increasing OPEC output by 800,000 bpd. This failed to have the desired effect. Baghdad threatened to postpone its plans to raise output if the United States held up Iraq's contracts for food, medicine, and economic infrastructure before the UN Sanctions Committee.

Albright offered an olive branch. Washington would not use force if Iraq failed to comply with the Security Council resolution of December 1999 requiring it to admit UNMOVIC inspectors into its territory. The turmoil continued at Nymex, where traders noted that crude oil inventories in the United States were 10 percent below the previous year's.

For the first time since his defeat in the 1991 Gulf War, Saddam found himself in a proactive position—all because of oil.

On September 20, WTI futures shot up to $37 a barrel. It caused panic at the White House. Two days later Clinton announced that he would release 1 million bpd for thirty days from the U.S. Strategic Petroleum Reserve, stored in the salt mines of Alabama. This was an unprecedented step to take in peacetime. Only then did the market calm down. On the next working day, September 25, oil futures fell by $3.

For the first time, Clinton found himself hidebound in his dealing with his nemesis, Saddam Hussein. His hands were tied further by the impending U.S. presidential vote on November 7,

BLOOD OF THE EARTH

which made him wary of even threatening to use force against Saddam for fear of the Iraqi leader retaliating by reducing or stopping altogether Iraqi exports—then running at a hefty 3 million bpd.

It was this state of the oil market that George W. Bush inherited from the preceding administration in January 2001.

The Bush Administration Eyes Iraqi Oil

At the first NSC meeting at the White House on January 30, 2001, the number-one item on the agenda was Iraq. And the next NSC meeting on February 1 was devoted exclusively to Iraq.

Advocating "going after Saddam," Defense Secretary Donald Rumsfeld said, "Imagine what the region would look like without Saddam and with a regime that's aligned with U.S. interests. It would change everything in the region and beyond. It would demonstrate what U.S. policy is all about." He then talked about post-Saddam Iraq—the Kurds in the north, the oil fields, and the reconstruction of the country's economy.[33]

Among the documents that were later circulated among NSC members was one prepared by the Defense Intelligence Agency, which had mapped Iraq's oil fields and exploration areas and listed companies that might be interested in participating in the oil industry. Another DIA document, titled "Foreign Suitors for Iraqi Oil Field Contracts," listed companies from thirty countries—France, Germany, Russia, Britain, and others—their specialties and bidding histories. Attached maps pinpointed "supergiant oil field," "other oil field," and "earmarked for production sharing," and divided the basically undeveloped southwest of Iraq into nine blocks to show areas for future exploration.[34]

According to Falah al Jibury, a stocky, middle-aged Iraqi-American oil consultant who had acted as President Reagan's "back channel" to Saddam Hussein in the 1980s, the U.S. administration began making plans for Iraq's oil industry "within weeks" of Bush taking office in January 2001. In an interview with the BBC's *Newsnight* program, aired on March 17, 2005, he described his participation in secret meetings in California, Washington, and the Middle East when, among other things, he interviewed possible successors to Saddam. By January 2004 a plan for the Iraqi oil crafted by the State Department and oil majors emerged under the guidance of Amy Myers Jaffe of the James Baker III Institute for Public Policy at Rice University in Houston. It recommended maintaining the present state-owned Iraq National Oil Company (INOC)—to be opened up to foreign investment after an initial period in which U.S.-approved Iraq managers would supervise the rehabilitation of the war-damaged infrastructure. Unknown to the architects of this scheme, the Pentagon planners, heavily influenced by neoconservatives, devised their supersecret plan, which involved the sale of all Iraqi oil fields to private companies with a view to increasing output well above the normal OPEC quota for Iraq in order to destroy OPEC.[35]

Earlier, in April 2001, Amy Myers Jaffe had directed the Independent Task Force appointed by Vice President Dick Cheney to produce a report on new energy policy. It was published under the title "Strategic Energy Policy Challenges for the 21st Century." Its authors said, "Perhaps the most significant difference between now and a decade ago is the extraordinarily rapid erosion of spare capacities at critical segments of energy chains. Today shortfalls appear to be endemic. Among the most extraordinary of these losses in spare capacity is in the oil arena." They noted that OPEC's spare capacity had declined from 25 percent of the global demand in 1985 to a mere 2 percent in 2001, and warned that without an adequate cushion of spare capacity, shortages could occur and prices could spike: "The world is currently precariously close to utilizing all of its available global oil production capacity, raising the chances of an oil supply crisis with more substantial consequences than seen in three decades."[36]

The authors concluded that the major problems were (a) concentration of resources in the Middle East Gulf region and (b) "the vulnerability of the global economy to the domestic conditions in the key producer countries." Of course, nothing could be done to alter (a), and so U.S. policy makers needed to focus on improving the internal state of affairs in major petroleum-producing nations.

9/11 and After

Immediately after the flying bomb attacks on the United States on September 11, 2001, Saudi crown prince Abdullah acted swiftly to counter the oil-price rise expected in the aftermath of the terrorist assaults. He instructed Oil Minister Ali al Naimi to renege on the agreement with OPEC to slash output and raise it. Then, by rushing 500,000 barrels in its tankers to the United States, Saudi Aramco succeeded not just in stabilizing the petroleum price but in actually lowering it from $28 to $20 a barrel in a few weeks.[37]

The fact that fifteen of the nineteen hijackers were Saudi citizens[38] created a surge of ill feeling against the Saudi kingdom among the people and politicians of the United States. It suddenly dawned on them that Saudi Arabia is an autocratic monarchy without a written constitution, and that it has been a fundamentalist state ever since its inception in 1932, where *sharia*—Islamic canon—is the sole source of legislation. Doubts also arose about the stability of the kingdom. "Like prerevolutionary Iran," reported Elaine Sciolino in the *New York Times*, "Saudi Arabia is an authoritarian, oil-rich monarchy. It is notorious for corruption and profligate spending, resistant to democratization, viewed increasingly as subservient to the will of Washington, dependent on American weaponry, and criticized by radicals in exile and some conservative clerics for not being Islamic enough."[39]

The American media was suddenly full of detailed allegations that several members of the House of Saud as well as other leading citizens of the kingdom had contributed large sums to Islamic charities, which then channeled some of the funds to Al Qaida.

On the other side, some leading religious figures in Saudi Arabia did not shed tears over what Al Qaida had inflicted on the Americans at home. While most senior religious scholars, called *ulema*, remained loyal to the House of Saud and were prepared to do its bidding, this was not the case with most of the younger, junior *ulema*. On the contentious issue of the continued presence of U.S. military personnel on Saudi territory, many among the latter shared the popular opposition to it on the basis that they were defiling the holy soil of Arabia. Some of them agreed, privately, with Osama bin Laden when he compared the U.S. troops in their country to the Soviet soldiers in Afghanistan in the 1980s.

This was at a time when three-quarters of twenty-two million inhabitants of Saudi Arabia were below the age of thirty, and one out of three college-educated young men were unemployed. The Saudi royal family's capacity to buy off opposition—a successful strategy deployed in the past—was much reduced due to its profligacy, incompetence, and avarice, which had resulted in the wastage of tens of billions of dollars of oil income over the past quarter century. Between 1981 and 2001, the per capita income fell by three-quarters, from $28,000 to $6,800.

To be sure, the Saudi royals were not unaware of the rising discontent. Nothing captured their dilemma better than the issue of the Pentagon operating its second command post at the Prince Sultan air base in Al Kharj to launch air attacks on Afghanistan. More than the technical advantage that the latest state-of-the-art command post would provide Washington, it would be a propaganda coup, U.S. policy makers calculated. To have the foremost Islamic state march shoulder to shoulder with the United States in its war on terror would reassure the Arab and Muslim world that its campaign was not against Islam.

Having secured permission for the use of the new facility at the air base, Washington publicized it. In so doing, it deeply embarrassed the Saudi government. Prince Nayef, the Saudi interior minister, publicly contradicted the United States. A few days later, a story by the reliable Al Jazeera TV contradicted Nayef. Indeed, following his visit to Riyadh on October 3, 2000, Rumsfeld announced that some countries were helping the U.S.-led coalition overtly and others covertly. This meant, in plain English, that the Pentagon was allowed to turn on its new command center at the Prince Sultan air base.

Yet the neoconservatives in the United States targeted Saudi Arabia. According to the *Washington Post*, Laurent Murawiec of Rand Corporation, in his capacity as a consultant to the U.S. Defense Policy Board, a quasi-official body appointed by the defense secretary, had designated Saudi Arabia as an enemy of the United States and called for the seizure of Saudi financial assets, *including oil fields*, if its government did not terminate its support for Islamic terrorism. He accused senior Saudi officials of complicity with terrorist attacks on the United States. "The Saudis are active at every level of the terror chain, from planners to financiers, from cadre to foot solider, from ideologist to cheerleader," he told the U.S. Defense Policy Board in his presentation. As "the most dangerous opponent" of U.S. interests in the Gulf area, he continued, Saudi Arabia must change its ways or face severe American reprisals. His presentation reportedly received strong support among prominent Republicans at the meeting, leading to speculation that key officials of the Bush administration had endorsed it.[40]

The report led to a flurry of activity. U.S. secretary of state

Colin Powell immediately telephoned Saudi foreign minister Prince Saud al Faisal to reassure him that the opinions expressed by "certain individuals" did not reflect the views of the president or of the U.S. administration. The State Department went on to dispense several briefings on the subject. Finally, on August 26, 2002, Bush, vacationing at his ranch in Crawford, Texas, held a twenty-minute telephone conversation with Crown Prince Abdullah to repeat that Murawiec's views "had nothing to do with the views of any senior-level government administration officials, including himself, the secretary of defense or the vice president." He followed this up with an invitation to Saudi ambassador Prince Bandar to his ranch to reiterate ongoing close cooperation with the Saudi kingdom, thus ensuring that Saudi Aramco would remain one of the top four oil providers to the United States—the others being Canada and Mexico, the immediate neighbors of the United States, and Venezuela.

On August 29, Bush authorized Rumsfeld to order Operation "Southern Focus," which allowed the Pentagon to hit Iraqi targets that were not involved in attacking U.S.-UK warplanes enforcing the no-fly zone in the south. With this, the Pentagon initiated an air campaign as a prelude to the ground invasion of Iraq. At the same time, the Bush administration's effort to build up the U.S. Strategic Petroleum Reserve quietly continued, propping up prices.

On October 11, 2002, the *New York Times* reported that the Pentagon had plans to occupy and take control of Iraq's oil fields. The next day the *Economist* described how the Americans were calling Iraq "Klondike on the Shatt al Arab," the waterway demarcating the southern borders of Iraq and Iran.[41] On October 30, *Oil and Gas International* revealed that the Bush administration wanted a working group of ten to twenty people to (a) recommend rehabilitation of the Iraqi oil industry, (b) consider Iraq's continued membership of OPEC, and (c) consider whether to honor contracts between Saddam's regime and foreign oil companies. It would transpire later that by late October 2002, Halliburton had prepared a confidential five-hundred-page document on how to handle the Iraqi oil industry after the invasion and occupation of Iraq.[42]

In public, however, the Bush administration built its case on Iraq without any reference to its oil. The rationale for military action against Saddam Hussein's government in Baghdad was that he was in league with Al Qaida and that he was busily producing weapons of mass destruction to be passed on to terrorists or deployed against the United States and/or its allies in the region.

What happened in concealed conclaves was another matter altogether. At a secret NSC briefing to Bush on February 24, 2003, a State Department economist told him that it would cost $7–$8 billion to rebuild Iraq's oil infrastructure. This official was part of the State Department group that, according to the *Wall Street Journal*, recommended the opening up of Iraq's previously state-owned oil sector to outside investment after an initial period in which U.S.-approved Iraq managers would supervise the rehabilitation of the war-damaged infrastructure.[43]

Concerned about the market's ability to absorb temporary deficits during a conflict in the Middle East, Bush specifically inquired about the spare production capacity of Saudi Arabia and the UAE. Based on the reassurances of Prince Bandar, there was an expectation at the White House that the Saudi oil policy would be "the saving grace." Actually, Bandar had his sights fixed beyond the Iraq war. He hoped Saudi Aramco would "fine-tune oil prices over ten months to prime the economy for 2004 . . . [to generate] the [right] economic conditions before a presidential election."[44] Bandar was conscious of how his friend and fellow hunter, Bush Senior, had become a victim of the economic downturn around the November 1992 presidential election.

While there was much forward thinking done by Bandar, on the immediate issue of letting the Pentagon use the Prince Sultan air base, with its state-of-the-art command center to coordinate bombing of Iraq from far-flung points scattered all the way from the eastern Mediterranean to Diego Garcia in the India Ocean to the Arabian Sea, his government this time refused to oblige the United States. As a result, the Pentagon shifted its command center to Al Udaid air base in Qatar.

However, it was only after the invasion of Iraq that Rumsfeld announced in Riyadh that the Pentagon was closing its military bases in the kingdom, and it was not until September 2003 that the U.S. combat troops finally departed—thirteen years after their arrival. By then, there were 370,000 U.S. Army troops deployed in 120 countries, including some 150,000 in Iraq, out of a total active-duty force of 491,000.[45]

In late 2002, as anti-Iraq hysteria built up, Saudi Aramco upped its output from 8 million bpd in December to nearly 9 million bpd in February 2003. Energy Secretary Spencer Abraham told Bush at a meeting of top advisers on energy issues on March 19 that the Saudis would make up any loss of Iraqi oil by increasing their production to 10.5 million bpd for 30 days. Robert McNally, an energy expert at the White House, informed those present that the Saudi government had pledged to preposition its oil tankers already in the Caribbean or headed there to be near the refineries on the Gulf of Mexico coast. With world supply exceeding demand by 1.5 to 1.9 million bpd, prices fell from $37 to $31 a barrel.[46]

Anglo-American Invasion of Iraq and Its Aftermath

When the Anglo-American troops invaded Iraq on March 20, 2003, from Kuwait, they expected to see hundreds of oil wells ablaze. That did not happen. Being an Iraqi nationalist at heart, Saddam Hussein did not want to go down in history as a leader who damaged his country's most precious natural resource.

On entering Baghdad on April 9, the U.S. troops stood by as looters burned and ransacked public buildings, including government ministries—except the Oil Ministry, which they guarded diligently. Within a few days of the fall of Baghdad, at a secret meeting in London, the Pentagon's scheme of the sale of all Iraqi oil fields got a go-ahead in principle.

The Bush administration's assertions that oil was not a prime reason for invading Iraq did not fool Iraqis.

A survey of the residents of Baghdad, forming a quarter of the national population, in July 2003 by the (London) *Spectator* showed that while 23 percent believed the reason for the Anglo-American war on Iraq was "to liberate us from dictatorship," twice as many said, "to get oil."[47]

As the principal occupier of Iraq, the Bush White House made no secret of its plans to dismantle Iraq's strong public sector. When the first proconsul, (Retired) General Jay Garner, focused on holding local elections rather than fiddling with the economic structure, he was promptly sacked.

Paul Bremer, who succeeded Garner in mid-May, had to deal with Philip Carroll, former chief executive officer of the American operations of Royal Dutch Shell in Houston, appointed by Washington as the boss of the Iraqi oil industry. "There was to be no privatization of Iraqi oil resources or facilities while I was involved," Carroll told Bremer.[48]

However, this was only part of the reason why Bremer excluded the oil industry when issuing his Order 39 in September, privatizing nearly two hundred Iraqi public sector companies and opening them up to 100 percent foreign ownership. The Bush White House realized that denationalizing the oil industry would be a blatant violation of the Geneva Conventions on War, which bar an occupying power from altering the fundamental structure of the occupied territory's economy. Another major reason was the disapproval of Bremer's privatization of leading Iraqi companies voiced by the highly revered Shiite leader Grand Ayatollah Ali Sistani. Along with most other Shiite theologians, he held that minerals belong to the "community," meaning the state. On the ground, according to Falah al Jibury, "We saw an increase in the bombing of oil facilities and pipelines built on the premise that privatization is coming."[49]

In the immediate aftermath of the invasion, much equipment was looted from pipelines, pumping stations, and other oil facilities. By August, oil output inched up to 1.2 million bpd, about two-fifths of the pre-invasion level. The plan that Iraq's oil output would jump to 6 million bpd in three years after Saddam's overthrow, with oil prices falling to $20 a barrel, was now seen for what it was—part of the hype disseminated by the American neocons to sell the idea of invading Iraq to the America public.

With the insurgency taking off, attacks on oil pipelines and pumping stations averaged two a week. The pipeline from the Kirkuk oil field, with the capacity of 550,000–700,000 bpd, to the Turkish port of Ceyhan, became inoperative. Oil was exported only from the southern fields. Bush was compelled to approach the U.S. Congress for $2.1 billion to safeguard and rehabilitate Iraqi oil facilities. The resulting Task Force Shield undertook to protect 340 key installations and 4,000 miles (6,400 kilometers) of oil pipeline. It was not until the spring of 2004 that the output reached 2.5 million bpd. That did not hold. Production fell again.

"It is bizarre, traveling through a country that has one of the largest oil reserves on earth, to observe the long queues of cars at petrol stations," reported Zaki Chehab.

"Drivers have become so resigned to this that they often bring their entire families along to keep them company. It is not unusual to see picnics being laid out along the roadside to pass the time, while someone guards the car for fear of losing that precious place in the queue. People even risk their lives to fill their tanks—bombs can explode at the rate of five or more per day. The black market is thriving, with gangs selling petrol at hiked-up prices to those willing and able to pay to avoid the dangerous queues. One driver I encountered in Kirkuk was disgusted at the length of a queue we joined. 'This city sleeps on a sea of oil and just look at us,' he lamented."[50]

Addressing the twenty-sixth Oil and Money conference in London on September 21, 2005, Issam Chalabi, a former Iraqi oil minister in the late 1980s, referred to the extreme lack of security and clean institutions and laws to manage the oil industry and said that "Iraq will be lucky" to maintain its current level of some 1.5 million bpd.[51] Refineries were producing only two-fifths of the twenty-four million liters of gasoline needed daily, and so there were often long queues at service stations. The government became dependent on oil revenue for 90 percent of its income, a record at a time when corruption became rampant. A U.S. congressional team found that almost $9 billion in Iraqi oil revenue disbursed to the ministries had gone missing. A subsequent congressional inspection team, headed by Inspector General Stuart Bowen, reported that the Task Force Shield failed to meet its goals due to "lack of clear management structure and poor accountability," and added that there were "indications of potential fraud" that were being reviewed by the inspector general.[52]

Issam Chalabi spoke in London as prices were rising worldwide. The Bush administration started releasing stocks from its Strategic Petroleum Reserve of 700 million barrels as oil prices closed at $69.81 on August 30, 2005; Hurricane Katrina had come onshore the previous day. On September 1, gasoline prices in the United States crossed the $3 a gallon barrier and reached $3.20. Two years earlier, the price had been $1.20 a gallon.[53]

The endorsement of the new Iraqi constitution by referendum

in October 2005 put paid to the prospect of oil privatization. Article 109 states that hydrocarbons are "national Iraqi property." That is, oil and gas will remain in the public sector.

In March 2006, three years after the Anglo-American invasion of Iraq, the country's petroleum exports were 30 to 40 percent below pre-invasion levels.[54]

This was the case in a region whose share of the global oil exports is set to rise from the current 40 percent to 70 percent in the next two decades despite all the hype being disseminated about the hydrocarbon bonanza to be unleashed by such areas as the Caspian Basin and West Africa's offshore region.

SIX

The Caspian Oil Bonanza and Other Pipe Dreams

The road to the Nardaran-Mastaga village was so potholed that it felt like our driver was negotiating an obstacle course. His sudden twists and turns had me lurch from one end of the backseat to the other like an oscillating pendulum. We were headed for Pir Shafa, the site of Imam Ali's footprint and the tomb of Fatima Khanoum, a revered saint of Shiite Muslims.

For me it was one more holy Shiite site added to my earlier visits to Iraq, topped by the tombs of Imam Ali in Najaf and his martyred son, Imam Hussein, in Karbala. For Elchin Amirbekov, my thirty-year-old translator, though, it was something totally novel. A graduate of the Institute of Foreign Languages, he had presented himself to me at the Azerbaijan Hotel—a hostelry of 1,200 beds where every dawn was greeted with the soft thump of pumps cranking up water sixteen stories high, peppered with the barking of stray dogs—wearing a black shirt, olive green pants, a patterned sweater, and shining patent leather shoes. Like most Azeri men, whenever he found himself in a lift with mirrors, he preened himself, tapping his hair or straightening up his shirt collar. Having been born and brought up in Baku, the capital of the Soviet Republic of Azerbaijan, Elchin had never set foot inside one of the two local mosques, much less journeyed forty kilometers (twenty-five miles) to a holy shrine.

It was May 1992, five months after the breakup of the Soviet

Union. The removal, by popular demand, of the statue of Lenin in front of the republic's secretariat, a vast, multistory administrative complex facing a wide boulevard near the shoreline, marked the end of one era—and the beginning of the next. The Communist hammer and sickle gave way to the Azeri logo of an oil rig, ears of corn, and flowers.

The Soviet Republic of Azerbaijan was gone. The Republic of Azerbaijan had arrived, unleashing a list of long-festering grievances against the central authority in distant Moscow—and an irresistible desire to do what had been forbidden for generations.

Departing from our hotel by the elegant promenade—built with earth imported by the early oil barons, intent on creating in Baku a seafront to rival the one in Cannes for walking and riding in their splendid carriages—in the clean heart of the capital, home to two million souls, with wide boulevards, which smelled of fresh sea breeze mixed with half-burned gasoline from over-flooded car carburetors, our driver steered his taxi to the northeastern suburb of Nizami, an industrial hub. Next he got on to the Balakhan Highway.

On both sides of the road was flat land covered with donkey pumps and abandoned oil rigs—like so many steely structures shooting out of the earth—only a small proportion of several thousand that had been deployed to sink holes into a terrain hiding the much-coveted hydrocarbons. We stopped. Elchin and I ventured into this jungle of steel. The oil derricks were rusty to the touch and looked hideous. Some pumps were rocking rhythmically; others were frozen in time. Around every rig lay a stagnant pool of oil and water. The decrepitude of the nightmarish landscape was unforgettable. I felt nausea. I struggled to say something complimentary to Elchin about the industrial enterprise that had ended up as a human-made wasteland. I failed.

Contrary was the case with Elchin. He jumped instinctively over the pools of oil and water and took off his dark glasses to savor the site. He seemed inspired by it. "The foreign explorers tell us now that we have lots and lots of oil," he declared with an air of bravura. "So much that it would be enough to finance a three-inch-thick golden road from Baku to Moscow." The image of a glittering highway from the western shores of the Caspian to the Russian capital did grip me, momentarily. I asked him to stand by a derrick to let me capture his euphoria on film. He did, smiling expansively.

We got back to the taxi. As Elchin settled into his seat by me, he whispered assuredly, "We have so much oil that we can be as rich as Kuwait." If wishes were horses, beggars would ride—such was my unexpressed response. He was probably alluding to the hydrocarbon riches that lay not under the land of Azerbaijan but below the bed of the adjoining Caspian Sea, the world's largest closed body of water, although he uttered not a word about off-shore oil wells.

His sentiments would find an echo in an interview with Daniel Williams of the *Washington Post* in 1998 by Sara Ashore-bely, a Baku-based nonagenarian historian, one of the last remaining members of the generation that grew rich off the pools of oil in the Caspian Basin, whose memories of Baku, the once graceful seaside capital of Azerbaijan, and its cosmopolitan life and optimistic ambience were like a dream for contemporary Azeris. "I think that when people hear about my world of the past, they see their world in the future," she told Williams. "Oil in the [past] centuries seemed as much a magic potion as an industrial commodity." Her life of private schools, tea under a grape arbor, and conversations in French ended with the Bol-shevik takeover in 1920, and her old family home became a Soviet museum.[1]

Late spring, 2002. Off the Caspian shoreline, on the windy, man-made, 120-hectare (295-acre) Sand Island—surrounded by countless hectares of deserted, rusting oil rigs—Huseynov Vaqif, the burly, silver-haired general manager of the local office of the State Oil Company of Azerbaijan Republic (SOCAR) welcomed a visiting American journalist, Paul Roberts, with endless glasses of sugary tea as he briefed him on the progress he had made since his posting there six years earlier. By retrofitting previously abandoned oil wells and drilling many new ones, he proudly told the visitor, he had almost trebled the output of the Sand Island complex. In absolute terms, however, he had merely raised production from 1,500 bpd to just over 4,200 bpd.[2]

The lunch of borscht, sturgeon, and vodka that Vaqif served Roberts that afternoon might as well have been a rerun of what U.S. president Bill Clinton had offered the visiting seventy-four-year-old Azeri president Haidar Aliyev at the White House on August 1, 1997, after a red-carpet welcome. The honor was all the more striking since Aliyev was the leader of a country that was barred by the U.S. Congress from receiving a single cent from Washington.

Haidar Aliyev assumed power in June 1993 after a tumultuous period in Azeri politics following the breakup of the Soviet Union nineteen months earlier and the emergence of an independent Azerbaijan. He was a small, dapper man with a wide mouth and intelligent eyes, whose calculated astuteness combined with subtle manipulation proved extraordinarily effective in advancing his career to dizzy heights. His was a classic apparatchik's tale. Born in the Azeri enclave of Nakhichevan in 1923, he started out as an agent for Smersh ("Death to Spies") during World War II, and rose to become the KGB station chief in Islamabad, Pakistan, in the early 1960s. On his return home he was promoted to KGB general, a first for an Azeri, and became chairman of the Azeri KGB in 1967. As a result of a successful anticorruption campaign, he was elected secretary general of the Azeri Communist Party in 1969, a position he held for eighteen years. In 1982 he was elected to the all-powerful twelve-member politburo of the Communist Party of the Soviet Union (CPSU), one of only two members bearing Muslim names. His star waned when Mikhail Gorbachev became the CPSU's secretary general in March 1985. He lost his Politburo position in late 1987 and retired to his native Nakhichevan. In the turmoil that followed the first free elections in Azerbaijan in 1992, Aliyev managed to get himself elected speaker of the Azeri Parliament. When President Abulfaz Elchibey fled the republic in June 1993 during violent turmoil in Baku, he assumed presidential authority. He won the subsequent presidential election. A year later he signed a contract with a Western-dominated oil consortium for oil prospecting and production.

Hyped-up Figures

During his Washington visit, the American media, taking their cue from the White House, breathlessly trumpeted the tale of the oil rush—involving 200 to 240 billion barrels—about to be unleashed from the Caspian Basin, of which Azerbaijan, along with Kazakhstan, forms an important part.

The high-octane razzmatazz was powerful enough to infect all but the cynical—and the truly knowledgeable. According to the 1994 British Petroleum annual *Statistical Review of World Energy*, the most reliable document in the industry, proven global oil reserves in 1993 were 1,009 billion barrels, and those of Azerbaijan and Kazakhstan were 1.31 billion and 5.2 billion barrels, respectively. Yet barely a year later, U.S. officials were talking of proven deposits in Azerbaijan of 4.5 billion barrels. By mid-1997 they had raised the figure to 9.2 billion barrels and given a similar thrust to the Kazakh reserves, producing the aggregate of more than 20 billion barrels.

On July 21, 1997, the U.S. deputy secretary of state, Strobe Talbott, a tall, athletic-looking man with a broad pate and intense

eyes, took a quantum leap. Dealing with the energy and investment flows in the southern republics of the former Soviet Union,
he stated that "it would matter profoundly to the United States if
failure of political and economic reform were to happen in an
area that sits on as much as 200 billion barrels of oil."[3]

In stark contrast, according to the 1998 BP *Statistical Review of
World Energy*, providing figures for the end of 1997, Azerbaijan
possessed 7 billion barrels of oil and Kazakhstan 8 billion,
adding up to a mere 15 billion barrels.

There has been something fishy about the petroleum potential of the Caspian Basin ever since U.S. oil companies began
sniffing around the region after the Soviet Union's breakup and
discovered an unparalleled interest by the White House in telling
them how to conduct business in the region.

Clinton noted that three U.S. petroleum corporations
(Amoco, Pennzoil, and Unocal) managed to obtain a 37 percent
share—twice the proportion held by British Petroleum—in the
Azerbaijan International Oil Consortium (AIOC) set up to
exploit Azeri oil in September 1994. He appointed a special task
force under Talbott to oversee American interests. It included
officials not only from the Energy and Commerce departments
but also the NSC and the CIA.

Its first important decision was to tell the American corporations that under no circumstances were they to allow the erection
of an oil pipeline passing through Iran on its way to a maritime
outlet. This was an order, not advice.

"Usually the American oil companies find other countries are
way ahead in using political influence," said Robert Ebel, director
of the energy and national security program at the Center for
Strategic and International Studies at Georgetown University in
Washington. "Not this time. And then the oil companies always
knew that this would end up being a political decision. The
stakes are just so high."[4]

The fact that the United States was becoming increasingly dependent on petroleum from a perennially unstable region—the venue of the modern world's first Islamic revolution and two Gulf wars, one of them the longest conventional armed conflict of the century—worried the policy makers in Washington. But they were unwilling to broadcast their unease for fear of accentuating the problem by turning it into a topic of popular debate.

Instead, top American policy makers and oil executives clutched at any straw that held the prospect of oil supplies from a region that was not Arab or Iranian. Azerbaijan and Kazakhstan fit the bill: they do not sound Arab or Iranian. Secondly, creating a hoopla about the incoming oil bonanza in the Caspian Basin made the oil-rich Arab states nervous and helped to keep the price subdued.

Like most politicians interested more in maintaining popularity and/or getting reelected than in spelling out unpalatable facts to voters, Clinton tried to engender a false sense among his constituents that they could go on indulging in ever higher consumption of petroleum and that limitless oil fields lay in Azerbaijan and Kazakhstan waiting to be exploited by American and other Western companies.

Clinton combined the public relations exercise with a military move. In October 1999 he extended the U.S. Central Command's area of responsibility to the littoral states of the Caspian Sea, excluding Russia. This was a preamble to promote a new pipeline to transport the Caspian Basin's hydrocarbons, bypassing both Russia and Iran—with its existing oil terminals in the warm waters of the Persian Gulf—and to cultivate military links with Azerbaijan, Georgia, and Kazakhstan. By so doing, the Clinton administration pursued its overarching policy of trying to isolate Iran and reduce Moscow's influence in the region, while increasing its own.

Bush's Non-Arab, Non-Iranian (NANI) List

The pattern of reassuring Americans that vast hydrocarbon fields lay outside the less-than-reliable Middle East continued with Clinton's successor, George W. Bush, a failed oilman, and Vice President Dick Cheney, former chief executive of Halliburton, a giant oil-servicing corporation. Indeed, within months of assuming office, the Bush administration published a formal policy paper on energy that said as much.

The National Energy Policy (NEP) Development Group, chaired by Cheney, issued a wide-ranging statement on May 17, 2001, on the new administration's energy policy. It estimated that between 2001 and 2020, oil consumption in the nation would grow by 33 percent and that of natural gas by more than 50 percent, and that demand for electricity would rise by 45 percent.

It stressed that energy security must be a priority of U.S. trade and foreign policy. With that in view, it produced a long list of non-Arab, non-Iranian (NANI) countries with promising oil prospects. Of these only the top nine, accounting for almost all of the potential oil and gas deposits, mattered. They were Angola and Nigeria (in Africa); Azerbaijan, Kazakhstan, and Russia (in the former Soviet Union); and Brazil, Colombia, Mexico, and Venezuela (in Latin America).

According to the 2002 BP annual *Statistical Review of World Energy*, the aggregate of the nine NANI countries at 208 billion barrels of proved reserves were a third of the Persian Gulf region's total of 680 billion. The NANI nine's total output amounted to 20 million bpd, and their consumption to 7.5 million bpd, leaving 13.5 million bpd for exports.

The following estimates by the U.S. Department of Energy for the first quarter of the current century provide a sobering scenario: the output of the Latin American states will grow by 61 percent and their consumption by 78 percent, resulting in the region becoming a net importer of oil. The increase in the former

Soviet republics will match the rise in domestic usage. By contrast, the gain in Africa will exceed the growth in local consumption by 56 percent. Taken as a whole, the aggregate increase in production will exceed total usage by a modest 12 percent.[5]

Since the case of Azerbaijan illustrates both the geopolitics of petroleum and how oil's wildly fluctuating price impacts on exploration and output, it deserves a detailed study.

Azerbaijan

During the Soviet era, the authorities drilled an average of 200 wells per year, and took the total to 9,000 by 1987, the peak year for production. Once the oil ministry set up the Sea Island platform township 70 miles (110 kilometers) offshore in 1949, the ratio of offshore output to onshore started to change. In 1980, the onshore contribution was down to about a third of the total of 300,000 bpd. Because of low investment by Moscow, output began to fall from 1987 onward. It was down to less than a quarter of a million bpd in 1990, with onshore wells contributing only about a fifth. After 1991 there was a steady decline in both onshore and offshore output. This continued for the next five years. Only in 1997 did a reversal occur.

On September 20, 1994, after Haidar Aliyev had stabilized Azerbaijan politically, SOCAR signed a $7 billion, thirty-year contract with the Azerbaijan International Operating Company (AIOC), a consortium of eleven companies from six countries, led by BP Amoco and including Norway's Statoil and Russia's Lukoil to develop Azeri, Chirak, and Gunseil offshore oil fields, believed to have reserves of 3 billion barrels.

This document was the seed that sprouted into the heady tales of the Caspian oil bonanza.

Such yarns downplayed the daunting challenge of shipping petroleum out of landlocked Azerbaijan and Kazakhstan. The existing pipelines ended in the Russian port of Novorossiysk in the Black Sea, which is shared also by Georgia and Turkey. Once loaded, the tankers had to navigate through the Bosporus to enter the Mediterranean on their way to European or North American destinations. The weekly flow of 1,000 ships through the narrow Bosporus—three times the number passing through the Suez Canal—was already hazardous. Increased petroleum traffic through this waterway heightened the danger of an accident that would play havoc with the lives and properties of Istanbul's twelve million residents. When, following a collision in March 1994, an oil tanker caught fire in the Bosporus, a disaster was averted only because of the direction of the wind.

Nonetheless, the drive by foreign petroleum corporations to exploit the Azeri segment of the Caspian continued. They had to deal with SOCAR, where Natiq Aliyev, a brother of Haidar, was the chief executive, and Ilham Aliyev, the playboy son of Haidar—whose addiction to gambling drove his father to shut down all casinos—was the vice president.

In November 1996 SOCAR signed a twenty-five-year contract for the Karabagh oil field, with a consortium led by Lukoil and ENI Agip of Italy.

By then, SOCAR had emerged as the number-one employer in the republic. Most Azeris and foreigners also viewed it as the largest corrupt organization in Azerbaijan, which had acquired worldwide notoriety for fraudulent transactions, with hundreds of millions of dollars disappearing into the pockets of SOCAR officials.[6]

Washington's policy of inflating the hydrocarbon riches in the Caspian Basin received a stunning blow when the annual *Strategic Survey, 1998–99* of the prestigious London-Based International Institute of Strategic Studies (IISS), published in April 1998, described its estimates as "divorced from reality." It cited a consensus of oil industry forecasts of the recoverable oil reserves at 25 to 35 billion barrels. Instead of comparing the Caspian petroleum reserves with those of Saudi Arabia at 250 billion barrels, it argued, they should be compared to the oil fields of Europe's North Sea, with deposits of about 35 billion barrels. Intervening in the controversy, the International Energy Agency would put the proven Caspian oil reserves at up to 40 billion barrels, with "possible reserves" of between 70 to 150 billion barrels. Thus, this region was expected to provide no more than a mere 5 percent of the global demand in 2020.[7] So much for the Caspian Basin cornucopia!

Later events in the Caspian region and beyond not only confirmed the more realistic estimates regarding petroleum deposits but also discouraged oil companies from investing in the Caspian energy projects. The economic sanctions imposed against Pakistan and India by the United States following their nuclear tests in May 1998 aborted any plans for their purchase of natural gas from Turkmenistan.

The crash of the Russian ruble in August 1998, which accentuated the international financial crisis caused by the collapse of the currencies of the erstwhile Asian tiger economies a year earlier, made Western oil companies, already weakened by falling petroleum prices, cautious.

"So far, the heralded oil boom is feeding more dreams than mouths," reported Daniel Williams of the *Washington Post* from Baku in early September. The AIOC was producing a modest 70,000 bpd from its offshore Chirag-Azeri-Gunshali oil field. The multinational North Absheron Operating Company test-drilled Dan Ul Duzu up to 3,100 meters (10,100 feet) and failed to find oil or gas. Its second test well also proved dry. This happened at a time when oil prices had collapsed. "The Caspian oil looks far less prospective on $12–$13 a barrel than it did on $18," said Mehdi Varzi, a renowned oil economist. "The Caspian is no longer the new Kuwait, more like the new North Sea."[8]

In October 1998, having failed to find commercially viable oil reserves, two consortia of Western-dominated companies in

Azerbaijan folded. "It was like a domino effect," said Robin Bennett, a founder of the British Business Group in Baku. "The oil price fell, many contracts were delayed, and everyone was affected."

However, the reelection of President Haidar Aliyev in that month with 78 percent of the popular vote reassured foreign petroleum corporations. They overlooked the harassment of journalists and lack of media access for opposition candidates during the election campaign.

Prodded by Washington, the presidents of Azerbaijan, Georgia, Kazakhstan, Turkey, and Uzbekistan signed a document in October 1998 favoring a pipeline from Baku to the Mediterranean port of Ceyhan in Turkey, thus circumventing both Iran and Russia. But AIOC executives told U.S. officials that the 1,740-kilometer (1,090-mile) Baku-Tbilisi-Ceyhan pipeline would be commercially viable only when it carried 1 million bpd, a figure unlikely to be reached before 2010. Their consortium's current output was less than about one-tenth of that figure. But Washington persisted. Its Trade and Development Agency gave Turkey a grant of $823 million to help it plan its part of the pipeline, covering two-third of the total length.

This led to the formation of the BTC (Baku-Tbilisi-Ceyhan) consortium of eleven companies, led by BP and SOCAR, to build the Baku to Ceyhan pipeline at the cost of $4 billion. The alternative route of Baku-Tbilisi-Suspa, the Russian port on the Black Sea, would have been half as long as the Baku-Tbilisi-Ceyhan route, which passed through highly seismic landscape, and would have cost half as much. With Baku only 200 kilometers (120 miles) from the border with Iran, which had extensive pipelines within its territory leading to the Persian Gulf ports, a link-up with Iran was the most economical solution. The longer crude oil travels through a pipeline, the more expensive it becomes to the buyer. In the end the United States' strategic interests prevailed.

On the exploration front, the situation improved somewhat in the following spring when oil prices picked up a bit. Three small deals were signed in April 1999 in Baku. "First Baku was hyped up too much, then it was talked down too much," said Robin Bennett. "Now people are starting to find the middle ground."[9]

At the turn of the century, Exxon Mobil was busily sinking a hole into an overtouted block, Nakhichvan (named after a land enclave of Azerbaijan), not too distant from the successful Chirag-Azeri-Gunshali complex. When Exxon's first attempt failed, its executives decided to drill deeper. Its engineers went as far as 22,000 feet (6,700 meters), more than four miles, into the Earth's crust, setting a record for the Caspian. Still no sign of a commercial flow of oil or natural gas. So company officials had no option but to plug the hole. Yet so steeped were SOCAR officials in their myopic optimism that Natiq Aliyev blithely told a visiting journalist, Paul Roberts, the following spring that his analysis had shown that "our foreign partner" had drilled "outside the oil-bearing structures."[10] If only that were so. The next year, again, Exxon Mobil's attempt to extract oil from another overhyped block called Oguz ended in dismal failure.

Exxon Mobil was not alone. Dry wells proved to be the fate also of Total, ChevronTexaco, BP, and Agip. This drove them to wiggle out of their contractual obligations without making too much fuss.

Political uncertainty descended on the republic when Haidar Aliyev fell critically ill in July 2003. To dissipate it, he promoted his forty-two-year-old son Ilham—a plump, balding, mustached man with pop-out eyes—as prime minister. Following Haidar Aliyev's death, the Central Election Commission (CEC) made preparations for the presidential election in October. It rejected such political stalwarts as Ayaz Mutalibov, a former president, and Rasul Guliyev, a former speaker, as candidates. And the authorities systematically harassed the supporters of Isa Gambar, who was allowed to contest the election.

The Son Also Rises

Ilham Aliyev won the election with 78 percent of the vote, matching his father's score. The International Election Observation Mission of the Organization of Security and Cooperation in Europe (OSCE) noted a number of irregularities in the counting and tabulation. "This election has been a missed opportunity for a genuinely democratic election process," Peter Eicher, head of the mission, said. "We were particularly troubled by the level of intimidation and unequal conditions for candidates during the campaign."

Yet neither the European Union nor the Bush administration took any steps to penalize the Azeri president, who went on to detain seven leaders of the opposition, four of whom were reportedly tortured. Indeed, Washington increased its military advisers to Azerbaijan to fifty and doubled its military aid to $25 million, all in the name of waging "war against terror."[11] The U.S. military officers began training Azeri and Georgian forces to guard the BTC oil pipeline. The Pentagon was permitted to upgrade the Nasosnaya military airfield north of Baku, thus acquiring greater flexibility in transporting troops and deploying its airpower in the region.

On May 25, 2005, Ilham Aliyev unveiled the BTC, the world's longest pipeline, named after his father, Haidar. The line has the capacity to carry 1 million bpd of Caspian oil, a figure it is unlikely to handle until 2010, if then. The total Azeri output was less than a third of that statistic.

As the parliamentary election approached in the autumn of 2005, Ilham Aliyev could claim that his government had passed an anticorruption law and established the State Oil Fund to finance extensive public works to reduce the poverty among two-fifths of the 8.5 million Azeris. Yet, with state-owned companies controlling half of Azerbaijan's wealth, corruption was rife among top officials. A survey showed that nine out of the ten richest men were government officials. Number one was head of the Customs Committee, number three the highest police commander, and number four the health minister, Ali Insanov.[12]

To ensure the defeat of the opposition alliance, Azadiliq ("Freedom"), Aliyev blocked the return of its foremost leader, Rasul Guliyev, from Turkey. A fortnight before the election on November 6, he dismissed two ministers on charges of corruption and ordered the arrests of two more, accusing them of planning a coup in conjunction with the opposition.

On election day, according to C. J. Chivers of the *New York Times*, came "reports of vote stuffing, vote buying, inaccurate voting lists, voter intimidation, and more." Observers and journalist watched "as officials panicked in several precincts as vote counts favored opposition candidates. Rather than certify the results, some officials fled with the ballots. Others called for the police, who arrived, seized the votes and carried them off."

The OSCE accused the government of using force against the opposition before and during the election, including the use of riot police to violently disperse antigovernment demonstrations. Even the United States admitted that the election did not meet "a number of international standards."

One OSCE spokeswoman told the BBC that she witnessed a ballot box being stuffed with voting papers before the polls opened. Based on the reports of its 640 monitors, it concluded that in 43 percent of the cases the vote count was bad or very bad. Both the United States and the EU called on the Azeri government to investigate allegations of vote rigging.

Responding to these calls, the government recounted or annulled the results of a handful of the contests, gave the opposition Azadliq 10 seats out of 125—with the ruling New Azerbaijan scoring 65—and the rest to its independent allies.

Aptly summarizing the pattern of democracy prevailing in the Caspian region, Chivers wrote: "The model [of managed democracy] consists of distinct parts: publicly embrace it at the top, while the government proper sticks to pinpointed repression and electoral crime. Win elections overwhelmingly. Then apologize, if necessary, a little bit, and as quietly as possible. Repeat pledges abut the value of democracy. Such is the case in Baku." Here, in Azerbaijan, he continued, "its leaders have become fabulously rich as they have clung to a strongman model, building power around a few families and clans, securing police loyalty, maintaining a state television network almost bereft of candor and honesty and resisting political pluralism."[13]

While Chivers painted a damning portrait of Azerbaijan under Aliyev, an editorial in the *New York Times* said, "Though corrupt and brutal, Aliyev's regime has provided security and stability, and with proceeds from the new Baku-Tbilisi-Ceyhan pipeline about to start filling state coffers to overflow, it also has the wherewithal to keep the masses quiet, if not content. The same pipeline . . . as well as Azerbaijan's location gives the country a high strategic value . . . the stability and security of Azerbaijan is very much in the interests of the West."[14]

The reasoning laid out by the normally liberal *New York Times* seemed to have clicked with the Bush administration. Having rebuffed Ilham Aliyev after his election in 2003, Bush now rewarded him for his rigged parliamentary election with an invitation to the White House.

As the preparations for Aliyev's visit to the White House on April 28, 2006, got under way, Sergei Markov, director of the Institute of Political Studies in Moscow, said, "Russian public opinion, when it looks at the United States policy in Azerbaijan, cannot ignore the fact that the United States has a desire not in favor of democracy but in favor of profits and geopolitical domination."[15]

While both the *New York Times* and Bush were prepared to turn a blind eye to corruption and brutality for the sake of "security and stability" in Azerbaijan, the hard-bitten oil executives had by and large given up on discovering a hydrocarbon cornucopia in the southern Caspian and turned instead to the northern end of the internal sea, which fell mainly under the jurisdiction of Kazakhstan.

Kazakhstan Looks West—Then East

The prospecting for oil and gas in Kazakhstan—onshore and offshore—has proved fruitful. During the decade of 1993–2002, Kazakhstan's proven reserves rose steadily from 5.2 billion barrels to 9 billion barrels. Then an eye-popping surprise followed. The new findings in 2003 amounted to three times the previous total! Azerbaijan never had such luck.

Unlike Azerbaijan, which, at Washington's behest, excluded its neighbor Iran from its hydrocarbon projects, Kazakhstan followed an equitable policy. By participating in the U.S.-backed BTC pipeline project, it pleased Washington. It then balanced this decision by cooperating with Moscow and Beijing in the construction of the Aktau-Novorossiysk and Kazakhstan–China pipelines. Indeed, the Aktau-Novorossiysk pipeline was the first to be finished, in March 2001.

In domestic politics, though, this vast republic—with an area of 2.72 million square kilometers (1.05 million square miles)—with a sparse population of fifteen million, has basically traversed a path similar to Azerbaijan's. Ever since its independence, it has been governed by President Nursultan Nazarbayev, a tall, balding man with Mongoloid features and a penchant for well-tailored business suits. Born into a peasant family in 1940, he studied metallurgy at a technical college. He started his working life as a steelworker and rose steadily through the ranks of the Communist Party of Kazakhstan (CPK). By 1984 he had become chairman of the Council of Ministers. He found rapport with Mikhail Gorbachev and .

became the CPK's secretary general in 1989. In the presidential election in December 1991, when he was the sole candidate, he won 98 percent of the vote. Later, a pliant parliament extended his five-year term to seven years.

His government invited foreign oil companies to bid for oil projects. It succeeded. The first major contract to develop the Tengiz onshore field was won by a consortium led by Chevron and Mobil, together possessing 70 percent of the equity, with the rest owned mostly by Kazakhstan Oil. Spanning 2,500 square miles (6,475 square kilometers) along the scraggly northeast shore of the Caspian, the Tengiz contained 6 billion barrels of proven, recoverable reserves of high-quality oil, making it one of the world's largest finds over the past quarter century. The cost to develop it was put at $20 billion.[16]

China, an oil-thirsty neighbor of Kazakhstan, wanted to exploit Kazakh hydrocarbon resources and made a determined bid. Its China National Petroleum Company (CNPC) succeeded in inking a $9 billion contract with Kazakhstan to develop oil and gas fields in the northwestern Aktyubink and Uzen regions and build a 3,000-kilometer oil pipeline between Kazakhstan and the Xinjiang province of China.[17]

By the time the next presidential election was held, in December 1998, Kazakhstan's capital had been moved from the historic Almaty in the south to the newly built Astana (formerly a small town of Aqmola) in the north. The election was widely criticized when the leading opposition candidate was disqualified on a technicality. The Nazarbayev government continued its policy of harassing independent media and arresting opposition leaders, and passed a law that made it almost impossible for new political parties to emerge.

On the hydrocarbon front, the Offshore Kazakhstan International Operating Company (OKIOC), a consortium of nine companies including Royal Dutch Shell and BP Amoco, was established in 1999 to explore and exploit an oil field named after a turn-of-the-last-century Kazakh poet named Kashagan.

It started drilling in the shallow waters of the northern Caspian near Atyrau to go to the depth of 14,000 feet (4,270 meters) below the seabed. Its $600 million investment in an exploratory well was the biggest ever. It went on to spend close to $1 billion doing a seismic survey of the entire Kazakh sector of the Caspian and drilling two exploratory wells at the opposite ends of Kashagan's oil-soaked limestone structure. Measuring 85 kilometers by 25 kilometers (53 miles by 16 miles), the Kashagan field was a 350- million-year-old coral reef buried 5 kilometers (3 miles) beneath the shallows about 50 kilometers (30 miles) south of the Caspian's northern coast. During the Soviet era, the authorities were aware of this field's high potential, but lacked the technology to develop it. So they opted for the easier sites in Azerbaijan and western Siberia.

In July 2000, Kashagan's first exploratory well yielded high-quality light crude. And in March 2001, the consortium announced that it had struck oil at 4,982 meters (16,340 feet), just 200 meters (670 feet) deeper than the first well located 40 kilometers (25 miles) away. This confirmed the initial belief that the Kashagan was similar in structure to the richly endowed Tengiz field. However, the overexcited optimists' early declaration that Kashagan was "the largest field ever found," putting it ahead of the Ghawar's eighty-seven billion barrels, finally settled down to thirteen billion barrels.

Prominent among those carried away by the euphoria of a gargantuan oil field was Nazarbayev. He confidently forecast that by 2015, when Kashagan, Tengiz, and a number of lesser fields would reach maturity, Kazakhstan would be producing 8 million bpd a year up from the current 750,000 bpd—on a par with the current world leader, Saudi Arabia. Robert Ebel of the Center for Strategic and International Studies in Washington described

Nazarbayev as "too optimistic by half" and added: "I understand he wants the income, but I wouldn't anticipate any significant production before 2008. And I know the companies are in no great hurry."[18]

Sure enough, three years later the Kazakhstan government would announce that production of the Kashagan field would start in 2008 instead of 2005, with the target of 450,000 bpd by 2010. The delay led a few of the consortium's constituents to sell their stakes.

But Ebel's professional warning was ignored by the Bush administration. Its National Energy Policy blithely mentioned the prospect of the Kashagan oil field exporting 2.6 million bpd "if pipelines like the BTC were operational." It recommended that President Bush order the State and Energy departments to "establish the commercial conditions" to facilitate Kazakh exports via the BTC." (The completion of the BTC pipeline in May 2005 would leave the Kashagan consortium's schedule unaffected.)

Nor did the persistent allegations of rampant corruption involving Nazarbayev and his family and many members of his government, and the specific charges that the president had stashed almost $1 billion in Swiss bank accounts, make any difference to the stance of the Bush administration, which strengthened its ties with Astana in its crusade against terror.

In April 2003, the U.S. federal grand jury in New York indicted James Giffen, an American banker, for acting as a middleman for $78 million in backhanders to Nazarbayev and his aides from several U.S. and European petroleum corporations, including Exxon Mobil and ChevronTexaco, seeking lucrative contracts in Kazakhstan. Also, the authorities in Switzerland began investigating charges that Giffen and his associates used Swiss bank accounts to transfer money to Nazarbayev and his cronies.[19]

Reciprocating the cordiality shown by Washington, in May

2005 Nazarbayev unveiled plans to link its oil port of Aktau to the BTC pipeline by an underwater pipeline through the Caspian, thus making one of the Bush administration's pipe dreams come true.

In a rerun of the past, during the run-up to the presidential election on December 4, 2005, there were arrests of opposition leaders, break-ins at political offices, and muzzling of independent media. Three weeks before election day, Zamanbek Nur Kadilov, a former mayor of Almaty, the republic's largest city and its commercial capital, who had parted with Nazarbayev a year earlier and become an opposition leader focusing on corruption, was found dead of gunshot wounds at his home. (In February 2006, Altinbek Sarsenbayev, forty-three, a former minister and ambassador and confidant of Nazarbayev until 2003, would be murdered and his body found on a road near Almaty along with his driver and bodyguard. This led to the arrest of five "rogue" members of the elite combat unit of the Kazakh National Security Committee as suspects.)

Nazabayev won the election with 91 percent of the ballots. While the vote was blatantly rigged, the protest by the United States was muted.

Hydrocarbons Restore Russia's Confidence

"Russia has increased its output in older fields, and new fields are being developed, including those with U.S. and other foreign investors," said Washington's 2001 National Energy Policy document.

In the decade following the disintegration of the Soviet Union in 1991, the Russian oil industry went through a dramatic change of fortune. Its output of 9.33 million bpd in 1991 dropped precipitately to 8 million bpd the next year—partly due to the union's breakup and the privatization of the nationalized oil and gas industry, and partly due to the violence that preceded and followed the capture by Chechnyan nationalists of the capital Grozny, an important petroleum refining center and a strategic transit point for transporting the Caspian crude to Russia, Ukraine, and eastern Europe. The Russian attack in December 1994 was repulsed by the Chechnyan nationalists two years later. The slide in production continued until 1998, the year of the crash of the Russian ruble, when it dipped to a little over 6 million bpd. Following the election of Vladimir Putin as president of Russia in 2000, the Russian army returned to Chechnya. By then the oil and gas industries were dominated by Lukoil (70 percent state-owned) and Gazprom (73 percent state-owned), which between them owned two-fifths of the country's oil reserves of 72 billion barrels.

Following their meeting in May 2002, Putin and Bush unveiled the U.S.-Russian Energy Dialogue to develop "bilateral cooperation in the energy sphere" and promote "access to world markets for Russian energy." Later, the U.S. Department of Energy hosted the U.S.-Russian Commercial Energy Summit in Houston to strengthen relations between the energy companies of the two countries. Though Western technology aided improvement in production, which equaled the 1991 figure in 2004, the problem of depleted oil fields did not lend itself to a feasible solution.

In any event, Russia's laws were designed to favor local companies and discourage foreign investment in its energy sector. This policy applies equally to Western oil corporations and their Chinese counterparts, despite increasingly cordial relations between Moscow and Beijing.

Following the sale of Russia's enormous natural resources, including oil and gas, to private companies at give-away prices during the presidency of his predecessor, Boris Yeltsin, Putin decided to steadily regain control over the energy sectors—"the inner sanctum of the Russian economy"—by extending the reach of state-owned oil companies such as Lukoil and Gazprom. This meant a thumbs-down on the Western oil majors. Putin went on to deploy oil and gas as instruments of the state's foreign policy to increase Russian influence abroad.

The fivefold increase in petroleum prices between 1998 and the spring of 2006, along with a steep rise in gas prices in 2005–06, brought economic and political gains for Russia. They enabled Moscow-based Gazprom to become the world's third-largest corporation by market value after Exxon Mobil and General Electric and ahead of Wal-Mart, Toyota, and Citigroup.[20] They enabled the Kremlin to put the 1998 ruble crash behind them and pay back the loans from the Western governments and the International Monetary Fund (IMF) and built up healthy foreign exchange reserves. They caused a two-and-a-half-fold increase in Russia's per capita GDP in five years (1999 to 2004), raising it to nearly $10,000. Such a surge in wealth enabled Putin to use the energy card to actively advance Russia's geopolitical interests.

In theory, Gazprom was like any other corporation, with its investors and directors and annual general meetings. In practice, its decisions were made by President Putin and his small coterie in informal meetings and passed on to Dmitri Medvedev, the company's chairman, who also happened to be deputy prime minister and a former Kremlin chief of staff.

Given such a setup, it was easy for Putin to use Gazprom, as well as Lukoil, as powerful instruments of foreign policy. He realized too that for once he had the means to arrest the inroads that the United States had been making into Russia's "near abroad," the former Soviet republics, in the name of furthering democracy.

His attempt to restore Moscow's influence in central Asia met with some success. He also tried to regain the influence the Soviet Union used to exercise in the Arab Middle East and North Africa. Following the surprise victory of Hamas in the Palestinian parliamentary elections in January 2006, Putin broke ranks with the United States and the EU when they decided to boycott the Hamas government unless it recognized Israel, renounced violence, and accepted the previous Israeli-Palestinian agreements, and Hamas refused. Instead, Putin invited the Hamas leaders to Moscow, thereby establishing direct contacts with them. Later, defying Washington's diktat that no government should assist the Hamas administration, the Kremlin gave a grant of $10 million to the Palestinian Authority.

Every time Putin stood up to the United States, his popularity soared. Most Russians saw their country being ringed by American bases and members of an ever-expanding North Atlantic Treaty Organization (NATO), and felt that for far too long Washington had been publicly lecturing their government on how it should administer the country, and that it was about time the Kremlin asserted its sovereignty.

In March, during his visit to Algiers, Putin wrote off the $4.7 billion Algeria owed to the Soviet Union and agreed to sell $7.5 billion worth of weapons to Algeria. This was a bold move. "Russia is coming back," said Alexei Malashenko, a senior analyst at the Carnegie Center in Moscow. "The geopolitical strategy has changed. The rapprochement with the West is over, and Russia is taking its own route."[21]

It soon turned out that Malashenko was reflecting an official position. Responding to Cheney's charge that Russia was using oil and gas as "tools of intimidation or blackmail, either by supply manipulation or attempts to monopolize transportation"—a reference to a Russian-Ukrainian spat on gas prices in January 2006—Andrei Kokoshin, head of the Russian parliament's committee of relations with former Soviet republics, said, "The United States has to deal with an absolutely different Russia today—a Russia that has restored its real sovereignty in many areas and is pursuing a course on the world arena that meets mainly its own national interests."[22]

Such a dramatic turnaround in Russia's geopolitical fortunes was directly related to its hydrocarbon resources and the official policy of restoring state control over them.

Corruption in Angola, Turmoil in the Niger Delta

In their eagerness to highlight the virtues of the NANI countries prolific hydrocarbon sources, the authors of the U.S. National Energy Policy overlooked the universally recognized fact that the emergence of an oil industry in an underdeveloped economy leads to severe economic distortions, which in turn contribute to widespread corruption and political instability. In Africa this is particularly true of Angola and Nigeria.

"Angola's growing offshore oil industry, with participation by U.S. and international oil firms, is also a major source of growth [and] is thought to have the potential to double its exports over the next ten years," stated the NEP report in 2001.

In the four years since then, Angolan output had increased by only about a third. Despite the arrival of the Chinese oil companies and fresh investment, production was still below 1 million bpd. The corruption in the industry involving the top politicians in power, which resulted in the loss of roughly $1 billion in public revenues, continued unabated.

"Nigeria . . . has set ambitious production goals as high as 5 million bpd over the coming decade; more than twice as much as in 2000," stated the NEP document cheerily.

Accepting a foreign government's wishful figure for growth in its oil industry was naive to say the least. With the increase of barely 16 percent achieved by 2005 over the 2000 figure of 2.15 million bpd, the target of gaining another 84 percent in the remaining five years was nothing short of a pie in the sky.

In between, Royal Dutch Shell—the leading Western company operating in Nigeria since the 1950s, when oil was first discovered—admitted in January 2004 that it had overstated its oil and gas reserves in Nigeria by 20 percent, or 3.9 billion barrels of equivalent oil.[23]

The hydrocarbon-rich Niger Delta, producing 500,000 bpd, has been rife with violence since 1991, when the Movement for the Emancipation of the Niger Delta (MEND) was formed to control the oil and gas resources of the region. It demanded a greater share of the petroleum income for the local Ijaw communities and a compensation of $1.5 billion for environmental damage. The federal government dismissed MEND activists as thieves and criminals stealing oil. It executed Ken Saro-Wiwa, a MEND leader and a writer, in 1995.

Stealing from oil pipelines—called scooping when done on a small scale and bunkering when on a large scale—had become commonplace and resulted in periodic fatal explosions. In one such case in May 2006, up to two hundred people were killed at Inagbe Beach, an offshore island near Lagos, when thieves reached a pipeline buried just under the sands carrying gasoline from a tanker jetty to a distribution depot inland and drilled holes in it. Most of the victims were local residents who rushed to collect gasoline spilling out of the pipeline in jerricans. "If you've got no job and you're hungry, you take advantage of anything to feed your family," explained Olanrewaju Saka-Shenayon, a government official. "Anyone who takes this kind of risk is desperate."[24]

As in central Asia, so here, the petroleum industry was a hotbed of corruption and nepotism. Among the many government officials charged with "bunkering" were two navy admirals. While Nigeria's oil output was a little more than twice that of Angola, the loss to the public exchequer due to corruption and criminality, estimated at $4 billion a year, was four times as high. The problem was so severe that it pushed Nigeria to the top of corrupt nations in an annual survey on corruption by Transparency International, and kept it there.

MEND's agitation continued with its well-armed units patrolling the creeks of the Niger Delta in open-topped boats equipped with powerful outboard motors. It escalated its activities as oil prices exploded. In February 2006, its guerrillas launched a series of attacks on oil facilities, which crippled exports. Oil output fell by a quarter amid the kidnapping of foreign workers, arson against offshore oil installations, and bombings of pipelines.

In the midst of this mayhem, the federal court in Port Harcourt, the heart of the oil industry, ordered that Royal Dutch Shell pay $1.5 billion to the local communities for degrading their creeks and spoiling crops and fishing for decades. Shell decided to appeal.[25]

MEND kept a low profile as local leaders and the federal government negotiated regarding the payment of compensation. But in April 2006 it claimed responsibility for a car bomb inside a military barracks in the eastern delta, which had until then been free from violence. It warned Chinese companies to keep out of the delta after they had signed a wide-ranging $4 billion infrastructure contract with Nigeria involving oil production and railways and pipelines.[26]

Latin America

Latin America and Canada account for nearly half of the oil and gas imports into the United States—with oil arriving from Canada, Colombia, Ecuador, Mexico, and Venezuela, and gas from Bolivia, Peru, and Trinidad.[27]

The reference to Brazil in Washington's 2001 NEP document as a promising center for oil exports would prove misleading within a few years. Brazil's consumption of 1.79 million bpd in 2004 exceeded its output of 1.54 million bpd, and this deficit was set to widen.

"Colombia also has become an important supplier of oil to

the United States," noted the NEP cheerfully. In reality, between 2000 and 2005, the country's oil production declined by almost a quarter. In any event, its exports in 2005 amounted to less than a third of a million bpd.

Colombia had become extremely risky for the American petroleum corporations. Their oil pipelines were the favorite targets of the guerrillas of the Fuerzas Armadas Revolucionarias de Colombia (FARC) and Ejercito de Liberacion Nacional (ELN). In 2001, for instance, these left-wing militants bombed the vital Cano Limon-Covenas pipeline almost three times a week, thus stalling the delivery of more than twenty-four million barrels of crude oil, resulting in a loss of $600 million in revenue. During the next four years, the guerrillas ruptured the pipeline so frequently that it was nicknamed "the flute."[28] Despite increased assistance by the Pentagon's Southcom to the Colombian government to guard the Cano Limon pipeline, guerrilla attacks showed little sign of declining.

"Mexico is a leading and reliable source of imported oil," stated the NEP document, "and its large reserve base . . . makes Mexico a likely source of increased oil production over the next decade."

Over the decade of 1995–2004, Mexico's reserves declined by two-thirds, and its annual growth in petroleum production slowed to a measly 1 percent.

Its giant offshore Cantarell field, in the Bay of Campechem, which yielded more than half of the nation's oil output, was in irreversible decline. The site, discovered in 1976, held the world's eighth-largest reserves at that time. To counter the field's declining internal pressure, Petroleos Mexicanos, popularly known as Pemex, the state-owned oil company—described by internationally renowned oil expert Daniel Yergin as "an impenetrable state-within-a-state"—has resorted to nitrogen-injection techniques to squeeze out more oil. Due to higher investments during the past years, Pemex had cranked up output, according to Luis Ramirez, head of exploration and production. "Thus we pushed back the decline, which would have taken place in 2003 until 2006, when Cantarell will begin to decline significantly, at a rate of 14 percent annually," he said in August 2004.[29]

Overall, though, the investment policies of Pemex, possessing the ninth-largest oil reserves in the world, have been so skewed that Mexico now imports a quarter of its gasoline and natural gas needs from the United States.

Mexico's constitution prohibits foreign investment in the exploration and production of hydrocarbons. With oil nationalization in 1938, Pemex became part of the political landscape, which, until recently, was monopolized by the Institutional Revolutionary Party (PRI). It is estimated that graft among Pemex officials and trade unions, and related criminal activities, cost the Mexican public exchequer about $1 billion annually.[30]

While Mexican output will rise by a third to 4.8 million bpd by 2025, its domestic consumption will more than double, to 4.1 million bpd. So its exports will decline to two-fifths of the present rate—not the kind of news policy makers in Washington want to hear.

Venezuela, an Emerging Nemesis of Washington

According to the 2001 U.S. National Energy Policy document, growing international investment in Venezuela's energy sector is "encouraging the country's ability to meet its development goals and to keep pace with a growing world energy market."

This is true. But with the election and reelection of leftist Hugo Chavez since 1998, Venezuela has been diversifying its nationalized oil industry in a direction that runs contrary to the interests of Washington. In any case, many of the country's oil sites have matured, and their yield is declining. Despite a jump of 14 percent in its output in 2004 over the previous year, Venezuela is more than half a million bpd behind its peak production of 3.5 million bpd in 1998.

The move toward hydrocarbon oil nationalization that started in 1971 gathered momentum after the price explosion of 1973–74. The oil nationalization act that came into force on January 1, 1976, created Petroleos de Venezuela, S.A. (PdVSA), a state holding company with a central financial, planning, and coordinating role, along with three vertically integrated operating corporations to encourage competition. That meant that the PdVSA was not quite a monolith like Pemex.

As a thirty-eight-year-old colonel, Hugo Chavez tried to mount a coup in 1992 against President Carlos Andres Perez. He failed and was jailed. He was released when huge corruption scandals drove Perez from office in 1995. During Perez's tenure, Venezuela, cheating on its OPEC quota regularly, became the largest supplier of oil to the United States.

On his release, civilian Chavez entered politics as the leader of the left-of-center Movement of the Fifth Republic. He was elected president in December 1998 on a populist platform. He and his oil minister, Ali Rodriguez Araque, a former leftist guerrilla, convinced other OPEC members and four non-OPEC countries—Mexico, Norway, Oman, and Russia—to restrain or cut output.

During Chavez's presidency, Venezuela fell behind Saudi Arabia and Mexico as an oil supplier to the United States but earned more than before due to higher prices. In 2000, as chairman of OPEC, Chavez visited all OPEC capitals, including Baghdad, then under UN sanctions, to invite the leaders to an OPEC summit in Caracas on the organization's fortieth founding anniversary in September. Most OPEC leaders attended the summit, which agreed to maintain the $22–28 price range for a barrel of oil.

The next month, Venezuela signed an agreement with twelve Caribbean and Central American countries that gave them fifteen years to pay with 2 percent interest at $20 a barrel, compared to the current market price of $30. This agreement was soon extended to Cuba during President Fidel Castro's visit to Caracas, with Venezuela accepting a barter arrangement for repayment.[31]

Chavez's relations with the Bush administration soured when it welcomed his arrest and overthrow in a coup by dissident generals and opposition media tycoons on April 12, 2002. The coup collapsed two days later partly because a million Venezuelans from the poor neighborhoods of Caracas demanded his release and partly because all other Latin American capitals refused to recognize the post-Chavez government. Many in the region saw the Bush White House's commitment to democracy as skin deep.

This setback did not quiet Chavez's adversaries, who retained Washington's support. When his opponents called a general strike in December 2002, the union officials of PdVSA took up the call and brought production almost to a halt. Chavez responded by assuming total control of PdVSA and replacing the old guard with those loyal to his government and party. This disruption resulted in reduced output in 2003. But production picked up next year. Nearly half of Venezuela's exports were shipped to the United States. And Venezuela remained the world's fourth largest oil exporter after Saudi Arabia, Russia, and Iran.

In 2005, Chavez set out to use oil as a diplomatic weapon to garner support in the region for those of his policies that clashed with those of the Bush administration. At a summit of fifteen Caribbean countries in Caracas in June, he announced an energy alliance, called the PetroCaribe Initiative, whereby Venezuela offered to sell them cut-rate oil, a move praised by the assembled leaders. According to this scheme, on an average the signatories received oil at $40 a barrel instead of the market rate of $60-plus.[32] The implicit payback for Venezuela was diplomatic backing in the regional organizations.

Such support was on display at the summit of the thirty-four leaders of the Organization of American States at Mar Del Plata, Argentina, in November. Here Chavez stole the show both at the summit table and, with Argentine soccer idol Diego Maradona in tow, described the soccer stadium where he addressed twenty-five thousand people as the "grave site of the Free Trade Area of the Americas (FTAA)." Bush had failed to get the OAS summit's endorsement for the neo-liberal FTAA, which aimed to turn the Americas into a free trade zone dominated by the United States.[33]

Soon after his return home, Chavez held out a helping hand to the poor in the United States. Venezuela signed a deal to ship twelve million gallons of home heating oil to low-income families in Massachusetts through Citgo, the Houston-based subsidiary of PdVSA—a deal arranged by local Democrat Congressman William Delahunt. The fuel was to be offered at 40 percent below market prices to thousands of homes during winter. The scheme was later extended to other New England states.

During Chavez's seven-plus years of presidency—during which oil prices have risen by over 500 percent—Venezuela has provided $16 billion in foreign aid or subsidies to more than thirty countries, ranging from Indonesia to Argentina to Cuba, and to U.S. citizens, while simultaneously shoring up its foreign exchange reserves.

By purchasing $2.5 billion in Argentine debt, Chavez enabled left-leaning President Nestor Kirchner to pay off $9.8 billion debt to the IMF. His subsidies have covered such diverse activities as free eye surgery for poor Mexican Indians and Nicaraguans and the above-mentioned heating oil for poor American families in the northeastern states. Under his leadership, Venezuela's annual foreign aid has exceeded the nearly $2 billion that Washington allocates for development programs and the drug war in Latin

America. "Chavez wants to spread his ideas beyond Venezuela to Colombia, Peru, Ecuador, and Bolivia," said Antonio Ledezma, an opponent of the president. "The instrument he uses is petroleum."[34]

In January 2006, welcoming the newly elected Bolivian president Evo Morales in Caracas, Chavez promised Bolivia 200,000 barrels of diesel a month at subsidized rates, donated $30 million in social programs, and sent Venezuelan literacy volunteers into Bolivian villages in exchange for Bolivian farm products. "The axis of evil is Washington and its allies, who go about threatening, invading, and murdering," he said. "We are forming the axis of good."[35]

Chavez had clearly turned into a nemesis of the Bush administration in the Western Hemisphere. Bogged down in the quagmire of Iraq, the White House chafed quietly at the antics of the Venezuelan leader. On his part, Chavez remained alert to the possibility of invasion by the Pentagon to bring about "regime change." Leaving nothing to chance, he introduced a program to give weapons training to 500,000 civilians. He remained alert, too, to the needs of underprivileged Venezuelans. In 2006 his government planned to deposit $10 billion into a fund for social programs called Bolivarianism—named after Simón Bolívar, an early-nineteenth-century Venezuelan and Latin American revolutionary leader prominent in the South American Wars of Independence—up from $8 billion in 2005. This program, which has introduced the first free and widespread health care to seven out of ten Venezuelans, rendered by and large by seventeen thousand Cuban doctors; funded a mass literacy program; provided subsidized food and medicine to three out of five Venezuelans; given low-interest start-up loans to aspiring businessmen and -women; and funded eye surgery for a quarter of a million people, aims to reduce poverty to below 30 percent.[36]

Here, for once, was an example of a popular, democratic, and uncorrupt leader making adroit use of hydrocarbon resources for the welfare of the needy among his nation and others abroad in a selective and effective way, while upholding national sovereignty and furthering his political party's progressive ideology. This was a stark contrast to the way the super-affluent rulers of the oil-rich monarchies and their hangers-on lined their pockets with kickbacks on hydrocarbon, weapons, and construction contracts, and squandered billions of dollars from the public exchequer on hare-brained projects and huge sums of personal cash on lavish lifestyles, gambling, and fornication at home and abroad.

To dissuade Washington from attacking his country, Venezuelan oil minister Rafael Ramirez warned that in that eventuality PdVSA would stop its exports, thus pushing up oil prices that were already running high, and would then take its petroleum away from the United States and sell it elsewhere. He pointed out that Venezuela's oil exports to China were growing fast and would double in 2006 to 300,000 bpd—a remarkable figure for a country thirty tanker days away from Venezuela.[37] Earlier the CNPC had acquired two marginal fields in Venezuela for $359 million.

SEVEN

China: A Dragon Crashes into the Global Geopolitical Game

Most of the oil-rich Arabian Peninsula is covered with deserts, some of them resulting from the fluid rock pouring out of volcanoes, long since extinct, others full of fine sand and dunes of many hues and tones, still others made up chiefly of ash white calcium sulfate flats ringed with green salt bushes, and the rest containing the elements of the above in varying proportions. What they all have in common is the virtual absence of vegetation or life, except lizards and flies.

Venturing into such a landscape, bereft of cloud or shade, travelers encounter a blinding glare as the sun grows fiercely hot, which, combined with the shimmer rising from the blazing sand, leads them to see mirages, optical illusions.

Near the village of Al Warsan, several kilometers from Dubai International Airport, the sight of a dark, dragonlike figure clasping a golden globe with its tail, or a tall gateway resting on four sturdy, blood red pillars supporting a narrow, serrated platform embellished with replicas of Chinese buildings with curved, slanting roofs, would summarily and firmly be dismissed by any sane person as a glaring example of a mirage.

Dragon in the Arabian Desert

Neither the globe-embracing dragon nor the Chinese-style gateway is an optical illusion. Both are solid realities, their desert surroundings notwithstanding. They belong to the Dragon Mart, inaugurated in December 2004 as one of the half a dozen major building projects that will collectively form the International City, covering 800 hectares (2,100 acres) by early 2007.[1]

Though planned earlier, the construction of the Dragon Mart began in earnest after the 9/11 terrorist attacks. In their aftermath, all Arabs, irrespective of their wealth or sophistication, found themselves being treated with circumspection at best and hostility at worst by Americans and most Europeans. This made them turn east—toward the Indian subcontinent, southeast Asia, and China. "No longer feeling welcome in their former playgrounds on the Riviera or in the United States, hordes of Arab tourists now flock to Malaysia to escape the desert heat in the summer—more than 200,000 a year," wrote Michael Vatikiotis, former editor of the Hong Kong–based *Far Eastern Economic Review*.[2]

Housed inside a 2-square-mile (5.2-square-kilometer) compound, the Dragon Mart is the biggest Chinese sales outlet outside mainland China, with the site being used as a showcase and distribution hub for the six Arab Gulf states. Commerce between them and China reached a record $20 billion in 2004. The trade consisted of state-owned oil corporations in China purchasing hydrocarbons from the Gulf states, and government-owned Chinese consumer and technological companies exporting their wares to the six members of the Gulf Cooperation Council (GCC).[3]

A two-story shopping and eating area in the shape of a colorful dragon's tail whose central spine is almost a mile (1.6 kilometers) long, the Dragon Mart is divided into twenty compartments and provides outlets to three thousand companies—managed by the giant Chinamex—in shops, showrooms, and offices. The place is so vast that battery-operated golf carts ferry shoppers from one segment to another.

The stores sell everything—from hairpins to herbal medicines, bathrooms to burglar alarms, clothes to computers, toiletries to televisions, vibrators to video games, shoes to shampoos, lawn mowers to leather goods, perfumes to pottery, food to furniture, phones to photographs, and wigs to washing machines.

Here a ladies' handbag sells for $5, and fake Gucci shoes or briefcases for a fraction of the price of the original. Even the genuine goods are dirt cheap. The word has spread. Over the Islamic weekend of Thursday–Friday, the Arabs from Dubai and the rest of the United Arab Emirates, as well as the neighboring states of Oman, Qatar, Bahrain, and Saudi Arabia, flock to the Dragon Mart.

Yet shoppers do not feel the crush characteristic of oriental bazaars. Each of the twenty segments is shielded from the rest. The surrounding compound is dotted with characteristically Chinese images of dragons and dark gray lions, resting on their haunches, acting as guards.

A more exotic site is in the making at the International City: a replica of Beijing's Forbidden City, the largest and best-pre-served complex of ancient buildings in China, which was off-limits to the rest of the world for centuries—along with its Chinese-style landscaped garden, museums and performance courts, covering nearly ten square miles (twenty-six square kilo-meters). The replica of the Forbidden City on the fringe of the Arabian Peninsula will house local and foreign nationals with deep pockets for the privilege of living in a complex that will, according to a slick brochure, transport "the magic of Chinese culture to the desert."

By sponsoring this venture, the Chinese leaders have given their country such a potent, positive profile in the Persian Gulf region that it has preempted any other nation even thinking of trying to rival, much less outshine, them.

It was in the mid-1990s that China's State Council, the

highest executive authority, decided to project a popular economic profile in this area. As a cosmopolitan metropolis with excellent port and dry dock facilities and financial services, and an established center for re-exporting gold and Western goods to Iran and the Indian subcontinent, Dubai appealed to them instantly.

Since then, the developments in this principality of 3,900 square kilometers (1,510 square miles) have proved them prescient. In 2006 Dubai's man-made Jebel Ali port was being expanded to the extent that almost a fifth of the world's cranes were deployed there. This and the construction of the tallest building in the world, along with four man-made islands to increase Dubai's sixty-five-kilometer- (forty-mile-) long beaches twenty-three times, were the leading projects in the construction boom worth $100 billion, twice the amount needed to rebuild Iraq's shattered economic structure. It had attracted 250,000 Indian and Pakistan workers to a principality with a settled population of 1.25 million. Dubai was being hyped as "the capital of the world."

Most of the investment came from Dubai's rich neighbors. A lot of the Arab money withdrawn from the United States after 9/11 needed an outlet. With oil prices running high, there was much surplus to be invested. And, over the past few decades, money has been draining out of Iran into Dubai.

The comparatively modest Dragon Mart and the Forbidden City replica were the brainchildren of Chinamex and the Nakheel Corporation in Dubai, headed by Sultan Ahmad bin Sulayem—a small, dapper, soft-spoken man of fifty-one with a luxuriant mustache—a confidant of the ruler Sheikh Muhammad bin Rashid al Mukatam.

The idea was conceived almost a decade earlier, at a time when rapid industrialization had turned China from an oil-exporting country into an importer.

China's Self-Sufficiency in Oil

It was in 1993 that the People's Republic of China (PRC) began importing petroleum—moderately, at 25,000 bpd. But in a couple of years that figure leaped sixteenfold. The Chinese dragon, it seemed, had acquired an unquenchable thirst for oil.

The Chinese have a long and checkered history in oil and drilling. As early as the fifth century, they developed drilling for salt with wells bored up to the depth of 3,000 feet (915 meters). It was their technology that Europeans emulated in the early nineteenth century. And it was from Europe that this technology was taken to the United States. There, Americans applied it to boring for oil.

By the end of the nineteenth century, Imperial China, whose coastline had been carved up by the Great Powers in the course of the Opium Wars, had become a lucrative market for kerosene produced by the Shell Oil Company. The establishment of the Republic of China in 1912 made little difference to the foreign domination of the oil market. Mobil, Texaco, and British Asia came to monopolize this sector.

On the eve of the Communist victory in the civil war between the Communists and the National Party (the Kuomintang) in October 1949, the total Chinese oil output was less than 2,000 bpd, most of it from the Yunan field in Gansu province. Oil and gas contributed less than 1 percent of energy in China.

After the founding of the PRC under the leadership of Chairman Mao Zedong and Premier Zhou Enlai, Beijing forged an alliance with Moscow. Soviet geologists and engineers arrived to help their Chinese counterparts develop China's petroleum industry. And the Soviet Union became the chief source of oil and oil products for China.

In 1956 the newly formed Ministry of Petroleum Industry began exploring large basins and discovered oil fields in Qinghai province and the Xinjian Uighur Autonomous Region. In 1959 it struck a giant field, Daqing, in the Heilongjiang province adjoining the Soviet Union, with reserves of fifteen billion barrels. Production began in May 1960 and was so copious that Daqing contributed as much as two-thirds of the national output.

The next month the Beijing–Moscow alliance collapsed due to irreconcilable ideological differences, with Soviet leader Nikita Khrushchev publicly criticizing Mao Zedong as an "ultra-leftist" for his policy of further collectivization of peasants into people's communes, and the organ of the Communist Party of China, *People's Daily*, denouncing Khrushchev as a "bourgeois revisionist." Though the Soviet oil experts left, the Chinese government had no option but to continue buying more than half of its oil products from Moscow. This did not last long. The discovery in 1962 of the Shengli oil field, the second largest, followed by Liaohe field three years later, enabled China to become self-sufficient.

Indeed, China soon became an oil-exporting country. Daqing achieved a record output of 1 million bpd in 1976—the year that witnessed the deaths first of pragmatic Zhou Enlai, and then of radical Mao Zedong. Soon after, Premier Hua Guofeng coordinated a successful move to arrest four foremost radicals—"The Gang of Four"—led by Jiang Qing, the widow of Mao, and consolidated his position as the Communist Party chairman.

The following year, the pragmatic Deng Xiaoping, who had lately fallen into disgrace, was restored to his previous status, making him number two in the Communist Party hierarchy. An acolyte of Zhou Enlai, Deng unveiled a program of Four Modernizations, originally proposed by his mentor, covering agriculture, industry, defense, and science.

Abandoning agricultural cooperatives and communes, the brainchildren of Mao, the government introduced a household contract system whereby peasants leased land from the authorities, grew crops of their choice, and sold their produce in free markets.[4] It allowed large-scale imports of foreign machines and technology. It entered into joint ventures with foreign companies and established "special economic zones" that offered tax concessions to non-Chinese investors. It depoliticized the People's Liberation Army (PLA) and curtailed its budget by a quarter. It set up a network of high-tech research centers. To encourage private enterprise, Deng came up with the very un-Marxist slogan, "To get rich is glorious." With the "retirement" of Hua Guofeng in 1981, he became the "paramount leader."

Deng's reforms unveiled the next stage of development in the petroleum industry, which produced a record 2 million bpd in 1978. Oil prospecting was extended to the Tarim, Junggar, and Turpan-Hami basins in the west—as well as the continental shelf in the Huanghai Sea and East China Sea in the east, and offshore islands in the South China Sea.

In 1982 the government established the China National Offshore Oil Corporation (Cnooc) to undertake offshore exploration and production, and permitted limited foreign participation in the offshore areas in order to gain expertise. It founded the China National Petrochemical Corp (Sinopec) to focus on refining and marketing.

In the mid-1980s, China's State Council concluded that controlling domestic oil usage was detrimental to the economy forging ahead at an average annual growth of 10 percent. So it abandoned its long-held policy of self-sufficiency in petroleum and let non-Chinese companies explore for oil onshore.

In 1988 the State Council transformed the Ministry of Petroleum Industry into the China National Petroleum Corporation (CNPC), with a mandate to carry out oil exploration and production onshore and in shallow waters.[5]

With 1.4 million employees, the CNPC was second only to the PLA army in size. A later reorganization would turn the CNPC into a mother corporation with three subsidiaries: PetroChina, with its focus on exploration and production in China; Sinopec, which erects and operates refineries and markets oil products; and Cnooc, 71 percent state-owned, which has most of its reserves either on the mainland or in Chinese territorial waters.[6]

The student protest at Beijing's Tiananmen Square in May–June 1989, and its suppression, which resulted in seven hundred to two thousand deaths—and which was aired worldwide, drawing wide-spread condemnation in the West and elsewhere—left the national economy unimpaired.

China's march toward prosperity continued. Buoyed by this, eighty-eight-year-old Deng undertook a tour of central and southern China in 1992 to garner backing for further economic reform. This proved to be the last year of China's self-sufficiency in oil.

China as an Oil Importer

Once China became an oil importer in 1993, its imports rose by an average of 24 percent a year, thus exposing it to the external pressure of the international oil market. That in turn led its State Council to devise a strategy to ensure energy security as an integral part of its foreign policy. It decided to participate in oil and gas prospecting and production projects abroad, as well as in transnational pipeline construction. Diversification of both the sources and transportation of oil became its leading credo. At home it opted for constructing refineries capable of handling heavy, sour oil, and vigorously developing the natural gas industry. It aspired to build up a Strategic Petroleum Reserve (SPR) just as the United States and Europe had done.

To enable the CNPC to invest abroad, the State Council changed its policy of requiring it to sell petroleum at government-mandated low prices to Sinopec and major industries. Due to the authorized successive price hikes, the CNPC's profits surged from $6 billion in 1993 to $21 billion four years later. By then, oil and gas produced 20 percent of all energy in China, a nineteenfold increase since the Communist revolution.

The state-owned petroleum companies followed the official dictum strictly: China's energy security is our primary concern, with our own economic interest playing a secondary role. "The Chinese take a long-term perspective to securing strategic resources rather than a short-term investment perspective," said Chris Stephens, who is involved in mergers and acquisitions in China. "They don't face those pressures to show investment returns on a quarterly basis [as do Western companies]."[7]

After small beginnings in 1993, four years later the CNPC inked deals worth $8 billion abroad, beating off competition from such long-established stalwarts as Amoco, Texaco, and Unocal of the United States, and Petronas of Malaysia. During the next decade, the CNPC and its subsidiaries acquired stakes in forty-four countries, from Angola to Azerbaijan, Myanmar to Mauritania, and Sudan to Saudi Arabia, altogether investing $15 billion.

In economic terms, it made sense for the Chinese companies to acquire oil and gas acreage abroad, as their production costs were a fraction of the international market price. As such, Chinese corporations stood to make windfall profits in the case of oil-price explosions. However, the State Council—committed to safeguarding the interests of the nation as a whole—was expected to pressure the oil companies to sacrifice high profits and sell the commodity to Chinese factories at artificially low prices in order to cushion the oil shock and keep the economy bouncing along almost as before. (This is what the State Council did when oil prices rose above $60 a barrel in 2005. Between May and September 2005, it mandated three rises in pump prices, totaling 25 percent, while the rise in the global crude price was 65 percent.[8]

By 1997, economic reform and industrial advancement had

acquired such a momentum that the incapacitation of Deng, caused by an irreversible coma in 1995, which would lead to his death in February 1997, left the economy unaffected, especially when the transition of full powers to the Communist Party chief, Jiang Zemin, went through smoothly.

The prospects for China's admission to the World Trade Organization (WTO) seemed rosy after U.S. president Bill Clinton's successful trip to China in June 1998, followed by Chinese premier Zhu Rongji's trip to the United States the following April. Most of the talks were related to the liberalization of China's service sectors, such as financial services and telecommunication. But there was a setback when the Chinese embassy in Belgrade was bombed by NATO warplanes in the course of its military campaign against Serbia in Kosovo. Beijing demanded a satisfactory explanation from Washington and in its absence suspended its talks with the United States on its entry into the WTO.

A further setback occurred in the early days of George W. Bush's administration following the midair collision between an American spy plane and a Chinese fighter in the South China Sea in April 2001, resulting in the death of a Chinese pilot.[9] Beijing demanded an apology and compensation while putting on hold the Sino-American talks on its WTO entry.

On the Eve of WTO Membership

On the eve of China's admission to the WTO in November 2001, its rulers could proudly claim that since 1978 the number of Chinese living below the poverty line—defined by the World Bank as those living on two-thirds of a U.S. dollar a day—had fallen from 260 million to 42 million in a country of 1.3 billion. That meant an annual decline of nearly 10 million. During this period, Chinese migrated from villages to urban centers at the rate of 12 million per year, amounting to 1 percent of the population.[10] On the other hand, the gap between the rich and the poor widened dramatically, and the social welfare system all but vanished.

Urbanization and industrialization, coupled with easy loans from banks and other financial institutions, fueled a construction boom—one of the main ingredients of its spectacular and sustained economic growth on the domestic front. From power plants to steel mills and car factories to the relentless expansion of expressways to high-rise office complexes and luxury apartment blocks, the skylines of China's urban centers became dotted with construction cranes. In barely two decades, the number of skyscrapers in Shanghai climbed from one to more than three hundred. And in the 1990s, China spent an average $33 billion a year on expanding its road network.[11]

Between 1978 and 2005, the percentage of the college-age population in higher education jumped from 1.4 percent to 20 percent. China boasted 100 million Internet users and 3.5 times as many mobile phone owners.[12]

The succession of Jiang Zemin as the Communist Party chief and president of the Republic in 2002–03 by Hu Jintao—a moon-faced, tight-lipped, bespectacled man of fifty-seven, with a head of thick black hair—left untouched China's dizzying economic advancement, which pushed its GDP to number four in 2004 after the United States, Japan, and Germany.[13]

The nation's economic miracle was reflected in the speed at which its oil needs galloped. By 2002, China was importing nearly a third of its oil demand. Three-fifths of these imports passed in tankers through the narrow, crowded, accident-prone Malacca Strait—dominated by the Pentagon's Pacom (Pacific Command), charged with patrolling the Indian Ocean, South China Sea, and western Pacific—on their way from the Persian Gulf or Sudan. In the absence of enough naval power of its own, China could not protect these oil lanes.

To overcome this strategic vulnerability, the State Council

favored building overland pipelines from adjoining Russia and the central Asian republics, thus reducing China's dependence on ocean routes. Here it made some progress.

But the one front where there was no advance was the idea of building up a Chinese SPR. Though the SPR's merits—overcoming interruptions and accidents in supplies, stabilizing the price domestically, and discouraging economically or politically motivated supply disruption—were obvious, the project was expensive. It would cost $5 a barrel for a salt cavern facility with a unit capacity of 100 million barrels.

The high outlay argument did not convince the military leadership. Xiong Guangkai, China's deputy chief of general staff, publicly called for a buildup of strategic reserves and a fleet to defend oil tankers.[14]

Surging Energy Demand Outstrips Supply

In 2002 China became the world's second-largest energy consumer, outstripping Japan. Fuel was needed to run transport and generate electricity. Demand for electric power rocketed as the number of air conditioners rose fiftyfold, refrigerators tenfold, and television sets fivefold between 1984 and 2003. There was also an explosion in the construction of new factories that required electricity.[15] In transport, air travel quadrupled in a single decade.

Though China's power supplies grew by an average of more than 10 percent a year, electricity shortages in cities had become endemic, with sudden blackouts a daily phenomenon. In Shanghai the problem was so acute that companies staggered their working hours; some shut down during the week and operated on weekends.

Demand for gasoline and diesel reflected the steep rise in car ownership, an unmistakable sign of personal prosperity. In the decade of 1995–2004, auto owners increased from 10 million to

27 million. In 2003, car sales jumped by a whopping 70 percent, with the government financing one out of three transactions. To keep pace with the demand, the Chinese car industry expanded at the fastest rate in the world, and employed 1.6 million workers at more than fifty car plants of varying size.[16] Several hundred thousand Chinese flocked to Beijing's Biennial International Auto Show at the breathtakingly large International Exhibition Center.

Such an explosion created its own problems. By 2004, auto ownership in Shanghai (population 13 million) had reached 2 million, a figure predicted for 2020 by the planners in the early 1980s. To solve the inner-city housing shortages, they had opted for a suburban constellation around the city center, thus inadvertently engendering a car culture. As recently as 1995, automobiles accounted for less than 5 percent of personal transportation—with cycles at 33 percent, buses 25 percent, and foot 31 percent. Then, within five years, car transportation trebled.[17]

Yet this national average, when boiled down, came to only eight cars per 1,000 people of driving age. So the potential for growth was immense. Some analysts estimated that currently, nearly 300 million Chinese earn more than $2,000 a year—the level at which, measured in terms of purchasing-power parity, auto buying had taken off in developing economies. For instance, between 1987 and 1997, South Korea registered a four-fold increase in auto ownership and a trebling of gasoline consumption.[18] A similar expansion in car ownership in China will push the total number of cars to 108 million by 2015, resulting in the trebling of gasoline usage.

As it was, an increase of 16 percent in oil consumption in 2004 took the annual figure to 6.7 million bpd, with China producing only about half of the demand. So there was tremendous pressure on the state-owned oil corporations to intensify oil and gas prospecting, if only to compensate for the declining production at Daqing and Shengli, which had traditionally contributed more than half of the national output.

China's State Council directed the government-controlled oil corporations to explore for oil in the East and South China Seas, raise the offshore contribution from a measly 6 percent in 1996, and actively seek foreign assistance. The initial scheme of encouraging non-Chinese companies to participate in expensive, technologically demanding offshore projects was later extended to some demanding onshore operations, including one in the Qiantang Basin in northern Tibet. Foreign firms began oil and gas prospecting in the Xinjiang province's Tarim Basin, much of it covered by the Taklimakan Desert and posing immense logistical and climatic challenges. With oil available only beyond the depth of 6,000 meters (19,700 feet), drilling proved costly and overly problematic.

To their credit, the Chinese had developed robotic underwater exploration submersibles and had extended a robot's ability to work at depths of 20,000 feet (6,100 meters) from the earlier 3,000 feet (915 meters).[19]

On the other hand, the nation's natural gas industry has lagged behind, for several reasons: the remoteness of the reserves, insufficient pipeline infrastructure, lack of a well-developed market, and insufficient funding.

Meanwhile, the Persian Gulf region remained the main source of China's oil and gas imports.

The Persian Gulf Region

In 1998, three of the five oil barrels that Beijing imported originated in the Persian Gulf region. That led the State Council to aggressively bolster China's profile on the Arabian Peninsula by establishing the Dragon Mart and the replica of the Forbidden City near Dubai.

Elsewhere in the Middle East, China signed a production-sharing contract with Baghdad for the Ahdab oil field, the second largest in Iraq, in 1997. It was to be implemented after the anticipated lifting of the UN sanctions on Iraq imposed in 1990. (Following the invasion and occupation of Iraq by the Anglo-American alliance in 2003, the legal status of Iraq's oil-development contract with China, as well as many other countries, became murky.)

Most importantly, Beijing forged strong hydrocarbon links with Saudi Arabia, with which it had enjoyed friendly ties since 1990. Riyadh was equally keen to reciprocate, well aware of the needs of the booming Chinese economy. "We are going to get the Chinese market just as we got Japan and the United States—through aggressive marketing subsidies," said one Saudi Aramco official.[20] Along with discounts went the Saudi Aramco's offer to supply sweet, low-sulfur oil, and not the abundant sour, high-sulfur crude that most of its fields have.

In exchange for Saudi Arabia's preferential treatment, China offered arms and technology transfers for which, unlike in the United States, no parliamentary approval was needed. Thus Riyadh obtained from Beijing such weaponry as long-range ballistic missiles—which neither the Unites States nor any of its Western allies would sell it.

Economic ties between the Middle Kingdom and the Desert Kingdom thrived. In 2004, when the two governments agreed to hold regular political consultations, Sinopec signed a $300 million deal to explore for natural gas near the Ghawar field even though the risk was high and profit low. Sinopec was motivated less by its commercial considerations and more by strategic and diplomatic gains for China. That year, at 440,000 bpd, Saudi Arabia became the top oil supplier to China, a position it has maintained since then.

In 2005 Beijing-Riyadh trade jumped 60 percent, to $14 billion.

Work was going apace at a huge refinery in China, a joint venture of Saudi Aramco and Exxon Mobil, to refine Saudi heavy oil.

Tellingly, the first foreign visit outside the Middle East that the freshly elevated King Abdullah ibn Abdul Aziz made in January 2005 was to Beijing, where he signed an agreement to bolster Sino-Saudi investment in oil and gas production and refining.

Chas Freeman, former U.S. ambassador to Saudi Arabia, remarked that until recently Washington had wanted Saudi oil and offered protection in return. "More recently [after 9/11], the simplicity of this bargain became embarnacled with all sorts of other agendas, including women's rights, human rights, religious freedom, and other issues that Saudis either find irksome or difficult to address," he said. "None of these issues arise with the Chinese or Indians." Both China and Saudi Arabia shared their preference for a faster pace of economic reform and development to political change. "Because China has criticized America's antiterror campaign and democracy plans—which too go well with the region's beliefs—scope for better ties between the two sides remains unlimited."[21]

China's president, Hu Jintao, reciprocated by visiting Saudi Arabia in the course of his three-continent tour in April 2006. He became the first non-Muslim foreign leader to address the Advisory Council in Riyadh.

His visit came after the vociferous protest by the U.S. public and politicians against the prospect of the management of six American ports being transferred from a British company to a Dubai-based corporation—further encouraging Arab businessmen to turn away from the West. "We are opening new channels; we are heading east," declared Prince Waleed ibn Talal of the royal family, the world's eighth richest man.[22]

Supping with the Mullahs

Since its establishment, the Islamic Republic of Iran's relations with China have been cordial. During the Iran-Iraq War, Tehran started buying mainly Soviet-designed warplanes and tanks from Beijing from 1983 onward. Later, anti-ship and air-to-surface missiles, as well as surface-to-air missiles, were added to the shopping list. Between 1986 and 1990, half of the $3 billion that Iran spent on weapons imports went to China.

During his visit to Beijing in 1992, President Ali Akbar Hashemi Rafsanjani signed an agreement with China for the supply of nuclear research reactors to be built near Tehran. But under pressure from the Clinton administration, China cancelled the deal.[23] However, the Chinese reportedly provided specialized equipment for the development of Iran's Shahab surface-to-surface missiles. In response, Washington slapped economic sanctions on the Chinese companies involved and pressured Beijing to terminate its military cooperation with Iran. This slowed the flow of China's missile technology to Iran but did not end it.[24]

In 1992, two dissident Iranian Kurdish leaders in Berlin were murdered. After a judicial conclusion in Berlin found that Iran's Supreme National Security Council was "the planning center for assassinations abroad," European Union members withdrew their ambassadors from Tehran. Iranian leaders turned determinedly eastward in the spring of 1997.[25] Rafsanjani announced that his government had decided to give priority to its ties with Asian countries, in particular China and India. This was viewed as part of Iran's larger strategy of frustrating the designs of the "hegemonist" United States by strengthening links with China, India, and Russia.

"Iran is a natural partner to fuel China's economy," said Iran's oil minister, Bizhan Namdar Zanganeh. "We [Iran] have invited Chinese companies to actively participate in our exploration and development projects by promising them the greatest incentives."[26]

Economic ties between China and Iran became tighter, with reciprocal trade reaching $1.3 billion in 2000, the year when Jiang Zemin led a high-level delegation to Iran. Two years later, Sinopec and CNPC collaborated with Iran on a 240-mile (385-kilometer) oil pipeline from Neka, a Caspian port, to Tehran for refining.

As petroleum prices rose, Beijing-Tehran trade climbed to $7 billion in 2004, with Iranian exports amounting to $4 billion, three-quarters of it in crude oil, gas, and oil products. By then Iran had become the second-largest oil exporter to China, after Saudi Arabia.[27]

In October, during the visit of Chinese foreign minister Li Zhaoxing to Tehran, there was an agreement on a $70 billion package deal whereby Sinopec would buy 250 million tonnes of LNG over thirty years and participate in exploring and developing the Yadavaran oil field in southwest Iran—with estimated reserves of 15 billion barrels—with the right to import 150,000 bpd of oil into China.[28]

Chinese companies were active in Iran outside the energy sector. They had constructed a number of super oil tankers and power stations as well as the Tehran metro and a highway from the capital to the Caspian. They built a television manufacturing plant and set out to establish a broadband network in the republic. Iran became the venue of the first foreign assembly plant for China's Cherry Automobiles, with plans to turn out fifty thousand cars a year in a joint venture with a local producer.

So it came as no surprise that of the five permanent members of the UN Security Council, China was the most reluctant to see Iran referred to the Security Council on the subject of its nuclear program.

And it was at the behest of China, which maintained the

secretariat of the Shanghai Cooperation Organization (SCO) in Shanghai, that the SCO summit in mid-2005 granted Iran observer status at its meetings while rejecting the United States' request for the same. SCO's members included Kazakhstan and other central Asian republics.

The Kazakh Embrace

In 1996 China hosted a meeting in Shanghai of the representatives of Russia, Kazakhstan, Kyrgyzstan, and Tajikistan, with all of whom it shared common borders. They issued an "Agreement on Confidence Building in the Military Field along the Border Areas."

In September 1997 the CNPC signed a grand deal with Kazakhstan involving oil fields east of the Caspian Sea and in the northwestern region of Aktyubink. After the signing of the agreement by Kazakh president Sultan Nazarbayev and visiting Chinese prime minister Li Peng, both sides described it as "the deal of the century," with the CNPC paying $4.7 billion and pledging to invest another $10 billion in the infrastructure.

This was an attempt by Kazakhstan to balance its pro-Western tilt while loosening its traditionally tight links with Russia. As part of the Soviet Union, engaged in a hostile rivalry with Communist China since 1960, contemporary Kazakhs had grown up thinking of China as an exotic and threatening place. However, by signing the latest economic agreement with Beijing, Kazakh officials recognized that China was a source of enormous economic opportunity. In a larger sense, they had concluded that while the East—China, Japan, and South Korea, in particular—had both money and technology, it was desperately short of energy, a firm basis for strong mutual commercial ties.

By tapping into the oil fields of a neighboring country and bringing the commodity to its own border province of Xinjiang, China wished to solve both its own problems, economic and political, and those of Kazakhstan. Of the three economic segments of China—the comparatively well-off east, the middle-income center, and the relatively poor west—Xinjiang was in the last category. Whereas the annual per capita GDP in the Shanghai province was $2,440, that in Xinjiang was $715. Xinjiang's drive for industrialization had faltered due to lack of energy and foreign investment, which, at $4 per capita, was minuscule compared to $278 in Shanghai.[29] Over the long run, the Chinese leaders visualized their investment in Kazakhstan as a means to expand China's influence there.

By shipping Kazakhstan's oil to Xinjiang,[30] the CNPC planned to boost the industrialization of the underdeveloped province. Moreover, oil imported overland from Kazakhstan cost China far less than oil shipped from the Persian Gulf region. A rise in the living standards of Xinjiang's population was expected to help Beijing contain the growing discontent among the ethnic Uighurs there, who were Muslim. For many years militant Uighurs, forming nearly half of the province's population, had been agitating to reestablish the sovereign state of East Turkistan, which existed in 1933 and again from 1944–50, with some of them exploding bombs in Beijing.

By 2002, the CNPC-led consortium boosted the production from these onshore oil fields to 550,000 bpd, amounting to half of the total national figure. The CNPC shipped some of its Kazakh oil by tankers in the Caspian to refineries in northern Iran, and in return the National Iranian Oil Company (NIOC) dispatched an equivalent amount to China by sea, thus giving China, Kazakhstan, and Iran a common economic interest—a throwback to the Silk Road of ancient times.

In July 2005 China signed an agreement with Kazakhstan to develop a strategic partnership. It set the scene for CNPC's acquisition of Canadian-registered PetroKazakhstan, which owned oil fields in southern Kazakhstan, for $4.2 billion.

This deal also heralded the arrival of the Chinese oil corporations in North America, a region already overcrowded with energy companies.

Contrary was the case with Africa, an underdeveloped continent three times the size of China, with many natural resources that Beijing was eager to exploit to feed its fast-growing industry. This industry led it to purchase 25 percent of the world's aluminum, steel, and copper (thus outstripping the United States) and 40 percent of its cement in 2003. It succeeded so well that its trade with Africa almost quadrupled in six years, to reach $48 billion in 2005. Nearly five hundred Chinese companies were active in Africa on their own or in partnership with local firms.[31]

The African Connection

China had targeted Africa before—in the 1960s to help the national liberation movements in the colonized parts of the continent through its Communist cadres. In a much-changed world, this time it was the CNPC—not CPC, Communist Party of China—that worked hard to gain a foothold in Africa. It succeeded so well that the *South China Morning Post* warned in May 2004 that China's "assertive inroads, notably in Nigeria and Gabon, threaten to blunt U.S. efforts to gain a foothold in West Africa." By then the contribution of the countries of Angola, Sudan, Congo, and Nigeria to Chinese petroleum imports were three-fifths the size of those from the Persian Gulf region.[32] In absolute terms, Angola became the second most important oil source for China in 2005 after Saudi Arabia, overtaking Iran.

Since the CNPC's moves were part of an overarching state policy—to translate the strictly commercial link into agreements on security cooperation and the building of the economic infrastructure of an African state—other Chinese firms followed soon after to help the African countries build roads, railways, and power plants. They did so not only in oil-bearing states like

Sudan but also in adjoining Ethiopia and Rwanda. Chinese workers and executives became as much of a common sight in Africa as they had become earlier in the Persian Gulf region.

It was not until 1995 that the CNPC won an oil exploitation contract in Sudan. Two years later it got a further break. Washington banned U.S. trade with Sudan after listing it as a country that supported state terrorism, resulting in Occidental Petroleum having to withdraw its oil and pipeline contracts. The CNPC purchased a 40 percent stake in the Greater Nile Petroleum Operating Company consortium, involving a total investment of $12.6 billion, to explore and develop the prolific Heglig and Unity oil fields. It went on to construct a 940-mile (1,500-kilometer) pipeline from the fields to an oil terminal at Suakin on the Red Sea in the record time of one year. Within three months of its completion in May 1999, the first tanker carrying 580,000 barrels of oil sailed off to China.

By 2005, Sudan, an oil importer before the CNPC's arrival, earned $2 billion a year in oil exports, half of which went to China. This made Sudan the second-largest African supplier of oil to China, after Angola.

What made the CNPC attractive to the rulers of Sudan as well as to other African countries was Beijing's willingness and ability to provide its economic partners with political-diplomatic cover when necessary. This unspoken understanding became manifest in 2004. When the issue of the massacres in the troubled Sudanese western region of Darfur was debated at the UN Security Council in September 2004, the United States wanted to impose economic sanctions against the Sudanese regime. Beijing threatened to veto such a resolution. So the Security Council passed a watered-down resolution on Darfur.

Although the CNPC arrived in Angola three years after its deal with Sudan, its progress was so rapid that by 2005 Beijing was purchasing a third of the Angolan petroleum output and had given its government a $2 billion line of credit to build railways and roads and to electrify parts of the capital, Luanda.[33]

In Nigeria, the CNPC's deal to develop the Chad Basin in 1997 was trumped by Cnooc in January 2006, when it paid $2.7 billion cash to acquire a large stake in oil and gas fields in the Niger Delta.[34]

During his visit to Nigeria in April, Chinese president Hu Jintao received a standing ovation at the National Assembly when he described China as "a developing country."

His statement was at odds with the fact that Beijing had promised $4 billion of infrastructure investment—railways, power plants, and telephones—in the oil-bearing area in return for preferential treatment in the allocation of upcoming exploration and production rights in the oil acreage.[35]

China's Other Neighbors

China's forays into faraway lands for hydrocarbons did not occur at the cost of overlooking its immediate neighbors, such as Myanmar and Russia. Indeed they were crucial to the State Council's overall strategy to cobble together a web of overland energy supply routes.

In November 2004, China concluded a major trade agreement with the ten-member Association of South-East Asian Nations (ASEAN). During that year, Beijing reinforced its economic and political ties with the military dictatorship in Myanmar, whose biggest trading partner and arms supplier is China. Myanmar possessed 18.5 billion cubic feet of natural gas, an energy asset that both of its powerful neighbors, China and India, eyed hungrily.

Thus, when, at the UN Security Council, the United States tried to initiate a discussion on the release from house arrest of the Myanmar dissident leader Aung San Suu Kyi, the winner of the 1991 Nobel Peace Prize, China, backed by Russia, refused to endorse the tabling of the motion, arguing that her continued detention had no bearing on international peace and security.

Following ASEAN's annual meeting in the Laotian capital of Vientiane in July 2005, Chinese foreign minister Li Zhaoxing flew to Yangon (formerly Rangoon). China was taking advantage of Myanmar's isolation despite its admission to ASEAN in 1997. Beijing offered Myanmar hefty aid while allowing a thriving cross-border trade to continue to offset the ill effects of the Western embargo. Describing the current situation, George Yeo, the prime minister of Singapore, said, "Myanmar has the back gate to China wide open. India, in its geo-strategic calculation, has decided to keep its side gate open. So it must be in the interests of ASEAN to keep our side gate open, whatever happens in Myanmar."[36] In return for Beijing's military and economic aid, Myanmar allowed China to build its first military base on the Indian Ocean on Myanmar soil in 2005.

While the relationship between China and Myanmar was grossly unequal, that was not the case with Beijing's ties with Tokyo.

In 2003, Chinese and Japanese petroleum companies competed for access to Russian oil fields and pipelines. While the Japanese corporations proposed a $5 billion project for a 2,300-mile (3,700-kilometer) pipeline from Siberia to coastal Japan to carry 1 million bpd, their Chinese rivals suggested a 1,400-mile (2,250-kilometer) pipeline from Siberia to its oil city of Daqing to transport 600,000 bpd. By offering not merely to finance the pipeline but also to invest a further $7 billion in the Siberian petroleum industry and another $2 billion on "social projects" in Russia, the Japanese won the contest.[37] However, the long-running battle between Beijing and Tokyo on oil and gas rights in the East China Sea, believed to contain 100 billion barrels of oil, remains unresolved.

Hugging the Russian Bear

For the People's Republic of China, first the Soviet Union and then Russia constituted a preeminent neighbor. Following the Soviet Union's disintegration in 1991, Beijing made large-scale purchases of Russian warplanes, submarines, destroyers, and missiles. Toward the end of the decade, it turned its attention to Russia's hydrocarbons.

At the Shanghai Cooperation Organization summit in Bishkek, Kyrgyzstan, in August 1999, Jiang Zemin and Russian president Boris Yeltsin formulated an "anti-NATO" pact and expressed their belief in a multipolar world—a concept at odds with the "sole superpower" status of the United States.

In July 2001, during his visit to Moscow, Jiang Zemin signed the Sino-Russian Friendship Treaty with Vladimir Putin, Yeltsin's successor.

From the modest imports of 50,000 bpd of Russian oil in 2002, shipments from Russia climbed to 300,000 bpd in three years. A fifth of this oil was delivered by rail.[38] Such a large volume made the idea of a 2,400-kilometer (1,500-mile) Russia-China pipeline costing $2 billion more feasible: it was expected to carry double the current amount.

In diplomatic matters, the interests of Beijing and Moscow converged in central Asia. They shared the common aims of curbing Islamist extremism, maintaining and improving their commercial interests, and frustrating Washington's agenda to dominate the region.

At the SCO's annual summit in July 2005, China and Russia called on Washington to name the date of its withdrawal of soldiers and military hardware from its bases in Qarshi-Khanabad in Uzbekistan and Manas in Kyrgyzstan, which it had acquired on the eve of the Afghanistan War in October 2001. To widen its influence, the SCO granted observer status not only to Iran but also to India, Pakistan, and Mongolia.[39]

The joint Sino-Russian military exercises conducted on China's Shandong Peninsula from August 18 to 25, 2005, "to test the capability of the two armed forces in jointly striking international terrorism, extremism, and separatism" were the first of its kind.[40] The maneuvers involved eight thousand Chinese and two thousand Russian troops equipped with a Russian navy squadron and seventeen long-haul aircraft, plus non-nuclear-powered submarines, and included amphibious and paratroop landings on the Shandong Peninsula in the Yellow Sea.

Admiral Gary Roughead, commander of the U.S. Pacific Fleet, told the Associated Press that he was "curious" to know how the two navies would operate and how they would command and control their forces, and how they would integrate in a combined way. He added that he had noticed Chinese submarines and surface ships pushing beyond their earlier areas of operation near the eastern coast of China during the past twelve years.[41]

The *Baltimore Sun* noted that China and Russia had been "cozying up" partly due to a shared aversion to a U.S.-dominated world. "Within that bond, these games accomplish multiple, and from a U.S. perspective, troubling aims," it wrote editorially. "It's a bazaar in which Russia, China's biggest arms supplier, is showing off long-range bombers and other equipment that would greatly expand Beijing's ability to project power; it's a display of China's intent on building capacity for a sea assault on Taiwan; and it's the latest twist in the long-running 'Great Game' of foreign powers in oil-rich central Asia where there is mounting resistance to the post-9/11 U.S. military presence."

The Dragon and Uncle Sam

Washington was unhappy about China acquiring oil resources abroad on a large scale. The tensions between the two powers came to the fore when Cnooc attempted in June 2005 to buy

Unocal, an American oil corporation, at $67 a share versus the offer of $64 a share by Chevron.

It failed because of the harsh political reaction in the United States, where the president is authorized to bar a takeover on national security grounds. This authority has been used only once before—by President George H. W. Bush in 1990, when he blocked the sale of Mamco Manufacturing, an airplane parts maker in Seattle, to a military-related agency of the Chinese government. "We should not forget that if it wanted to, the U.S. Navy could block China's access to Cnooc's foreign oil any day of the week," Amy Myers Jaffe, an oil specialist at Rice University, wrote. "China, however, would have difficulty imposing such a blockade on American companies."[42]

Reflecting the Bush administration's hostility toward Cnooc, on August 10 Unocal shareholders rejected its higher bid ($19.5 billion) in favor of the lower bid of $18 billion by Chevron. "It's a tremendous precedent-setter for a government to interfere and declare that national security is at risk," Daniel Yergin, president of Cambridge Energy Research Associates, told the *New York Times*. "What is this going to mean for American oil companies from Algeria to Zanzibar?" Another critic was David Goldwyn, former assistant energy secretary under President Bill Clinton. "What this misguided policy did was to say that the United States will not advocate fair trade when it comes to American assets."

Overall, relations between Beijing and Washington remained equivocal. Trade between the two nations was thriving, with Chinese exports to the United States in 2005 at $243 billion and imports from the United States at only $41 billion. The respective figures for 2000 were $52 billion and $16 billion.[43]

Sino-American trade took off once China became a WTO member in November 2001. It allowed China to expand its exports dramatically and to become deeply integrated into the world economy. Its plentiful supply of cheap, skilled labor led four hundred of the United States' top five hundred corporations to set up manufacturing plants in China. In 2004, Wal-Mart alone bought $18 billion worth of goods from China; it sourced four-fifths of its products worldwide from China.[44]

According to a report by Morgan Stanley, China's low-priced products had saved U.S. consumers an annual average of $60 billion over the past decade. Overall, Western consumers benefited, with clothes, shoes, and electrical appliances becoming cheaper by 42, 31, and 63 percent, respectively, during 2001–04.[45]

Due to the imbalance in Chinese-American trade, Beijing's foreign exchange reserves soared to nearly $854 billion by March 2006, a shade higher than Japan's, which were built up over four decades.[46] China invested these funds mostly in U.S. Treasury bonds, American mortgage-backed securities, and a variety of other financial instruments that earned a meager return but provided political leverage to be used in the future.

As it was, on the diplomatic and energy fronts, Beijing-Washington relations remained choppy.

Tensions between the two capitals remained high on the lingering issue of the long-term status of Taiwan. The United States disapproved of the way Beijing had been bolstering the SCO, which in August 1999 set up a joint antiterrorism center in Bishkek. At the behest of China, it added Uzbekistan to its ranks even though it does not share borders with all other SCO members. The SCO adopted a new charter in May 2003, which was not immediately released. Its later publication showed that it pledged "noninterference and nonalignment" in international affairs while aiming to create "a new international political and economic order"—implying thereby to end the role of the United States as the sole superpower. After Uzbek president Islam Karimov had been heavily criticized for the massacre of 167 to 500 unarmed protestors by security forces in Andijan in May 2005, the Chinese government greeted him with a twenty-one-gun salute when he visited Beijing in July. He departed with a $600 million joint venture for oil.[47]

During his visit to Singapore, a leading naval and maritime hub, in June 2005, U.S. defense secretary Donald Rumsfeld said, "China's defense expenditures are much higher than Chinese officials have published. Since no nation threatens China, why these continuing large and expanding arms purchases?" The Chinese officials retorted that there was no hidden military budget. Rumsfeld conveniently overlooked the fact that the Pentagon's 281 ships and the half a million members of the U.S. Navy exceeded the total of the next seventeen naval nations.[48]

On the eve of President Hu Jintao's visit in April 2006, U.S. officials ominously let it be known in their briefings to the media that Chinese oil companies should not "lock up" energy supplies or seek to direct markets and should "open" them up. Such homilies were delivered from Washington, which since the early 1990s has been actively guiding Big Oil on how to bolster its share of oil acreage outside the Middle East.

Nor, of course, was there any mention of the decision made by the Bush administration to build up India as a countervailing power to China.

EIGHT

India: A Giant Rising, Thirsty for Oil

It all started with tea—more specifically tea from China, which Scottish entrepreneurs successfully grew in the foothills of the Himalayas in India's northeastern region of Assam in 1834. Tea gardens flourished in the area, and their produce was exported in ever-growing quantity from the port city of Calcutta. In the mid-1860s the British built a railway from Calcutta to the garden region using both men and elephants. While working near a site—now called Digboi, a derivative of the "Dig, boy, dig" call that the Scottish foremen frequently issued to their workmen— an elephant appeared with his feet smeared in oil. That was sufficient evidence for James Goodenough of Mckillop, Stewart and Company to persuade his employer to drill for petroleum. The firm struck oil in 1867, the first successful discovery in Asia, at Nahorpung near the Myanmar border about 540 kilometers (340 miles) east of the provincial capital of Gauhati. But the yield was poor.

The resulting interregnum lasted until 1889—four years after the victorious British annexed what was then Burma into their Indian Empire. Success now came to the Burmah Oil Company (BOC), established in Glasgow, Scotland, in 1886 by local entrepreneurs who had made their fortunes in the trading businesses they had set up in the Far East. Their company would transform the traditional, manual collection of petroleum by Burmese villagers into a commercial enterprise, erect a refinery, and export kerosene to India.

Commercial production of petroleum started in 1890 with a well named Discovery, drilled by the Assam Railways and Trading Company, which nine years later would establish the Assam Oil Company (AOC) to take over its oil interests, later bought by the BOC. Its rig still stands as a living epitaph to the pioneering oilmen, and the field continues to yield petroleum, albeit a modest 300 bpd. So too does the nearby refinery, which went onstream in 1901 and has continued operating nonstop—a world record.

Just as in Midland, Texas, visitors are welcomed to an oil museum in Digboi, Assam, a town of forty thousand souls. But the parallel ends there. In contrast to the flat settlement in the arid zone of Texas, Digboi nestles in verdant blue hills and undulating plains covered with emerald green tea plantations, providing it with a setting for the most breathtaking and challenging eighteen-hole golf course on the planet—as well as a distant glimpse of the snow-capped Himalayas. Unlike the petroleum museum in Midland, where outmoded drilling rigs and equipment are stored in its large compound, visitors to Digboi come across outdated oil derricks of yesteryear in situ as they walk up Ridge Hill and, while sauntering down the hill on the other side, find themselves trespassing into a wildlife sanctuary, most likely encountering a herd of elephants.

For more than six decades, the Digboi field was India's sole petroleum source. During World War II, its oil and its proximity to the Pangsu Pass on the Indo-Burmese border made it a prime target of Japanese invaders after they had captured Burma. They came within three days' marching distance of Digboi but were first halted and then repulsed by the Allied forces at a heavy cost in men and materials to the defenders. The vast size of the local war cemetery provides a dramatic testimony.

As in the prewar days, so in the postwar period, selling kerosene remained the main business of the Burmah Oil Company and other foreign oil companies like Caltex (later Esso) and Royal Dutch Shell, with their subsidiaries based in India.

Independent India's Hydrocarbon Policy

The Anglo-Iranian Oil Company's conflict with the democratically elected government of Iran in 1951 was noted with keen interest by the leaders of freshly independent India.

The overthrow of the Iranian government in 1953 by the British and American intelligence agencies made India's ruling Congress Party, and particularly its charismatic leader, Jawaharlal Nehru, determined to keep India's oil resources under public ownership.

In 1956 the Indian parliament placed oil in the public sector with the creation of the Ministry of Petroleum and Natural Gas, which was given a virtual monopoly in future oil and gas exploration and production. Its operating arm, the Oil and Natural Gas Corporation (ONGC), found Western oil corporations unwilling to help it acquire expertise to explore and produce oil on its own. So it sought and received assistance from the Soviet Union, including the education and training of Indians as geophysicists and petroleum engineers. From the late 1950s, Soviet oil experts began working with the ONGC, and together they discovered oil in the Assam and Tripura-Cachar basins as well as in the Cambay area of the western state of Gujarat.

In 1961 the government of India and the BOC became equal partners in Oil India Limited (OIL), set up to engage exclusively in exploration and production. Both OIL and the ONGC made a number of oil and gas discoveries in different regions in the coming years.

During the mapping of the Gulf of Cambay in 1964–67, an Indo-Soviet exploration team discovered the Bombay High offshore oil and gas field about 160 kilometers (100 miles) north of Bombay. And it was the Soviet experience of setting up offshore installations in the Caspian that was applied in this instance. The result was a complex of fifteen wells and massive pumps to shift the petroleum to the coast. The oil began flowing in 1974.

At the time, the world was reeling from the quadrupling of oil prices in the wake of the October 1973 Arab-Israeli War. India was no exception. High inflation, caused mainly by the surge in petroleum prices, led to massive popular protest. In mid-1975 Prime Minister Indira Gandhi, Nehru's only daughter, was found guilty of electoral malpractices and disqualified from holding public office. On her advice, President Fakhuruddin Ali Ahmad declared an emergency and suspended the constitution. In essence, Indira Gandhi carried out a constitutional coup. The emergency continued until early 1977, when Gandhi's Congress (I) Party was defeated heavily by an alliance of opposition parties.

By then, the Indian government had nationalized the Burmah Shell Refineries and renamed it Bharat Refineries (later Bharat Petroleum), and bought the remaining 26 percent equity in Esso (earlier Caltex) and renamed it Hindustan Petroleum. Both Bharat Petroleum and Hindustan Petroleum operated as refining and marketing companies in competition with each other and with the state-owned Indian Oil Corporation (IOC) to provide better value and service to customers.

Prospecting by the ONGC and OIL yielded oil-bearing acreage in the western regions of India (chiefly Rajasthan and Gujarat) as well as the southern regions (in the Cauvery and Krishna-Godavari basins). But their cumulative production failed to rival the Bombay High's. The latter achieved an output of 400,000 bpd in 1985 and maintained it for the next four years before declining steadily.

Oil consumption in India, however, was puny. At less than

half a barrel of oil per capita, it was 1.5 percent of the figure for the United States. Since the domestic companies met two-thirds of India's oil needs until the late 1980s, the central government was complacent; and the three rounds of bidding for exploration blocks it invited between 1980 and 1986 were modest.

During this period, India's annual economic growth of 5.8 percent against a population increase of 2.2 percent was lackluster.[1] It was not until 1990, when India faced a severe balance of payment crisis, that those in the government favoring accelerated economic reform prevailed.

Under the premiership of P. V. Narsimha Rao of the Congress (I) Party in 1991, economic liberalization, initiated three years earlier, gathered pace. The GDP began to expand faster than before. During the decade, India's average annual economic growth rose to 6.4 percent while its population increase fell to 2 percent—with the per capita GDP, adjusted for different purchasing power of currencies, registering an accumulated total growth of 60 percent over the 1990 figure.[2]

The demand for oil and oil products soared. India's policy makers were compelled to move boldly on the oil and gas prospecting front. In 1992 the Ministry of Petroleum and Natural Gas offered, for the first time, already discovered fields in its 1992 round of bidding for exploration blocks—open to both domestic and foreign companies. The following year it inaugurated a data inspection facility in Houston to let U.S. corporations have instant access to documents and answers to field queries.

In 1997 the United Front Alliance government of Prime Minister Inder Kumar Gujral inaugurated a New Exploration Licensing Policy (NELP) for oil and gas, designed specifically to attract private companies both at home and abroad. It offered fresh exploration sites for oil and gas to international bidders.

Due to accelerated economic growth, demand for hydrocarbons

surged while domestic output stagnated. At the end of the 1990s, the indigenous production met only two-fifths of the demand of a shade over 2 million bpd. Just one oil field, the Bombay High, provided more than a third of the national aggregate. India was then governed by a coalition government headed by the Hindu nationalist Bhartiya Janata Party (BJP, Indian People's Party) led by Prime Minister Atal Bihari Vajpayee.

Hydrocarbon Vision 2025

Within months of the BJP-led coalition coming to power, with Ram Naik as the petroleum minister, the government published a document titled *Hydrocarbon Vision 2025*—prepared jointly by various ministries—to invite public debate.[3]

Hydrocarbon Vision 2025 was overly ambitious. It aimed to achieve energy security by raising domestic output and investing in equity petroleum abroad; shoring up capacity in all phases of the industry; creating a free market in hydrocarbons; and promoting healthy competition among explorers, producers, and retailers.

The document predicted that by 2025 petroleum product demand would quadruple, from 95 million tonnes to about 370 million tonnes a year, whereas domestic output would only double, to 52 million tonnes. In other words, India's self-sufficiency in petroleum would halve, from 30 percent to 15 percent. (By 2010, India was projected to become the fourth-largest consumer of energy, after the United States, China, and Japan.[4])

Hydrocarbon Vision 2025 visualized exploration of all of India's twenty-six basins by 2025. The hope was that this massive effort would lead to fresh reserves and raise the present proven reserves of 5.6 billion barrels, barely 0.5 percent of the global total. It specified building a Strategic Petroleum Reserve (SPR) of thirty-five million barrels by 2008 to cover fifteen days' domestic demand—to be achieved by prospecting for fresh reserves, augmenting supplies from traditional suppliers, and sealing acquisition deals abroad.

Laudable though this was, Indian leaders were late in responding to the looming crisis. During the previous three decades, demand for energy had grown by an average of more than 5 percent. Despite the predominance of such noncommercial forms of energy as dried cow-dung patties and firewood among rural Indians—who form seven-tenths of the national population of over 1 billion—the share of commercial energy rose from 41 to 68 percent.

Even so, the per capita energy consumption in India was less than a third of the global average,[5] which was also the case in China. So the potential for increase in energy consumption was enormous.

Liberalizing the Hydrocarbon Sector

Petroleum Minister Naik sanctioned twenty-five new exploration blocks in the first seven months of his taking office under the 1997 New Exploration Licensing Policy, with a plan to announce twenty-five more before the end of 2000. (During the 1990s, only twenty-three exploration blocks were sanctioned.) Most of these were offshore. It was the first time that a deep-water block was opened up for bidding. Just as in China, in the coming years India would resort to deep-water drilling by both state- and privately owned companies, especially on the east coast of India.

In January 2001 Naik flew to Houston to arouse interest among American oil executives in bidding for exploring rights for oil and gas—onshore and offshore—in the "proven and promising" sedimentary basins of Gujarat, Uttar Pradesh, West Bengal, Orissa, and Rajasthan.

To expedite the process and encourage the entry of the private sector, the government deregulated the whole of the oil sector in April 2002—from exploration to marketing. It allowed private and foreign companies to undertake the marketing of gasoline, diesel, and aviation fuel, provided they agreed to invest a minimum of $50 million in oil exploration or production, refining, pipelines, or terminals.

This gave an impetus to private companies at home, about a dozen of which became major players. Reliance Industries, for instance, became so successful in its downstream activities of refining and petrochemicals that it competed with the longer-established state-owned Indian Oil Corporation, Bharat Petroleum, and Hindustan Petroleum. In mid-2005 its quarterly profits were an astounding $530 million.

Reliance Industries was equally active in prospecting and production. In 2003, its discovery of 14.5 billion cubic feet of natural gas in the Krishna-Godavari Basin was the highlight of the year. It not only improved the energy security of the country by boosting possible gas production by 50 percent, but also raised the prospects of Indian sedimentary basins in the international market. Its two ultra-deep water oil rigs off the east coast, built at the cost of $1.5 billion, were scheduled to start operating by June 2006. And its gas field in the Krishna-Godavari Basin was set to yield forty million cubic meters a day from August 2006.[6]

To reverse the falling output of the Bombay High oil field, the ONGC initiated an investment of $2.6 billion in 2001 to redevelop it. Its output of 261,000 bpd in 2005 amounted to about a third of the national aggregate.[7]

To intensify its activities abroad, the ONGC set up a wholly owned subsidiary, ONGC Videsh,[8] to focus on overseas exploration and production projects. It visualized an investment of $25 billion to acquire oil and gas fields abroad. It obtained a 20 percent stake in the Exxon-led Sakhalin-I project in Russia. It also acquired rights to explore oil acreage in Iraq before the Anglo-American invasion in 2003. Later it would acquire a 25 percent equity participation in a producing field in Sudan. And its parent, the ONGC, would start building a pipeline in Sudan while negotiating to erect a refinery.[9]

With oil prices exceeding $60 a barrel in June 2005, India, like China, realized as never before the economic wisdom of importing oil from their own foreign fields at a cost of $10–12 a barrel after fees and royalties rather than purchasing it on the open market. At the same time, record-high petroleum prices made the ONGC the largest Indian company by value, with a market capitalization of nearly $42.3 billion.

Aiyar's Pan-Asian Initiative

By the end of 2005, India's oil and gas companies had established their stakes in twelve countries—Australia, Bangladesh, Egypt, Iran, Iraq, Ivory Coast, Libya, Myanmar, Qatar, Russia, Sudan, and Vietnam—with exploring possibilities in seven more: Ecuador, Kazakhstan, Kuwait, Oman, Turkmenistan, Venezuela, and Yemen.

Under the leadership of Mani Shankar Aiyar, who became petroleum minister in May 2004, with the installation of the Congress (I)-led coalition government, the ministry had acquired a higher profile at home and abroad. A highly energetic man of medium height with a full head of graying hair and a neatly trimmed salt and pepper mustache, Aiyar, a sixty-three-year-old Cambridge graduate, applied his sharp intellect and clear vision to his new job. In an early move, he secured the services of a senior civil servant of the Ministry of External Affairs, Talmiz Ahmad—a soft-spoken, erudite former Indian ambassador to Saudi Arabia—as an additional secretary in his ministry in charge of "oil diplomacy."

Sitting in his well-appointed reception lounge in March 2006, studded with bookshelves and enlarged photographs of his family and his leading political allies, in the annex of a sprawling bungalow surrounded by a large, well-kept garden in New Delhi, Aiyar articulated his policies.

"Oil diplomacy is aimed at mitigating the risks of our inevitable and growing dependence on imported hydrocarbons," he told me. "I have a three-track policy. One, we should exploit fully our domestic hydrocarbon potential. Two, we should network into the global hydrocarbons community to ensure stability, security, and sustainability in hydrocarbon supplies. Three, we should acquire overseas assets to reinforce our energy security."

By inserting his own concept of networking into the global hydrocarbons community, Aiyar expanded the framework of *Hydrocarbon Vision 2025*. He then tried to engender a pan-Asian perception rooted in the facts on the ground.

"Two-thirds of humanity lives in Asia, and the majority of the Asian oil is bought by Asian customers," he continued. "My idea is to create an OPEC-like organization for Asia, an Asian oil organization. If you consider Siberia as north Asia—as we do in India—then the oil business is now mainly Asian. The increase in hydrocarbon usage is greatest in Asia. But there is as yet no Pan-Asian Economic Union, or a Union of Asian Economic Organizations, or even a Pan-Asian Economic Forum. The present price mechanism is based on Saudi Arabia and its oil output. You get FOB [free on board] prices for the Saudi oil loaded at Yanbo or Ras Tanura. But the international price quoted is the West Texas Intermediate or Brent." He pointed out that the output related to the West Texas Intermediate had declined by 75 percent over the past two decades, and that related to Brent by 60 percent in recent years.

Aiyar's research showed that about two-fifths of the oil output of the Arabian Peninsula and the Persian Gulf region—together called West Asia by the Indian government and media—was purchased collectively by fellow Asian countries. In India's case, four of its five top suppliers were from the Gulf region—Saudi Arabia, Iran, Kuwait, and Iraq. This was a far cry from the days when the bulk of Asian oil was shipped to North America and Western

Europe. In those days, competition among West Asian producers to improve their individual share of the Western market led to the practice of pricing crude oil on the FOB basis, thereby paying for the transportation cost. As these suppliers did not give such a concession to non-Western customers, the latter ended up paying $1.50 to $2 a barrel more than their Western counterparts. Taking into account the changed oil market of today, this "Asian premium" should be discontinued. "We want to make the market price more rational," Aiyar said.

"With a view to creating a sense of Asian identity in the global oil market," Aiyar convened a roundtable conference of the seven principal western and southeast Asian oil suppliers—Iran, Kuwait, Oman, Qatar, Saudi Arabia, and the United Arab Emirates (UAE)[10]—and the four principal Asian consumers—China, Japan, India, and South Korea—in New Delhi in January 2005.

The assembled oil ministers issued a statement that identified substantial commonality of interest and areas of cooperation. They agreed to strive for a benchmark price for Asian oil and urged oil producers to invest in the downstream facilities of the consumer countries.

In November 2005 Aiyar hosted a meeting in New Delhi at which the four leading Asian petroleum consumer countries conferred with the oil producers of northern and central Asia, including Azerbaijan, Kazakhstan, Russia, Turkmenistan, and Uzbekistan. "The main difference between the two roundtable meetings was that whereas the north and south Asian producers are outside OPEC, almost all of the west and southeast Asian oil producers belong to OPEC," Aiyar continued. The outcome of the second roundtable was similar to the first. "We thus had the beginnings of a cooperative relationship between producers and consumers which should help establish among Asian importers an Asian equivalent of the International Energy Association, which provides a common forum for OECD importers—as well as help lay the foundations of an Asian oil and gas community."[11]

Delhi's Bilateral Links

In between the two conferences, Aiyar strengthened Delhi's hydrocarbon links with Riyadh and Tehran.

His move was welcomed by a Saudi Arabia keen to have its market share in both China and India. Indeed, its shipment of 450,000 bpd to India made it Delhi's number-one oil supplier.[12] In return, the Indian companies assisted Saudi Arabia in boosting its refining capacity.

As it was, India became self-sufficient in refining in 2000. To keep pace with rising demand for oil products, the Indian Oil Corporation, Hindustan Petroleum, and Bharat Petroleum completed a new batch of refineries by the end of 2003.

Ever since its independence, India had maintained cordial relations with Iran, a country whose ties with the Indian subcontinent date back to ancient times. In recent decades, the emergence of an Islamic Republic in Iran left Delhi's diplomatic and other links with Tehran unaffected. Indeed, following the revolutionary overthrow of the pro-American shah of Iran, the succeeding regime adopted a nonaligned foreign policy and became an active member of the Non-Aligned Movement (NAM), founded in 1955 by India, Egypt, Indonesia, and Yugoslavia.

During the 1980–88 Iran-Iraq War, Delhi maintained strict neutrality between the warring nations. After the UN sanctions against Iraq following its invasion of Kuwait in August 1990, India became more reliant on Iranian oil than before. The trend accelerated as the Indian economy picked up pace from the mid-1990s onwards. A decade later Iran became the third-largest supplier of crude to India after Saudi Arabia and Nigeria.

In November 2004, the Indian Oil Corporation—which had turned itself into a vertically integrated company by embarking on exploration and production—decided to invest $3 billion in developing gas fields along with Iran's Petropars Company. The following April, Iran gave the ONGC a 20 percent stake in the Yadavaran oil field, where China's Sinopec had a 50 percent stake, a 300,000 bpd project.[13]

In January 2005 three state-controlled Indian oil companies concluded a $40 billion contract with Iran for the purchase of LNG over twenty-five years, starting with 5 million tonnes in 2009 and rising to 7.5 million tonnes in 2011. Among other things, LNG is needed in India for domestic cooking, where the demand will rise from 170 million cubic meters per day to 400 million cubic meters per day in 2025.[14]

Outside the hydrocarbon sector, Indian companies were helping to develop Iran's Chah Bahar port along the Arabian Sea, along with other infrastructure projects.

The trend toward tightening links between Delhi and Tehran received a jolt, however, in September 2005. Defecting from the fourteen-strong NAM bloc at the meeting of the thirty-five governors of the International Atomic Energy Agency (IAEA) in Vienna, India voted with the United States for a resolution that stated that Iran's "many failures and obligations to comply with its Nuclear Non-Proliferation Treaty [NPT] Safeguards Agreement . . . constitute noncompliance" and that "the resulting absence of confidence that Iran's nuclear program is exclusively for peaceful purposes has given rise to questions that are within the competence of the Security Council."

The switch-over in the Indian position stemmed from U.S. president George W. Bush's agreement with the visiting Indian prime minister Manmohan Singh in July to aid India's civilian nuclear program. The reason India cut this deal was that it was running out of uranium ore and needed expertise in high-tech fast-breeder technology. For its part, the United States wanted to open new markets for American nuclear reactors, including

Westinghouse's AP-1000 rector. Bush had earlier tried to help sell it to China by backing it with the largest-ever loan by the U.S. Export-Import Bank, but in vain.[15]

There were wider diplomatic implications. Bush's move meant that Washington accepted India as a nuclear weapons power even though it had not signed the NPT. The Indian side saw the agreement as implying that the United States was entering into a strategic alliance with Delhi—with the tacit aim of counterbalancing the rising power of China.

The downside was the cooling of diplomatic relations between Delhi and Tehran, and tension between Singh's minority government and the United Front Alliance, whose backing it needed to stay in power. Nonetheless, the Indians were not abandoning their plans to participate in the building of a gas pipeline from Iran through Pakistan to bring nearly 90 million cubic meters a day to fuel power and fertilizer projects in north and northwestern India.[16]

Nearer home, in January 2005, India concluded a deal with the military government of Myanmar to construct a gas pipeline. The Myanmar-Bangladesh-India pipeline will not only transport the Myanmar gas, but will also probably carry gas from the Indian state of Tripura to other parts of India, and the Bangladesh gas from its eastern fields to the western part, where it is needed.[17] The next next year, Myanmar's military leader, General Than Shwe, was received with full honors in Delhi; and the following March, Indian president Avul Pakir Jainalabdeen Abdul Kalam visited Yangon when the conclusion of several cooperation agreements between the two countries was announced.

"The scramble for oil resources poses a unique challenge to Indian oil diplomacy in that it requires us to explore new engagements or, alternatively, to imbue traditional political relationships with a new, hydrocarbon-related value," said Talmiz Ahmad at a seminar on India's energy security in Delhi in July 2005. "Taking into account the geopolitical situation and the competitive edge that informs the global hydrocarbon scenario, some of the major challenges to Indian oil diplomacy are examined in the following paragraphs. . . . These proposed engagements involve refreshing traditional relationships with a new hydrocarbon-related content, such as the proposed links with Russia and Rumania; or replacing old suspicions with the new building blocks of cooperation, understanding, and friendship with countries such as Pakistan, Bangladesh, and China. It also has the potential of expanding India's diplomatic penetration across continents to new areas such as Norway, Latin America, and countries of North and West Africa that have traditionally been at the margins of India's diplomatic consciousness and imbuing them with a new importance and urgency."[18]

By then the Petroleum Ministry had suggested to the Indian cabinet that an *Energy Security Vision 2025* be drafted and adopted to complement the *Hydrocarbon Vision 2025*.

As it was, in order to protect the sea lanes used by oil and gas tankers from the Persian Gulf to India, the Indian government had embarked on building an aircraft carrier group, the first of its kind by any non-Western state, at the cost of $660 million. This was part of a larger Indian plan to expand its navy.[19]

In the commercial field, in its quest to acquire hydrocarbon assets abroad, the ONGC and its subsidiary, ONGC Videsh, had met with partial success. While they succeeded in Bangladesh, Myanmar, Cuba, Iran, and Vietnam, to great acclaim in the Indian media, in obtaining exploration and productions rights for oil and gas, they lost out to China in four other countries.

Aiyar realized that fierce competition between Delhi and Beijing in securing hydrocarbon acreage abroad was counterproductive. It inflated prices, benefiting the host country excessively at the cost of India and China. He felt that cooperation, rather than competition, should be the modus operandi between the two Asian giants. His sentiment was reciprocated by the Chinese.

As a result, during his visit to Beijing in January 2006, Aiyar signed a memorandum of understanding with his counterpart, Mai Kai. According to this agreement, Indian and Chinese companies will exchange information about a possible bid for a hydrocarbon project abroad before agreeing to cooperate formally. The agreement applied to all aspects of the industry, from prospecting to marketing.[20]

Desirable though this was, most analysts were skeptical that the Chinese, with a longer and wider experience in foreign bidding, would share their plans with the Indians, whom they had outbid in Angola, Ecuador, Nigeria, and Kazakhstan—even when, in the last case, the ONGC had formed a joint-venture company called ONGC–Mittal Energy with India-born Lakshmi Mittal, a steel tycoon worth $27.5 billion, the richest man in Britain. The last case was exceptional because the Kazakh oil company was registered in Canada, and the Chinese were determined to get a foothold in North America at any cost. In the absence of such a compelling reason, the chances of the two meganations refraining from competing against each other were, realistically speaking, about even.

Indian Ties with the Persian Gulf Region

Trade between the Indian subcontinent and the Persian Gulf region goes back to ancient times. In the modern era, the British administered the region's principalities, treated as protectorates, from Bombay. The Indian rupee was the local currency in these territories until their independence from Britain during the decade of 1961–71.

Today some nearly four million Indian expatriates work in the six Gulf monarchies of Bahrain, Kuwait, Oman, Qatar, Saudi Arabia, and the United Arab Emirates, constituting the Gulf

Cooperation Council (GCC). They are to be found in all economic and social fields, from the oil industry to catering to retail
trade to teaching to information technology. Every year they
remit home $5 billion while their country's trade with GCC
amounts to $15 billion, mainly in oil purchases.

About a third of the Indian workers come from the southern
state of Kerala, which has almost universal literacy and an abundant supply of university graduates. One such was Abdul Jalil, a
heavily built, mustached man in his early forties with a rich
thatch of black hair. A native of Kottayam, he obtained an
undergraduate degree in history from Calicut University, and
then acquired an undergraduate degree in education. Despite
such qualifications, he could not get a permanent job as a
teacher, only a temporary one to teach history and geography in
a secondary school. Luckily, his elder brother, Yunus Jalil,
worked as a semiskilled worker for the Abu Dhabi–based
National Petroleum Construction Company (NPCC) in the
UAE. At Yunus's recommendation, the NPCC interviewed Abdul
Jalil in Bombay and hired him as a laborer to work on an offshore drilling rig in Qatar for a year. After that the NPCC gave
him a year's contract to work as a helper on the rig. Then he was
promoted to an administrative clerk and transferred to the
onshore office in Doha.

"What I earned in India in rupees, I earn the same in Qatari
rials, which means ten times more," Abdul Jalil told me in Doha.
"And there is no income tax here. In my eight years of service
with the NPCC, I have been home seven times, each time for two
months. I am married and have two daughters." Why did he not
bring the family to Doha? "It is expensive to maintain a family in
the Gulf states. In Qatar you must have water and electricity connection in your name before you are allowed to bring your
family. Also you have to pay school expenses for your children.
Some companies give family allowance, and others don't. Over

the past few months house rents have gone up so much that about a third of my salary goes on rent."

How would he sum up changes in Kerala during the years he has spent in Qatar? "One out of five families in Kerala has someone working in the Gulf," he replied. "Somebody is a helper, somebody is a computer technician, and somebody has a shop here. In Kerala everybody wants to move up. The one who has a bicycle wants to own a scooter, and the one with a scooter wants a motorcycle, the one with a motorbike wants a car, and the one with a car wants a more expensive model. We in the Gulf save money and when we return home we invest it in a house or a car. That is the status symbol for us now, a house or a car."[21]

Not just in Kerala, but all over India.

Car Explosion in India

Fueled by the massive growth of its economic infrastructure and domestic and foreign investment and trade, the Indian economy has been booming for the past decade. During 2004, GDP grew by 8 percent. But the number of vehicles rose by twice as much. Urban streets built initially for two-lane traffic are now choked with four or six lanes of cars, scooters, auto-rickshaws, motorcycles, buses, and trucks.

The explosive growth in the automobile industry followed India's most ambitious infrastructure project since independence, involving the upgrading of its decrepit two-lane national highway network to a sleek four- or six-lane superhighway system. The most prized part of it was the toll-paying 5,840-kilometer (3,650-mile) Golden Quadrilateral Highway, connecting Delhi with Bombay, Madras (aka Chennai) and Calcutta. Built at the cost of $4.5 billion, it was part of the $65 billion road project. "We had to link the country up," said B. C. Khanduri, a former major general of the Army Engineers Corps, who as federal minister of roads from 2000 to 2004 supervised the accelerated road construction. "This was the mission of greatest importance for the economy. We gave the deadlines and made sure people met them. There were penalties for poor performance and bonuses for those who delivered on time."[22] For the first time in Indian history, autos could travel fast.

For many years India banned foreign imports and limited car manufacture to two models: the Ambassador, modeled on the 1959 Oxford Morris of Britain, and the Premier Padmini, a licensed version of Fiat Italy's 1100D. For nearly four generations, they held sway on narrow, rickety roads while the national output of cars remained below 200,000 a year.

Economic liberalization, combined with the expanding size of the middle and upper middle classes, easy credit to finance automobile purchases, and focused marketing strategies, often involving such movie stars as Shah Rukh Khan and Preity Zinta as brand ambassadors to hype a new model, changed the situation radically. Along with the increased number of vehicles came a wide array of models, ranging from the modest, home-made, small Maruti[23]—modeled on the small car produced by Suzuki of Japan—to imported Toyota Innova luxury vans priced at $23,000, the average annual income of forty Indians. For the prospering classes, cars became a means to mobility, choice, privacy, and status.

"Car showrooms, the bigger the better, are temples to consumerism here," reported Amy Waldman of the *New York Times* from Visakhapatnam, a port city of a million on India's eastern seaboard, situated on the Golden Quadrilateral Highway. The city had witnessed the rise of a string of car showrooms, with spanking white floors, high ceilings, large windows, and advertising posters of cheerful buyers many shades lighter than most locals. "Cars are the idols of a new individualism taking root," wrote Waldman. "Compared to the state-run rail network representing a certain egalitarianism in its chaotic, crowded stations and jam-packed trains, cars represent the atomization that prosperity brings."[24]

Smooth, multilane highways have reduced fuel and maintenance costs of trucking companies and generally speeded up deliveries, thus augmenting commercial and industrial activities and bolstering economic growth. Unlike in China, with its astronomical exports, the rise in the GDP in India is driven primarily by domestic demand.

"Twenty years back, one car was an achievement," said Khanduri in Bangalore, the capital of the southern state of Karnataka. "Luxuries are now necessities, and children are more focused on earning for themselves than caring for their parents. We are gradually adopting [the value of] 'everyone for himself.'"[25]

By "we," Khanduri meant the Indian middle class, estimated to be 250 million strong. Of these, an estimated 40 million middle-income households can afford an automobile, a number likely to leap as Tata Motors introduces their small car at half the price of the present cheapest model.

So India has become one of the fastest-growing automobile markets on the planet, and foreign companies are building factories all over the country to meet the rising demand. The sale of 1 million automobiles in 2005 amounted to a fivefold increase in just over a decade. Half of these were produced by Maruti, majority-owned by Suzuki of Japan. At the present growth rate, Suzuki's sales in India will exceed those in Japan by 2007 Already India is the world's third-largest manufacturer of small cars.

Yet the eight million autos on India's roads are a tiny fraction of the total in the United States, which has about a quarter of India's population. The potential for the market can be judged by the fact that at present only 1.5 percent of the Indian population aged fifteen to sixty-four owns a car.

Overall, transport in India accounts for almost half of the total energy consumed, twice as much as the manufacturing industry does. As for energy sources, coal contributes nearly 55 percent and oil 34 percent.[26]

The rising living standards of the Indian middle classes also translate into a jump in demand for electrical appliances—fans, refrigerators, air conditioners, television sets, and personal computers. That means ever-increasing consumption of electricity, part of which is generated in plants fueled by oil or natural gas.

Hunger for Electricity

Since independence, India has witnessed a phenomenal surge in its installed generating capacity. Between 1947 and 2005, it shot up nearly a hundredfold, from a mere 1,300 megawatts (MW) to 123,000 MW. Most of it was in the public sector. Thermal power stations, fueled by gas oil, diesel, or natural gas, provided seven-tenths of the electrical energy.

Now, to satisfy the voracious needs of the Indian population, the utility companies will have to raise the national electricity generating capacity *sixfold* by 2020.[27]

Meanwhile, there is a chronic deficit of more than 10 percent in the installed power-generating capacity. "Indian's bankrupt utilities [run by the state governments] are unable to satisfy the demand," noted Professor David Victor, an energy expert at Stanford University, California. "Blackouts are commonplace. Farmers, who account for about two-fifths of all the power consumed, can barely rely on getting power for half of every day. In industrial zones, the lifeblood of India's vibrant economy, unstable power supplies are such trouble that the biggest companies usually build their own power plants."[28]

The situation is equally grim in urban centers, home to 330 million Indians. Outages occur almost daily, especially during late spring and summer, when the demand of electric fans and air conditioners overwhelms the system.

What happened in Delhi in May 2006 was typical of towns

and cities throughout India. Faced with high temperatures, the local authorities issued a list of emergency orders: all shops must close by 7:30 P.M.; no neon lights outside stores should be switched on; all shopping malls must shut down for an extra weekday; all offices must turn off their air conditioners by 6 P.M.; and all those at home are banned from using air conditioners between sunrise and sunset. "Some areas [of Delhi] are regularly without power for eight-hour stretches," reported Amelia Gentleman of the *International Herald Tribune.* "Those who can afford to wire up individual generators are better off—but these provide only erratic relief. . . . Everyone complains of sleepless nights." A group of irate locals queued to pay only half of their electric bills in protest at the power cuts. "The capital of the world's largest democracy does not have enough electricity to power traffic lights," scoffed Sanjay Kaul, a leader of the protestors.[29]

No wonder that by now it is standard practice for all major hotels, hospitals, and public buildings to have standby generators to go into action the moment supplies from the local electrical grid stop.

During my visit to the Institute for Defense Studies and Analysis in New Delhi in comparatively temperate March 2006, I discovered that an employee was stationed at the top of the elevator to manually operate it in case of power failure.

This finding brought home to me the stark fact that whereas in the West the energy crisis is widely believed to be on the horizon, in India—as well as China—it has actually arrived. That makes it incumbent upon the world community to develop rapidly and urgently all alternatives to oil, be they finite or renewable.

Part III
Alternatives to Oil:
Finite and Renewable

NINE

Finite Alternatives to Oil: Natural Gas, Coal, and Uranium

A cursory sighting in downtown Washington, D.C., in June 2004, got implanted in my mind because it recurred the next day during my foray into the adjoining Montgomery County of Maryland. In both cases, it was a slogan in bold black letters running across the full length of local buses, just below the roof and above the windows: "Running on Clean Natural Gas."

The sign took me back to my trip to Tehran three years earlier. It reminded me of the interview I had had with Massoumeh (aka Nilufar) Ebtekar, the first female vice president of Iran, who ran the Environment Protection Department. As I checked in at the reception on the ground floor of a multistory building in downtown Tehran, I instilled into my mind a crucial instruction: do not extend your hand to shake hers, as in public women are allowed to touch only men closely related to them.

Ebtekar had a tastefully furnished, air-conditioned office on the top floor of a multistory building with an alert personal assistant half her age. I remembered Ebtekar's drooping eyelids and winsome smile, framed strictly by a *hijab* (head scarf) covering her hair, from her pictures taken at the time of the American hostage crisis a quarter century earlier. A student of the local Polytechnic University, she had acted as a spokesperson for the militant Iranian students who had seized the United States embassy and taken diplomats hostage. She surprised the international reporters covering the crisis—she used the nom de guerre "Mariam"—with her American East Coast accent, a result of her education at Highland Park Elementary School in Philadelphia, where her father had pursued a doctorate at the University of Pennsylvania. By now, married with two children, she had acquired a doctorate in immunology at Tehran University and was a part-time medical teacher there.

Since her 1997 appointment to the environmental job, she had applied herself to it with extraordinary vigor and enthusiasm. She had dealt with the problem of the smog that blights Tehran during winter, standing as it does at the foot of the deforested El Borz Mountains. At her behest, in April 2000, the cabinet adopted a ten-year plan to tackle air pollution head-on. Soon a huge electronic bar chart went up at a busy square in Tehran flashing the percentage of pollutants in the air—carbon monoxide, carbon dioxide, and sulfur dioxide.

With nine out of ten Tehranis using a car to get to work, this city of six million adults had 1.6 million cars. Her ten-point official plan aimed at reducing pollution included the fuel used in automobiles, car design and manufacturing, exhaust emission controls, and public transport. Within a year all gasoline stations would stop selling leaded gasoline. Starting with fifty buses running on compressed natural gas (CNG) during that period, Ebtekar told me, the number of such buses was set to rise to a thousand the following year.

In other words, the authorities in Tehran switched to natural gas for public transportation long before their counterparts in Washington did so.

The Iranian government's lead was followed by an increasing number of individuals who, at the modest expense of $550, installed a device in their automobiles that enabled them to switch from gasoline to CNG if and when they wished.

This practice has spread over most of the non-Western world.

For example, taxis and auto-rickshaws bearing the CNG sign and a green stripe on the chassis have become a common sight in the cities of India. One of the reasons for this was summed up in an advertisement that BP ran in American and British newspapers in October 2005. Under the headline, "We've Been Burning the Midnight Natural Gas," the advertisement read: "By switching from coal to natural gas, carbon dioxide emissions in new power generation can be reduced by up to 50 percent. That's why, since 1997, we've been working to increase natural gas to about 40 percent of our energy portfolio."[1]

Evidently, BP's management had taken seriously a February 2005 report by the Washington-based Science Applications International Corporation (SAIC) on the future of oil. "The world has never faced a problem like this," it concluded. "Without massive mitigation more than a decade before the fact, the problem will be pervasive and will not be temporary. Previous energy transitions (wood to coal and coal to oil) were gradual and evolutionary; oil peaking will be abrupt and revolutionary."[2] Expanding on the report, its main author, Robert Hirsch, told George Monbiot of the *Guardian* that without "timely mitigation, the economic, social, and political costs will be unprecedented." It was possible to reduce demand and to start developing alternatives, but this would take ten to twenty years and cost trillions of dollars. "Waiting until oil production peaks before taking crash program action leaves the world with a significant liquid fuel deficit for more than two decades," which would cause problems "unlike any yet faced by a modern industrial society."[3]

In short, a switch-over from oil to other fuels, especially natural gas, was long overdue.

The virtues of natural gas are manifold. It can be used not only in automobiles but also as fuel for electricity-generating plants. It is suitable as feedstock for fertilizer and petrochemical manufacture, as well as an agent to increase underground pressure in declining oil fields to boost output. Since it contains more hydrogen and less carbon than crude oil, it provides more energy than an equivalent volume of oil, and its carbon dioxide emissions are much lower. In its liquefied form, LNG can be transported cheaply because of its low volume. It can be converted into gasoline or diesel—a process that becomes economical when an oil barrel sells above $35.[4] It can also be refined to yield pure hydrogen for hydrogen fuel cells.

Its main disadvantage is that, due to its diffuse form and massive volume, it is difficult and expensive to transport.

Fuel of the Twenty-First Century

Natural gases fall into two categories: combustible and non-combustible. The combustible natural gases comprise methane (CH_4), ethane (C_2H_5), propane (C_3H_8), butane (C_4H_{10}), and hydrogen (H_2). The noncombustible ones include nitrogen (N_2), carbon dioxide (CO_2), and hydrogen sulfide (H_2S). The combustible gases are subdivided further as dry—methane—and wet, butane and propane. On an average, three-quarters of the gas accumulated in oil or oil-and-gas traps consists of combustible gases, with methane constituting more than four-fifths. Since methane is the most abundant in nature, it has the least value.

Natural gases are to be found either in fields of their own—as nonassociated gases—or along with oil, when they are labeled as associated gases.

Before 1970, oil corporations considered associated natural gas—meaning primarily methane—something of an irritant interposed between the prospectors and the petroleum they were seeking. After all, a single barrel of oil contains more energy than a houseful of natural gas. Unsurprisingly, when Royal Dutch Shell discovered the North Field gas field in 1971 in Qatar, it regarded the new find as useless because it contained no petroleum. And transporting gas was costly. So, gas was universally viewed as a by-product of negligible value—below 5 cents for 1,000 cubic feet—which was better flared than processed.

It was the oil-price explosion of the mid-1970s that caused a radical reevaluation of natural gas. Such large consumers of petroleum products as power stations and big factories were forced to seek an alternative fuel.

Major Western hydrocarbon companies also faced an unprecedented problem during that period. The oil nationalization by the Gulf monarchies, initiated in the mid-1970s and completed by the end of the decade, caused a deep cut in their petroleum reserves.[5] Then the state-owned oil companies in the region extended their activities to refining and marketing, thus depriving Western corporations of another lucrative business. This led the Western oil majors to focus more on finding gas reserves outside the Persian Gulf region. BP, Royal Dutch Shell, and Exxon purchased exploration and production rights in gas-rich areas or entered into joint ventures with such gas-producing countries as Algeria, Indonesia, Nigeria, Russia, and Trinidad.

As gas technology developed, oil corporations saw profit in marketing not only the cheap methane but also the more expensive ethane—as feedstock for plastics and synthetic rubber—and butane and propane, used for domestic cooking.

These developments coincided with an emerging awareness of the environmental degradation caused by the wide-scale use of chemicals and the burning of petroleum products, and the rise of environment protection lobbies in the West. Since methane produces one-third less CO_2 than oil, and only half as much CO_2 as coal, natural gas became a preferred fuel.

But the subsequent rapid rise of the natural gas industry in the United States hit a snag: the Fuel Use Act of 1978. Passed by Congress at the behest of powerful coal corporations, it excluded the use of natural gas as fuel for electricity generation and industrial power. The 1978 act remained in force for nearly a decade. In the late 1980s, therefore, the percentage of electricity generated from natural gas was about the same as that before the 1978 act: 18 percent.

However, the use of natural gas in other spheres of the economy rose, especially after the Second Oil Shock, in 1979–81, which turned natural gas into a valuable commodity, priced at $3 for 1,000 cubic feet. Oil explorers became interested in drilling below the oil window in order to tap into the zone of nonassociated gases.

"Gas wells are ten to twelve thousand feet deep," explained Bruce Brady of the Great Western Drilling Company in Midland, Texas, to me. "This is old formation under pressure, it is more cooked, and is older and hotter—and that is why it is gas, not liquid."[6]

Following the pattern of petroleum prospecting, the gas explorers discovered prolific gas reserves at first. In the early 1980s, in the offshore fields of the Gulf of Mexico, for instance, it was common to find gas fields of 100 billion cubic feet or more. Two decades later, the average size of a gas field had plummeted to 5 billion cubic feet.

Globally, though, since 1980, proven gas reserves have increased 2.5 times, to 179 trillion cubic meters in 2004. Yet during that quarter century, the share of gas in the world energy basket rose only marginally—from 18 to 22 percent.

As with petroleum, the United States consumed many times more gas than its reserves would allow. Its reserves were a puny 3 percent of the global total while it burned 24 percent of the world aggregate. Gas consumption reached a peak in 2001 at the height of an investment surge in gas-fired electricity-generating plants that lasted from 1999 to 2003 and raised the contribution of gas-fueled power stations to the national grid to 30 percent.

In the developing world, where coal is the predominant fuel

for power stations, gas has proved to be a cheaper alternative. "One dollar invested today in gas-fired generation capacity produces three to four times the amount of electricity [as] the same dollar invested in coal-fired generation capacity," said John Browne, group chief executive of BP, at the World Gas Conference in Tokyo in June 2003.[7] That is why by 2020 gas consumption by developing nations will nearly treble.

From the consumer's perspective, an additional attraction of gas is that since there is no Organization of the Gas Exporting Countries, the industry is free from a quota system. This may change. In 2001 Qatar helped establish the Gas Exporting Countries Forum (GECF), whose fluctuating membership has included Algeria, Azerbaijan, Bolivia, Egypt, Indonesia, Iran, Iraq, Kazakhstan, Libya, Malaysia, Nigeria, Oman, Qatar, Russia, Saudi Arabia, Trinidad and Tobago, Turkmenistan, the United Arab Emirates (UAE), and Venezuela. Together these countries possess 70 percent of the world's gas reserves and produce more than 40 percent of its output. The main function of the GECF so far has been to exchange information among its members.

Since gas facilities are far more expensive than those for oil, gas supply contracts involve many billions of dollars and tie up government and large corporations for decades. "Natural gas is not as flexible a commodity as oil and is sold in longer-term contracts," Abdullah bin Hammad al Attiyah, the energy minister of Qatar, told me.[8]

The cheapest way to transport gas is by overland pipeline. But when the distance between the source and the destination is very long, the commodity is best transported as LNG, which occupies a fraction of its volume in vaporous form. The downside is that handling supercool LNG is expensive due to the heavy initial outlay. LNG, pumped into superheavy sealed containers on specially designed ships, is discharged into specially constructed storage tanks at the destination terminal—to be sent by special pipes to re-gasification units that must be warmed gradually to let the LNG expand to its natural vaporous form. So the LNG trade requires special containers, ships, terminals, and pipelines. Also, LNG can only be used for generating electricity. But by 2020, whereas the global population will rise by 25 percent from the present six billion, demand for electricity will rocket by 85 percent.[9]

Tiny Qatar has emerged as a leader in producing LNG, for several reasons. Its scanty population makes minimal demands on the government, which possesses the third-largest gas reserves in the world, and the cost of lifting one million calorific units (mcu) or one million British thermal units (BTUs) of gas is 50 cents to $1, whereas the selling price fluctuates around $6.60. (The cost of lifting one million mcu or one million BTUs in West Texas in 2005 was $2.50.)

Russia, the Top Gas Holder

During its existence, the Soviet Union, possessing two-fifths of the global gas reserves, was at the top of the table. Now Russia, containing the planet's largest gas field—Urengoy in the West Siberian Basin—stands at the head of the league table.[10]

Following the 1973–74 oil shock, Western European governments became interested in buying natural gas from the Soviet Union. Moscow started supplying gas to West Germany in 1975 in modest quantities through transnational pipelines.

When, in the aftermath of the 1979–81 oil shock, West Germany and its neighbors tried to raise their intake of Soviet gas by building additional pipelines, the Reagan administration protested. It argued that increased Soviet gas imports would provide Moscow with additional diplomatic leverage, and that the hard currencies earned by it would strengthen its economy and military. Washington banned the export of U.S. equipment to build the pipeline and then tried to ban the export of European equipment containing American technology. Western Europeans objected. Once again, the geopolitics of hydrocarbons came into play.

Controversy raged across the Atlantic for a long while. Finally, according to an agreement reached in May 1985, Western Europe agreed to limit its imports of Soviet gas to 30 percent of the total, and help develop Norway's gas industry.[11]

In the 1990s, President Boris Yeltsin's government allowed Russia's key assets—oil, gas, and metals—to be sold off at scandalously cheap prices to private companies. Under Vladimir Putin, who assumed the presidency in 2000, the Kremlin began reclaiming oil and gas resources, starting with Mikhail Khodorkovsky's Yukos Oil Company. Now Gazprom, the country's biggest corporation, with a market value of $250 billion—ahead of BP and lagging behind only Exxon Mobil—owns more than a fifth of the world's gas deposits. That is setting off alarm bells again in Washington.

More than a dozen European countries wholly or overwhelmingly dependent on Gazprom for their gas needs include Finland, the three former Soviet republics of Estonia, Latvia, Lithuania, the Czech Republic, Slovakia, Austria, Hungary, Poland, Belarus, Georgia, Bulgaria, and Turkey. Germany receives almost half of its gas supplies from Gazprom, and France and Italy nearly a quarter each.[12] Such a predominant position in the gas market strengthened Russia's hand in playing the geopolitical game of hydrocarbons. When Ukraine failed to meet Gazprom's demand to accept a higher price for natural gas being sold to it at below-market rates, Gazprom shut off supplies on January 1, 2006, freezing Ukrainians and hurting their industry. Ukraine relented.

Rising hydrocarbon prices boosted Russia's economy and gave it the sort of clout it had previously lacked. This was particularly true of its dealings with Germany, the third-largest economy in the world. "What has happened over the past five years is that Germany's energy dialogue with Russia has turned into an energy alliance," said a Russian analyst in September 2005.[13] Plans were well advanced to build a $12 billion north European gas pipeline to bring the Siberian gas to Vyborg and then to the German port of Greifswald via the Baltic Sea.

A confident Kremlin undertook foreign policy initiatives. It proposed to enrich uranium for Iran inside its territory to dissipate the diplomatic impasse between Tehran and its U.S.-backed European negotiators—Britain, France, and Germany—over Iran's nuclear program. It also invited Hamas leaders to Moscow after their election victory in the Palestinian territories.

"We have to take into account the overall energy needs of the world and the obsessions to democratize the [Middle Eastern] region overnight," said Russian foreign minister Sergei Lavrov during his visit to Berlin in April 2006. "We can't take sides in the [likely] conflict of civilizations. We want to help to bring both sides together." He stressed the need for global energy security. "Even if all the ambitious plans are implemented to save energy, the world's need for energy security will not diminish," he added. "That is why a new concept of international relations is needed."[14]

The weight of Lavrov's words will increase with time. By 2030, Russia will satisfy half of the gas needs of Europe, which will rise sharply.

On the supply side, Russia's gas riches are followed by Iran's. Together they possess two-fifths of the global reserves.

Iran in the Gas Forefront

A striking fact about Iran is that between 1984 and 2004 its proven gas reserves doubled—to 27.5 trillion cubic meters.

The unexpected cornucopia led the government to decide in 1994 to encourage the use of gas and its products domestically, thus enabling it to export more oil. With this in view, it decided to extend the existing arc of its gas pipeline to form a loop around the country, with plans for future spurs to Pakistan and India, central Asia, and Turkey for exports.

By almost trebling gas production during the next decade, the Iranian government raised its contribution to the energy basket to 40 percent, one of the highest in the world.

It succeeded on the exports front as well. On August 12, 1996, Turkish prime minister Necmettin Erbakan signed a $20 billion natural gas deal with Iran, to run until 2020.

The agreement was inked just a week after U.S. president Bill Clinton signed the Iran-Libya Sanctions Act (ILSA). It authorized the president to impose sanctions against any individual or company anywhere in the world that invested more than $40 million in the oil or gas industry of Iran or Libya.[15]

The Clinton administration sent a delegation to Ankara to pressure the Turkish government to cancel its contract with Tehran. But Erbakan refused, arguing that he was implementing Turkey's long-established policy of diversifying its energy resources. Here was one more example of the geopolitics of hydrocarbons trumping all other considerations, including Turkey's membership in NATO and its close ties with Washington.

Turkey was not alone. The European Union (EU) and Japan argued that ILSA violated the rules of the World Trade Organization, to which they and the United States belonged. Aware that at current rates of extraction, Iran's gas reserves would last more than three centuries, European, Japanese, and Chinese companies were in no mood to kowtow to American legislation, especially when they were convinced that its extraterritorial application was illegal.

Indeed, in September 1997, an oil consortium led by Total Societé Anonyme (later TotalFinaElf) of France, and including

Gazprom of Russia and Petronas of Malaysia, with 40/30/30 shares in equity, signed a $2 billion contract with the National Iranian Oil Company (NIOC) to develop its offshore South Pars gas field, holding 6,800 billion cubic meters of gas. The plan was to extract twenty billion cubic meters of gas by 2001, enough to satisfy two-thirds of France's demand. Washington declared that Total, Gazprom, and Petronas had violated ILSA and that it would penalize them. It never did.[16]

The rising energy needs of China and India led those countries to forge strong hydrocarbon links with Iran. As mentioned earlier (in chapter 7), in 2004, China signed a $20 billion gas deal with Iran extending over a quarter century, and reached an agreement in principle on a $70 billion contract involving Sinopec's purchase of Iranian LNG for a quarter century. At the present modest extraction rate, China's domestic gas reserves would be exhausted by the middle of the current century.

India, too, inked an agreement with Iran for the supply of LNG. And the plan to erect a gas pipeline from Iran to India through Pakistan remained in the cards. It was not viewed as a barrier to the growing entente cordiale between Delhi and Washington following President George W. Bush's visit to India in March 2006. Evidently, he accepted Delhi's argument that gas supplies from Iran were vital to maintain its high growth rate.

The next in the gas reserves league is Qatar. Between it and Iran, they possess three-quarters of the gas reserves of the Middle East.

Tiny Qatar, a Gas Giant

The North Dome field, straddling Iranian and Qatari territorial waters, is the globe's largest nonassociated-gas field, with proven reserves of more than 10 billion cubic meters.

The natural gas industry got a massive push with the overnight change of Qatar's ruler in June 1995. In that month, while

Qatar's ruler, Sheikh Khalifa al Thani, was on vacation in Switzerland, his son and crown prince Sheikh Hamad al Thani—a tall, dark, heavily built man of forty-five—mounted a bloodless coup.

He immediately ordered huge investments by the state-owned Qatar General Petroleum Company (later Qatar Petroleum) in its massive North Field gas field and its LNG facilities in Ras Laffan. Within a decade, Ras Laffan Industrial City, eighty-five kilometers (fifty-two miles) north of Doha, furnished with quays, industrial plants, and specialist ships bearing vessels to carry LNG, became a beehive of activity.

A tightly guarded and self-enclosed settlement, Ras Laffan Industrial City is closed to outsiders. To enter the place, an authorized visitor must secure a permit from the Ministry of Industry. Despite restricted movement inside the Industrial City, it is not hard to notice yellow buses transporting thousands of south Asian workers from their makeshift camps to work sites crammed with a maze of pipes, tanks, and cylinders of assorted sizes—and vast turbines embossed with an oryx, the national symbol.

When I arrived there along with an official of Qatar Petroleum in February 2005, I was greeted by Joseph Angelil, an ebullient, stocky Lebanese Christian with wavy black hair. After watching a short film on the Industrial City and looking at a series of charts and graphs that illustrated what had been achieved and, more importantly, what was planned for the coming years, it became evident that Qatar had become the globe's major LNG supplier. "Qatar's exports of LNG will rise from twenty million tonnes a year in 2004 to seventy-seven million tonnes in 2010," Angelil concluded with a flourish. "It will export LNG to America, to Japan and South Korea, and Britain and India in between."

A year later, during my visit to Delhi, an official of the Ministry of Petroleum and Natural Gas told me that LNG imports from Qatar, starting with five million tonnes a year in 2005, would quadruple in the next decade.

The first domestic production of gas in India occurred in 1961. With the development of the Bombay High offshore oil and gas field, a sizeable natural gas industry grew, with Bombay High having three-fifths of India's gas reserves. In 1994 India consumed 16.6 billion cubic meters of gas, mostly obtained from Bombay High—a figure that would double in a decade.[17] With fresh discoveries of gas in Krishna-Godavari Basin onshore and offshore in 2000 by the ONGC and later by Reliance Industries, the total reserves rose to 920 million cubic meters. At the present rate of extraction, they will last only three decades.

India is feverishly building additional LNG terminals and pipelines along its western and eastern coasts. "India's energy security over the next twenty-five years is critically linked to the import of LNG from our gas-rich neighbors and completion of transnational pipeline projects from Turkmenistan and Iran," Talmiz Ahmad, India's senior civil servant focused on oil diplomacy, told me.[18]

As it happened, a large majority of the fifty thousand workers toiling in Ras Laffan Industrial City to build a factory—which, according to Wayne Harms, president of operations in Qatar for Exxon Mobil, the largest foreign investor in the country, "may be the largest plant facility anywhere in the world"[19]—were from India. They were engaged in a project to carry LNG to Britain for the next twenty-five years, starting in 2008.

LNG, a Favored Commodity of the Future

Between 1983 and 2004, Britain's consumption of natural gas doubled. Due to the rising output from the hydrocarbon riches of the North Sea, it became self-sufficient in natural gas in 1995. That state of affairs, however, lasted barely a decade. Output began declining after reaching a peak in 2000, as predicted by M. King Hubbert's followers.

In 2004, when gas-fired stations produced a third of total electric power, Britain became a net importer of gas. Following a sharp decline in domestic production during the next two years, the rise in wholesale gas prices was so steep that it forced many gas-burning power stations to switch to coal and struggling small factories to turn to alternative fuels.

By design or by accident, this set the scene for importing LNG from Qatar. Britain started equipping itself to receive seventeen million tonnes of LNG a year at its Milford Haven port in South Wales to meet a quarter of its gas needs. By 2020 Britain will be importing 80 percent of its gas from abroad.

To their alarm, the locals discovered that the two LNG terminals at Milford Haven were being built in an area that already had an oil refinery. There were fears that oil tankers heading for the refinery could collide with the moored LNG tankers and cause a cataclysmic explosion. "The emphasis has been, 'This is great for the area, good for the local economy; don't knock it,' " said Lisa Francis, a member of the Welsh Assembly. "But . . . there are real safety concerns." This was all the more true in light of the British gas company BG publicly admitting that cracks had been discovered on one of its new LNG containers and that the ship had been returned to the foreign yard where it was built. More than four thousand local people signed a petition expressing concern that the risks had not been properly weighed. Some of them displayed posters on their windows: WARNING: LNG DANGER ZONE.[20]

Similar concerns were expressed in the United States, as well. "Many regard the big LNG ships and re-gasification terminals as safety risks, especially with the threat of terrorism," wrote Paul Roberts. "Even before 9/11 few American communities wanted LNG facilities nearby out of fear that LNG is polluting and likely to explode—despite the fact that being frozen it is far less flammable than gasoline."[21] Such fears explain why, during the past three decades, when LNG became technically feasible, energy companies in the United States had constructed only four LNG receiving terminals capable of handling a mere 2 percent of the nation's needs.

Three factors forced a change in the policy. One, the United States' natural gas deficit rose from 70 billion cubic meters to 96 billion cubic meters a year during 1995–2004. Two, at the present rate of extraction, the nation's gas reserves will be exhausted in a decade. Three, by 2020 gas demand will rise by 50 percent. That is why ten new LNG terminals capable of handling 140 billion cubic meters a year are now being constructed.[22]

The increase in LNG trade will benefit Qatar hugely. Its economic growth of 29 percent in 2005 was the highest in the world; and it was on course to head the per capita income league table by the end of the decade. But then, Qatar was an exceptional case.

Taking a global view, Talmiz Ahmad said, "The problem pertaining to gas . . . has to do with the need for fresh investments over the medium term to develop new fields, albeit in the traditional areas where production in old fields is declining. It is estimated that investments of about $1–1.2 trillion would be required over the next ten years to develop the potential to meet global requirements."[23]

At the same time, there is no escaping the fact that, like oil, natural gas is a finite commodity, and that the Hubbert's peak for it is predicted a mere generation after petroleum's. More specifically, a study by BP in 2005 pegged the world's supply of natural gas at sixty-seven years, assuming 2004 exploitation rates, and oil supplies at forty-one years.[24]

As yet there is a fuel outside the hydrocarbon family that has come to the fore to run electricity-generating stations: uranium.

Power of the Atom

Nuclear power is the most recent entrant in the field of energy, having arrived as a commercially viable process only in 1957.

In the subsequent half century, it came to account for one-sixth of global electricity, with countries as varied as the United States, India, Japan, Argentina, and South Korea acquiring nuclear power stations.[25] In 2006, more than thirty reactors were being built in a dozen countries. Reflecting the upsurge in demand, the price of uranium oxide, popularly known as yellow cake, shot up from $6.70 a pound in early 2001 to $41.50 in May 2006.[26]

It was in 1938—more than a century after the invention of an electric generator by Michael Faraday in Britain and Joseph Henry in the United States—that German scientists Otto Hahn, Lise Meitner, and Fritz Strassman conducted the first successful experiment with nuclear fission in Berlin, the capital of Nazi Germany. Four years later, Enrico Fermi achieved a self-sustaining nuclear chain reaction at the University of Chicago. In 1946, U.S. president Harry Truman, who had earlier ordered the devastation of Hiroshima and Nagasaki in the war against Japan, established the United States Atomic Energy Commission to foster and control peacetime development of atomic energy. However, the National Reactor Testing Station in Idaho did not produce usable electricity from nuclear fission until 1951.

In his "Atoms for Peace" speech in 1953, at the height of the first nuclear missile race of the cold war, U.S. president Dwight Eisenhower proposed international cooperation to develop peaceful applications of nuclear energy. But the credit for establishing the first nuclear-fueled electric-power station, on June 27, 1954, went to the Soviet Union for its plant at Obillioninsk. Britain was next, with its nuclear power plant at Calder Hall in Cumbria in October.

The year 1957 witnessed the establishment of the International Atomic Energy Agency (IAEA) as a nuclear watchdog—as well as the first industrial accident at Britain's Windscale (later renamed Sellafield) nuclear reactor, when its graphite core caught fire and spilled radiation into the environment, causing widespread ill health.

The Nuclear Non-Proliferation Treaty (NPT) was launched under the aegis of the IAEA in 1968, to halt the spread of nuclear weapons, and became effective in 1970. In exchange for refraining from developing nuclear arms, the signatories were to receive assistance to develop civilian nuclear power stations by the five "recognized" nuclear weapons powers—the United States, Britain, China, France, and the Soviet Union.

In the United States, the oil shock of 1973–74 had led to a large-scale harnessing of nuclear power. Before the price explosion, nuclear plants had generated only 4.5 percent of total electricity. Within a decade, it would leap to 20 percent.

The construction of fifty new atomic power stations engendered a corps of antinuclear activists who were alarmed about the havoc that an accident at a nuclear station could cause. Their fears were realized in 1979 when, soon after the release of the Hollywood movie *The China Syndrome*—which showed the cooling systems at a nuclear power unit failing and the melting reactor core penetrating the floor and pouring down into the earth—an actual partial-core meltdown happened at Three Mile Island nuclear plant in Pennsylvania. The Carter administration responded by ending authorization for new reactors. As a result, no atomic power stations have been built in the United States since 1980–81.

The Chernobyl Nuclear Plant Disaster

In Western Europe, the accelerating construction of nuclear power plants, begun in the mid-1970s, came to a virtual halt in the aftermath of the explosion at Reactor 4 at Pripyat's Chernobyl nuclear plant in the Soviet Republic of Ukraine on April 26, 1986. The Soviet Union followed Western Europe's lead and stopped building any more nuclear power stations.

On the night of April 25, 1986, inadequately supervised operators at Chernobyl reportedly conducted an ill-conceived safety test and caused an explosion. In the absence of a containment building, a mile-high plume of radioactive particles drifted over 40 percent of Europe, including the Scandinavian countries, France, and Britain, and as far away as Japan to the east and the East Coast of the United States to the west. Between 50 and 250 million curries of radiation, almost equal to 100 medium-sized atomic bombs, were released into the atmosphere.[27]

It was by far the most disastrous civilian nuclear power accident. "On April 25 to 26, I was in the on-call crews, in the escadrille. I was given the task of flying directly to the town of Chernobyl," recalled fifty-two-year-old Sergei Volvodin, a burly, snub-nosed helicopter pilot, on the twentieth anniversary of the accident. "The weather was wonderful . . . When we went toward the final point of the route, reversed and flew toward Pripyat, I saw that all of the steam and smoke from the station was nearby, and that it was all going mainly toward this village. There are people planting potatoes in their gardens, and all of this is falling on their heads. I give a command to the crew, 'Shall we go and measure what is there?' They nodded, 'Let us go,' right into smoke and steam. The technician began to report, '15, 20, 50, 100—Commander, it has gone off the scale.' . . . We made a decision to leave the zone immediately."[28]

The accident resulted in the destruction of the plant and the deaths of thirty-one workers and firefighters and serious injuries to nearly three hundred workers. The carnage caused by the flames and the chaotic evacuation of those surrounding the site were dreadful. The severe contamination of large zones of Ukraine, Belarus, and Russia led to some 200,000 people being relocated. What was equally shocking was the fact that the Kremlin publicly acknowledged the explosion only after radioactive particles had been detected in Sweden, partly because initially the Soviet authorities themselves were confused.

"I had to enter the zone immediately," remembered sixty-three-year-old Svetlana Rudneva, the steely-eyed head of the radiation center. "It's unbearable to remember those moments when we passed through the countryside from which people had been evacuated—you couldn't hear children laughing, you couldn't hear voices—it was utter silence. And I've also been left all my life with the images of apples, which were hanging in a big, huge garden—they should have been long since picked off the trees and eaten. They were needed by no one. That was terrible."[29]

Once the Soviet authorities recovered from the initial shock and confusion, they acted with vigor, speed, and imagination. Soviet engineers and workers promptly built a gargantuan sarcophagus of 700,000 tonnes of concrete to seal the volcanic reactor.

"Here everything collapsed, and it stood like a fire-breathing volcano," recalled sixty-eight-year-old Yevgeny Akimov, the sad-eyed, wide-mouthed builder of the sarcophagus. "This volcano could disgorge for a huge amount of time, for years, this radioactive hellfire, radioactive dust. It had to be closed."[30] What Akimov and his workers buried under the concrete were 200 tonnes of uranium, almost a million tonnes of elements, including plutonium, and vast amounts of radioactive water and dust.

The power plant has remained sealed for twenty years. Now leaks are appearing. The plan is to build a vast steel arch over the sarcophagus. The Belarusian government claimed that a sixth of Belarus was still contaminated and that the disaster had cost $235 billion so far. In Ukraine the health of 200,000 workers who took part in the cleanup had been badly affected.[31]

Post-Chernobyl Europe

By the late 1980s, Western Europe had acquired 190 reactors, with only half a dozen authorized to be erected after the Chernobyl disaster, even though the pro-nuclear lobby pointed out that a Chernobyl reactor design would never be allowed in the Western world. As it was, the nuclear power stations in Europe and the United States were equipped with light water reactors, where water acted not only as a coolant but also as a moderator. That made the plants far safer than the one at Chernobyl, it was argued.

France became the leader in Europe. Its fifty-nine nuclear power plants and treatment facilities produced nearly three-quarters of the nation's electricity. After the terrorist attacks in New York and metropolitan Washington in September 2001, all these installations were put under the protection of armed guards and aerial radar.[32] Its nuclear industry was well advanced. Its leader, Areva S.A., was a nuclear giant. As such, there was no move afoot to phase out the nuclear stations.

Contrary was the case in Germany. Until the mid-1980s, the energy sector in West Germany was dominated by coal and nuclear companies and the powerful coal miners' union. The Chernobyl accident galvanized the antinuclear lobby, which was dominated by those favoring environmental protection, called Die Grünen (the Greens). New antipollution laws and falling coal production made coal-fueled power plants unappealing.

Following German reunification in October 1990, the East German Bündnis 90 and West German Die Grünen agreed to form a larger Die Grünen, known in the English-speaking world as the Green Party. Following the federal elections in 1998, the Green Party formed a coalition government with the Social Democrats. Two years later, Jürgen Trittin, the Greens' minister of environment, nature conservation, and nuclear safety, reached an agreement with energy companies on the phased closure of the nineteen nuclear power plants, producing 25 percent of electricity, by 2020.

The deal was codified in the Nuclear Exit Law. Assuming thirty-two years to be the average life of a nuclear power station, the law specified how much electricity a power plant was permitted to produce before its shutdown. As a result, the share of nuclear power in Germany fell to 12 percent in 2006.

Germany's lead was followed by the Netherlands and Belgium, where nuclear-powered stations' contribution to the national electric grid was as high as 55 percent.

Britain was way behind, with nuclear power amounting to only 22 percent of total electricity. Britain had twenty-eight nuclear stations, all but eight state-owned. As the closure of most of these plants at the end of their natural life approached, a national debate ensued about whether or not to initiate a new round of atomic power stations against the background of Britain's commitment to lower CO_2 emissions.

Debate in Britain

In May 2004, in his article in the *Independent*, Professor James Lovelock, a former National Aeronautical and Space Agency (NASA) scientist and nuclear expert, caused a stir among his fellow environmentalists when he argued that the sole immediately available source of energy that did not cause global warming was atomic energy, and that only a massive expansion of nuclear power as the world's main energy source could prevent climate change from overwhelming the globe. "Civilization is in imminent danger and has to use the nuclear—the one available safe source of energy—now or suffer the pain soon to be inflicted by our outraged planet," he concluded.

To establish the environmental friendliness of nuclear fuel, Professor F. Duggan of London cited figures from the January 1995 edition of *Nuclear Issues*. The levels of CO_2 emissions in tonnes per gigawatt-hour were: coal, 870; oil, 750; gas, 500; nuclear, 8; wind, 7; and hydro, 4. Four years after the Chernobyl accident, he added, the most contaminated area, thirty kilometers (twenty miles) from the reactor, registered background radiation similar to that of Cornwall in Britain.[33]

Surveys revealed a disjunction between popular feeling and expert opinion. The BBC *Newsnight* poll in May 2005 showed 52 percent were opposed and 39 percent in favor.

By contrast, a poll of British legislators in September 2005 found that 53 percent favored nuclear power becoming a major contributory factor to energy supplies and 34 percent opposed. Two months later, a report based on the deliberations of 150 scientists, engineers, economists, and sociologists in London concluded: "Nuclear power will inevitably have a key role in a future clean energy mix." Without it, the report added, Britain will struggle to plug an anticipated 10,000 MW energy gap—almost 20 percent of the total demand—expected to open by 2015 as existing nuclear and coal-fired stations are retired.[34]

Those in the antinuclear column mentioned security, proliferation, financing, climate change, resources depletion, degree of transparency by nuclear companies, and waste management. In each instance, their opponents offered a credible counterargument.

The antinuclear activists reasoned that more nuclear sites and more transported nuclear waste would increase the probability of terrorist attacks. Those in the opposite camp referred to the safety measures the French government had taken following 9/11. On a much wider scale, they proposed that there be rotating international teams of experts to monitor the running and auditing of the plants to ensure safety.

Building nuclear power stations will stimulate construction of more such plants in other countries, with the increased possibility of weapons of mass destruction (WMD) developing. Insulating nuclear power from nuclear weapons was "fanciful," asserted the antinuclear lobby. Their rivals pointed out that the major blame must be laid at the door of the five "recognized" nuclear weapons powers, who had failed to take any steps to get rid of their atomic arms as required by the NPT. It was true that the centrifuge that purified uranium to 4 percent for civilian nuclear power plants also did so to 90 percent and above for atomic weapons. A solution lay in the international funding of a project to produce a centrifuge that would seize up when it purified uranium to 89 percent.

According to the opponents of nuclear power, as most utility companies are now privatized—which was not the case when atomic stations were first constructed—private capital will be required to build them, and the private sector will not risk financing such plants unless there are cast-iron government guarantees in the form of massive subsidies. This was quite true, their adversaries agreed. The undisputed fact was that although nuclear power is expensive to build, it generates electricity steadily and cheaply.

Also, the efficiency of the nuclear stations had risen steadily. In the United States, for instance, whereas in 1986, an average American nuclear plant produced electricity 57 percent of the time, it now did so 90 percent of the time.[35] As for funding, both private and public finance could be harnessed to build nuclear power stations, the pronuclear lobby argued.

A new nuclear program will have no effect on CO_2 emissions until 2015–2020, asserted the anti-nuclear lobby. Leaving this statement unchallenged, pronuclear activists said, "Better late than never."

The opponents of the nuclear industry argued that confidence and trust in the industry was being depleted by such incidents as the recent massive leak at Thorpe, registered by instruments but ignored by the staff. The pronuclear lobby, taking a realistic view of men and machines, noted that no matter how safe designers and manufacturers made an industrial process, it was impossible for them to eliminate human negligence.

The major problems, in the view of George Monbiot, an anti-nuclear commentator, were the spent fuel rods and the prohibitive cost of decommissioning old power stations. British Nuclear Fuels Ltd. (BNFL) refused to let EU inspectors visit the Sellafield plant to examine one of the dumps. (Some 1.3 tonnes of plutonium has been sitting around in ponds for about thirty years.) So the European Commission was taking the British government to court. Monbiot referred to the recent revelation made by the *Guardian* that BNFL had secretly buried ten thousand cubic meters of nuclear waste from other countries and that the Ministry of Defense had dumped seventeen thousand cubic meters of nuclear waste on the seabed off the coast of Alderney.[36]

So far the British government had spent £50 billion ($90 billion) to clean up the nuclear plants, which had ceased to function. Since the authorities did so when electricity was in the public sector, there was no separate account to apply to the one generated by nuclear stations to include the cost of dealing with spent fuel and waste products and the decommissioning of the expired plants. An estimate offered by the government in April 2006 put the cost of decommissioning Britain's nuclear power plants at £56 billion ($108 billion).[37]

While the behavior of the nuclear industry's executives has often been far from transparent and their statements either misleading or "economical with the truth," thus engendering public distrust, there has been much improvement in nuclear technology since the building of the Sellafield power station.

Take, for instance, Westinghouse Corporation's design for the third-generation AP-1000 (Advanced Passive) reactor. It was so named because the reactor has far fewer moving parts in its safety systems. It heats water in the reactor, but under high pressure, so it does not boil, and that water is then run through a heat exchanger to generate steam that goes through the turbine. Then there is the new "pebble bed" reactor, which uses graphite instead of water to control reactions, and is therefore safer. It is being pioneered in different countries, including China. Donald Johnston, secretary general of the OECD, pointed out in an op-ed that a single 1,000-MW nuclear plant produced only five cubic meters of high-level waste, and that the total nuclear waste in Europe was five hundred cubic meters, or 0.005 percent of the total industrial waste.[38]

On waste management as well as safety, the Finnish nuclear authority Posiva seems to have found a satisfactory solution. After twelve years of public debate, it allowed the construction on a remote island of a $3.5 billion nuclear plant to be equipped with an Olkiluoto-3 French–German evolutionary "Pressure Water" reactor by Teollisuuden Voima Oy, to be completed in 2009.

The first new atomic power station in Europe for a decade, it was the most advanced and was designed to last sixty years, twice the normal life. If its control rods failed, triggering a core meltdown, a special basin of concrete would hold the debris, preventing the release of radioactive material. The nuclear waste would be set in cast iron, to be encased in copper and dropped down a half-kilometer-deep borehole, which would be saturated with bentonite, a kind of clay. According to Posiva's metallurgists, under such conditions the copper barrier would be good for a million years. The new station would raise the nuclear power percentage in Finland from 27 to 37 percent.[39]

The United States, with a much larger nuclear industry, faces a more intractable waste-disposal challenge. The problem of thirty-six thousand tonnes of radioactive waste, stored at the plants that produced it, remains unsolved. The Energy Department's plan to open an underground storage facility in Nevada has been stalled because of lawsuits and local resistance.

An inkling of the debate in the United States could be gleaned from the National Energy Policy unveiled by the Bush administration in May 2001.

Nuclear Renaissance in the United States and India?

After asking rhetorically, "How many Americans know that nuclear power already supplies one-fifth of the country's electricity?" the U.S. National Energy Policy paper called for a new evaluation of nuclear reprocessing which would take advantage of the fact that as reactors consume uranium, they also produce plutonium. "If the plutonium is chemically scavenged from the fuel, it can be used to run reactors," the document said. "But the technology is dirty and expensive. For the last decade, it has been cheaper to fuel reactors with new uranium than to recover plutonium. Also, plutonium can be used for making weapons. At present Japan, France, and Britain reprocess the uranium fuel."[40]

Yet it was not until four years later that a rethinking of atomic power started among U.S. legislators and a consensus was codified in the Energy Policy Act of 2005, which provided for public funds for new nuclear power stations. They had acted against the background of rising petroleum prices and the imminent moves by several state governments to tighten CO_2 emissions. The United States had at that time sixty-four nuclear sites in thirty-one states, with 103 reactors managed by private companies, and a further eleven plants for nuclear weapons and materials run by the Department of Energy. In the case of more than half of the functioning reactors, their owners were applying for renewals of their soon-to-expire licenses.

In March 2006, U.S. energy secretary Samuel Bodman referred to sixteen new nuclear reactors on the drawing boards. But not a single one had yet been ordered. "It is hard to imagine people putting a $5 billion bet on new reactors, as matters stand now, with uncertainty around climate change policy and the impossibility of getting financing for them in private markets," said Peter Bradford, a former member of the U.S. Nuclear Regulatory Commission. On the other hand, a dizzying scope for expansion was pointed out by Thomas Homer-Dixon and S. Julio Friedman, nuclear power experts. Meeting the growth in American energy demand until 2050, they said, would require building 1,200 nuclear power plants—that is, two per week.[41]

Bodman talked of the nuclear plans for the United States while President Bush was in Delhi. He and Indian prime minister Manmohan Singh signed an agreement to implement a nuclear pact that would help India satisfy its fast-rising energy demand while continuing to manufacture nuclear arms. India agreed to place fourteen out of its twenty-two reactors—existing and under construction—under an IAEA inspection regime over the next eight years. The remaining reactors, as well as India's program of fast-breeder reactors—highly efficient producers of plutonium used for nuclear weapons—were to remain in the military sphere, allowing Delhi to continue manufacturing atom bombs.

"The agreement offers us access to civilian nuclear energy," said Amitabh Mattoo, a member of the Indian prime minister's Task Force on Global Strategic Development. "It protects our strategic program, and it mainstreams India." Critics argued that the agreement would make it more difficult for Washington to persuade Iran and other nations to give up their nuclear arms ambitions. "You cannot break the rules and then expect Iran to play by them," said Democrat representative Ed Markey of Massachusetts.[42]

The claims of nuclear help from the United States were exaggerated. In reality, the earlier visit to Delhi of French president Jacques Chirac, who signed a nuclear cooperation agreement with Singh, was more meaningful. "We are the only ones today who can propose nuclear technology, equipment, everything," said Dominique Girard, the French ambassador to India. "Russia has less sophisticated technology, and the Americans have not been constructing nuclear plants for ages. They have the technology, but they have not put it to use for many, many years [since 1979]." Anne Lauvergeon, president of the nuclear giant Areva, which put India's need at twenty-five to thirty reactors, said, "We have the technology because the Indians require large reactors and we have been working with these for a long time." Summing up, Chirac declared: "The agreement is inspired by a moral desire to help India realize its economic potential unhampered by the stranglehold of energy constraints, and without it having negative fallout on the world as a whole as a result of greenhouse gas emissions."[43]

In practical terms, with all the assistance of the United States *and* France, the contribution of nuclear fuel to India's overall energy demand will rise from the current 1.5 percent to a mere 6 percent by 2020. "Nuclear energy is like a vitamin supplement to a balanced diet to feed the country's power needs," remarked Talmiz Ahmad.[44] In general, electricity accounts for one-third to one-half of the total energy in most countries.

India had progressed greatly since 1948, when the Indian Atomic Energy Commission was set up in the Department of Scientific Research, and exploration for uranium was initiated. Eight years after the Department of Atomic Energy was established under the direct charge of Prime Minister Jawaharlal Nehru, India acquired its first nuclear reactor. In 1958 this department absorbed the Atomic Energy Commission, which became the policy-making body for developing and utilizing atomic energy for peaceful purposes.

India began refining uranium ore in the eastern state of Bihar in 1967. It built its first nuclear power station in collaboration with General Electric Corporation of the United States at Tarapur near Bombay, which supplied the enriched uranium as fuel. In that design, the heat from the nuclear rods makes the water in the reactor vessel boil, and the resulting steam runs the turbine, which operates the electric generator. The Tarapur plant, with two 160-MW reactors, was connected to the electric grid in 1969. After that, India built electrical power reactors of the Pressurized Heavy Water type, which use natural uranium as fuel and heavy water as a moderator.

By 2006 India had fourteen working reactors, which provided less than 3 percent of the nation's electricity.

In contrast, China had nine nuclear power stations, generating only half as much electricity as in India. Even when the number of such plants rises to fifty by 2020, their contribution to the national grid will be a meager 4 percent. Russia was set to play a vital role in China's nuclear industry. In 1997 the Chinese authorities purchased two reactors from the Russian nuclear technology exporter Atomstroyexport, to become operational in 2006–07. Being "very close to leading-edge Western designs," according to Ian Hore-Lacy, a spokesman for the London-based World Nuclear Association, a pronuclear group, "the Russian units are very good. I would be happy to live next door to one of them." Atomstroyexport was competing with France's Areva and U.S.-based Westinghouse, a recently acquired unit of Toshiba of Japan, for a new $8 billion contract for four third-generation reactors in China.[45]

At the end of the twentieth century, India had proven uranium reserves of some fifty-three thousand tonnes and an annual output of two hundred tonnes. At that rate, India's reserves will be exhausted by 2020. This was one of the main reasons why its government cut a deal with Washington that, if approved by Congress, would likely persuade the forty-member Nuclear Supply Group, which controls the exports of sensitive nuclear material and technology, to acquiesce to the U.S. request for an exception for India—which has not signed the NPT.

Globally, assuming that the use of uranium continues at the

present rate, the low-cost uranium reserves will be used up by 2055—barely a century after the mineral became a commercially viable fuel for generating electricity.

However, another uranium source is being exploited: nuclear fuel derived from deactivated atomic warheads. A twenty-year U.S.-Russian program—"Megatons to Megawatts"—aims to eliminate five hundred tonnes of Russian nuclear warhead material by diluting it into nuclear fuel and selling it to utility companies in the United States. By September 2005, half of the twenty thousand Russian nuclear warheads were deactivated, and the recycled fuel was used by almost all the civilian nuclear sites to produce 10 percent of the nation's electricity. The remaining Russian warheads will be deactivated by 2013. A similar project has been initiated in the United States to transform enriched uranium from the atomic warheads into fuel suitable for civilian power stations.[46]

The implementation of the "Megatons to Megawatts" program could be beneficial both to the environment and to the cause of the nonproliferation of weapons of mass destruction.

Overall, though, such a project will prolong the use of uranium for power generation by merely a decade or so. The inescapable fact is that the only other fuel in nature that can provide energy to humankind for a few more centuries is coal.

Coal, Dirty and Clean

In the hydrocarbon family, coal is the least efficient fuel. Since hydrogen and carbon atoms exist in an almost one-to-one ratio in coal, it provides the least energy among hydrocarbons. By possessing two hydrogen atoms to one carbon atom, oil releases twice the energy of coal. And, with its four hydrogen atoms to one carbon atom, methane (the main component of natural gas) is almost twice as energy-efficient as oil.

Coal has the longest history of providing energy to modern

societies. By the turn of the twentieth century, the globe's coal output was almost one billion tons, a staggering figure at the time. In 1926 when the coal miners' union in Britain—then a superpower—called a strike, one million miners, accounting for one-sixteenth of the nation's labor force, stopped working.

By 2000 coal was still one of the leading players on the world stage in generating electricity. Today it provides 28 percent of electric power worldwide, marginally less than the 1970s figure. Countrywide, percentages vary widely, from twenty in the United States to four times as much in China.

Despite a long history of exploitation, the U.S. coal belt of Virginia, West Virginia, Kentucky, and Tennessee continues to be a prolific supplier of fossil fuel. At the current rate of mining, the coal reserves of the United States will last two and a half *centuries*. As it is, coal's role in generating electricity is set to rise. The Energy Policy Act of 2005, heavily influenced by the coal lobby, supported coal-fueled electric plants. The relaxed Environmental Protection Agency guidelines gave carte blanche to the coal industry to expand its operations in the eastern states. By 2020, the coal output, enhanced by a quarter, will fuel plants that will generate 44 percent of the nation's electric power. In purely economic terms, coal, which produces electricity at two cents per kilowatt-hour, is unbeatable.

In Europe, coal continues to be an important energy supplier in the countries that entered the industrial age early on, such as Britain and Germany. In Britain it is the source of nearly a third of total electric supplies, and in Germany about a quarter.

These figures pale in comparison with those in China, which burns a third of the world's consumption of 4.1 billion tonnes of coal. Though China has one-eighth of the world's coal reserves, assuming the present rate of extraction remains static, it will exhaust them in less than six decades. But coal consumption will rise, as China plans to construct two large new coal-fired power stations each year until 2015. In contrast, by 2020, most of the coal-fired power stations in Britain will close, as they will violate EU regulations requiring expensive filters to be fitted to counter acid rain.[47]

In India, coal is the most abundant fossil fuel resource, and coal-fueled plants generate nearly three-quarters of the country's electricity. It also powers steel, cement, fertilizer, chemical, paper, and many other medium- and small-scale factories. At the present rate of mining, India will exhaust its recoverable coal reserves in two and a quarter *centuries*.

As a public sector industry, coal has suffered from inefficient management along with a poor safety record. The coal mines are all in eastern India. So the coal-fueled power stations outside this region have to rely on the state-owned railroad network, which is a byword for inefficiency. Quite often power plants find themselves within a few days of closure due to shortage of coal. With economic liberalization initiated in 1991, private companies have penetrated the industry and are improving their market share. At the same time, with the upgrading of the national high-tension power grid, it has become economically feasible to set up power plants near the coal mines and transmit electricity to distant locations.

Worldwide, the most disturbing aspect of coal is that it is the leading pollutant, generating more CO_2 than any other fossil fuel. It is not surprising, therefore, that seven of the ten most polluted cities on the planet are in China.

At the Asia-Pacific Security Forum during the Association of Southeast Asian Nations summit in Vientiane in July 2005, the following nations decided to form the Asia-Pacific Partnership for Clean Development and Climate: the United States, Australia, China, India, Japan, and South Korea. Its priority was to develop a technology to burn coal more efficiently and capture CO_2 before it reaches the atmosphere.

A solution to coal's polluting problem lies in producing decarbonized coal, or converting coal into petroleum products, thereby reducing demand for crude oil.

Decarbonizing Coal or Natural Gas

A hybrid technology involving decarbonizing natural gas or coal already exists.

In the case of natural gas—mostly methane—superhot steam is deployed to break down the methane molecule into hydrogen and carbon, with the hydrogen used for industrial purposes and the carbon either released into the atmosphere as CO_2 or stored in abandoned mines and oil fields or in the deep seas.

"You smash up the coal completely before you use it," explained Tony Juniper, head of Friends of the Earth in England, in his London office. "You extract the hydrogen and therefore the carbon. You burn the hydrogen, and all the CO_2 gets sequestered. That technology is out there. We should be taking it up now."[48]

What Juniper was referring to, in lay terms, was a process called Integrated Gasification Combined Cycle (IGCC), which converts coal or heavy crude oil into a synthetic gas—syngas—composed of hydrogen, carbon dioxide, carbon monoxide, and steam, along with traces of methane, sulfur, and other pollutants. Once syngas has been scrubbed of sulfur and other pollutants, it is subjected to extreme heat and pressure. This results in the separation of hydrogen molecules, ready to be accumulated, and a stream of liquid CO_2 suitable for storage—underground, or under seabed by an offshore oil company. It is cheaper to take CO_2 out of coal in an IGCC than out of natural gas.

The syngas acts as fuel for a gas-fired turbine, which in turn generates electricity, while the exhaust heat produces steam, which assists in running the coal conversion cycle. When the exhaust is subjected to high pressure, the consequence is the separation of hydrogen and liquid CO_2, each ready to be stored.

The disadvantage of the IGCC is that an IGCC station needs one-fifth more coal as fuel than a conventional plant to produce the energy needed to power the carbon-capturing mechanism, and is therefore quite costly. Also, the resulting liquid CO_2 is three times bulkier than the original coal.[49] The price of electric power thus generated is a third to a half higher than the present one.

Yet, a $1.2 billion IGCC station erected in Italy has been converting 16 million tonnes of heavy oil into 550 MW of electricity and several tons of hydrogen for the past several years.[50]

With the paucity of oil, followed by natural gas and then uranium, facing humanity as the present century unrolls, the future for clean coal in the energy basket seems quite bright—maybe as high as 50 percent by 2201

Coal into Petroleum Products

Another alternative is to convert coal into petroleum products. On average, one ton of coal should yield 1.5 barrels of oil and a variety of chemicals.

The process, patented by German scientists Franz Fischer and Hans Tropsch in 1923, was first used in the United States five years later. The federal government continued making investments in several test plants in the 1930s and 1940s, which altogether yielded nearly one million gallons of synthetic gasoline. Seeing the development as a threat to their prosperity, major oil corporations persuaded the federal authorities to abandon the project.

Following the example of Nazi Germany, the seven-year-old apartheid regime in South Africa established South Africa Synthetic Oil Ltd. (Sasol) in 1955 to use synfuel technology to convert coal into petroleum products, including diesel. The apartheid system is gone, but Sasol is very much alive. It now produces 150,000 bpd from forty million tonnes of coal.[51]

Elsewhere, China and Malaysia are building large synfuel facilities. In April 2006, scientists at Rutgers University and the University of North Carolina in the United States published a paper in the journal *Science* outlining a new two-step process for converting coal into diesel—an improvement on the Fischer-Tropsch process.[52]

In 2004, after much research, the Pentagon concluded that it was desirable to operate all battlefield equipment on a single multipurpose synthetic fuel, and that synfuel was "ideal" as "a stable, clean, domestically made battlefield fuel."[53] So in 2006 plans were in place to build the first coal-to-gasoline plant in Pennsylvania.

Historically, what has worked against synfuel is that it costs an average of $35 a barrel, far more than petroleum has cost on average until recently. However, with the oil price now firmly above $50 a barrel since mid-2005 and no downward trend on the horizon, the price disadvantage of synfuel has disappeared.

Yet, as Governor Brian Schweitzer of coal-rich Montana said in his *New York Times* op-ed in October 2005, "There will be significant start-up costs for private companies, but risk can be alleviated with long-term buyers like the military and with new federal loan guarantees." He also recommended that the U.S. administration give subsidies and tax breaks to the new industry, as it has been doing in the case of oil.

With the worldwide number of cars set to grow from the present 750 million to 1.2 billion in 2020, with eight billion humans inhabiting the Earth, demand for gasoline and diesel will rise correspondingly.[54] On the other hand, by then, with any luck, the much-anticipated divorce—or at least separation—between the automobile and the internal combustion engine might have become a welcome reality.

TEN

Car and Internal Combustion Engine: A Divorce on the Horizon

February 29, 2004: The two-year-old Kodak Theater, at the corner of Hollywood Boulevard and Highland Avenue in Los Angeles, with Hollywood Boulevard cordoned off for eight blocks on both sides of the theater with a heavy police presence. It is, of course, Oscar night.

Ahead of the ceremony, televised live globally, stars parade into the 3,300-seat theater in a complex that contains a hotel, a ballroom, and retail shops. For the men, basic black tuxedo is de rigueur. For the women, though, it is an occasion to display their skills in impressing the worldwide audience with the uniqueness of their exclusive haute-couture gowns, designed and given to them by Yves St. Laurent, Giorgio Armani, or Prada, their diamond necklaces and jeweled earrings glittering in the flash of cameras. There is a wide variety of color, from pale fuchsias and blues to beige and midnight black. Where this eye-catching diversity gives way to monotony is in the uniformity with which every one of the glittering stars steps onto the red carpet from an SUV.

But wait. What Charlize Theron, a best actress nominee, alights from is *not* a SUV, not a Hummer H2, the most "bling-bling" car—as the New Orleans rapper B. G. put it—big, showy, and expensive, with leather upholstery and every electronic gadget known to humanity, a PlayStation games console, a DVD player, and a stereo system with Richter-style bass.

Theron is not the only one to shun SUVs. Her example is emulated by her rival for the best actress award, Keisha Castle-Hughes, as well as Tim Robbins, Will Ferrell, and Robin Williams. They all travel in their Toyota Priuses.

The Prius is a hybrid automobile, a Japanese-made four-door family car, with an engine capable of doing 60 miles per gallon (mpg) and upstaging the Hummer H2, whose admirers dismiss the Prius as "deeply unsexy" and "far too ugly on the inside."

What happened on that February 2004 evening in Los Angeles was not a coincidence. The "Oscar stunt" was carefully orchestrated by an advocacy group called Global Green USA. "We want to get the American public to see that driving these [Prius] cars is chic and fun," said the organization's president, Matthew Petersen.[1]

Arnold Schwarzenegger, the Hollywood actor-turned-state-governor, held onto his five Hummer H2s, a civilian version of the Humvee, the American military vehicle, each of which cost $53,000 and consumed its thirty-two-gallon tank at the rate of a gallon every twelve miles. He also possessed two Hummer H1s; each is a five-ton behemoth burning a gallon every ten miles and costing $140,000.

Across the Atlantic, in April 2006, hoping to rebrand the Conservative Party of Britain, its newly elected leader, David Cameron, emerged from his freshly bought sky blue Toyota Prius T Spirit with a shine in his eyes and a huge smile on his lips for the cameras.[2]

President Clinton's Early Move

The profligate burning of gasoline in the United States of the early years of the twenty-first century was a far cry from the project launched by the newly elected President Bill Clinton in 1993: to design a commercially viable automobile that would do 80 mpg (or 35 kilometers per liter). He assigned the task, to be funded by $1.5 billion from the federal budget, to Vice President Al Gore. Gore compared it to the Apollo space program "in its urgency and technological complexity."

Working in conjunction with the three automobile supergiants— General Motors, Ford, and Daimler-Chrysler—Gore established the Partnership for a New Generation of Vehicles, a joint industry- government undertaking, to produce an affordable car doing 80 mpg by 2004. From then on, the automobile troika collectively matched federal dollar for dollar to develop related technologies, particularly when the Clinton administration removed the earlier freeze on the statutory Corporate Average Fuel Economy (CAFE) standards.

The federal government's attempt to economize on fuel con- sumption went back to 1975, when Americans were suffering the trauma caused by the 1973–74 oil shock. Until then, the average passenger car did 15 mpg. During the Gerald Ford administra- tion, the United States implemented the CAFE standards as required by a congressional law, which was passed in the teeth of bitter opposition by automakers who were required to improve mileage. However, Vice President Nelson Rockefeller's plan to get the U.S. administration to help develop alternative energy sources and reduce dependence on petroleum and Saudi Arabia got nowhere in the face of opposition from the president's pow- erful chief of staff, Dick Cheney.[3] A quarter century later, Presi- dent George W. Bush's chief of staff, Andrew Card, was an automobile lobbyist before taking up his new post.

Once car manufacturers reconciled themselves to the new law, their designers and engineers produced automobiles that com- bined fuel efficiency with elegance. Their design improvements went beyond the engine to the transmission and chassis aerody- namics. The average fuel consumption of an American passenger car in 1985 dropped to three-fifths of its figure a decade earlier. But as oil prices plummeted in the spring of 1986, the U.S.

administration of President Ronald Reagan froze the CAFE standards at the 1985 level—that is, the average of 25 mpg for a car.

The law was kinder to light trucks, chiefly pickups, on fuel economy standards as these vehicles were run primarily for business. In 1975, one out of five vehicles sold was a light truck.

Freed from the statutory demand and keenly aware of the plentiful and cheap oil, the American automakers—intent on reclaiming those buyers who had forsaken them for their Japanese rivals—now opted for bigger, heavier, and more powerful automobiles and trucks that would transport heavier loads, accelerate more quickly, and be equipped with far more features than before. As a result, fuel efficiency suffered.

Yet, once more the American automakers would be wrong-footed in their race against their Japanese counterparts. They were overtaken by Toyota. At the annual Tokyo Motor Show in October 1995, Toyota introduced a "concept" automobile, called Prius, powered by a hybrid engine—part gasoline, part electric—a space-age wedge of an automobile that seemed to be a cross between *Star Trek* and *The Jetsons*. It would stay ahead not only of its later American competitors but also of such domestic rivals as Honda. Two years later the Toyota Prius made its market debut in Japan. But it was not until 2000 that Toyota started selling Prius in the United States. By 2005, sales of Prius and Lexus RX hybrids would surpass 300,000.

Bush Junior Regresses

In Detroit, the automobile capital of the United States, the federal-backed endeavors of the American automakers came to naught in January 2002. The Bush administration unceremoniously disbanded Al Gore's Partnership for a New Generation of Vehicles, with the new energy secretary, Spencer Abraham, asserting that the project had "no chance" of meeting its target of coming up with a reasonably priced automobile doing 80 mpg within the next two years. He conveniently ignored the fact that the program had not just developed useful technologies but had also made crucial contributions to the design of a viable hybrid gas-and-battery-powered car capable of doing 40-plus mpg.[4] Indeed, this would enable the American auto supergiants to introduce hybrid models by 2004.

At the same time Abraham announced that the Department of Energy would pursue a $1.7 billion program called FreedomCAR— Cooperative Automotive Research—as well as a fuel initiative aimed at developing hydrogen-powered fuel cells to power automobiles of the future, hydrogen production and delivery infrastructure, and advanced automobile technologies. The new project was to be operated jointly by his department and the automobile troika. Critics argued, rightly, that by focusing on hazy, long-term objectives, the Bush administration and the car industry were ducking the more demanding challenge of improving mileage by undertaking the politically fraught task of raising fuel efficiency standards for existing car and light truck models.

"Any regulations requiring greater fuel efficiency will initially favor Japanese and German automakers, whose fleets are already more fuel efficient, thereby costing American companies more of their market share and U.S. autoworkers more of their jobs," explained Paul Roberts. "Such losses are consequential to American politicians."[5]

Between 1990 and 2003, the American transport industry contributed $256 million to the two leading political parties' election campaigns, with the Republicans receiving more than twice than the Democrats. No wonder that between 2001 and 2005 the House Republicans defeated three bills to raise the average fuel efficiency of cars to 33 mpg. In the 2004 presidential election campaign, they dismissed Democratic candidate John Kerry's proposal to that effect as one of his several "job-losing" proposals.[6]

By 2003, light trucks formed more than half of the total annual sales of some seventeen million vehicles. Families gravitated to minivans, SUVs, and family-style pickup trucks with two rows of seats. SUVs, accounting for more than half of light truck sales, produced almost 1.5 times the pollutants that an average passenger car did. Due to the high proportion of gas-guzzling SUVs in the light truck category, the overall fuel efficiency of the light truck fleets fell to such an extent that overall fuel economy of *all* vehicles hit a twenty-two-year low in 2002.

On the other side, there was a strong incentive for carmakers to manufacture cars such as the Hummer H2 and Ford Excursion, the latter doing less than 5 mpg in urban areas, because they were exempt from fuel regulations and provided hefty profit margins for the producers, and because most buyers could claim tax breaks for them. The new proposals for fuel efficiency unveiled by the Bush administration in August 2005 pointedly exempted the Hummer H2.

The CAFE standard for light trucks remained fixed at 20.7 mpg, while that for new passenger cars was 27.5 mpg in 2003, unchanged by the proposals made by the Department of Energy two years later. By comparison, the respective averages for vehicles in Europe and Japan were 35 mpg and 34 mpg.

The claim made by the Bush administration that its proposals for fuel efficiency to be applied between April 2006 and January 2008 would save 10 billion gallons of gasoline was described by the Union of Concerned Scientists as "minuscule," amounting to less than one month's gasoline saved over fifteen years—or 1/180th of the total—and would do virtually nothing to reduce U.S. dependence on oil or address high fuel costs.[7]

With nearly 240 million vehicles on American roads, even a fraction of a mile gained out of a gallon of gasoline amounts to millions of gallons saved daily. It is estimated that by improving fuel efficiency to 40 mpg, the United States would save about 2.5

million bpd of oil by 2020—the amount it is currently importing from the Middle East.

Bright Side of High Gasoline Prices

What conservationists and environmentalists failed to achieve over decades, nature and market forces did in a few months.

A surge in oil prices in the wake of the hurricanes that shut down refineries and drilling rigs in the Gulf of Mexico region of the United States in 2004–05 pushed a gallon of gasoline beyond $3 (or 80 cents a liter). This was up 80 cents a gallon in a little over a year, and public sentiment turned decidedly against fuel profligacy. During August–September 2005, sales of SUVs fell by a staggering 40 percent. "People in the United States love power and performance, but big SUVs are getting hurt real bad as the gasoline prices are high and the folks know they are going to stay so," said George Maglianao, a car industry analyst at Global Insight in New York. This was the background against which General Motors (GM) announced its ending the manufacture of the Hummer H1.[8]

At the opening of the 2005 Motor Show in Tokyo on October 19, 2005, the United States' Big Three automakers vied with one another in draping their sexiest models over their new concept automobiles, powered by some sort of alternative source—fuel cells, hydrogen, or gasoline-electric engines. Even President Bush, in his 2006 State of the Union speech, made a passing remark about reducing Americans' addiction to oil.

Hybrid Cars

In a Toyota Prius, an internal combustion engine is paired with an electric motor, with the two subsystems functioning as a tag team based on road and environmental conditions. On a highway, where less fuel is needed to make the car travel, the small, efficient gasoline or diesel engine takes over. But on an incline or other terrain or in slow-moving city traffic, where more power is required, the electric motor starts operating.

Even before the gasoline price surge of 2005, the Prius, with sales of 100,000 in the previous year, had become a status symbol, a growing favorite of movie stars and executives, upstaging the Hummer in Los Angeles, widely regarded as its spiritual home.

Its merits became apparent to a growing mass of Americans, and a long waiting list of buyers emerged. First of all, it was economical to run. For instance, Mark Cappellano, a vintner in California who had waited eight months for his 2004 Toyota Prius, found that his journey to Los Angeles and back cost him half of the $80 he would have spent on his earlier conventional sporty Saab. "My Toyota Prius gets fifty-two miles per gallon—in the city," said movie star Cameron Diaz. "Isn't that exciting?"[9]

Secondly, unlike other alternative cars, powered exclusively by electricity, ethanol, or natural gas, the gasoline-electric hybrids do not need special fueling stations or recharging apparatus. Therefore they do not pose an imminent threat to the vested interests in the energy system, with assets of a staggering $10 trillion in oil wells and tankers, refineries, marketing networks for gasoline and diesel (with 180,000 gasoline and diesel service stations in the United States alone), and electric generating stations and transmission lines.

Thirdly, unlike the earlier models, resembling eggs rather than passenger cars, the latest hybrids look stylish and come with most of the options available for a conventional car—a computerized, keyless ignition system, wireless connectivity, the latest stereo systems, and leather upholstery.

Fourthly, a hybrid costs only $2,000 to $6,000 more than its gasoline-powered counterpart. Finally, it reduces pollutants by 90 percent and CO_2 emissions by half, especially in cities, when its electric motor takes over. Little wonder that in the British capital, registered hybrid motorists who travel through central London are exempt from the surcharge of $14 a trip.[10] To encourage its employees to purchase a hybrid car, Bank of America, the world's largest retail bank, announced bonuses of up to $3,000.[11]

Looking ahead, there is the option of redesigning the hybrids to consume natural gas, ethanol, or methanol if the continued burning of gasoline or diesel creates unacceptable political or environmental problems.

Pioneering Toyota, enjoying a three-year technological lead over its American and European rivals, was bolstered further by the record $10.5 billion profit it made in 2004–05—partly due to the huge sums it invested in the research and development of hybrid engines and systems, including lithium batteries—compared to the third-quarter loss of $1.6 billion that General Motors suffered.[12] Toyota was deploying part of its enormous profits in new fuel-saving technologies that it visualized as the new wave in an age of high prices at gasoline pumps.

This made the globe's other car giants anxious to lease or buy hybrid technology from Toyota, further boosting its coffers.

In August 2005, when Toyota announced that, by 2012, all Toyota cars would be offered in hybrid versions and that the company would sell one million hybrids a year, the announcement sent a shock wave through the spines of the American automotive supergiants. The following month, Bill Ford of Ford announced plans to increase their hybrid production tenfold, to 250,000 by 2010.

"Toyota has this big cash hoard," said David Iida of Honda (USA) in Detroit. "They can lose as much as they want to, and use the car as an advertisement." He was apparently referring to the $30 million advertising campaign mounted by Toyota to hype the hybrid and to burnish its image as an environmentally friendly company.[13]

Taking into account both the merits and demerits of hybrid vehicles, John Simister, the car correspondent of the *Independent*, concluded: "The hybrids are giving carmakers excellent feedback about electric power trains in the real world. They are an interim solution and an impure one as they carry duplicate power units. But they are usable now because they are easy to refuel. They also get people used to electric power."[14]

Outside the framework of an internal combustion engine—the heart of a traditional automobile—exists the concept of a hydrogen fuel cell, which is an electrolyte in reverse.

Hydrogen Cell Fuel

Hydrogen and carbon form all organic compounds, the basis of all life on the planet, and the root of all fossil fuels—coal, petroleum, and natural gas. Energy is proportional to the content of hydrogen in a fossil fuel.

Hydrogen stores and sheds energy in the making and splitting of the bonds between it and carbon. Through photosynthesis, green plants transform water, air, and sunlight into sugar. Sunlight causes a water molecule to break into oxygen and hydrogen, with solar energy attaching itself to hydrogen. This makes the newly released hydrogen atom unstable. To regain stability, the hydrogen must share its extra energy by binding with a new partner—an atom of carbon—to form carbohydrate or sugar. That explains why sugars are high-energy compounds: their bonds contain the solar energy conveyed by the hydrogen.

When an animal masticates a plant, he splits the hydrogen-carbon bond. The hydrogen separates from the carbon and unites with oxygen in the lungs of the animal, thus producing a molecule of water, but only by giving up its store of solar energy, which warms the animal and provides the chemical-electrical energy to move its muscles and ensure the growth of its tissues. The carbon that is released reunites with the oxygen in the animal's lungs, a process known technically as oxidation, and popularly as burning. When exhaled, it releases its own share of solar energy.

"In either metabolism or actual combustion," writes Paul Roberts in *The End of Oil*, "the energy-carrying cycle is essentially the same: hydrogen takes on solar energy at the beginning, releases it through oxidation at the end, then reverts to water, in which form it is ready to take on another load of solar energy in the next round of photosynthesis."[15]

Hydrogen is manufactured most efficiently by electrolysis. In electrolysis, an electric current is introduced into a conducting liquid known as an electrolyte, where it flows between two electrodes, causing the splitting of water or other chemical compounds into their ionic (charged) components, which then react chemically.

Hydrogen cells work on the principle of cold oxidation, where hydrogen is oxidized, but most of the energy is released as electricity, not as heat (as happens in nature).

A manufactured fuel cell is a box with two chambers divided by an electrolyte. One chamber, lined with platinum, is fed pure hydrogen in the form of pairs of hydrogen atoms, and the other pure oxygen. On contact with platinum, which acts as a catalyst, hydrogen divides into two single atoms, which, being unstable, are attracted to the oxygen atoms in the adjoining chamber. The partitioning electrolyte permits only the proton, the nucleus of the hydrogen atom, to pass through it to join with the oxygen in the other chamber. The hydrogen atom's electron—the minuscule electrically charged particle that orbits the proton—is separated from the hydrogen core and siphoned off through a metal wire. Each electron is in effect a bit of electricity.

As electrons penetrate the electrolyte barrier and reach the metal wire, they set in train a flow of electric current that powers an electric motor in a car. After performing the function of running an automobile, electrons return to the fuel cell through another metal wire on the other side of the electrolyte. They combine with the proton of the hydrogen atom. The re-created hydrogen atoms join with the oxygen in the other chamber and form steam in the process, releasing some heat.

To put it simply, fuel cells make use of stored hydrogen and freely available oxygen in the air to create electricity. And the only exhaust from the engines that they power is steam.

The attractions of hydrogen are many. It is the simplest and cleanest of fuels. Only water results from its combustion. There is no carbon dioxide and no sulfur compounds. One, hydrogen can be used in the present internal combustion engine in a compound like LPG, or more efficient compressed natural gas (CNG). Two, hydrogen is obtainable from fossil fuels, including coal, nuclear reactions, natural gas, and biomass. It is a by-product of fertilizer production. With solar, wind, or hydroelectric power, it can be electrolyzed from water. Three, there are no different grades or types of hydrogen, no diesel or super–unleaded gasoline, so there is no need for different storage systems. Four, hydrogen can be had in gaseous, liquid, or solid form (as hydride within a solid, but that is a ways off). Five, the production of hydrogen is unaffected by geopolitical instability. Six, when burned inside an internal combustion engine, hydrogen produces almost three times the energy as the same weight of gasoline, and far less polluting emissions. Seven, quiet hydrogen cells cause no vibrations, start instantly, and exhaust nothing more harmful than steam.

Evolution of a Hydrogen Cell Car

Once again it was the 1973–74 oil price explosion that compelled governments and automotive companies in the West and Japan to invest funds into the research and development of fuel cells. But a decade later, as petroleum prices began to fall rapidly, interest in such a project declined.

What had emerged by then were cells that were powerful enough to run an automobile but were much too bulky and weighty, due to heavy electrolytes, to merit a practical application. A viable contrast emerged in the form of a Proton Exchange Membrane (PEM) cell produced by Willard Grubb and Leonard Niedrach of General Electric Corporation in 1962 for the Gemini space program. In it, a thin polymer film functioned like a conventional electrolyte and separated electrons from protons. But the trouble was that such a cell, requiring platinum catalysts, was prohibitively costly. On the positive side, PEM cells were powerful enough to move a car and could easily be accommodated inside it.

Geoffrey Ballard of Ballard Power Systems, based in a suburb of Vancouver, Canada, began working on a project to boost the power of PEM cells. Though he made an important leap in 1986, the overarching challenge was still daunting. A few cells put together needed to generate 75 KW of electrical power or 100 horsepower. By 1992, Ballard managed to push the cell power to 10 KW.

The following year he got a much-awaited business break. Daimler Cars of Germany decided to produce a fuel-cell auto and formed a joint venture with Ballard Power Systems. The Clinton administration, sensitive to environmental issues, invested in fuel-cell technology for mobile sources of pollution such as automobiles as well as for static sources like buildings.

Success came in 1996, when Daimler had become Daimler-Benz. It unveiled NECAR II, a normal-looking minivan powered by two Ballard cells each of 25 KW. With room for six passengers, it had a maximum speed of 70 mph and a range of 150 miles between fuel stops. Other companies joined the race. In 1999, Royal Dutch Shell set up a hydrogen division, and BP followed soon afterward.

The pioneering company, however, wanted to maintain its

lead. In 2000, DaimlerChrysler, as it was now named, announced its intention to market 40,000 cell cars by 2004, rising to 100,000 within two years. Stock markets took note. Fuel cells shone brightly in the technology sector. Nearly $600 million was channeled into an industry that had yet to prove itself by delivering its first promised unit: a car powered by hydrogen cells. Regrettably, analysts and investors misconceived the cell technology by bracketing it with the earlier software technology, which was mainly used to provide services and information more efficiently. In reality, fuel cells are solid objects whose value can only be judged after they have been produced and deployed to evaluate their performance.

Soon the hydrogen cell bubble collided with reality, and burst. Shares of Ballard Power Systems crashed, from its peak of $140 to a derisory $6, leaving the company with little cash to invest in fresh research and development, and forcing it to shed staff.

DaimlerChrysler, a company with a long track record of manufacturing and selling traditional autos, gradually introduced its hybrid version. It lowered its hydrogen cell ambitions to 50,000 such cars by 2010 "at the earliest."

The project attracted the attention of other car giants, among whom GM Europe-Vauxhall was the most advanced. In June 2004 it tried out a hydrogen cell car, called Zafira, at Vauxhall's engineering center at the Millbrook Test Center. It was to do a test run of 6,000 miles from Hammerfest, Norway, to Caboda Roca, Portugal, via London and Salzburg. The idea was to test durability and iron out manufacturing problems as the target date of 2010 drew near for a large-scale production of a hydrogen car.

Zafira used liquid hydrogen. It had two hundred fuel cells wired in series to deliver 94 KW of power. They were installed under the hood in an aluminum case topped by a cover like that of a regular engine—with a 60-KW electric motor behind and below. The stainless steel hydrogen tank was under the rear seat—just as in cars with internal combustion engines. There was no battery to give an extra surge of energy for acceleration. (Yet it had a starter battery.) Within fifteen seconds of switching the fuel cell the car's air compressor built up the pressure, the cells were running, water was dripping out of the exhaust pipes, and the driver was ready to go, reaching the maximum speed of 90 mph.

But hydrogen cells are not for trucks and buses. "What you will not see soon is fuel cell power for trucks and buses," said John Simister, the car correspondent of the *Independent*. "These are already more efficient than lighter vehicles because internal combustion engines are at their most effective when working hard, whereas fuel cell's efficiency advantage comes at light loadings."[16]

Three months later BMW announced they had developed a car that had a dual petrol/hydrogen engine.

Hydrogen Network, a Mammoth Challenge

The mass manufacture of a hydrogen cell car faced colossal challenges, including the cost of production and the establishment of a fuel supply infrastructure. The prototype was both costly due to the use of platinum and unusually heavy due to weighty electrolytes. Using polymer film instead of electrolytes jacked up the price further.

Whereas car owners expected a range of three hundred to four hundred miles between fuel stops, even the largest fuel tank could keep the vehicle running for only two hundred miles. The cost of a prototype cell car remained prohibitive, and the future looked bleak until and unless it was reduced to twice that of a traditional internal combustion automobile.

But then Toyota proved itself once again to be far ahead of its rivals. By early 2006 it had produced its Fine-X model, which ran on hydrogen fuel cells and could cover three hundred miles at the maximum speed of 125 mph. A few Fine-Xs were on the road in Tokyo, a city with a few hydrogen stations to fill the onboard battery.[17]

Setting up a hydrogen-fueling infrastructure will be prohibitively expensive. To replace the American surface transportation system with vehicles running on hydrogen cells fuel, the United States would have to produce 230,000 tons of hydrogen *daily*.[18]

Offering hydrogen fuel at even a third of the present gasoline stations in the United States would involve an investment of $30 billion. It is very expensive to handle or transport hydrogen. As in the case of natural gas, a solution can be found in liquefying hydrogen, which contains nine times the energy of its vaporous counterpart, to cut the cost of transportation. As such, major oil companies—excepting Exxon Mobil, which fails to see any future for hydrogen fuel—are conducting feasibility studies. The alternative of supplying compressed hydrogen through pipelines, as is the case with cooking gas, is unacceptable to governments. They want to tax transportation and not home cooking or heating. Moreover, labor-intensive carbon-fiber storage tanks to be used for compressed hydrogen are very expensive.

The cost of the new fuel is another major barrier. The cheapest and most convenient solution would be to have an onboard system for converting natural gas into hydrogen. But such a device is, by most estimates, decades away.[19]

Nonetheless, the following factors are pushing the world toward the hydrogen fuel cell: ever-growing CO_2 emissions, the rising price of oil, an inexorable growth in the global vehicle fleet, and continuing political-military turmoil in the Middle East.

By the end of the decade, there will be 900 million vehicles worldwide requiring 360 billion gallons of gasoline a year. By 2050, with petroleum supplies at their end, the planet is expected to have 1.5 billion vehicles, all hopefully running on hydrogen cells and requiring 260 billion kilograms of hydrogen fuel.

Producing that much hydrogen will mean generating an extra 15 to 25 percent electricity. That is where nuclear power plants come in, according to a paper delivered by Professor Paul Kruger of Stanford University at the conference of the World Nuclear Association (WNA), a pronuclear group, in London in 2004. He stated that if future nuclear stations were built slightly larger than usual, they could be used to produce hydrogen at very little extra cost.[20]

Such proposals deserved serious consideration by governments and companies as the need for controlling and then reducing greenhouse gas emissions to counter the unprecedented rate of global warming became more urgent by the month.

ELEVEN

Renewable Energy and Rising Global Temperature: A Race

February 16, 2005—the day the Kyoto Protocol became international law—was a singularly infelicitous choice for a gala dinner by the sponsors of International Petroleum Week in London. On that date they invited Lee Raymond, the $53 million a year chief executive officer of Exxon Mobil, the world's largest and most profitable oil giant, to deliver an after-dinner speech to 1,200 petroleum industry executives and their wives at the luxurious Grosvenor House Hotel. The event was widely known.

Five activists of Greenpeace UK turned up at the enormous, chandeliered dinner hall. Without much ado, they picked up the wine bottles and emptied them unceremoniously on the tables. Before the dazed oil executives in black ties and their expensively dressed female consorts could respond and summon the hotel staff to eject the intruders, the latter had drenched sixty tablecloths with expensive wine.

As it turned out, what transpired at Grosvenor House Hotel was merely an epilogue to the main drama, enacted by a larger posse of Greenpeace agitators. Their target was the International Petroleum Exchange (IPE), dealing with Brent crude, which covers nearly two-thirds of oil transactions worldwide.

The IPE is housed in a modern, streamlined, five-story ochre building, a dramatic contrast to its neighbor, the ornate Victorian Gothic Tower Bridge. The back of the IPE opens to an inlet of water from the Thames crammed with moored boats. It was from that side of the building that three Greenpeace protestors, using mountaineering implements, managed to climb to the flat roof, and, at the appointed lunch hour, unfurled a vast banner reading: CLIMATE CHANGE KILLS, STOP PUSHING OIL. Their more numerous colleagues, mainly men of assorted ages, applauded. Then they stood quietly outside the IPE building carrying large printed signs reading CLIMATE CHANGE KILLS against a background of oil barrels.

Inside the building, mayhem broke out as protestors rushed through the only door in the basement leading to the trading floor and headed for the viewers' gallery. They were led by Stephen Tindale, executive director of Greenpeace UK, a veteran activist whose imaginative campaign against Esso (later Exxon Mobil) in mid-2002 drew worldwide publicity. Greenpeace members, wearing masks of President George W. Bush, stood in the middle of city traffic, carrying signs bearing the oil company's logo as E$$o followed by "ATE MY BRAIN" as a riposte to the oil giant's relentless campaign against the 1997 Kyoto Protocol. As a result, Esso faced a consumer boycott and a shareholder campaign in Britain.

Now, on a cold but sunny February afternoon in 2005, in the melee that ensued from the entry of Tindale and his followers into the IPE building, security guards waded in to punch and kick those trapped in corridors, resulting in serious injuries to a dozen intruders. "They [traders and guards] were in a frenzy," said Peter Mulhall, a protestor from Liverpool. "They were trying so hard to hit us they were falling over each other." The Greenpeace protestors, explained Tindale later, had intended to discuss the issue with the oil traders and the IPE management. "We were nonviolent and we made it clear. But there were quite a few blows raining down on our heads. There was not much of a discussion. We decided to retreat for everyone's safety." Yet thirty of them got left behind. Ten of them were arrested by the police and the rest were held inside until the trading stopped at 5:30 P.M.

Overall, they did manage to disrupt oil trading on the floor. One oil trader said, "We were disappointed with the security for allowing this commotion just at a time when the market was pushing higher on the back of reports that a missile had been fired at Iran."[1]

The firing of a missile at Iran was not a happy augury for the upgrading of the 1997 Kyoto Protocol to a legally binding international treaty on the environment.

The Kyoto Protocol

In 1988 the United Nations appointed the Intergovernmental Panel on Climate Change (IPCC) to study the subject. The IPCC submitted its first report in 1990. It warned that if greenhouse gases were not curtailed drastically over the next few decades, global temperatures would rise between 1.5 and 5.8 degrees Celsius by 2100. *Greenhouse gases* is the collective name used for nine gases: carbon dioxide, carbon monoxide, and sulfur dioxide arising from the burning of fossil fuel; methane from agriculture and landfill; nitrous oxide from vehicle exhausts; and sulfur dioxide, hydrofluorocarbons, perfluorocarbons, and sulfur hexafluoride from other industrial processes. By far the major pollutant is carbon dioxide. These gases trap heat and thereby raise temperatures.[2] Such temperature rises will cause the polar ice caps to melt, leading to the oceans and seas rising by twenty inches, drowning not only such island communities as the Seychelles and the Maldives, but also all those living along the coastal areas throughout the world, disrupting traditional agriculture, turning tropical landmasses into deserts, and resulting in increased weather-related disasters such as furious storms blowing more frequently than ever before.

This scenario was based on a study of past phenomena. In the five millennia after the last Ice Age, the Earth grew warmer by only 3 degrees Fahrenheit (1.7 degrees Celsius). But due to the abrupt warming period brought about by the colossal burning of fossil fuels—first coal and then petroleum—during the twentieth century—when carbon emissions, as measured by carbon dioxide, jumped twelvefold—polar ice caps had shrunk by about a sixth, the sea levels had risen an average of four inches, winters had become warmer and summers hotter, and hurricanes and floods had become more frequent.[3] In the prehydrocarbon age, carbon emissions had been totally and easily absorbed by forests and seas.

Taking note of the IPCC's warnings, the United Nations Framework Convention on Climate Change at the Earth Summit in August–September 1992 in Rio de Janeiro, Brazil, decided to act. It required every signatory to the convention to reduce greenhouse emissions without specifying figures. The United Nations in New York set up the secretariat of the UN Climate Change Convention.

Even in the absence of specific targets, world attention—outside the United States—turned increasingly to using renewable sources for producing energy. According to Lester Brown of Worldwatch Institute, during the last decade of the twentieth century, wind power generation grew by 24 percent a year, solar cell production by 17 percent, and geothermal power by 4 percent. These figures looked impressive simply because the base in each case was tiny.[4]

The follow-up conference to the UN Framework Convention on Climate Change in Kyoto, Japan, in December 1997 came up with a protocol. Its template was the 1987 Montreal Protocol to eliminate chemicals called chlorofluorocarbons, manufactured by a few chemical companies, that harmed the ozone layer in the atmosphere, and which had proved successful. The Kyoto conference agreed that the buildup of greenhouse gases over the past two centuries in the atmosphere was almost entirely caused by the industrialized nations. "Indeed, we became rich through these emissions," as Britain's chancellor of exchequer, Gordon Brown, would put it succinctly some years later.[5] Between 1912 and 2004 alone, carbon emissions rocketed sevenfold, from 1 billion tonnes a year to 7 billion tonnes.

Therefore the Kyoto conference specified a collective 4.8 percent reduction in greenhouse gas emissions by 2012 for 38 industrialized countries out of the 156 signatories. The list included all thirty members of the OECD, a club of rich nations, which accounted for 70 percent of the global output. The listed country could easily estimate its carbon dioxide emissions by calculating the fossil fuel its population burned through its taxation system and imports. The conference decided that the Kyoto Protocol would become operational only when the signatories responsible for 55 percent of the total emissions had their parliaments ratify it.

Though U.S. president Bill Clinton, a Democrat, signed the Kyoto Protocol, the Senate refused to ratify it. Since the United States was then responsible for a third of global greenhouse gases, its failure to ratify the Kyoto Protocol was a major setback for those eager to see the document implemented.

So it became incumbent upon most of the 37 remaining nations to ratify the Kyoto Protocol. In mid-December 2004, after much prevarication, the Russian parliament did so, and pushed the emissions total to 61 percent. And, two months later, the Kyoto Protocol became international law, whose arrival in London was marked by media-grabbing protests by Greenpeace.

Details of the Kyoto Protocol

The first ever international environmental law, based on the Kyoto Protocol, treated 1990 as the base year and required industrialized states to achieve their targets by 2018–2020. The EU, then consisting of fifteen nations, negotiated an overall reduction of 8 percent, with the percentage for each member state varying. Britain agreed to the figure of 12.5 percent.

To encourage the signatories to meet their targets, there were three innovative provisions. Any two countries could agree to reduce emissions jointly. Another provision, called Clean Development Mechanism (CDM), allowed rich nations to invest in poorer nations to help them install a green method of generating power, and in return appropriate the resulting carbon credit for themselves. The third method was straight carbon trading. Former eastern and central European countries that were members of the Moscow-led Warsaw Pact had lost most of their heavy industry after the collapse of the Soviet Union in 1991, thus saving huge amounts of harmful emissions. They could sell their carbon credit to such industrializing countries as Ireland, Spain, and Portugal, who were then exceeding their targets.

While developing countries were not subject to the climate change regime—at least not until the second round of the Kyoto Protocol in 2012—the debate surrounding the subject and the Kyoto Protocol has had a profound impact on the policies of such rapidly developing countries as China, India, and Turkey. It was estimated that greenhouse gas emissions in these three countries would have been one-fifth higher if they had not implemented energy-saving policies inspired by the UN Framework Convention on Climate Change and the Kyoto Protocol.[6]

Whereas, in 2002, China and India were number two and five respectively in the league of carbon dioxide emissions in absolute terms, their per capita emissions were very low. The figures in tonnes per capita were: the United States, 5.5; Canada, 4.5; Russia, 2.8; Britain, 2.7; Japan, 2.6; Germany, 2.5; China, 0.7; and India, 0.25.[7]

Uncle Sam, the Odd Man Out

Driven mainly by short-term considerations, successive U.S. administrations have pursued inconsistent policies on fuel conservation and power generation by renewable means, both of which directly impact global warming.

President Jimmy Carter, a Democrat, tried to encourage alternative sources of energy. He declared May 3, 1978, "Sun Day." Andrew Young, the U.S. ambassador to the UN, inaugurated the day with a ceremony at the UN while the rest of the country witnessed hundreds of appropriate events. Carter announced a further $100 million federal spending on solar power research and development and set a personal example by installing a solar water heater on the White House roof. The newly appointed White House Council on Environmental Quality declared that a goal of producing more than half of our energy from solar sources by 2020 should be "achievable" and proudly noted that it was Russell Ohl, an American scientist at Bell Telephone laboratories, who'd invented a silicon solar cell, the building block of solar photovoltaic (SPV) panels—devices that transform sunlight into electricity.[8]

The Republican administrations of President Ronald Reagan in the 1980s failed to back the solar energy project. Reagan removed the solar panels from the White House roof as well as tax credits for solar energy. His actions were in tune with popular sentiment. The collapsed oil prices in the mid-1980s effectively pushed energy as well as environmental concerns off the nation's agenda. In 1990, under the Republican presidency of George H. W. Bush, federal funding for solar power fell to $81 million from $557 million a decade earlier.[9]

In the private sector, U.S. utilities cut their investments in energy efficiency by half. As a result, Japan forged ahead. By making their electrical and electronic consumer items and factories more energy efficient, Japan's usage of oil rose by a mere 1 million bpd from 1975 to 2003 despite a large increase in its population. (During the same period, U.S. oil consumption rose by 4.3 million bpd.) Today, Japan produces one tonne of steel using 20 percent less energy than the United States and 50 percent less than China.[10]

On the other hand, by 2003 global climate change had emerged as a subject of major importance and concern outside the United States. Initially, there was considerable doubt about the link between the rising temperature and human activity. The findings of the 1990 IPCC report to that effect were challenged by the Global Climate Coalition (GCC), consisting of companies from the oil, automobile, and allied industries. The coalition was opposed to imposing limits on greenhouse gases.

At the White House, Clinton accepted the mounting evidence linking global warming with the burning of fossil fuels. He strengthened the EPA. And, as stated earlier, his second administration signed the 1997 Kyoto Protocol. It failed to convince the Senate, though, the majority of which held that ratifying the Kyoto Protocol would award China and other developing countries a competitive edge over the United States as they would be exempt from incurring the expense of reducing emissions.

The installation of Republican George W. Bush in the White House in January 2001 signaled a dramatic policy reversal on global warming, fuel conservation, and renewable sources of energy. He assembled a team with long and deep ties to the coal, petroleum, and automobile industries. Vice President Dick Cheney had represented Wyoming, a leading coal-producing state, in the House of Representatives for almost two decades. As President Gerald Ford's chief of staff, he helped squash Vice President Nelson Rockefeller's ambitious scheme to assist the development of alternative energy sources and reduce dependence on oil. As a director of Chevron, Condoleezza Rice had an oil tanker named after her. Energy Secretary Spencer Abraham, a former senator from Michigan, was better known as "The Senator from Detroit." Andrew Card, the President's chief of staff, worked for a car lobby group before taking up his White House job. And Commerce Secretary Donald Evans was a former chief executive of a petroleum exploration company.

"In all their years in government, Cheney and the Bushes have never done anything to hold the oil companies' feet to the fire, or get Americans' feet off the gas pedal," noted Maureen Dowd, a columnist for the *New York Times*.[11]

Oilmen in the Oval Office

Addressing a meeting of businessmen in Toronto a month before the publication of the National Energy Policy of the freshly installed Bush administration in May 2001, Cheney referred to the rolling blackouts then blighting California and warned that the same fate might befall the rest of the United States. He promised a new energy policy—one firmly in supply-side economics. It would encourage petroleum corporations to explore new areas, including the Arctic National Wildlife Refuge, upgrade the fuel transportation and refining infrastructure, and construct up to 1,500 coal, gas, and nuclear power stations. He then rounded on the advocates of a dual strategy of energy conservation and development of alternative sources of energy. Pledging that consumers would not be urged to curtail their energy usage as they had been in the past, he criticized environmentalists for demanding that the administration step in and "force" Americans to use less energy as if "we could simply conserve or ration our way out of the situation we are in." Conservation, he declared, might be "a sign of personal virtue," but it was an insufficient basis for a sound, comprehensive energy policy.

The $12.3 billion, 1,724-page Energy Policy Act, passed by Congress in July 2005, basically reflected Cheney's speech. It contained no provision on raising the fuel efficiency of cars and trucks, reducing oil consumption, or lowering atmospheric temperature. Senator Byron Dorgan failed to get the Senate to endorse the House of Representatives' provision requiring the president to lower the projected petroleum oil demand by 1 million bpd by 2015.[12]

"Bush and his advisers have long hewn to a strain in conservative thought that regards environmental protection, energy conservation, and climate policy mainly as misguided liberal efforts to 'save the planet' by weakening the economic and political power of the business community," noted Paul Roberts in his book *The End of Oil*. "In Bush's view, only a strong business community can keep the economy healthy enough (and America) powerful enough to take care of environmental concerns."[13]

Though lambasted by the scientific community and environmentalists, Bush's energy policy had a majority backing in the Republican-majority Congress. In August 2001, for instance, the House of Representatives passed a law that contained $27 billion worth of incentives to traditional energy producers and only $6 billion for conservation. "The problem with the Congress is that it always looks at the supply side while giving short shrift to the demand," noted the *New York Times* in its editorial of October 22, 2001.

Assured of congressional support, top officials in the Bush administration resorted to manipulating the findings of the EPA on climate change and even undermining its standing. In mid-2003, following White House instructions, the EPA scrubbed most of the references concerning climate change from its report on the global environment. According to the *New York Times*, the excised material included the EPA's conclusions about the part played by human activity in climate change based on the National Research Council report in 2001, which was commissioned by the White House, and which Bush had publicly endorsed.[14]

Then came a further revelation. Bush administration officials, reported the (London) *Observer*, had enlisted the help of conservative lobby groups funded by the oil industry to attack U.S. government scientists if they produced work seen as accepting too readily that pollution is an issue. Central to the revelations of double-dealing was the discovery of an e-mail sent to Phil Cooney, chief of staff at the White House Council on Environmental Quality, by Myron Ebell, a director of the Competitive Enterprise Institute (CEI). The CEI is an ultraconservative lobby group that had received more than $1 million in donations since 1998 from oil giant Exxon. The e-mail, dated 3 June 2002, revealed how White House officials wanted the CEI's help to play down the impact of a report the previous summer by the EPA in which the United States admitted for the first time that humans are contributing to global warming. "Thanks for calling and asking for our help," Ebell told Cooney. The e-mail discussed possible tactics for playing down the report and getting rid of EPA officials, including its head, Christine Todd Whitman.[15]

Part of the reason why the Bush White House was able to get away with its assertions on global warming was that the mainstream press and electronic media in the United States maintained neutrality on the subject. In their study of reporting on the subject in major American newspapers in 2003, researchers Maxwell Boykoff and Jules Boykoff found that a majority of reports gave the skeptics—amounting to a few dozen people—approximately the same space as the scientific consensus reached by thousands of independent researchers.[16]

The Boykoffs' research was confirmed by Ross Gelbspan in his book *Boiling Point: How Politicians, Big Coal and Oil, Journalists, and Activists Have Fueled the Climate Crisis*, published in 2004. He discovered that on matters of scientific facts, journalists employed an essentially unfair idea of "balance"—treating global warming as if it were still a matter of conjecture, with equal weight given to both sides. "Accurate coverage would have reflected the position of the mainstream scientists in 95 percent of the story—with the skeptics getting a paragraph at the end," wrote Gelbspan.[17]

Remarkably, this was the case in 2004—three years after the first sentence of the executive summary of the National Academy of Science report on climate change read, "Greenhouse gases are accumulating in Earth's atmosphere as a result of human activities"—followed later by a warning that "[g]lobal warming could well have serious adverse societal and ecological impacts by the end of this century."[18]

No wonder it has proved a Herculean task for scientists and environmentalists to make the majority of Americans recognize the grim scientific truth and act. This has led to an alarming situation where the United States—a continental country responsible for the most profligate usage of energy and possessing a tremendous potential for devising new energy technologies—has written itself out of a scenario of vital importance to the human race.

The Big Oil Lobby

Three powerful factors are at work to blinker the vision of the majority of Americans: short-term self-interest, powerful lobbying by the hydrocarbon, automobile, and allied industries, and the complacency of the Bush administration, which is in cahoots with fossil fuel industrialists and their allies.

Americans are addicted to their cars as status symbols and their extravagance in the use of domestic heating and air conditioning to such an extent that they seem oblivious to the long-term cost of their profligate ways to humanity at large.

The highly skewed nature of the worldwide ownership of oil and gas deposits makes it easy for the petroleum lobby to further its interests. Between them, a mere half a dozen corporations—

Saudi Aramco, National Iranian Oil Company, Petroleos de Venezuela SA, Petroleus Mexicano, Exxon Mobil, and Royal Dutch Shell—own the reserves that are now yielding a third of the total global oil output.

Though they are divided between OPEC and non-OPEC categories, they close ranks swiftly when they sense a development— be it technological, legal, or environmental—they consider threatening to their interests.

Individually and collectively, they want the world to remain hooked on oil and gas. The most effective tool at their disposal is price: the lower it is, the higher the demand. Yet such oil-producing states with large populations as Iran, intent on raising the living standards of their citizens, are opposed to cheap oil. Contrary is the case with the oil-rich countries with small populations that exist on the Arabian Peninsula. They favor low prices. In the past they have achieved this by flooding the market with oil in violation of their OPEC quotas. But with the recent surge in demand by quickly industrializing China and India, their ability to depress prices has diminished greatly. Nonetheless, they have the option of giving price discounts to attract new customers or raise their market share in a given country. Their hydrocarbon reserves are so vast that any such concessions make only a small dent in the value of their assets or profits.

While giant oil corporations in the West vie fiercely with one another in securing market share, they collaborate actively when it comes to influencing legislation on energy or the environment. As described in chapters 3 and 4, links between oil companies and Western governments have always been intimate. In the United States, for instance, the generous depletion allowances given to the oil and gas industry benefited the industry to the tune of $140 billion between 1968 and 2001.[19] The oil nationalization in the Middle East in the latter half of the 1970s, followed by the local companies' entry into refining and marketing, resulted in a steep drop in the oil and gas reserves of the Western petroleum corporations. Their position became precarious with the oil-price collapse during 1986–88. This led to a series of mergers and acquisitions. The process culminated around the turn of the century and produced supergiant oil corporations: Exxon Mobil, ChevronTexaco, TotalFinaElf (originally Total, Elf of France, and Fina of Belgium), and an enlarged BP swallowing up Amoco and Arco. With that, a small coterie of Big Oil executive officers was assured of an even more receptive hearing by the upper echelons of Western governments than before.

In Washington, the executive officers of Exxon Mobil, Chevron, BP, and Royal Dutch Shell became big players with powerful lobbying power to delay, dilute, or defeat laws and rules they considered hurtful to their companies.

Their resistance to the rise of alternative energy sources is based partly on the huge stake they have in the current oil and gas infrastructure. In the United States alone, there are more than 150 oil refineries, 4,000 offshore platforms, 160,000 miles of oil pipelines, facilities to handle 15 million bpd of imports and exports, 10,400 power plants, 160,0000 miles of high-voltage electric power transmission lines and millions of miles of electric power distribution wires, 410 underground gas storage fields, and 1.4 million miles of natural gas pipelines—as well as 180,000 gasoline service stations.[20]

Early on, to counter the rise of the environmentalist lobby, oil companies joined the Global Climate Coalition to oppose limits on the emissions of greenhouse gases. As the scientific evidence linking temperature rise with fossil fuel consumption mounted, many oil and non-oil members quit the coalition. Among them were BP, the second-largest oil corporation in assets and revenue, and Royal Dutch Shell. BP and Shell went on to concede the necessity of action to counter global warming, and acted accordingly.

After launching BP Solar as its subsidiary in 1997, BP constructed solar plants in India, Spain, and the United States, and a decade later was well within its planned annual revenue of $1 billion. After establishing a separate alternative energy division in 2005, BP announced that it would invest $8 billion over the next decade.

The following year it undertook a project to build a $1 billion hydrogen-fueled plant in California that would convert waste products from refineries into hydrogen and separate carbon dioxide for capture and storage. It also decided to group together solar, wind, and hydrogen power stations.[21]

By 2006, BP was in the thick of rebranding itself by a massive advertising campaign that announced that its logo, "bp," stood for "beyond petroleum"—and no longer for British Petroleum. "We are leading plans to develop a power station in Scotland that will run on hydrogen," read its full-page advertisement in the *Sunday Times* of October 23, 2005. "This will produce electricity with 90 percent lower carbon emissions for 250,000 homes." An equally prominent ad in the *Guardian* four days later read: "We've been burning the midnight natural gas. By switching from coal to natural gas, carbon dioxide emissions in new power generation can be reduced by up to 50 percent. That is why since 1997 we've been working to grow natural gas to about 40 percent of our energy portfolio." Its full-page advertisement in the *Independent* of November 8, 2005, titled, *Knowing your carbon footprint is a step in the right direction*, read: "A carbon footprint is the amount of carbon dioxide emitted each year due to the energy we use. The average UK household footprint is 10 tonnes each year. That's like 100,000 people all putting the kettle on at the same time. We all need to do something to reduce today's emissions and avoid serious environmental damage in the future. Here at BP, we're trying to reduce our footprint. Since 2001, our energy efficiency projects have reduced emissions by over 4 million tonnes. Visit bp.com/carbonfootprint to calculate your household's carbon footprint and to see how it can be reduced."

Not to be seen as lagging behind, Royal Dutch Shell, which made a record profit of £13 billion ($23 billion) in 2005, announced that it had so far spent $1 billion on wind, biofuels, and solar sources.[22] On June 11, 2006, in association with the *Observer*, Shell published a special twelve-page supplement and a colorful chart on energy and energy conservation in Britain.

In stark contrast, Exxon Mobil continued the policy implemented by Exxon under the leadership of Lee Raymond. Its top officials were part of a cabal at the American Petroleum Institute whose deliberations became known in a leaked memorandum in 1998. The document outlined a strategy to give "logistical and moral support" to climate change dissenters and raise questions about and undercut the "prevailing scientific wisdom" about global warming.[23]

Generous grants by Exxon Mobil have sustained a body of skeptics on the issue of climate change who deny any link between human activity and temperature rise. Their research provides the foil for the mainstream journalists to "balance" their stories on climate change.

The Citizens' Green Lobbies

In contrast to the behemoth fossil fuel lobby, environmental pressure groups are diffuse. Lacking any economic clout, they depend solely on persuasion and occasional media-grabbing direct action protest. Greenpeace, Friends of the Earth, and World Wildlife Fund (WWF) are the leaders and the best known.

Of these, Greenpeace has acquired the highest profile. It was established in 1971 when a group of anti–Vietnam War activists in the United States decided to stage a nonviolent protest against U.S. nuclear testing in Alaska. They chartered a fishing vessel called *Phyllis Cormack*. After renaming it *Greenpeace*, they sailed to the testing zone and grabbed headlines in the press in the United States and elsewhere. In 1972 the Richard Nixon administration abandoned its tests in the area. Since then Greenpeace has widened its fields of activity. They include not just global warming but also the hunting of whales and genetically modified foods.

"We have to be credible and use good science, but if we can be a credible threat then we can do better things," John Passacantando, the executive director of Greenpeace USA, told the *Pittsburgh Post-Gazette* in February 2003. Since becoming the top official of Greenpeace USA in 2001, the wavy-haired, forty-one-year-old former economist and investment analyst has continued the organization's audacious, confrontational—albeit nonviolent—tactics. "To paraphrase [Henry David] Thoreau, I regret only our good behavior."

Under his leadership, Greenpeace activists installed mock oil rigs in the Capitol's reflecting pool in Washington to protest against major oil corporations' influence on the official energy debate, as reflected in the National Energy Policy of May 2001. They delivered an ice sculpture of a melting nuclear reactor to a conference of nuclear power industrialists in Washington. In January 2001, they blocked Exxon Mobil tankers from mooring in Australia and staged a worldwide boycott of the company because it produced and sold shale oil, one of the dirtiest fossil fuels. "Greenpeace is a global organization and we can put pressure on corporations around the world," Passacantando said.[24]

In Britain, Greenpeace scored its most sensational victory in June 1995, when Royal Dutch Shell decided to abandon its plan to dump its 66,000-ton oil rig, used in the North Sea, in the Atlantic Ocean, following harassment at sea by helicopter-borne Greenpeace activists, the threat of a gasoline station boycott, and condemnation by several European governments.

Greenpeace has consistently refused funds from governments, political parties, and companies. In the United Kingdom, 90 percent of its 200,000 supporters donate small amounts monthly by direct debit.

The Friends of the Earth (FoE) was founded in 1969 in America by David Brower, who quit the environmentalist Sierra Club as the executive director when his colleagues failed to take on nuclear issues or establish international contacts. Two years later it became an international network when environmentalists from the United States, Britain, France, and Sweden met in the Swedish town of Roslagen. They decided *not* to be tightly organized or directed from the top. Initially they focused on opposing nuclear power. The accidents at Three Mile Island in 1979 and Chernobyl in 1986 gave an impetus to their movement.

Out of this grew Friends of the Earth International (FoEI), a federation of FoE groups in seventy-one countries with 1,200 staff members and some 5,000 local activist groups. It was assisted by the small International Secretariat, based in Amsterdam. In 2002, it had 72,000 members and many more supporters, the total reaching about a million. Besides climate change, the FoE groups focus on genetically modified organisms, forests, and international financial institutions and trade.

Friends of the Earth England, Wales, and Northern Ireland, led by Tony Juniper, became the United Kingdom's leading pressure group in the struggle to protect the environment. Almost all of its income comes from members and supporters. It engages in campaigning, citizens' action, and providing information and ideas, the key doctrine being, "Grow the economy only in ways that focus on quality of life and protection of the planet."

Both FoE and Greenpeace were preceded by the World Wildlife Fund, which is more focused on conservation of nature and species. Established in 1961 as part of the UN in Geneva as IUCN—The World Conservation Union—it was renamed World

Wildlife Fund (WWF), with the panda logo, the following year, and became an international organization with scientific, technical, and financial resources to fund and conduct conservation efforts around the globe. Since then the World Wildlife Fund has grown into the largest privately financed international conservation organization in the world, with national affiliates in more than thirty countries and a global membership of more than five million—with nearly a quarter in the United States alone.

The WWF, the FoE, and Greenpeace are all part of the Stop Climate Chaos lobby, which wants CO_2 stabilization by 2015. This umbrella organization cites scientific studies which show that 60 to 80 percent reductions would be required by 2050 to stabilize the climate by keeping it within 2 degrees Celsius above preindustrial levels.[25]

Green Grassroots Rebellion in the United States

In the United States, campaigning by the green lobbies, combined with Bush's failure to produce a promised alternative to the Kyoto Protocol, has produced positive results at the local and state levels. By the autumn of 2005, nine states and 192 cities and towns had acted to cut emissions. The northeastern states, from Maine to New Jersey, announced plans to require large power stations to freeze CO_2 emissions by 2009 and then reduce them by 10 percent by 2020. They were devising a price mechanism to make it costlier for coal-fueled electric stations to operate. California, Oregon, Washington, and Arizona were considering similar measures.[26]

But there was no change at the federal level, despite the fact that between 1990 and 2003 greenhouse gas emissions had risen by 13 percent, and that a survey of 928 published research papers on climate change in scientific journals in 2005, published in *Science*, the weekly journal of the American Association for the Advancement of Science, showed that there was no disagreement about the consensual conclusion that the globe was getting warmer and that human activity was the reason for it.[27]

The second Bush administration continued to attack the Kyoto Protocol. Its director of environmental quality, James Connaughton, maintained that the Kyoto target for the United States to reduce emissions was "so unreasonable . . . that the only way we could have met it was to shift energy-intensive manufacturing to other countries."[28] His statement was at odds with the estimate that the United States' 2 percent loss of its GDP to implement the Kyoto Protocol was only slightly larger than the European Union's 1.5 percent.[29]

Equally, there was no change in the White House's policy of intimidating those officials who provided evidence contrary to its unscientific stance. In December 2005, the *New York Times* noted editorially on February 9, 2006, James Hansen, the top climate specialist at NASA, "called for accelerated efforts to reduce industrial emissions of CO_2." He was threatened by George Deutsch, a twenty-four-year-old presidential appointee at NASA's public affairs department, with "dire consequences" if he continued to call for "aggressive action" on climate change.[30] "The Bush administration has been muzzling those who disagree with it on global warming, birth control, forest policy, and clean air. It edited out and censored inconvenient truths from the Environmental Protection Agency reports in 2002 and 2003."

Bush's Ostrichlike Stance

The following facts and computer-based predictions failed to make a dent in Washington's official "no action" policy on climate change:

* A study by Sergei Kirpotin of Tomsk State University in western Siberia and Judith Marquand of Oxford University— published in the September 2005 issue of the London-based

New Scientist—showed that the entire sub-Arctic region of western Siberia, spanning 1 million square kilometers (equal to France and Germany combined) had started to melt for the first time since it was formed 11,000 years ago at the end of the last ice age. Methane is trapped within the peat bog below the permafrost, which lies below the topsoil. If permafrost thaws, then methane will be released. The 70 billion tonnes of methane is a quarter of the worldwide total. As a greenhouse gas, methane is twenty times more potent than CO_2.[31]

* By 2100, the top layer of the Arctic permafrost will thaw and release vast amounts of carbon stored in the soil, which will threaten ocean currents and wreck roads and buildings in Alaska, Canada, and Russia.[32]

* Simulation studies carried out at Stanford University's Department of Global Ecology, covering the years 1870 to 2300, showed that CO_2 will double from 1870 to 2070, then treble in 2120 and quadruple in 2160. Temperatures in Arctic Russia and North America will rise by 25 degrees Fahrenheit (14 degrees Celsius) around 2100. Alaska will become a largely temperate state.[33]

* A study by Jonathan Overpeck, director of the Institute for the Study of Planet Earth at the University of Arizona in Phoenix, and Bette Otto-Bliesner of the U.S. National Center for Atmospheric Research in Boulder, Colorado, published in the U.S.-based journal *Science*, showed that if "nothing is done to put the brakes on climate change, Greenland, the west Antarctic ice sheet, and other expanses of polar ice will be warmed beyond 'the tipping point' after which their melting is inevitable." Professor Overpeck said, "We showed that that level of warming [of 3 to 5 degrees Celsius] will come later in

the century unless we act on carbon emissions [now]. An Arctic warming of 3 to 5 degrees Celsius is enough to cause four to six meters [thirteen to twenty feet] of sea level rise . . . A one-meter sea-level rise would see the Maldives disappear, make most of Bangladesh uninhabitable, and put cities such as New Orleans out of business."[34]

* Of the world's eighty-eight largest glaciers, seventy-nine are receding; 95 percent of the Himalayan glaciers are shrinking. Glaciers in western China's Qinghai-Tibet Plateau, accounting for nearly half of China's glaciers, are melting at 7 percent a year.[35]

* The Greenland ice gap is breaking up at twice the rate it was five years ago, according to a satellite study done by James Hansen, director of NASA's Goddard Institute for Space Studies in New York.[36]

* Whereas over the past 5,000 years, the seas have risen by one millimeter per year, they have risen by twice as much annually over the past 150 years. The expected forty-centimeter rise in sea levels by 2100 will alter coastlines, erode beaches, and destroy houses.[37]

On the eve of the follow-up climate-change conferences—one of all UN members and the other of the Kyoto Protocol signatories—in December 2005 in Montreal, the Associated Press published the results of a study with two major conclusions. One, CO_2 has increased from 280 parts per million (ppm) to 380 ppm in two centuries, and will rise to 550 ppm by 2050 at the current rate of fossil fuel use. Two, there is more CO_2 in the atmosphere now than at any time in the past 650,000 years.[38]

At the Montreal conference of all UN members in December,

the U.S. delegation walked out when the Canadian hosts criticized its policy. Later it returned to "nonbinding talks" on long-term measures. "Talk is cheap and nonbinding talk is even cheaper," noted the *New York Times* on December 13. "And talk alone will not get the developing world into the game. Why should India and China make major sacrifices while the United States in effect gets a free ride?"

To their credit, however, China and India agreed to play an active role in future talks while insisting that they did not want targets imposed on them after 2012 because by then they would not be rich industrialized nations. Despite its dazzling economic growth over two decades, on a per capita basis China is still in the lower half of the league table of UN members, and its development plans call for it to be "moderately prosperous" by 2020. For their part, the rich nations agreed to implement deeper emission cuts.

None of this made an iota of difference to the administration in Washington. Leading U.S. corporations took their cue from the Bush White House and vice versa. A study commissioned by Ceres, a coalition of investors and environmental groups, surveyed one hundred global corporations, seventy-four of them based in the United States, covering ten major industries, including oil and gas, chemicals, coal, food, industrial equipment, and airlines. It showed that European and Asian companies cared more about global warming than their American counterparts. This contradicted the official line that Bush's program of voluntary reductions by individual companies had resulted in a decrease in emissions, when the reality was to the contrary. Overall, the American companies were "playing catch-up" with international competitors like BP, Toyota, Alcan, Unilever, and Rio Tinto, many of which operate in countries that regulate greenhouse gases. "Dozens of U.S. businesses are ignoring the issue with 'business as usual' responses that are putting their companies and their shareholders at risk," said Mindy Lubber, president of Ceres.[39]

Bush's fanciful scenario reached its apotheosis in his reference to "energy independence" in his State of the Union speech on January 31, 2006. He announced that the Advanced Energy Initiative would increase federal funds for research into clean fuels by 22 percent and that the research would include "zero-emission coal-fired plants, revolutionary wind and solar technologies, and clean, safe nuclear energy." He said that the ethanol that U.S. scientists were exploring would come from wood, chips, stalks, or switch-grass—tall, tough grass found in marshes. (The next day the Houston correspondent of the *New York Times* pointed out that the federal government continued to support traditional ethanol made from corn, a process that consumes large quantities of expensive natural gas. It was thought that the technology of using plant fiber to make ethanol, though feasible, would not be commercially viable until the mid-2010s. In Brazil ethanol comes from sugar cane. In the United States so far the focus has been on corn.)

"Breakthroughs on this and other new technologies will help us reach another great goal: to replace more than 75 percent of our oil imports from the Middle East by 2025," Bush declared. The following day his energy secretary, Samuel Bodman, explained that replacing 75 percent of our oil imports from the Middle East by 2025 was "purely an example." (It's worth recalling that Richard Nixon promised oil independence by 1980, and that Gerald Ford moved the date forward to 1985, and that his successor, Jimmy Carter, in 1979 named 1990 as the date for ending dependence on foreign oil.) On February 1, the *New York Times* reported that the National Renewable Energy Laboratory, billed as the centerpiece of Bush's Advanced Energy Initiative, was about to dismiss staff, which had been told that cuts would be concentrated "among researchers in wind and biomass, which includes ethanol."

Renewable Energy

While renewable energy sources include solar, wind, and wave, wind was the only technology that had developed to the extent that it became commercially available for large-scale development worldwide by the end of the last century. Already on the Great Plains of the United States, across windswept northern Europe, the flat coastal terrain of the Indian state of Tamil Nadu, the hills of Spain, and the mountains of California, wind-powered turbines had become a common sight. At the turn of the twenty-first century, investment in the wind-power industry reached $7 billion to produce 7,000 MW of electricity, enough to light up 3.5 million homes in Europe. Progress continued unabated in the European Union.

In the United States, except during Carter's presidency, research and development of renewable sources of energy has been treated with skepticism at best and hostility at worst. Since World War II, the federal government has invested thirty times more money, at $150 billion, into nuclear research and development than into renewables. Whereas natural gas production has received two-thirds of federal production tax credits in the recent past, renewables have obtained a niggardly 1 percent.[40]

America's stepmotherly attitude toward green energy continues and is reflected by its Congress. At the end of the Clinton presidency in 2000, yielding to opposition from utilities and the nuclear and fossil fuel industries, the U.S. Congress reduced the fiscal 2000 federal budget for renewables research by $20 million from the previous year. No surpise then that solar, wind, and geothermal energy sources provided only 2.1 percent of electricity.[41] In the fall of 2003 the Republican-majority House of Representatives rejected a bill specifying that renewable energy should form 10 percent of the national energy by 2010.

Of the $12.3 billion provided in the 2005 U.S. Energy Policy Act, $2.9 billion will go to the coal industry, $4.3 billion to nuclear power, and $1.5 billion to oil and gas companies, leaving a mere $3.6 billion for energy conservation measures and incentives to renewable energy.

The United States has lost the lead it once had in solar power. In the 1980s, Exxon Mobil spent $500 million in an abortive attempt to develop solar cells. It then turned its back on all alternative energy sources. It was not until 2001 that its senior vice president, Rene Dahan, called for a reappraisal of barriers to renewable energy such as wind and solar power. By then Japan had emerged as the world leader in solar power, producing almost half of the global total.

According to the U.S. Solar Energy Industries Association (SEIA), solar photovoltaic (SPV) panels covering a mere 0.3 percent of the country—a quarter of the land occupied by railroads—could provide all of the nation's electricity. But the $5 trillion cost, amounting to nearly half of the GDP at $9 trillion, would raise hackles in Congress.[42]

It is the same story in the wind-energy industry. In the 1980s, California produced more than 90 percent of the world's wind energy. Since then, it and the rest of the United States have fallen behind European countries and even India. In 2002, the wind-driven capacity in the United States was 4,000 MW, a fifth of the European statistic. The potential remains high. It is estimated that the eleven states between North Dakota and Texas could become "the Saudi Arabia of wind energy," with enough gushes to supply a substantial part of the nation's electricity.

The European Wind Energy Association estimates that if the trend toward declining costs continues, wind power will provide one-eighth of global energy by 2020.

One of the important side effects of the 1997 Kyoto Protocol was that it encouraged the signatories to accelerate their green power generation in order to reduce their carbon emissions. This was particularly noticeable in the European Union, which established the European Renewable Energy Council (EREC).

European Union and Wind Power

Since 1998, EU member-states have supported renewable energy projects with a combination of tax benefits, legal mandates, and pricing mechanisms.

This has gone down badly with the opponents of the Kyoto Protocol in Europe, who have increasingly emulated the tactics of their fellow travelers in the United States and received active backing from Exxon Mobil.

"It is clear that a number of well-funded and well-orchestrated media campaigns were carried out by groups that are opposed to the Kyoto Protocol and measures to restrict greenhouse gas emissions," said a leaked internal memo of the Royal Society in London. "There are signs that these groups are preparing similar media and political offensives [in the EU and Canada] ahead of the publication of the IPCC's fourth assessment report in [early] 2007."[43] The leaked document referred to "the concerted efforts" undertaken by these groups in 2004–05 to change the way the British media covered climate change after Prime Minister Tony Blair had declared that "[c]limate change is the single most important issue we face as a global community." It mentioned Exxon Mobil attempting to "influence public opinion" about the threat of climate change.[44]

On the other hand, the EREC's 2002 estimates showed that to meet its Kyoto Protocol commitments, the EU will have to produce, from renewable sources, 22 percent of electricity, or 12 percent of all energy. That means doubling its current total green energy percentage of 6 percent.[45]

In the EU, wind-driven energy grew at an impressive 20 percent a year. European firms became the lead players in the wind turbine market, with annual sales of almost $12 billion. With a capacity of 20,000 MW installed on land alone in 2002, the EU accounted for three-fourths of the globe's wind power output. The capacity will treble by 2008.

Outside Europe and North America, the UN Environment Program's Solar and Wind Energy Assessment report focused on fourteen developing countries, including Brazil, China, and Vietnam. By relying on information provided by satellite measurements and computer models, it found that in Nicaragua, Vietnam, and Mongolia, as much as 40 percent of the land was sufficiently windy to generate electricity. As a result, the estimate for wind-generated electric power was raised from the earlier 200 MW (based on information supplied by the countries' meteorological departments, using outdated techniques) to 40,000 MW—equal to the output of forty typical nuclear stations.

Going by the proportion of electricity produced by wind turbines, Denmark emerged as the world leader, producing a fifth of its electric power by that method. As early as 1999 the Danes had captured half of the market for wind technologies.

Actually, for some European countries, using wind as a source of power meant a return to the past. For centuries, tapping the wind was the domain of the miller, his family, and his hand-set wind sails. In seventeenth century England and Scotland, an estimated ninety thousand windmills were an integral part of rural life. Windmills were a common sight in the Netherlands and Denmark, too. Indeed, the ubiquity of windmills in the Netherlands turned the contraption into a national emblem. It was in 1888 that Charles Francis Brush, an American scientist, built the first large wind turbine for electricity generation.

In more recent times, a revival came in the wake of the oil shock of 1973–74. Members of socially conscious groups erected one or two private windmills in a field or an orchard, especially in Denmark, Germany, and the Netherlands. These continue to function, but they are no longer the norm.

Today windmills are not the charming, stubby type seen in old paintings but are wind turbines—tall, slender, sleek poles supporting shining, stainless steel blades—growing more powerful by the year, the largest one now producing 250 times more electricity than the ones built two decades earlier. "Twenty-eight windmills stand in a perfect lineup near the shore, anchored in about six meters [twenty feet] of water," reported Marlise Simons in the *New York Times* in December 2002, describing a wind farm near the coast of Lelystad in the Netherlands. "The swoosh of wind going over the blades is barely audible, even drowned by the squawking of the seagulls." At any given time, except in winter, hundreds of high-powered turbines, equipped with the latest computer technology, are being erected in the offshore waters of northern Europe. They will contribute most of the increase in wind-driven energy in the EU in the coming years.[46]

Following the successful demonstration of wind farms offshore, governments and companies went full steam ahead with marine wind parks. "Power companies are staking out suitable tracts of sandbanks, reefs, and shallow open waters from the shores of Ireland to the Baltic Sea," reported Simons. "They are joining up with offshore oil and gas companies, including Shell, that have the capability to drill and rig up to 100-ton towers at sea." Offshore, wind blows harder and more steadily than on land, and there are no protestors complaining about the wind farms spoiling the landscape.

On the downside, construction costs for offshore turbines are 50 percent higher than on land, and maintenance is problematic in a region that faces Atlantic gales in winter.

Onshore, engineers solve most maintenance problems with a mobile phone and a laptop computer. When the mobile phone rang, the engineer searched through his laptop, checked the disturbance, and sent a telephone signal back to the computer aboard the wind turbine. If it was the blades that had become stationary, given the right command, they would start spinning again, yielding electricity.

Germany Leads the Way

In postwar West Germany, coal and nuclear firms, along with the strong coal miners' union, had a tight grip over the energy industry. That changed with the 1986 Chernobyl nuclear accident. It revived the flagging antinuclear opposition and gave an impetus to the leaders of the Green Party (officially called the Greens), founded in 1980. The resulting antipollution laws combined with declining coal output put coal-fueled power stations in a disadvantageous position.

Following German reunification in 1990, the federal government passed the Electricity Feed-In Law (FEL). It mandated that utility companies purchase part of their electric power from producers using renewable sources. That unveiled the "wind revolution." The windy north of Germany was the place to launch it. The initial investments were small, with an odd wind turbine popping up over wide areas. This made it expensive for the electric power companies to link their grids to these tiny units. They lobbied the federal government. It yielded in 1997 and imposed a limit of 5 percent on electricity generated by renewable sources.

The next year the political situation changed. The Green Party secured enough parliamentary seats to become the junior partner in the coalition government dominated by the Social Democrats, led by Gerhard Schroeder. Germany thus acquired the distinction of having environmentalists share power at the federal level, an unprecedented development in Europe or elsewhere.

The new red-green administration passed the Renewable Energy Law (REL), which lifted the 5 percent limit on the purchase of green energy. It introduced a nominal surcharge on all energy sales to subsidize the producers of electric power from renewable sources.

"Wind energy is expensive, that is true," said Stephan Kohler, head of Germany's energy agency. "Conventional methods are cheaper, but you have to do both."[47]

Unconvinced, utility firms objected vehemently. They took their case to court, arguing that government subsidies breached the free-trade provisions of the EU. The administration lawyers reasoned that these subsidies were only balancing the accumulated costs of what coal-fired energy had inflicted on the nation at large over many decades. They won.

With this, the construction rate of wind turbines doubled. In December 2002, half of the twenty-eight million people using wind-produced electricity worldwide were in Germany. By mid-2004, Germany became the world's largest producer of wind energy, its fifteen thousand wind turbines generating 15,000 MW, or 6 percent of its total supply.[48]

The German government also actively encouraged small electrical generating units to consume biofuels from crop waste, wood chips, and other plant-based fuel. The progress has been so rapid that the country is reported to be running short of crop wastes, opening up the possibility of an agro-industry growing only fuel crops.

The solar-energy systems, the biofuel power units, and other renewable sources added a further 4 percent to Germany's electric supplies, making the country the leader in green energy. By the end of the decade, the total green energy proportion was set to rise to 15 percent.[49]

Britain's Catch-up

Though Britain is endowed with a mightier wind source than Germany—with winds blowing harder and longer, especially in Scotland—it was far behind Germany in exploiting it commercially. Unlike in Germany, Britain's Green Party was a political cipher. But public opinion very much favored energy from renewable sources.

Yet it was only in 2004, when Britain produced only 2 percent of electricity from green sources, that its Labour government got serious about promoting wind energy by offering subsidies. It announced its plans to increase the number of wind turbines from the existing 1,034 to 4,000 by 2010, divided almost equally between onshore and offshore, to produce 9,000 MW of electricity. This would require a £10 billion ($18 billion) investment in wind power by the utility companies, subsidized by the government to the tune of £1 billion ($1.8 billion).[50] At the end, wind would account for half of the power generated by green sources and supply one-tenth of the national requirement.

The British government's focus fell on Scotland, with the prospect of turning the rugged mountain territory into a Klondike of wind energy. "Twenty-five percent of Europe's wind blows across Scotland, so this is an opportunity and can be cost-effective here," said Matthew Smith, chief executive of Scottish Renewable Forum.[51]

The twenty-one small wind farms built in Scotland so far hold a certain attraction—at least for Elisabeth Rosenthal of the *International Herald Tribune*, reporting from Dumfries, Scotland, in February 2005: "Up close there is a certain eerie beauty about the clusters of turbines that have already started to dot this magnificent landscape [in Dumfries]. Massive structures with spindly, slowly spinning blades that sweep the sky and nearly brush the ground, they look like giant humming insects in a [Salvador] Dalí painting. They are hospital white. Sheep graze about their bases." For each thrumming 400-foot (120-meter) wind turbine, the landowner received an annual rent of £10,000 ($18,000), a substantial sum.

Yet progress was not as smooth as the government and the green lobby would have liked, due to resistance by rural inhabitants. When Scottish Power announced plans in April 2004 to build a wind farm with more than one hundred turbines in Ae

Forest, it faced objections. They fell into four categories: cost, environmental, aesthetics, and technical.

According to the Royal Academy of Engineers, wind-generated electricity costs twice as much as that produced by natural gas, nuclear power, or coal.

As laying a thousand-ton block of concrete for a wind turbine base requires heavy-duty roads for transport to the site, this results in damage to the landscape. Already, the protestors pointed out, peat bogs in northern Scotland had been damaged and fish populations decimated by construction. In the case of offshore wind parks, environmentalists feared they would disturb fishing and spawning grounds and endanger birds that migrated at night. Strangely, the list of protestors in Britain and Norway included the military. Their officers objected to certain windy coastal sites, contending that wind farms were likely to produce false radar echoes and disturb telecommunications.

The more fundamental problem was that even in windswept Scotland, northern Germany, or Denmark, the wind often blows only either intermittently or too strongly to be harnessed commercially. That meant wind parks had to be backed up constantly by conventional power centers. In the pioneering countries of Denmark and Germany, energy regulators have had to scramble to import energy at short notice when the wind was unobliging—through cross-border connectors that link their electrical grids to their neighbors'. The island nation of Britain, however, lacked such links and could not depend on continental European backup. On the other hand, since Scotland already produced 30 percent more electric energy than it needed, it would not require connectors to import power in case winds failed to oblige at the right time.

However, these objections paled when they were juxtaposed with the staggering energy deficit facing Britain in the near future. By 2020, only three of the current twelve nuclear power units will be in operation, reducing nuclear input into the national grid by 16 percent, and most of the coal-fired power stations, now supplying 30 percent of electricity, will also close as they will be unable to meet EU regulations requiring expensive filters to be fitted to counter acid rain—accessories that increase CO_2, which rose by 50 percent between 1990 and 2002 chiefly due to a rise in transport, especially air transport. Even if Britain met its current target for wind power by 2020, wind will barely fill the vacuum left by the near collapse of the nuclear-powered supplies.

Unlike the tardiness on developing and tapping renewable sources of energy shown by successive British governments, their counterparts in India, a former British colony, acted with some foresight.

India's Mixed Results

As early as 1982, India established a Department of Non-Conventional Energy Sources, which it soon upgraded to the Ministry of Non-Conventional Energy Sources (MNES). Besides harnessing traditional wind, solar, and hydro energy, the MNES implemented projects on chemical sources of energy, hydrogen energy, alternative biofuels for surface transportation, geo-thermal energy, and ocean energy.

Also, India has made much use of its hydraulic resources to generate electricity. By 2000, nearly a fifth of the country's electric power came from this source. Yet, in the case of small hydro projects, only a tenth of the potential of 15,000 MW has been realized so far.

A similar situation prevailed in the field of green energy. Though the potential for expanding the use of technologies for green energy generation was vast, actual progress was slow because of the high initial outlay. At the turn of the twenty-first century, green energy amounted to only 4,000 MW against a potential of nearly 100,000 MW.

In 1985 the government launched the extensive Wind Resource Assessment. The initial estimates of wind energy at 20,000 MW were later raised to 45,000 MW as the height of a typical wind turbine rose to 50 meters (165 feet). Besides the coastal terrain of eastern, southern, and western states, some inland areas of other states have potential. The newly established Center for Wind Energy Technology, based in Tamil Nadu, is the nation's technical headquarters for wind power development at home and abroad.

In 2001, with its installed wind turbine capacity at 1,700 MW—up from a puny 32 MW in 1990—India then ranked fifth on the planet. Since then, with the participation of the private sector in the industry, the pace has quickened, with the total wind energy capacity rising 2.5 times in four years. India has also spawned a wind turbine manufacturing industry. Indeed, by 2005, Suzlon Energy, an Indian company, became the fifth-largest wind turbine fabrication company in the world. It grabbed newspaper headlines when it started work on a $60 million factory in the eastern Chinese port city of Tianjin to produce wind turbines there.[52]

India is richly endowed with sunshine. The daily solar radiation of 4 to 7 KWH per square meter received in the country is one of the highest on the planet. Unsurprisingly, the MNES's solar energy program—covering both solar thermal and solar photovoltaic technologies—has expanded to become one of the largest in the world.

Its solar thermal program involves 500,000 square meters (5,380,000 square feet) of collector area and 485,000 solar cookers, and is focused on popularizing solar water heaters and cookers. Solar water heating is applied at a variety of sites, from residences to hotels to industrial processes. Solar air heating is used in timber kilns and for drying agricultural produce. Solar stills are deployed to supply distilled water in rural hospitals and battery-charging stations, and as drinking water in remote arid areas. After promoting the sale of the box solar cooker—designed to cook food for up to five people, and supplied with or without electrical backup—the MNES came up with the dish solar cooker, designed to serve up to fifteen persons.

The MNES has also installed solar photovoltaic systems in rural areas to supply power for street and home lighting and running water pumps. These systems have been integrated into local electrical grids. However, the aggregate capacity of 107 MW is unimpressive.

By comparison, in rural areas there has been substantial progress in the field of chemical sources of energy.

Of an estimated potential of 12 million bio-gas plants, about 3.44 million family-type plants have been set up so far.

While the Indian Republic has a thriving democratic system, an all-India environmentalist party has not yet emerged. Much of the conservation and green energy campaigning is done by a small number of urban-based activists often belonging to Friends of the Earth or Greenpeace, who receive much sympathetic media coverage and comment. They play an important role in raising consciousness about green energy and the environment among the urban middle and upper-middle classes, who count most in the day-to-day functioning of a democracy.

Such is not the case in China, where the Communist Party and government remain the sole repository of decision-making, with little or no role for nongovernmental organizations.

China, a Late Arrival

The breakneck growth in China's economy over a quarter century has wrought immense damage to its environment. Due to the extraordinarily rapid increase in urbanization and industrialization, China, with one-sixth of the world's population in 2004, accounted for one-sixth of global greenhouse emissions due to the 50 percent increase in pollutants in the Chinese atmosphere. Sulfur pollution created acid rain across much of the country, affecting forests and agriculture and causing damage to buildings. Acid rain fell not only on a third of China but also on parts of its neighbors. Seven out of ten Chinese rivers and lakes were so polluted by toxins that they could no longer be used for potable water.[53]

By 2004, China was home to sixteen of the twenty most air-polluted cities in the world. More than 100 million Chinese lived in places where air quality was described as "very dangerous."

Smoggy gray skies, caused by coal-burning power stations and fast-multiplying cars, choked every major Chinese city. Beijing in the spring of 2006 was typical. A combination of dust storms, exhaust gases from vehicles, and dust and rubble from construction sites choked the skies and covered the streets in a yellow haze, forcing the local authorities to issue health warnings and advise that children be kept indoors behind closed doors and windows. The number of outpatients with respiratory complaints at the two biggest hospitals exceeded the average by a third.

Such a situation arose despite the fact that by the mid-1990s, China had acquired a substantial body of environmental legislation, including many sector-specific laws. The Environmental Protection Law set up the Environmental Protection Agency, and required environmental impact assessments and reports for new construction projects to be issued by environmental protection bureaus and environmental protection offices at the city or county level or higher.

But it was only in 1996 that the Chinese authorities, backed by financial aid from the European Commission's Environment Directorate General, set up an interministerial committee to implement the program on economic planning and environmental protection, with an important role assigned to the State Environmental Protection Administration (SEPA).

As a result, between 1997 and 2000, total spending on the environment doubled, from 0.8 percent of the GDP to 1.5 percent.

In its May 2000 report, the China Council for International Cooperation on the Environment and Development outlined the practical problems, which applied as much to China as they did to India. "Rapid industrialization combined with underpricing of natural resources and energy has provided little incentive to use them efficiently," it said. "Although the legal framework is comprehensive, implementation has been weak. However, as the Chinese government has been confronted with billions of dollars in damage by floods and significant health costs due to pollution, the environment has become a higher priority." But, it added, charges and fines levied on those producing industrial emissions were too low to act as an incentive for investment in reducing industrial pollution. "The authorities often have difficulty to enforce compliance by both urban-based state-owned enterprises and rural township and village enterprises, where highly polluting, outdated technologies exacerbate environmental problems. Multinationals often follow international standards as a matter of internal policy, and foreign investors are more likely to comply with high environmental standards."[54]

In October 2005, Zhang Lijun, deputy director of the Environmental Protection Agency, warned that pollution levels could quadruple in fifteen years due to energy consumption and a big jump in car usage. When such statements issued periodically went unheeded, Chinese prime minster Wen Jiabo intervened publicly.

"Environmental protection has become the weakest aspect in social and economic development," he told a top-level environmental policy group in April 2006. "The implementation of green laws is not strict at all." He revealed that the government had failed to achieve eight of the twenty environmental goals. Most disturbingly, the plan to cut emissions of pollution chemicals by 10 percent and energy consumption by 20 percent by 2011 was not on track.[55]

In the sphere of renewable energy, after a period of long neglect, the authorities decided to act. In 2005 the National People's Congress passed its first Renewable Energy Law, to become effective January 1, 2006. "Strengthening the development and use of renewable energies is a must for us to address increasingly serious energy and environmental issues," asserted President Hu Jintao at a renewable-energy conference in Beijing. The plan was to double renewable energy—including hydropower, currently at 4.5 percent—from the present 7 percent by 2020. China aimed to increase its wind-energy capacity from 1,260 MW to 20,000 MW by 2020—which will still be a mere one-twelfth of its potential.[56]

The major hurdle to these ambitious plans in China is the same as in India—a high capital outlay in a country where there are other, more lucrative channels for investment.

TWELVE

Summary and Conclusions

"The Stone Age did not end for lack of stones, and the oil age will end long before the world runs out of oil."
—Sheikh Ahmad Zaki Yamani, oil minister of Saudi Arabia, 1962–86[1]

Whereas an average American uses 69 oil barrels a year and a Briton 32, a Chinese consumes only four barrels and an Indian two.[2]

"None of us in Asia should fall victim to the strategies of outsiders. The only way to counter the geopolitics of others is to have our own geopolitics."
—Mani Shankar Aiyar, petroleum minister of India, 2004–06[3]

"In the developing world they use twice as much oil as industrialized countries do to produce each unit of output."
—Kofi Annan, United Nations secretary-general, 1997–2007[4]

By 2020 the world population will be up by 20 percent to 8.1 billion, but electricity demand will rise by 85 percent, and total energy demand by 57 percent.[5]

There is no historical precedent for a single mineral coming to dominate human life as completely as petroleum has since it was first extracted in commercial quantities in the mid-nineteenth century. But then, it has taken natural processes tens of millions of years to produce oil and gas reserves underground.

Oil, the end product, is such a unique combination of carbon and hydrogen—the elements of life on the planet—that it provides not just fuel for machines and electric-generating plants but also heat for buildings and cooking food, and feedstock for manufacturing fertilizers, fibers, glues, lubricants, plastics, pharmaceuticals, and rubber.

The use of oil in its heavy form of bitumen in building roads and coating walls and hulls of ships goes back to antiquity. Equally ancient are the roots of worshipping fire, originating in the eternal flames caused by natural gas leaks from under the rocks in the Caspian region.

It was in this area, near Baku, that a Russian mining engineer, Fyodor N. Semyonov, successfully deployed a cable rig to drill a well and struck petroleum in 1846. It would be a dozen years later that the first commercial oil well would be drilled in Ontario, Canada, to be followed by a lucky strike at Titusville, Pennsylvania, in 1859.

Americans were vigorous in exploring and extracting petroleum, using it mainly as an illuminant in the form of kerosene. Enterprising engineers and industrialists were quick to build the first motor car with an internal combustion engine, invented by a German scientist, Carl Benz, in 1882.

Within a decade of George Selden in 1885 securing a patent for a gasoline-powered automobile—which had outperformed its rivals run on steam or electricity—Henry Ford had introduced his Model A. This would unveil a new chapter in Western civilization.

With drillers striking a gusher at Spindletop, Texas, in 1901, the United States was set to displace the Russian Caucasus as the world's largest oil producer.

With fuel oil replacing coal around 1908, the use of petroleum spread to cargo ships in the United States. The advantages of switching from steam engines to internal combustion engines were obvious: reduction in fuel cost by three-quarters, gain in cargo volume by a third, and further savings resulting from shedding engineers and coal stokers.

In Europe, Germany's kaiser Wilhelm II emulated American ship owners by ordering the German Navy to switch from coal to oil. This step heralded a change in international relations as profound as the introduction of gunpowder in 1040.

The Oil Age

In the century that has passed since, oil has established itself as the preeminent commodity both in war and in peace.

The ubiquity of cars, the universal use of polyethylene bags and plasticware, the popularity of air travel, and the global spread of chemical fertilizers: despite their diversity, they are all rooted in the same source—oil. Oil is truly Big Business, with an annual turnover of $2.4 *trillion*. Two of the top three corporations in the world by market value are Exxon Mobil and Gazprom, well ahead of Wal-Mart, Toyota, and Citigroup. And four of the seven most profitable companies in the world are in oil.

In the United States, the preeminence of petroleum can be traced to the Standard Oil Company, owned by John D. Rockefeller's family. It came to dominate the petroleum scene not only as a virtual monopolist in oil refining and marketing but also as the leading exporter of kerosene. By 1891, Standard Oil accounted for 90 percent of American exports of kerosene and controlled 70 percent of the world market. The astronomical profits from the petroleum industry enabled Rockefeller to get into coal, copper, iron, shipping, and banking, and to push his personal wealth ultimately to a staggering $2 billion ($30 billion today).[6] Contrary to all expectations, following the breakup of the Standard Oil Company in 1911, the stock prices of the successor companies almost doubled, with Rockefeller, holding shares in the latter, benefiting greatly.

The entry of the United States into World War I in the spring of 1917 on the side of the Allies made a huge difference. Important though the deployment of American soldiers was, the supply of abundant oil from the United States, then pumping two-thirds of the world's output, was even more critical given the paucity of petroleum that dogged the opposing Central Powers. For the first time in history, tanks and warplanes equipped with internal combustion engines, fueled by oil products, had become the chief weapons of warfare.

Washington's massive military intervention in Europe and the Middle East widened the horizons of the U.S. industry, especially oil, which had until then focused on central and southern America. The war ended with the Allies tacitly agreeing to adopt an "open door" doctrine toward one another, which translated into giving U.S. capital equal access into the Middle East.

Participation in the war had brought about active collaboration between the U.S. administration and the petroleum industry, led by Standard Oil of New Jersey. Following the armistice, this nexus between government and oil continued. When, in 1920, Walter Teagle, the successor to Rockefeller at Standard Oil of New Jersey, decided to branch out into oil exploration and production abroad, he received the active support of the administration of U.S. president Woodrow Wilson.

In a sense, what Washington did was to follow the example of the European governments, especially London's. It was in Britain that the government intervened directly to save the sinking fortunes of a private citizen, William Knox D'Arcy, who had been financing a never-ending venture to find oil in Iran since 1901. It then progressed to buying a majority share in the Anglo-Persian Oil Company (APOC) after it had struck lucky in Iran, with the proviso that APOC guarantee oil supplies to the British Navy for the next two decades. This agreement, codified into law on the eve of World War I, became the modus operandi of economic imperialism exercised by Britain, which was also then foremost in political imperialism, controlling territories populated by a quarter of humanity.

A foreign power exercising economic domination over another country is freed from the expense and responsibilities of administrative-political control while exploiting the labor and natural resources of the territory. As it was, over the past many generations, the United States had practiced economic imperialism in its relations with most Caribbean and Latin American countries, providing diplomatic-military backing to American commercial interests.

The Middle East, however, had been the playground mainly of the British, keen to keep their sea lanes to the Indian Empire secure. After World War I, a reluctant acceptance of the Open Door Policy by Britain and France—the main beneficiaries of the collapse of the Ottoman Empire—allowed American oil companies a foothold first in Iraq and then in Bahrain and Kuwait. Their big break came in Saudi Arabia, when King Ibn Saud awarded a massive oil concession to Standard Oil of California (Socal) in 1933. With the finding of oil five years later, American petroleum corporations were poised to outperform APOC and the smaller Compagnie Française des Pétroles in the Persian Gulf region.

Later, U.S. president Franklin Roosevelt would succinctly summarize the carve-up thus: the Iranian oil is British, the Saudi ours, and the rest is to be shared. The oil nexus between the United States and Saudi Arabia continues unabated, albeit slightly impaired by the preponderance of Saudi citizens among the hijackers who attacked New York and metropolitan Washington in September 2001.

Roosevelt made the above statement in 1944 during World War II. As with World War I, the universal verdict after the end of the second global conflict was that petroleum was the number-one determinant of the Allied success.

The Postwar Era

Unlike in the post–World War I era, the United States now became the lead player in the geopolitics of oil, determined to keep Soviet influence and the Soviet military as far as possible from the hydrocarbon resources in Iran, Iraq, and the rest of the Middle East—a doctrine announced by the U.S. Joint Chiefs of Staff in November 1946. Five months later, U.S. president Harry Truman put an ideological gloss on it by promising aid to any nation "threatened with Communist subjugation."

The anti-Communist crusade suited the hereditary rulers in the Persian Gulf region. During World War II, when Iran was occupied by Britain and the Soviet Union, the Tudeh (Communist) Party was allowed to function. It gained strong support among oil workers. By staging a series of strikes in 1946, the pro-Tudeh union won concessions from the British-owned Anglo-Iranian Oil Company (AIOC). This worried both the AIOC and Muhammad Reza Pahlavi. When the Soviets joined the Allies in mid-1941, the Iraqi government of pro-British King Faisal II permitted the Iraqi Communist Party to function openly. It organized oil workers. But when it called a strike in mid-1946, it faced government repression. Yet it managed to maintain its standing among oil employees. On the Arabian Peninsula, King Ibn Saud was staunchly opposed to communism because of its adherence to atheism.

With the discovery of the gigantic Ghawar oil field in Saudi Arabia in 1948–50, the Persian Gulf region reserves rose to a half of the global total, leaving those in the United States far behind.

The Washington-Riyadh links tightened further. American weapons and other military aid began arriving in the region, and the U.S. Navy established a permanent presence in Bahrain. The Pentagon's strategic aim was to safeguard oil supplies in the area. That objective remains unchanged to this day.

The oil revolution swept through a postwar Europe busily reconstructing its shattered economy, and the United States witnessed mammoth highway construction, giving birth to a suburban civilization. During the 1950s, the demand for oil doubled in a decade to 21 million bpd. American oil corporations were in the forefront to exploit the hydrocarbon riches of the Persian Gulf region.

In the underpopulated Arab Gulf monarchies, with their subjects living in a tribal social system bereft of a public education scheme and manufacturing industry, there was no discernible opposition to Western petroleum corporations. The semi-independent hereditary rulers, propped up by the British (except in the case of Saudi Arabia), were the final arbiters of authority.

Contrary was the case in Iran, which had experienced a constitutional revolution in 1906–07, resulting in an elected parliament. Within four decades of that revolution, an educated, politically conscious middle class, imbued with national pride and led by the charismatic Muhammad Mussadiq, emerged to challenge economic imperialism in the form of the Anglo-Iranian Oil Company (AIOC). Its employees, organized by the pro-Tudeh unions, formed the backbone of the confrontation with imperialist Britain. Together they succeeded in putting the shah to flight in August 1953—only to be countered by a coup masterminded by the American and British intelligence agencies. The AIOC returned to Iran but not as the sole operator. It took a minority stake in a consortium dominated by American petroleum corporations—an unmistakable sign of their ascendancy in the critical region.

For the next two decades, five American oil majors dominated the hydrocarbon world, providing enough evidence for their critics to come up with the slogan "Oil, Power, and Empire." And yet an alternative title, "Seven Sisters," pertaining to the Anglo-Dutch-American cartel of seven corporations, seemed more appropriate. Coined by the late Anthony Sampson, a British journalist, for his book on oil, it applied to (American) Esso (later Exxon), Gulf, Socal, Socony (later Mobil) and Texaco; (Anglo-Dutch) Royal Dutch Shell; and British Petroleum. This cartel produced four out of five barrels of the world's oil and refined three out of five barrels. Since it controlled a majority of the marketing facilities, it fixed prices to protect its profits without any regard for the interests of the oil-producing countries.

To be sure, the cartel encountered periodic resistance and competition. In 1958 the Soviet Union attempted to enter the international petroleum market by releasing cheap oil. The cartel responded by slashing its prices at the expense of the oil-producing countries. That in turn led to the formation of OPEC in 1960 by Iran, Iraq, Kuwait, Saudi Arabia, and Venezuela. Its aim was to make the Western oil companies coordinate their production plans in consultation with the host governments. But the oil cartel was too power-drunk to pay attention to OPEC.

The Six-Day War in June 1967 wrought a sea change in the Arab Middle East and in the geopolitics of oil. The swift and degrading defeat Israel inflicted on Egypt, Syria, and Jordan highlighted the Arabs' military weakness. That drove them to wield the oil weapon.

On the initiative of Kuwaiti ruler Sheikh Sabah III ibn al Salim I, five oil-producing Arab states formed the Organization of Arab Petroleum Exporting Countries (OAPEC) in 1968. Its significance would rise considerably when it emerged that two-thirds of the increased demand of 21 million bpd during the 1960s was met by the growth in oil output in the Persian Gulf region and North Africa.

Rising Resistance to Western Oil Cartel

Encouraged by the formation of OAPEC and the Soviet Union's assistance to develop its oil fields, the Iraqi government, run by the Arab Baath Socialist Party since 1968, nationalized the Western-owned Iraq Petroleum Company in 1972 and later took over the American and Dutch interests in the Basrah Petroleum Company, operating in the south. Its actions had the active support of the oil workers, influenced by the Iraqi Communist Party.

In October 1973, Egypt and Syria mounted preplanned attacks on Israeli forces in the occupied Arab territories with the aim of regaining Egyptian or Syrian land. OAPEC members imposed an oil embargo on the United States and the Netherlands for helping Israel militarily. Algeria doubled the price of its crude to $9.25 a barrel. And the Persian Gulf producers pushed the figure to $11.65 a barrel, amounting to 4.5 times the prewar price. OPEC backed the hike.

For the first time since its inception, OPEC made its price stick. And OAPEC's oil embargo hurt the American economy.

Neither of OAPEC's conditions about the return of the Arab territories seized by Israel in 1967, nor the restoration of the Palestinians' rights, was fulfilled by Israel. Yet its members ended up lifting the oil boycott after five months, listening to the pleas especially of British prime minister Edward Heath not to weaken the West and thus strengthen the Communist bloc.

Still, members of the Organization for Economic Cooperation and Development (OECD), a group of the richest nations, suffered an economic recession that persisted until late 1976—when OPEC accounted for more than half of the world's oil output and seven-eighths of oil exports.

The First Oil Shock highlighted several facets of the global economy and politics, and set off chain reactions in different spheres.

One, it validated Henry Kissinger's statement that "cheap and plentiful oil" was the "basic premise" on which post–World War II Western capitalism was built.[7] Two, it illustrated dramatically oil's primacy in Western economies and politics. For instance, its ill effects—high inflation followed by rising wage demands feeding the inflationary spiral—paved the way for the defeat of Britain's Labour government in 1979. Indeed, its fallout caused political turmoil even in such developing countries as India, where Prime Minister Indira Gandhi declared a state of emergency in mid-1976. Three, the First Oil Shock left the global economy more volatile than before. Four, it underscored the West's dependency on Arab and Iranian oil. Five, it led to greater efforts to develop hydrocarbon resources outside OPEC and OAPEC. They would bear fruit a decade later, with non-OPEC production outpacing OPEC's. Six, high petroleum prices made many exploratory projects in the hitherto inaccessible areas of the North Sea and Alaska economically feasible. Seven, expensive offshore prospecting and drilling became economical. Eight, natural gas, which before was routinely burned, now became valuable.

Nine, for the first time Western governments took energy conservation seriously. The U.S. Congress passed the Energy Policy and Conservation Act of 1975 to set the Corporate Average Fuel Economy (CAFE) standards for automobiles.

Ten, the overflowing treasuries of the oil-rich states led governments to nationalize Western petroleum corporations, thus drastically reducing their hydrocarbon assets. Eleven, the nationalized oil companies enabled the rulers and their hangers-on in the Gulf monarchies and Iran under the shah to line their pockets, thus increasing the already wide disparities between the superaffluent and the rest of the populace.

War between Two Oil-Rich Nations

As in the early 1950s, so now, the petroleum industry in Iran determined the course of its history. The oil boom caused a vast influx of rural migrants into cities, who backed the Islamic revolutionary movement. And it was the oil workers' indefinite strike in December 1978 that dried up the shah's exchequer and delivered the final blow to the monarchy.

The toppling of the shah in 1979—in which pro-Tudeh oil workers played a vital role by going on an indefinite strike at the height of the anti-shah revolutionary movement in 1978—caused a political earthquake in the region, resulting in another major price hike. The instability increased when Iraq's president Saddam Hussein invaded the Islamic Republic of Iran in September 1980. Oil prices rose again. So the period 1979–81 became associated with the Second Oil Shock. As a result, as mentioned above, natural gas, which had until then been flared, came to the fore, and its value rose sixtyfold.

The war between two oil-producing neighbors opened a new chapter in the geopolitics of petroleum. The commodity became a crucial factor in determining the course of the eight-year-long conflict.

Saudi Arabia stepped in to cover the oil deficit caused by the war, thereby making it even more indispensable to the United States as well as France and West Germany. U.S. president Ronald Reagan declared in October 1981 that the United States would not stand idly by and see Saudi Arabia "taken over by anyone who would shut off the oil."

By then a 50,000-strong joint task force, called the Rapid Deployment Force, at the MacDill Air Force Base in Tampa, Florida—established by President Jimmy Carter to safeguard Gulf oil supplies and build up the American Fifth Fleet, based on the British-controlled island of Diego Garcia in the Indian Ocean—was well established. Reagan would later rename it the Central Command (Centcom).

What ultimately compelled Iran to accept the UN-mediated cease-fire was the collapse of oil prices in spring 1986 to $10 a barrel due to the flooding of the market by Kuwait and Saudi Arabia, aimed at reducing Tehran's income.

Thus oil and its price proved to be *the* determining factors in the last century's longest conventional war.

In the West, the return of cheap, plentiful petroleum led to the abandonment of the official programs of energy conservation, and consumers resumed their old profligate ways with a vengeance.

Iraq as Swing Producer

The year 1993 was a turning point in the Great Game of Oil. China became a net importer of the commodity as a result of a decade and a half of economic reform that brought prosperity to tens of millions. The state-owned China National Petroleum Corporation (CNPC) eyed Iraq's oil hungrily. Russia and France wanted Iraq's petroleum industry freed from the United Nations sanctions to enable Baghdad to return the loans it had secured from them during the Iran-Iraq War.

Thus the Chinese-French-Russian axis that emerged at the UN Security Council by 1995 was guided as much by hydrocarbon interests as it was by strategic considerations.

Later, since Iraq was exempted from OPEC quotas due to the suffering of its people caused by UN sanctions, and since it was given carte blanche by the UN Security Council to rehabilitate its petroleum industry, the resulting flexibility transformed it into a swing producer. This was ironic. What had driven U.S. president George Herbert Walker Bush in August 1990 to reverse Iraq's invasion of Kuwait was the prospect of Saddam Hussein annexing Kuwait and thus doubling the oil deposits under his control and challenging Saudi Arabia's status as the swing producer stemming from its top position in the reserves league table.

In 2000, when oil prices reached a ten-year-high of $34 a barrel due to the robust global economy, Bill Clinton realized, gloomily, that a dip in the record Iraqi output of 3.6 million bpd would lift prices even higher when the United States was importing three-fifths of its petroleum needs.

When oil futures hit $37 a barrel on September 20, Clinton ordered the release of 1 million bpd for thirty days from the U.S. Strategic Petroleum Reserve, an unprecedented move in peacetime.

Rice's Astonishing Ignorance

The above analysis establishes unequivocally the central role oil has played since 1910 in shaping the foreign policies of not only the United States and major European powers in war and in peace but also the leading Middle Eastern countries. Yet, appearing before the U.S. Senate Foreign Relations Committee in April 2006, Secretary of State Condoleezza Rice said, "Nothing has taken me aback more as secretary of state than the way that the politics of energy is—I will use the word 'warping'—diplomacy around the world." The statement was all the more astonishing as it came from a former director of Chevron—who had one of the company's oil tankers named after her.[8]

For many years, the United States' increasing dependence on oil from an unstable region—the site of the world's first Islamic revolution and two wars, one of them the longest of the twentieth century—has been a matter of deep concern in Washington. But instead of coming clean on the subject with the public and adopting a twin-track policy of energy conservation and vigorous development of renewable energy sources, governmental policy makers and oil executives have resorted to exaggerating the hydrocarbon potential of the non-Arab, non-Iranian areas.

Clinton and his aides painted the Caspian Basin as the Klondike of oil. His successor, George Walker Bush, an oilman, followed this policy with redoubled enthusiasm.

Oilmen in the Oval Office

Once George W. Bush had installed his team of oilmen (Dick Cheney and Donald Evans) and automobile lobbyists (Andrew Card and Spencer Abraham) in the White House, he appointed a National Energy Policy (NEP) Development Group, chaired by Cheney.

The NEP document published in May 2001 outdid the Clinton administration in presenting a rosy scenario. Of the long list of non-Arab, non-Iranian (NANI) countries with promising hydrocarbon prospects, only nine mattered: Angola and Nigeria; Azerbaijan, Kazakhstan, and Russia; and Brazil, Colombia, Mexico, and Venezuela.

The NANI states' proven reserves were only a third of those of the Persian Gulf region, which has two-thirds of global oil reserves. The Latin American countries' consumption would rise by nearly 80 percent by 2025—well above the increase of about 60 percent in their output. In the three former Soviet states, the growth in their production would barely meet the rise in domestic usage. Only in Africa would there be an excess for export.

As for the Persian Gulf region's hydrocarbons, the Bush administration maintained a studied silence in public about Iraqi oil even though its top officials had started making clandestine plans for it within weeks of taking office.

After Saddam's overthrow in 2003, a plan for Iraq's petroleum industry prepared jointly by the State Department and Big Oil recommended maintaining the status quo, with the state-owned Iraq National Oil Company (INOC) to be opened up to foreign investment after the industry had been rehabilitated under Washington-approved Iraqi managers. But there was a competing supersecret Pentagon plan that recommended selling all Iraqi oil fields to private firms to boost production beyond Iraq's normal OPEC quota in order to destroy the cartel.

As the word about denationalization spread among INOC employees and their relatives, a concerted sabotage of oil pipelines and other facilities ensued. Earlier, in the chaos of the invasion and its aftermath, much equipment was looted from pipelines, pumping stations, and other oil installations. Petroleum production fell to 1.2 million bpd and later stabilized at around 1.8 million bpd, half of the record high under the ousted regime.

Article 109 of the Iraqi constitution endorsed by a referendum in October 2005 described hydrocarbons as "national Iraqi property." The Iraqi constitution thus became the latest in a series upholding state ownership of hydrocarbons dating back to the Mexican constitution of 1917. It was this constitutional provision that President Lazaro Cardenas, a hugely popular leader, invoked when he nationalized the petroleum industry, until then dominated by British interests, much to the acclaim of the oil workers' unions and the rest of the citizenry.

The enforcement of the latest Iraqi document reduced Western petroleum corporations' full access to only 6 percent of the world's oil reserves and partial access—through joint ventures or production-sharing agreements—to another 11 percent.[9]

In sum, the dialectical tension between the oil-hungry West, led by the United States, and the oil-rich, predominantly non-Western countries, centered chiefly around prices, continues. Since the latter group consists largely of Muslim states, which together possess nearly three-quarters of the global oil reserves and many of which are ruled by laws derived from *sharia*—Islamic canon—there is a need to examine the relationship between hydrocarbons and Islam.

Oil and Islam

For all practical purposes, the latest Iraqi constitution, drafted by its elected representatives and reflecting popular opinion, has turned the country into an Islamic republic of Iraq. An article in the constitution states that *sharia* is the fundamental source of Iraqi legislation. Another article says that no Iraqi law shall violate the undisputed principles of Islam.

Article 109, pertaining to the oil and gas resources of Iraq, derives from the view held by Islamic scholars, both Shiite and Sunni, that minerals belong to "the community"—that is, the public at large, represented by a legitimate government.

This religious opinion, or fatwa, determines the hydrocarbon policy not only of the overwhelmingly Shiite Islamic Republic of Iran but also of the predominantly Sunni kingdom of Saudi Arabia. The same is true of the remaining Sunni-ruled monarchies of the Persian Gulf region. Altogether, these eight countries possess more than three-fifths of the global petroleum reserves, and will provide 84 percent of the world's oil exports in 2020.[10] The Gulf Arab monarchies are authoritarian or semi-authoritarian. In Kuwait, the most liberal of them, voting for the parliament is limited to only a quarter of adult citizens.

Those who advocate democracy in the Arab world in its own right and also as a stabilizing factor in the hydrocarbon-rich part of the world should recognize the fact that Islam—in both its religious and political aspects—has a strong hold over Arab masses. Witness the electoral success of the Muslim Brotherhood in Egypt in 2005, and the landslide victory of Hamas—the Arabic acronym meaning Islamic Resistance Movement—in the Palestinian parliamentary election of 2006. Any sustained progress toward a representative government in the oil-rich Gulf monarchies can only be made if there is a marriage between Islam and democracy.

Muslims demanding a representative government derive their inspiration not from the practice of Grecian towns in antiquity but from the Koran. They quote the verses that read: "Take counsel with them in the affair," and "Those who answer their Lord and perform the prayer, their affair being counsel between them" (3:159 and 42:36).[11] These Koranic verses appear in the preamble to the constitution of the Islamic Republic of Iran. It is noteworthy that the official title of the country says "republic"—not "state" or "emirate." That means power in Iran lies with the public.

It is also worth noting that in the twenty-seven years since the Islamic revolution, the regime has held nine presidential, seven parliamentary, four Experts' Assembly, and two local elections, not to mention three referendums on the name of the country and the constitution. Iran's supreme leader is chosen by the popularly elected Assembly of Experts.

As Iran is anathema to the George W. Bush administration— although not Saudi Arabia, a fundamentalist state run strictly according to *sharia* since its inception in 1932—there was no mention of it in the NEP document's forecasts. Nor did it dwell on the dramatic entry into the oil market of China and India, fast-industrializing giant nations.

The Dragon Enters the Oil Market

When China found Iran keen to get its oil companies to participate in its hydrocarbon industry, it responded positively. Other Chinese firms got involved in Iran's automobile and telecommunications industries and built railroads and highways.

It was at China's behest that the six-member Shanghai Cooperation Organization (SCO) conferred observer status on Iran in 2005. The SCO included China's central Asian neighbors and Russia.

Within five years of the disintegration of the Soviet Union in 1991, China and Russia came together under the umbrella of the SCO with the common aim of fighting extremism and irredentism. In 2001, the two neighbors signed a friendship treaty based on their common belief in a multipolar world. This proved to be a preamble to the import of Russian oil into China, which reached 300,000 bpd in three years.

In central Asia, the CNPC turned to Kazakhstan with a $4.7 billion oil deal in 1997. By so doing, freshly independent Kazakhstan balanced its pro-Western tilt while loosening its close ties with Russia. By bringing the Kazakh oil to its underdeveloped, politically restive Xinjiang province, China intended to raise local living standards and pacify irredentist elements.

By investing heavily in Angola and Sudan, China increased its African imports to about half those of the Persian Gulf region. However, this is unlikely to last. It is estimated that by 2020, the Persian Gulf shipments will cover four-fifths of China's imports. By then China's middle class will have doubled to 40 percent of the population, with the Chinese economy becoming number two in the world.[12]

India's Asian Perspective

In 1947 independent India inherited a privately owned, eighty-year-old oil field in the northeastern region of Assam with a modest output.

The Indian government's decision to place oil and gas in the public sector went down badly with Western companies. When they refused to share their expertise in prospecting and production with the state-owned Oil and Natural Gas Corporation (ONGC), India turned to the Soviet Union. Indian students enrolled in the geophysics and petroleum engineering faculties of Soviet universities. Soviet oil engineers and geologists working with their Indian counterparts discovered oil not only in northeast India but also in the western state of Gujarat.

But domestic reserves were not expected to amount to much, and India's policy makers were reconciled to the fact that their country would continue to rely heavily on imports from the Persian Gulf region. So they decided to build an aircraft carrier group primarily to safeguard the oil and liquefied natural gas (LNG) tanker sea lanes.[13]

BLOOD OF THE EARTH

However, India's naval achievement will pale before the 281 ships and half a million members of the U.S. Navy—outnumbering those of the next seventeen naval nations combined—to ensure inter alia the security of the United States' oil supplies.[14]

The three-and-a-half-fold increase in oil prices to $70 a barrel between 2002 and 2006, with gasoline rates showing no sign of dropping below $3 a gallon, focused the minds of American politicians as never before. They knew that while U.S. industry had so far managed to absorb higher fuel costs, consumers—endowed with voting powers—were struggling to cope with the high gasoline price.

Fierce Competition in a Tight Market

"The balance of world oil supply and demand has become so precarious that even small acts of sabotage or local insurrection have a significant impact on oil prices," said Alan Greenspan, chairman of the U.S. Federal Reserve Bank from 1987 to January 2006, in his congressional testimony in June 2006. He added that among oil producers, only Saudi Arabia had unveiled a $50 billion plan to raise output by 1.5 million bpd by 2009, and that he doubted that others would be able to pump enough crude to meet future demand.[15]

In other words, the much-dreaded Hubbert's Peak for oil production predicted between 2006 and 2017 is fast approaching. What is worse, the subsequent rapid fall in output will occur at a time when the demands of China and India in particular will be moving sharply in the opposite direction.

Given the continued tightness of the energy market, the battle for hydrocarbon reserves will escalate, its intensity reaching the level of the European nations' violent scramble for colonies in the nineteenth century. The crucial difference this time will be that the impending struggle will go beyond a handful of European powers and will include China and India as independent players.

"The renewed focus on energy," noted Daniel Yergin, the famed oil expert, "is also fueled by the threat of terrorism, instability in some exporting nations, a nationalist backlash, fears of a scramble for supplies, geopolitical rivalries, and countries' fundamental need for energy to power their own economic growth."[16]

In other words, the century-old geopolitics of oil have become more complicated with two more ravenous meganations in dire search of hydrocarbons led by politicians who are determined to prevent debilitating energy deficits that could trigger sociopolitical turmoil, and debilitating terrorist activity in the oil-rich Iraq that threatens to spill over into the rest of the region.

Its spread to the oil-rich eastern province of Saudi Arabia is particularly worrisome to the international market. In a well-planned attack on the Abqaiq oil facility in February 2006, Al Qaida operators, wearing the uniforms of Saudi Aramco guards and driving company cars, managed to pass through two of the three perimeter gates of the facility and were only challenged at the last gate. The subsequent gun battle lasted two hours, resulting in the deaths of the infiltrators and damage to pipelines. Had the terrorists managed to sabotage the facility, which processes a staggering 7 million bpd to be loaded onto tankers for export, petroleum futures would have registered a rise of as much as $20 a barrel.[17]

For the present, oil- and gas-producing nations are feeling a rush of power as never before.

Growing Power of Hydrocarbon–Haves

Nothing illustrates the growing clout of hydrocarbon-rich nations better than the case of Venezuela, a country of twenty-six million ruled by Hugo Chavez, a popular, leftist leader, since late 1998. During his tenure in office, Venezuelans participated in eight elections and referendums in eight years, with his opponents controlling 170 of the 180 newspapers and magazines and all of the five privately owned television channels.[18] By making adroit use of oil revenues at home and abroad, and by selling petroleum at a discount to the Caribbean and Central American nations, he has broken new ground in the deployment of hydrocarbon assets as instruments of constructive diplomacy.

Chavez's example was followed by the freshly elected president of Bolivia, Evo Morales, who, as promised, nationalized the gas fields on May Day 2006.

As expected, Washington disapproved. "Let me put it bluntly," said President Bush. "I am concerned about the erosion of democracy in Venezuela and Bolivia." However, leaders of small Latin American republics did not cower, unlike in the past. Instead, Chavez fired a salvo the next day. "We have to tell the U.S. president that . . . his imperialist, war-mongering government is dangerously eroding the possibility of peace and life on this planet."[19]

At about the same time, a bigger and a more potent spat erupted between Russia and the United States when Dick Cheney chose the capital of Lithuania, Vilnius, to deliver a stinging attack on the Kremlin. "No legitimate interest is served when oil and gas become tools of intimidation or blackmail, either by supply manipulation or attempts to monopolize transportation," he said. This was a reference to the Russian-Ukrainian dispute on gas prices, which led to Gazprom shutting off supplies to Ukraine in January. Cheney also lambasted the Kremlin for cracking down on dissent. And then—in a self-defeating move—he flew to the Kazakh capital of Astana to express "admiration and friendship" for President Sultan Nazarbayev, a leader whose government routinely rigged elections and suppressed opposition.

Russian president Vladimir Putin used his State of the Nation speech to the parliament on May 10 to hit back. Noting that the U.S. defense budget was twenty-five times Russia's and that the United States had turned itself into a castle, he remarked, "As they say, 'Comrade Wolf knows whom to eat. He eats without listening and he is clearly not going to listen to anyone.' " By "Comrade

Wolf," he clearly meant "Uncle Sam." He added, "Where is all the pathos about protecting human rights and democracy when it comes to the need to pursue their own interests?" In short, while Washington had no qualms about advancing its interests by any means, it was criticizing Moscow for pursuing its own interests.[20]

Such a robust rejoinder from Russia to the world's sole superpower would have been unthinkable a few years earlier when oil and gas prices were low and the Russian ruble was recovering from its 1998 collapse.

More seriously, and quietly, Russia was forging an energy-and-defense alliance with energy-hungry China. It held joint military exercises with Beijing in August 2005. Together they named 2006 as the "Year of Russia in China," with Chinese President Hu Jintao remarking that Sino-Russian relations were stronger than ever.

The two neighbors formed the core of the Shanghai Cooperation Organization. On its tenth anniversary in June 2006, President Hu chaired a summit of the six members and four observer nations—India, Iran, Pakistan, and Mongolia—stressing the SCO's aim of pursuing "joint security, energy, and development goals, including enhanced cooperation against terrorism, Islamist extremism, and separatism."

Putin proposed that the SCO form an "energy club." Iranian president Mahmoud Ahmadinejad invited SCO members to a meeting in Tehran to discuss energy exploration and development in the region—just as Mai Kai, head of China's economic planning and energy ministry, visiting Tehran, declared: "The economies of China and Iran are closely tied together." Not to be left behind, Pakistani president Parvez Musharraf highlighted the geostrategic position of his country as an energy and trade corridor for SCO members in his plea for full SCO membership.

Hu's statement that the SCO was not directed at "third parties" failed to reassure the United States (whose application for observer status had been rejected)—and its closest Asian ally, Japan. "The SCO is becoming a rival block to the U.S. alliance," noted a senior Japanese official. "It does not share our values. We are watching it very closely."[21]

To offset the rising power of the SCO, the United States and Japan will have to pursue a medium-term policy of actively developing and exploiting alternatives to oil.

Oil Alternatives

It is most unlikely that oil prices will fall below $40 a barrel in the short to medium term. Indeed, they might rise above the recent high of $78 a barrel. Such prices have made secondary and tertiary methods of oil recovery economical,[22] and so helped marginally to raise supplies.

As for lowering consumption, hybrids provide the best short-term alternative. Experts in the United States agree that corn ethanol can play only a minor part in fuel replacement.

The longer-term alternatives to oil remain cellulosic ethanol as well as clean coal and nuclear power, since natural gas can only be a bridging fuel: the peak of gas production will be reached only a generation later than that for oil.

Given the disasters caused by the nuclear power plant accidents in the United States and Ukraine, the issue of reviving this industry has proved deeply contentious in the West. In the United States, lawmakers had a chance to debate the issue during the passage of the Energy Policy Bill of 2005. The provision providing $4.3 billion of public money to build new nuclear power stations received bipartisan support in Congress. A poll conducted in the spring of 2006 by Bisconti Research revealed that seven out of eight Americans viewed nuclear energy as an important element in meeting future electricity needs and three out of four agreed that utilities should prepare now to build new nuclear power plants in the next decade.[23]

For their part, American utility companies remain hooked on coal-fired power plants because they are the most economical and because the United States has abundant coal supplies. As many as 140 such projects were on the drawing boards in 2006. Only 12 of these will use the Integrated Gasification Combined Cycle (IGCC) process—which converts coal or heavy crude oil into a synthetic gas, and converts carbon into liquid CO_2 suitable for long-term sequestration—simply because they will cost 15 to 20 percent more to construct.[24] So much for the Bush administration's claims that American industry was acting voluntarily to reduce environmental pollution.

In a world acutely aware of the perilous consequences of a polluted atmosphere, the fact that nuclear power releases minuscule pollution into the air has become one of its leading merits. But then again, uranium supplies are finite. At the present rate of consumption, low-cost uranium will be exhausted by 2055.

Beyond our present technology, there is the prospect of controlled nuclear fusion—which powers the sun as well as the awesome explosion of a hydrogen bomb—used for peaceful purposes. In nuclear fusion, energy is obtained from fusing light nuclei into heavier ones. Initially, the fuel would be deuterium (a form of hydrogen present in seawater), and tritium, super-heavy hydrogen, which can be manufactured from lithium. But the tasks of capturing nuclear fusion and putting it to practical, peaceful ends have proved fiendishly daunting.

A European project to build an experimental fusion reactor, called the Joint European Torus, was started in 1983 at Culham near Oxford, Britain. It took eight years before the reactor was ready to use fusion fuel. This was a preamble to building a demonstration fusion power plant. It was not until 2005 that the EU and six countries—the United States, Russia, China, Japan, India, and South Korea—agreed to let France host the site near the southern town of Cadarache. Finally, in May 2006 the parties signed a treaty to build a €4.6 ($5.8) billion International Thermonuclear Experimental Reactor (ITER). Once it is ready in 2017, it will take twenty years of experiments at the cost of $10–15 billion to have a fusion power plant working. It is estimated that between 10 to 20 percent of global energy could come from fusion by 2100.[25]

This is truly a long-term project. Meanwhile, to cover the rising energy deficit, and to counter the disaster that awaits humanity due to rising temperatures, it is urgent that governments and companies tap renewable sources of energy.

Green Renewables

The major sources of renewable energy are wind, sun, and tide.

Despite improvements in wind turbine technology, wind-generated electricity costs twice as much as that produced by natural gas, nuclear power, or coal. Yet the demand for electricity is rising so rapidly that this more expensive technology must be harnessed along with the conventional methods.

Europeans are forging ahead. By 2004 the EU had reached seven-eighths of its 2010 wind energy target of 40 gigawatts of electricity-generating capacity.[26] And Japan is foremost in the solar-power sphere.

In this sphere, Germany stood out primarily because the Green Party, a substantial political entity, exercised power in coalition with the Social Democrats for seven years. As a result, the total green energy proportion in Germany is set to rise to 15 percent by 2010.

In March 2006 the Energy Savings Trust in Britain estimated that home generation of power through wind turbines and solar hot water panels on the roof, as well as fitting photovoltaic tiles on the roof and a ground-source heat pump in the garden, could potentially provide 30 percent of all electricity by 2050, and that scores of small companies were offering solar panels, rooftop wind turbines, heat pumps, solar thermal panels, photovoltaics, hydropower turbines, wood fuel boilers, and fuel cells.[27]

The United States, the biggest consumer of fossil fuels and the largest pollutant in the world, presents a lamentable contrast. Unlike China or India, the United States lacks a coherent energy policy or long-term strategy. The periodic Energy Laws that got passed ended up as a hodgepodge of rewards and penalties for several special interest groups or states (Texas and Alaska) or regions (coal-bearing states) or senior legislators. Of the $12.3 billion provided in the 2005 U.S. Energy Policy Act, less than a third was allocated for energy conservation measures and incentives to renewable energy.[28]

The interests of the oil and auto industries remained deeply entrenched. "The United States derives much of its wealth from a global economy that is dependent on fossil fuels," notes Paul Roberts. "So . . . any effort to move away from a hydrocarbon system—or worse, to use less energy—poses alarming economic and political risks to the U.S.—a reality that tends to reinforce the status quo."[29]

Also, the mainstream media in the United States remain scandalously neutral on the subject of global warming and its relationship to human activity, despite the more alarming recent reports from researchers. According to the Potsdam Institute for Climate Impact Research in Germany, greenhouse gases not only lead to higher temperatures but are themselves increased by higher temperatures, and global warming may be up to 78 percent worse than previously predicted.[30]

In short, the situation is so grim that we have no choice but to adopt and implement the slogan "All at Once." That is, we must pursue all the avenues of alternatives to petroleum for our energy needs at the same time. It is no longer a question of implementing this option *or* that. The only sensible and responsible course to follow is to pursue this option *and* that.

The future of the human race is at stake. The task is urgent. It brooks no delay.

Notes

Introduction

1. Today western Texas produces one-fifth of all U.S. oil, and the offshore fields of the Gulf of Mexico a quarter. *New York Times*, September 2, 2005.
2. Now the houses in that neighborhood are worth about $250,000 each.
3. Kenneth S. Deffeyes, *Hubbert's Peak: The Impending World Oil Shortage* (Princeton, NJ and Oxford, UK: Princeton University Press, 2001), 140; *New York Times*, December 27, 2002; *BP Statistical Review of World Energy*, June 2005, p. 6.
4. The cost of extracting a barrel of oil onshore in Saudi Arabia is 80 to 90 cents. *The Times*, March 5, 2005.
5. See further, *BP Statistical Review of World Energy*, June 2005, p. 6.
6. *New York Times*, March 9, 2005.
7. The Al Wajbah Palace is the official name of the ruler's administrative-residential complex.
8. *Guardian*, September 11, 2004.
9. Arthur Blessitt had been invited earlier to Midland in April 1984 in the wake of the bankruptcy of the First National Bank of Midland the previous October—the largest independent bank failure in Texas at the time—to console the distraught and the ruined.
10. Unable to pay its debts of $12 billion, the BCCI would go bankrupt in mid-1991.
11. Cited in Craig Unger, *House of Bush, House of Saud: The Secret Relationship between the World's Two Most Powerful Dynasties* (New York: Scribner, 2003/London: Gibson Square Books, 2004), 127.
12. Before Enron Inc. went bankrupt in late 2001 with debts of $30 billion, it exercised more influence in the new George W. Bush administration than any other corporation in recent times.
13. *Sunday Times*, June 4, 2006.

Chapter 1

1. According to the most widely accepted interpretation, Azerbaijan is a derivative of *Azarpayagan*, meaning "Land of Fire" in Persian. A less accepted

357

version has it that Azerbaijan was known in ancient times as Aagban/Aagbaan, meaning "An Arrow" or "Forest of Fire" in Sanskrit.

2. In recent times, the elderly caretaker at the site fondly told visitors from the Indian subcontinent that Indian prime minister Jawaharlal Nehru and his daughter, Indira Gandhi, had visited the temple during their trip to Soviet Azerbaijan in the mid-1950s.

3. Cited in Kenneth S. Deffeyes, *Hubbert's Peak*, 125.

4. *Washington Post*, September 5, 1998.

5. In the Titusville area, cart drivers controlled the supply lines for petroleum. When competitors built wooden pipelines in the 1860s, the cart drivers responded with armed attacks, arson, and sabotage.

6. The Beaumont–Houston area would become the manufacturing center for the Texan oil industry.

7. Cited in Roger Olien, *Black Gold: The Story of Texas Oil and Gas* (San Antonio, TX: Historical Publishing Network, 2004), 14.

8. Daniel Yergin, *The Prize: The Epic Quest for Oil, Money and Power* (New York and London: Simon and Schuster, 1991), 235.

9. The name Turkish Petroleum Company was changed to Iraq Petroleum Company in 1931 when its equity was redistributed to include two American companies.

10. Cited in Aileen Keating, *Mirage: Power, Politics and the Hidden History of Arabian Oil* (Amherst, NY: Prometheus Books, 2005), 45–46.

11. Daniel Yergin, *The Prize*, 283.

12. Cited in Daniel Yergin, *The Prize*, 302.

13. One British pound sterling was then worth five U.S. dollars.

14. David Holden and Richard Johns, *The House of Saud* (London: Sidgwick and Jackson, 1981), 120–21.

15. Colin J. Campbell, *The Coming Oil Crisis* (Brentwood, UK: Multi-Science Publishing Company and Petroconsultants, S.a. 1998), 55.

Chapter 2

1. *Guardian*, April 29, 2006 and May 20, 2006; *International Herald Tribune*, September 3–4, 2005; Associated Press, April 3, 2005. Exxon Mobil Corporation, based in Irving, a suburb of Dallas, Texas, is the parent of Esso, Mobil, and ExxonMobil companies around the world, with a presence in 180 countries. The annual turnover of BP, the number-two company, was $280 billion in 2005.

2. For further details, visit http://www.fhwa.dot.gov/policy/ohim/hs03/mv.htm. See also Matthew Yeomans, *Oil: Anatomy of an Industry* (New York: The New Press, 2004), 101.

3. *The Times*, March 20, 1999. The six economic recessions since World War II cost the world more than $1.2 trillion in direct losses. Paul Roberts, *The End of Oil: On the Edge of a Perilous World* (New York: Houghton Mifflin, 2004/London: Bloomsbury, 2004), 108.

4. Colin J. Campbell, *The Coming Oil Crisis*, 16.

5. Cited in Michael Klare, *Blood and Oil: The Dangers and Consequences of America's Growing Petroleum Dependency* (New York: Metropolitan Books/London: Penguin Books, 2004), 9.

6. September 13, 2005.
7. Dilip Hiro, *The Essential Middle East: A Comprehensive Guide* (New York: Carroll & Graf), 381.
8. Dilip Hiro, *Inside the Middle East* (London: Routledge & Kegan Paul, 1982/New York: McGraw Hill, 1982), 333.
9. Ibid.
10. Michael Klare, *Blood and Oil*, 37. In 1972, while constituting a mere one-twentieth of the human race, Americans consumed a third of the global oil output, a proportion that has changed little since then.
11. Kenneth S. Deffeyes, *Hubbert's Peak*, 164–65.
12. As late as the 1930s, Alice Hobart's novel, *Oil for the Lamps of China*, later turned into a movie, proved a runaway success.
13. Alternatively, naphtha is put through a reformer to get gasoline.
14. For the details and products of Jordan Petroleum Refinery Company in Zarqa, Jordan, visit www.jopetrol.com.jo/pages.php?menu_id=29&local_id=0&local_det.
15. Dilip Hiro, *The Essential Middle East*, 373.

Chapter 3

1. Kenneth S. Deffeyes, *Hubbert's Peak*, 2–3.
2. Colin J. Campbell, *The Coming Oil Crisis*, 52. The discovery of giant fields of more than half a billion barrels peaked in 1965.
3. Joseph Riva's report is available online at peakoil.blogspot.com/2005_12_01_peakoil_archive.html
4. David Goodstein, *Out of Gas: The End of the Age of Oil*, (New York and London: W. W. Norton, 2004), 16.
5. Over the past decade, fresh oil discoveries have amounted to about two-fifths of consumption.
6. *New York Times*, March 3, 2003; *International Herald Tribune*, March 26, 2005; *Daily Telegraph*, February 4, 2005.
7. *International Herald Tribune*, December 23, 2005; *New York Times Magazine*, August 22, 2005.
8. Op. cit., p. 62
9. After recalculating its proven oil reserves in 2003, Iran raised its total from 89.7 billion barrels to 125.8 billion barrels, thus overtaking Iraq with its 100 billion barrels.
10. The full text of the report is available at www.informationclearinghouse.info/article3535.htm.
11. *New York Times*, October 22, 2002.
12. *Economist Survey of Oil*, April 30, 2005, 11. ChevronTexaco Corporation came into being in 2001 when Chevron acquired Texaco.
13. August 22, 2005.
14. Of the 1,410 rigs active in the United States, 1,228 were drilling for gas and only 181 for oil. *Platts Oilgram News*, July 25, 2005, 6.
15. Cited in *New York Times Magazine*, August 22, 2005.
16. Interview in Al Dukhan, Qatar, in February 2005.
17. Kenneth S. Deffeyes, *Hubbert's Peak*, 166–67.

18. *Financial Times*, April 28, 2006.
19. Interview in Midland, Texas, June 2005.

Chapter 4

1. Cited in Daniel Yergin, *The Prize*, 142.
2. Cited in Matthew Yeomans, *Oil*, 7, 101.
3. It proved to be an incredibly lucrative investment. In 1923 Winston Churchill reported that the British government had earned £25.6 million on an investment of £2.2 million. Larry Everest, *Oil, Power and Empire* (Monroe, ME: Common Courage Press, 2004), 51.
4. According to Webster's dictionary, the term *geopolitics*, coined by Swedish political scientists circa 1916, applies to a systematic study of internal and continental features, physical, economic, and anthropographic factors in shaping governmental policies, especially foreign policy, for achieving national security. It is distinguished by its dynamic quality, viewing the state as an organism requiring growth, from political geography, which is based on static conditions.
5. Matthew Yeomans, *Oil*, 8.
6. Cited in Daniel Yergin, *The Prize*, 183.
7. Cited in Ibid., 183.
8. Oil production in Iraq would reach such proportions by World War II that in 1941 Britain would intervene militarily to overthrow the anti-British government of Rashid Ali Gailani.
9. Cited in Daniel Yergin, *The Prize*, 276.
10. In 1923, Franz Fischer and Hans Tropsch, German coal gasification researchers, patented a process to convert coal into liquid hydrocarbons using iron and cobalt catalysts. The Fischer-Tropsch process, adopted by Nazi Germany, was known as "ersatz," meaning "substitute" in German. A ton of high ash coal yields two hundred liters of oil, with by-products ranging from tar to rare chemicals. *Mainstream* (December 23–29, 2005), 111.
11. *Petroleum Review*, February 1992, Baku, 64.
12. Cited in Daniel Yergin, *The Prize*, 337.
13. Michael Klare, *Blood and Oil*, 28–29.
14. Daniel Yergin, *The Prize*, 394.
15. Cited in Dilip Hiro, *The Iranian Labyrinth: Journeys through Theocratic Iran and Its Furies* (New York: Nation Books, 2005)/*Iran Today* (London: Politico's Publishing, 2006), 253.
16. In Europe, it was the head of Shell Oil, Marcus Samuel, who coordinated oil supplies to the Allies. Shell Oil workers in the Dutch East Indies, now Indonesia, played a vital role in destroying oil wells that the Japanese were aiming to capture. *Daily Telegraph*, February 4, 2005.
17. Cited in Daniel Yergin, *The Prize*, 401.
18. Daniel Yergin, *The Prize*, 404.
19. William Eddy, *F.D.R. Meets Ibn Saud* (New York: American Friends of the Middle East, 1954), 34; David Holden and Richard Johns, *The House of Saud* (London: Sidgwick and Jackson, 1981), 138; Robert Lacey, *The Kingdom* (London: Hutchinson, 1981), 272.
20. Cited in Daniel Yergin, *The Prize*, 404.

21. Cited in Howard Zinn, *A People's History of the United States: 1492–Present*, (New York: Perennial Classic, HarperCollins, 2001), 413.
22. Cited in Michael Klare, *Blood and Oil*, 40.
23. Dilip Hiro, *The Essential Middle East: A Comprehensive Guide*, 269, 560.
24. Cited in Aileen Keating, *Mirage*, 500.
25. Cited in Ibid., 510.
26. Muhammad Mussadiq surrendered on August 20, 1953. He was sentenced to three years solitary imprisonment, and then kept under house arrest until his death in 1967.
27. Cited in Daniel Yergin, *The Prize*, 509.
28. In the 1950s, foreign oil accounted for 10 percent of total U.S. oil consumption. Michael Klare, *Blood and Oil*, 10.
29. Dilip Hiro, *The Essential Middle East*, 392–93.
30. King Saud formally abdicated in 1964.
31. Colin J. Campbell, *The Coming Oil Crisis*, 49.
32. Dilip Hiro, *The Essential Middle East*, 393.

Chapter 5

1. The International Monetary Fund estimates that a $5 increase in oil price cuts global economic growth by about 0.25 percent a year. *Financial Times*, May 1, 2006.
2. *The eXchange of change, 1872–2002*, (New York: New York Mercantile Exchange, 2003), 43. This trading place was founded in 1872 as Butter and Cheese Exchange, with eggs added eight years later. In 1882, it became the New York Mercantile Exchange. It added potatoes in 1941. Now a seat at Nymex costs $2.5 million.
3. Trades at Nymex are financial papers, called futures, which are derivatives, not the real thing. Under them come the swaps of cargoes which actually take place. Under those are the terms of the transactions, one cargo per month for twelve months, a unit being a tanker full of oil worth about $40 million at $60 a barrel. These are the actual cargoes that are handled at the Antwerp-Rotterdam-Amsterdam (ARA) conurbation at the confluence of the Rhine, Wall, and Scheldt rivers. The market price is a benchmark, and the actual price for each cargo is adjusted for the quality of the crude being sold and how easily it can be refined into high-value products. Interview with Peter Stewart of *Platts Oilgram News*, November 2005.
4. *New York Times*, May 1, 2006.
5. In 1986 Arabian Light became Dubai Oil and was traded at the Petroleum Exchange in Singapore.
6. Steven Emerson, *The American House of Saud* (New York: Franklin Watts, 1985), p. 128.
7. Paul Roberts, *The End of Oil*, 151–152.
8. *Wall Street Journal*, May 1, 1981.
9. Until recently the Singapore Petroleum Exchange traded in Dubai crude oil.
10. Steven Emerson, *The American House of Saud*, 136.
11. Dilip Hiro, *War without End: The Rise of Islamist Terrorism and Global Response*, (London and New York: Routledge, 2002), 158.

12. Dilip Hiro, *Inside the Middle East*, 346.
13. After Hijra—meaning "migration." The Islamic era began with the migration of Prophet Muhammad from Mecca to Medina on July 22, 622 AD.
14. Dilip Hiro, *War without End*, 135–40.
15. Cited in Dilip Hiro, *The Essential Middle East*, 103.
16. *Guardian*, January 7, 1981.
17. *The Times*, October 17, 1975.
18. Dilip Hiro, *Inside the Middle East*, 350.
19. *New York Times*, October 2, 1981.
20. In October 1999, U.S. president Bill Clinton extended the area of responsibility of the Central Command to the littoral states of the Caspian Sea, except Russia. All told, Centcom's area of responsibility covered twenty-nine countries—thirteen Arab, eight central Asian and Caucasian, five East African, and Iran, Afghanistan, and Pakistan. In 2006 the beach-front headquarters of Centcom had liaison teams from sixty-three nations. *Daily Telegraph*, April 10, 2006.
21. Daniel Yergin, *The Prize*, 748.
22. Research shows that only 5 percent of SUV drivers ever leave the asphalted roads.
23. At the U.S. National Security Council meeting at the White House on August 2, 1990, President George H. W. Bush argued that with 20 percent of the world's oil, "Saddam would be able to manipulate world prices and hold the United States and its allies at his mercy. Higher fuel prices would fuel inflation, worsening the already gloomy condition of the U.S. economy." Bob Woodward, *The Commanders* (New York: Simon & Schuster, 1991), 226.
24. Dilip Hiro, *Desert Shield to Desert Storm: The Second Gulf War* (London: HarperCollins/New York: Routledge, 1992), 111, 116, and 121.
25. Dilip Hiro, *The Essential Middle East*, 160–61; *The Nation*, September 12, 2005. 26. The reason Russia fought so hard to pacify Chechnya was that the main oil pipeline starting at Baku ran through Grozny, the site of a refinery and a switching station where the Baku oil was split into two pipelines, one going west to Novorossisk and the other east to Astrakhan to join the pipeline system running to Kazakhstan. *Guardian*, October 3, 1995.
27. This is also the case with Iran. Kenneth Deffeyes, *Hubbert's Peak*, 41. However, in 2003 Iran raised its proven oil reserves by 40 percent.
28. See further, Dilip Hiro, *Neighbors, Not Friends: Iraq and Iran after the Gulf Wars* (London and New York: Routledge), 2001, 220.
29. Dilip Hiro, *Neighbors, Not Friends*, 229–30.
30. In 2003 the company renamed itself Total S.A. Its oil reserves amount to 11 billion barrels.
31. *Washington Post*, February 20, 2002.
32. Dilip Hiro, *Neighbors, Not Friends*, 187.
33. Ron Suskind, *The Price of Loyalty: George W. Bush, the White House, and the Education of Paul O'Neill* (New York: Simon & Schuster, 2004), 85.
34. Ibid., 96.
35. For the BBC *Newsnight* report, visit http://news.bbc.co.uk/1/hi/programmes/newsnight/4354269.stm. Iraq nationalized its oil industry in 1972.

36. Cited in Larry Everest, *Oil, Power and Empire*, 252.
37. So secretive is Saudi Arabia that this critical gesture by its de facto ruler Abdullah, meant to cushion Western economies against the shock of the terrorist attacks, was leaked to the *Washington Post* five months after the event. February 12, 2002.
38. The reason for this lopsidedness was more practical than ideological. The non-Saudi Al Qaida volunteers found it hard to get American visas. Due to warm Riyadh-Washington relations, it was easy for a Saudi citizen to obtain a U.S. visa.
39. November 4, 2001.
40. August 6, 2002.
41. October 12, 2002, 78.
42. In her column in the *New York Times* of December 28, 2005, Maureen Dowd referred to the lack of response by the Pentagon to the newspaper's request for a copy of the Halliburton document on Iraq's oil industry.
43. March 3, 2003.
44. Bob Woodward, *Plan of Attack* (New York and London: Simon & Schuster, 2004), 323–24.
45. Larry Everest, *Oil, Power and Empire*, 275.
46. Bob Woodward, *Plan of Attack*, 381.
47. Cited in Dilip Hiro, *Secrets and Lies: Operation "Iraqi Freedom" and After* (New York: Nation Books, 2004); *Secrets and Lies: The True Story of the Iraq War* (London: Politico's Publishing, 2005), 398.
48. BBC *Newsnight*, March 17, 2005.
49. There was also the vexatious problem of sorting out the thirty major oil-development contracts that the Saddam Hussein regime had signed with companies based in Canada, China, France, India, Italy, Russia, Spain, and Vietnam. All those factors cooled the ardor of the Bush team to denationalize Iraq's oil industry.
50. *New Statesman*, March 20, 2006.
51. *International Herald Tribune*, September 22, 2005. Issam Chalabi doubted if Iraq could return to the 1979 peak of 3.5 million bpd before 2009.
52. *Guardian*, May 1, 2006.
53. At the New York Mercantile Exchange, oil prices rose 28 percent in 2004 and 45 percent in 2005. *New York Times*, September 1, 2005, and May 1, 2006; *Guardian*, September 6, 2005.
54. *Foreign Affairs*, March–April 2006, 73.

Chapter 6

1. September 5, 1998.
2. Paul Roberts, *The End of Oil*, 44–45.
3. *Financial Times*, July 22, 1997.
4. Cited in *Middle East International*, September 12, 1997, 19.
5. Michael Klare, *Blood and Oil*, 121.
6. In September 2003 a New York Court indicted a Swiss banker for providing bribes to Haidar Aliyev, who was then seriously ill. As SOCAR's vice president,

Ilham Aliyev was also involved. During the proceedings, which continued well into the spring of 2006, three accused international speculators described huge shakedowns and bribes in the late 1990s at SOCAR. *New York Times*, April 19, 2006.

7. *Seminar*, November 2005, p. 20.
8. Reuters, September 21, 1998.
9. Gemini News Service, July 11, 1999.
10. *The End of Oil*, 62–63.
11. *Guardian*, July 2, 2004.
12. *New York Times*, October 31, 2005.
13. Ibid., November 17, 2005.
14. November 11, 2005.
15. *New York Times*, April 19, 2006.
16. Ibid., August 18, 1999. Chevron set up a joint venture, Tengizchevroil, to exploit the large Tengiz oil field in the Caspian Basin.
17. *Middle East International*, October 10, 1997, 19–20; Reuters, April 15, 1998.
18. *The Times*, April 2, 2001. Large advertisements by the Kazakh government in Western newspapers now mention an oil output of 3 million bpd by 2015, a realistic figure.
19. Michael Klare, *Blood and Oil*, 125–26.
20. Bloomberg News, May 3, 2006.
21. Agence France-Presse, March 11, 2006.
22. *Guardian*, May 5, 2006.
23. The figure for the oil alone was 1.5 billion barrels.
24. Reuters, May 12, 2006. Five years earlier a similar fire in the same area killed 250 people. And in 1998 a fiercer explosion from a leaking gasoline pipeline led to 1,000 deaths.
25. *Guardian*, February 25, 2005.
26. *Financial Times*, May 1, 2006.
27. *International Herald Tribune*, January 20–21, 2006.
28. In 2001, the raids on Colombia's big oil pipeline shut it down for 266 days, resulting in a loss of $600 million in revenue. *The Business*, September 4–5, 2005; *New York Times*, May 14, 2006.
29. Reuters, August 15, 2004.
30. *International Herald Tribune*, September 21, 2005.
31. Ibid., November 1, 2000.
32. *Wall Street Journal*, June 30, 2005; *Economist*, July 2, 2005, 36.
33. *International Herald Tribune*, November 5–6, 2005. By then Venezuela's oil deals benefited twenty countries in the Caribbean and Central America. *Guardian*, November 25, 2005.
34. *New York Times*, April 4, 2006.
35. *Daily Telegraph*, January 5, 2006; *New York Times*, May 2, 2006. On May Day, President Evo Morales took control of Bolivia's oil and gas fields and gave foreign energy companies six months to agree to new contracts with his government, thereby fulfilling one of his major promises during the election campaign.

36. *Observer Review*, May 7, 2006; *Guardian*, May 15, 2006.
37. *International Herald Tribune*, February 28, 2006.

Chapter 7

1. The International City, reflecting the architectures of Britain, China, France, Greece, Indonesia, Iran, Italy, Morocco, Russia, Spain, and Thailand, will accommodate sixty thousand.
2. *International Herald Tribune*, November 17, 2004.
3. *New York Times*, January 13, 2005. It was against this backdrop that China began negotiating a free trade agreement with GCC states in 2006, from which Dubai expected to gain a great deal.
4. In 1984 China achieved a record grain output of 400 million tonnes.
5. In 1998, Sinopec and CNPC were turned into vertically integrated companies to engage in all aspects of the hydrocarbon industry.
6. Michael Klare, *Blood and Oil*, 168.
7. *New York Times*, July 9, 2005.
8. *Financial Times*, September 14, 2005.
9. See further, Dilip Hiro, *War without End: The Rise of Islamist Terrorism and Global Response*, 311–12.
10. *Financial Times*, June 16, 2002; *Guardian*, September 17, 2005.
11. *Time*, June 27, 2005, 33; *Guardian*, May 2, 2006. In the first quarter of 2006, new loans soared by 61 percent compared to the previous year, causing investment in factories and fixed assets to climb 30 percent. *New York Times*, April 28, 2006.
12. *New York Times*, October 28, 2005; *International Herald Tribune*, November 10, 2005.
13. In 2004, China's $1,700 per capita income made it richer than Morocco. But urban dwellers, accounting for 44 percent of the population, earned three times as much as the rural folk.
14. *Observer*, April 30, 2006.
15. For all that growth in electric power, the per capita electricity usage in China was about one-eighth of the average for an industrialized Western nation. Paul Roberts, *The End of Oil*, 248.
16. Michael Klare, *Blood and Oil*, 167.
17. Paul Roberts, *The End of Oil*, 159.
18. Ibid., 156–57. By 2010 China will have *ninety times* the number of cars it had in 1990! *New York Times*, April 20, 2006.
19. *Observer*, July 3, 2005.
20. Cited in Paul Roberts, *The End of Oil*, 257.
21. *International Herald Tribune*, January 27, 2006.
22. *New York Times*, April 24, 2006.
23. Anoushiravan Ehteshami, *After Khomeini: The Iranian Second Republic* (London: Routledge, 1995), 179, 190–91.
24. Overall, total Chinese arms exports to the Middle East in 1995–2002 were $1.6 billion versus the United States' $46.7 billion. Michael Klare, *Blood and Oil*, 174.

25. Dilip Hiro, *Neighbors, Not Friends*, 221.
26. Cited in FrontPageMagazine.com, January 6, 2005.
27. Iran would yield that position to Angola in 2005.
28. *New York Times*, January 13, 2005, and April 20, 2005. China planned to import oil from the Yadavaran field by a pipeline running through central Asia. *Observer*, April 30, 2006. In March 2004, Zhuhai Zhenrong, a state-backed Chinese oil-trading company, signed a $20 billion contract to buy 110 million tonnes of liquefied natural gas from Iran over twenty-five years starting in 2008.
29. *Middle East International*, October 10, 1997, 19–20.
30. The proposal of the 3,000-kilometer (1,880-mile) Kazakhstan–China pipeline, costing $3.5 billion, was dropped in August 1999 because the oil price fell to $12 a barrel, and it required a flow of 500,000 bpd, far more than the expected output of 150,000 bpd.
31. *Guardian*, March 28, 2006.
32. The individual breakdown was: Angola, 14 percent; Sudan, 5 percent; Congo, 4 percent; and Nigeria, 2 percent.
33. *Guardian*, November 9, 2005.
34. Earlier Cnooc had invested in oil and gas exploration rights in Australia, Azerbaijan, Bangladesh, Indonesia, Thailand, and Vietnam. *New York Times*, January 10, 2006.
35. *Financial Times*, May 1, 2006.
36. *International Herald Tribune*, July 29, 2005.
37. Paul Roberts, *The End of Oil*, 256.
38. *Platts Oilgram News*, August 2, 2005, 3.
39. *International Herald Tribune*, August 2, 2005; *Boston Globe*, May 25, 2006.
40. The deployment of fighter aircraft and heavy weaponry militated against the claim of fighting terrorism.
41. August 18, 2005.
42. *International Herald Tribune*, July 28, 2005. Earlier, Nanjing Automobiles had bought the assets of MG Rover in Birmingham, in the UK, and the Chinese computer maker Lenovo had purchased IBM's personal computer business for $1.25 billion without any hitch.
43. *China Daily*, April 18, 2006. Worldwide Chinese exports leaped from $250 billion in 2000 to $580 billion in 2004. *Time*, June 27, 2005, 35.
44. *Time*, June 27, 2005, 32; *Guardian*, March 25, 2006.
45. *Daily Mail*, August 26, 2005. In 2004, China's worldwide exports of information and communication technology at $180 billion, registering a 46 percent growth over 2003, were higher than those of the United States, at $149 billion. *International Herald Tribune*, December 12, 2005.
46. China's foreign reserves were set to exceed $1 trillion by the end of 2006. *The Times*, March 29, 2006.
47. *Guardian*, July 6, 2005, and June 6, 2006.
48. *Time*, June 27, 2005, 34; *Observer*, April 30, 2006.

Chapter 8

1. Dilip Hiro, *The Timeline History of India* (New York: Barnes & Noble, 2006), 302.

2. Ibid., 308; *The Times*, June 8, 2006.
3. The Vajpayee government adopted *Hydrocarbon Vision 2025* as official policy in December 2000.
4. *Daily Star*, August 12, 2005.
5. *Seminar*, November 2005, 18.
6. *Platts Oilgram News*, July 28, 2005, 5.
7. *Sunday Telegraph*, July 28, 2005.
8. *Videsh*, a Hindi word, means foreign.
9. *New York Times*, February 18, 2005.
10. Indonesia had agreed to attend, but its oil minister cancelled his visit at the last minute due to commitments emerging from the tsunami disaster on December 26, 2004.
11. Interview in New Delhi, March 2006.
12. Riyadh's exports to China amounted to 500,000 bpd, and to the United States 1.7 million bpd. *New York Times*, February 18, 2005.
13. *Financial Times*, November 11, 2004; *New York Times*, April 20, 2005.
14. *Daily Star*, August 12, 2005.
15. *Guardian*, July 20, 2005.
16. During his one-day stop in Pakistan on March 4, 2006, U.S. president Bush said that he had "no beef" against the proposed Iran-Pakistan-India gas-pipeline project. *Times of India*, March 14, 2005.
17. *New York Times*, February 18, 2005.
18. *Seminar*, November 2005, 22. Visit www.india.seminar.com.
19. Dilip Hiro, *The Timeline History of India*, 333.
20. *Financial Times*, January 13, 2006.
21. Interview in Doha, February 2005.
22. *Guardian*, May 2, 2006.
23. Maruti is the Hindu goddess of storms.
24. December 26, 2005.
25. *New York Times*, December 26, 2005.
26. *Alexander's Gas Connection*, August 25, 2004.
27. Interview with Talmiz Ahmad in New Delhi, March 2006.
28. *International Herald Tribune*, March 17, 2006.
29. May 13, 2006.

Chapter 9

1. *International Herald Tribune* October 29, 2005.
2. Cited in *New York Times Magazine*, August 22, 2005.
3. September 27, 2005.
4. At present the only plant converting gas into diesel is operated by Shell in Malaysia as a pilot project, producing 15,000 bpd. Over the next five to seven years, however, Exxon Mobil, Chevron, Royal Dutch Shell, and Sasol of South Africa will invest $14 billion to produce 1 million bpd of diesel from natural gas. *New York Times*, January 18, 2006.
5. In 1972 Exxon and Mobil together had a combined output of 7.3 million bpd; today it is 4.2 million bpd, whereas Saudi Aramco produces nearly 9 million bpd.

6. Interview in June 2005.
7. Visit www.bpgas.co.uk/perspectives/hot.060203.html.
8. Interview in Doha, February 2005.
9. *Pioneer*, March 12, 2006.
10. When converted into oil barrels, Urengoy's gas deposits amount to the third largest in the world, falling behind only those of Saudi Arabia's Ghawar and Kuwait's Burgan oil fields.
11. At the same time, an underwater gas pipeline from Algeria to France was built speedily.
12. *New York Times*, April 25, 2006.
13. From 2000 to 2004, German exports to Russia increased from 6.7 billion ($8.4 billion) to 14.8 billion. *International Herald Tribune*, September 8, 2005.
14. *International Herald Tribune*, April 7, 2006.
15. The sanctions menu included the U.S. federal government banning purchases from the banned entity; prohibiting the sanctioned entity from acting as a primary dealer of U.S. Treasury bonds; and a denial of licenses for the export of controlled technology to the sanctioned entity. Dilip Hiro, *Neighbors, Not Friends*, 220.
16. Dilip Hiro, *Neighbors, Not Friends*, 229.
17. *Mainstream*, December 23–29, 2005, 112.
18. Interview in New Delhi, March 2006.
19. *New York Times*, December 22, 2005.
20. *Guardian*, January 31, 2006.
21. *The End of Oil*, 250.
22. In 2005 Qatar Petroleum signed a $7 billion deal with Royal Dutch Shell to supply LNG to North America and Europe.
23. *Seminar*, November 2005, 20.
24. Cited in *Foreign Affairs*, March–April 2006, S3.
25. For the Organization of Economic Cooperation and Development (OECD), a group of the richest nations, the figure was nearly a quarter of the total capacity. In 2005 there were 441 nuclear generating units in thirty countries.
26. *Guardian*, May 18, 2006.
27. Only a limited number of the Chernobyl-type reactors were operating in the Soviet Union at that time.
28. *International Herald Tribune*, April 25, 2006.
29. Ibid., April 25, 2006.
30. Ibid., April 25, 2006. Vince Novak, director of the European Bank for Reconstruction and Development, in charge of the Chernobyl project, said, "How the Soviets built [the sarcophagus] in 1986 for me is almost a miracle. I can't think of anyone else being able to do it in the way they did it." *Guardian*, April 27, 2006.
31. The World Health Organization estimated that perhaps nine thousand people will eventually die as a result of the Chernobyl disaster. *New York Times*, April 26, 2006.
32. *Time*, June 25, 2005, 40.
33. *Metro*, December 23, 2005.

34. *Observer*, October 2, 2005; *Guardian*, November 10, 2005. This was the largest interdisciplinary gathering of experts on the subject—at least in Britain.
35. *New York Times*, April 26, 2006.
36. *Guardian*, September 7, 2004.
37. Ibid., October 2, 2005.
38. *Sunday Times Magazine*, June 11, 2006, 19; *International Herald Tribune*, March 22, 2005.
39. *Guardian*, September 7, 2004 and March 11, 2006.
40. Cited in *New York Times*, May 18, 2001.
41. *New York Times*, March 2, 2006; *International Herald Tribune*, March 26, 2005.
42. *New York Times*, March 3, 2006. The agreement had to be ratified by the U.S. Congress to become operational. India built its nuclear program from scratch and in isolation, following Washington's sanctions in the aftermath of its nuclear test in 1974.
43. *International Herald Tribune*, February 21, 2006.
44. Interview in Delhi, March 2006.
45. *International Herald Tribune*, April 14, 2006.
46. *Pioneer*, March 12, 2006; *Foreign Affairs*, March–April 2006, the inside back page advertisement by USEC and TENEX.
47. But these filters increase CO_2.
48. Cited in *Guardian*, August 22, 2005.
49. If done on a large scale, the end result would be handling and storing waste materials that would exceed those currently being stored in the iron and steel industries of the United States.
50. Paul Roberts, *The End of Oil*, 208.
51. *Mainstream*, December 23–29, 2005, 111–12; *New York Times*, January 18, 2006.
52. *The Times*, April 14, 2006.
53. Cited in *New York Times*, October 3, 2005.
54. *Pioneer*, March 12, 2006.

Chapter 10

1. *The Times*, March 11, 2004. By staging the stunt outside the most widely filmed cinema in the world, Global Green USA shifted the venue of a heated confrontation between the drivers of Hummers and Priuses from the parking lots of upscale Los Angeles to a worldwide audience.
2. *Metro*, April 25, 2006.
3. *International Herald Tribune*, February 18, 2006.
4. *New York Times*, January 10, 2002. This decision ran counter to the statement in the Bush administration's National Energy Policy of May 2001 that promised a $4 billion tax credit for a new generation of highly fuel-efficient cars.
5. *The End of Oil*, 296.
6. *Guardian*, September 1, 2004. The automobile industry contributed three times more money to Republican candidates than to Democratic candidates. In the past eighteen months the industry's Political Action Committees have contributed eight times more money to Republicans as they have to Democrats, according to Political Moneyline.com. *New York Times*, May 4, 2006.

7. *Guardian*, August 24, 2005.
8. Cited in Ibid., October 25, 2005; *Sunday Times*, May 14, 2006.
9. Cited in *Sunday Times*, May 14, 2006.
10. In Britain, the sales of hybrids, which started in 2000, rose to 7,100 in January 2004. *Independent*, June 8, 2004.
11. Others who had joined Bank of America in their drive to promote cleaner, more fuel-efficient cars were California-based Internet giant Google, footware maker Timberland, and the city of New Haven, Connecticut. Associated Press, June 8, 2006.
12. With a net income of $12.3 billion in 2005–06, the Toyota Group became the globe's most profitable manufacturing corporation. And with its targeted output of nine million units in 2006–07, it was set to become the largest carmaker in the world, ahead of General Motors, the industry's leader for a record seventy-five years. *New York Times*, May 11, 2006.
13. Ibid., October 20, 2005.
14. June 8, 2004.
15. Paul Roberts, *The End of Oil*, 70.
16. June 8, 2004.
17. *Guardian*, March 31, 2006.
18. *International Herald Tribune*, March 26, 2005.
19. *Guardian*, December 2, 2003. New studies suggested that leaking hydrogen could damage the ozone layer in the atmosphere and exacerbate global warming.
20. *Guardian*, September 10, 2004. The Bush administration's Department of Energy decided to construct a demonstration nuclear reactor in Idaho Falls to produce hydrogen.

Chapter 11

1. *Guardian*, February 17, 2005.
2. The draft fourth report of the IPCC Working Group said that temperatures could rise by 2 to 4.5 degrees Celsius when CO_2 reached 550 particles per million (ppm), twice the pre-industrial level, most probably by 2050, and that 3 degrees Celsius was the most likely value for such changes. *The Times*, May 4, 2006.
3. Of the sixteen warmest years since records were first kept in 1860 in the United States, fifteen have occurred since 1980. The seven warmest years occurred during the 1990s. Paul Roberts, *The End of Oil*, 120.
4. By contrast, during that decade, world oil consumption rose by a mere 1 percent per year, while coal use declined by nearly 1 percent. *International Herald Tribune*, September 22, 2000.
5. *International Herald Tribune*, March 26, 2005.
6. *Guardian*, February 7, 2005.
7. The absolute figures in millions of tonnes were the United States, 1,600; China, 908; Russia, 415; Japan, 322; India 280; Germany, 229; Canada, 161; Britain 151. *Guardian*, November 2, 2005.
8. *In These Times*, February 7, 2000, 14.
9. Ibid.
10. *Guardian*, February 17, 2006.

11. April 26, 2006.

12. *Platts Oilgram News*, July 27, 2005, p. 5; July 29, 2005, p. 5. Also excluded from the new law was the opening of Alaska's Arctic Wildlife Refuge to oil and gas drilling, which the Bush administration wanted, reversing the Senate's earlier 51–49 vote to allow oil drilling in that region.

13. Paul Roberts, *The End of Oil*, 298.

14. Cited in Paul Roberts, *The End of Oil*, 301.

15. September 21, 2003.

16. Cited in *New York Times*, April 17, 2006.

17. *New York Times Book Review*, May 30, 2004, 32.

18. Cited in *International Herald Tribune*, March 26, 2005.

19. Howard Geller, *Energy Revolution: Policies for a Sustainable Future* (Washington, D.C.: Island Press, 2003), 38.

20. *Foreign Affairs*, March–April 2006, 78; *Financial Times*, April 28, 2006.

21. BP Solar's latest plan was to build 278 small solar power plants in Spain by 2008 to supply power to 12,500 homes. *Guardian*, April 22, 2006.

22. Ibid., February 14, 2006.

23. Cited in *New York Times*, April 17, 2006.

24. February 17, 2003.

25. *Observer*, December 11, 2005; *Guardian*, February 28, 2006.

26. *Financial Times*, October 31, 2005; *Observer*, December 11, 1005; *Guardian*, December 22, 2005.

27. Cited in *New York Times*, April 17, 2006. The leaked draft of the fourth report of the IPCC Working Group pointed to "decisive new evidence" that the rising temperatures recorded over the past fifty years were the result of human activity and not natural variation. *The Times*, May 4, 2006.

28. *International Herald Tribune*, March 26, 2005.

29. Paul Roberts, *The End of Oil*, 135.

30. It transpired that George Deutsch had inflated his résumé, and this revelation led to his quitting the job.

31. *Guardian*, August 11, 2005.

32. Ibid., December 21, 2005.

33. *New York Times*, November 1, 2005. Between 1950 and 2000, total annual carbon emissions measured rose more than fourfold, from 1.3 billion tonnes to 7 billion tonnes, whereas in the earlier half century, the total had only doubled, from 0.7 billion tonnes to 1.3 billion tonnes.

34. *Guardian*, March 24, 2006.

35. *Observer Magazine*, December 18, 2005, 35; *Observer*, November 20, 2005; Associated Press, May 2, 2006.

36. *Independent*, February 17, 2006.

37. *Guardian*, November 25, 2005.

38. November 24, 2005.

39. *New York Times*, March 21, 2006.

40. Vaclav Smil, *Energy at the Crossroads: Global Perspectives and Uncertainties* (Cambridge, MA: MIT Press, 2003), 36 and 84.

41. *In These Times*, February 7, 2000, 14.

42. Ibid.; *International Herald Tribune,* March 26, 2005.
43. The IPCC's fourth report was expected to say that new computer models predict a rise of 11 degrees Celsius instead of the previous 1.5 to 5.8 degrees Celsius by the end of the current century.
44. *Guardian,* April 15, 2006 and April 21, 2006.
45. The EU's energy mix was oil, 49 percent; gas, 23 percent; nuclear, 16 percent; coal, 16 percent; and renewables, 6 percent. *International Herald Tribune,* December 9, 2002.
46. December 9, 2002.
47. Cited in *Guardian,* February 26, 2005.
48. The figure will double by 2010.
49. Germany's energy mix was oil, 37 percent (all imported, a third from Russia); gas, 23 percent (80 percent imported, half of it from Russia); coal, 22 percent (about a fifth imported); nuclear, 12 percent; and renewable, 6 percent. *International Herald Tribune,* April 7, 2006.
50. *Independent,* March 24, 2004.
51. Cited in *International Herald Tribune,* February 26–27, 2005.
52. *The Hindu,* March 16, 2006.
53. *Guardian,* October 31, 2005; *Independent,* December 6, 2005.
54. For the full text of the report, visit www.harbour.sfu.ca/dlam/newsletters/0004.html.
55. Cited in *Guardian,* October 31, 2005, and April 21, 2006. By 2020, China may become the world's largest producer of greenhouse gases.
56. *Guardian,* November 8, 2005; *The Hindu,* March 16, 2006.

Chapter 12
1. Cited in *New York Times Magazine,* August 22, 2005, 7.
2. *BP Statistical Review of World Energy,* June 2006, 11.
3. Cited in *New York Times,* February 18, 2005.
4. *Los Angeles Times,* October 2, 2000.
5. *Pioneer,* March 12, 2006.
6. Howard Zinn, *A People's History of the United States: 1492–Present,* 301.
7. Henry Kissinger, *Years of Upheaval* (Boston: Little, Brown and Company, 1982), 862.
8. *International Herald Tribune,* April 6, 2006. Rice seemed unfamiliar with the widely quoted statement by a top State Department official in August 1945: "A review of the diplomatic history of the past thirty-five years will show that petroleum has historically played a larger part in the external relations of the United States than any other commodity." See chapter 4, p. 89.
9. *New York Times,* May 7, 2006. Most of the Western oil companies' full access was limited to North America.
10. In 2020 the Persian Gulf region will produce 56 million bpd and consume only 9 million bpd.
11. Arthur J. Arberry, *The Koran Interpreted,* Oxford University Press, Oxford and New York, 1964.
12. *Guardian,* September 17, 2005. Using the purchasing-power parity method, the CIA in 2004 ranked the Chinese GDP as the second largest in the world,

about 62 percent of the American and 1.94 times Japan's, the third largest. *New York Times*, July 20, 2005.

13. The amount of natural gas crossing oceans as LNG will triple to 460 million tons by 2020. *Foreign Affairs*, March–April 2006, 79.

14. *Observer*, April 30, 2006.

15. Reuters, June 7, 2006; *Financial Times*, June 8, 2006.

16. *Foreign Affairs*, March–April 2006, 69.

17. Associated Press, February 25, 2006.

18. *Guardian*, May 18, 2006.

19. Ibid., June 2, 2006.

20. Ibid., May 11, 2006.

21. Mercury News, June 15, 2006; *Financial Times*, June 16, 2006; *Guardian*, June 20, 2006. India had lobbied hard through Russia to be accorded observer status at the SCO.

22. Chevron claimed that by using steam flooding to extract heavy oil, it had recovered 1.3 billion barrels of oil from one field alone. A Chevron advertisement on January 16, 2006.

23. *Boston Globe*, May 14, 2006.

24. *New York Times Magazine*, May 29, 2006. Worldwide, more than 1,000 coal-fired power stations were being planned in 2006.

25. The EU will pay 40 percent of the cost and the remaining six signatories 10 percent each. Bloomberg, May 22, 2006; Associated Press, May 29, 2006.

26. Associated Press, May 22, 2006.

27. *Guardian*, March 21, 2006. A WhisperGen boiler costing £3,000 also generates electricity. And a quiet, low-visibility rooftop wind turbine costs £1,500 Both devices sell any surplus electricity to the grid.

28. Of the $12.3 billion provided in the 2005 U.S. Energy Policy Act, $4.3 billion was allocated to nuclear power, $3.6 billion to energy conservation measures and incentives to renewable energy, $2.9 billion to the coal industry, and $1.5 billion to oil and gas companies.

29. *The End of Oil*, 288–89.

30. Researchers have also found that the warmer the planet gets, the more CO_2 gets released naturally by soil and oceans. *Guardian*, May 23, 2006; *Metro*, May 23, 2006.

Chronology

1846: The first modern oil well is drilled near Baku, Azerbaijan, by Russian engineer Fyodor Semyonov

1848: News of Semyonov's achievement reaches the czar's court in Moscow and is given official recognition

1858: The first commercial oil well is drilled in North America—in Oil Springs, Ontario, in Canada—by James Miller Williams

1859: The first commercial oil well is drilled in the United States in Titusville, Pennsylvania

1860: Etienne Lenoir in France invents an internal combustion engine

1861: Nikolaus Otto in Germany invents a gasoline-fueled internal combustion engine

1867: The first successful discovery of oil in Asia is at Nahorpung in the northeastern region of Assam in India

1870: John Davison Rockefeller establishes Standard Oil Company

1877: The practice of replacing coal with oil as fuel to power steamships originates in the Caspian's Baku region when the Nobel brothers build the world's first oil-fueled steamship; for the first time oil is transported by a pipeline of wood from Baku to the Black Sea coast of Georgia

1882: Carl Benz in Germany runs the first automobile with an internal combustion engine

1888: Charles Francis Brush, an American scientist, builds the first wind turbine for generating electricity

1895: George Selden in the United States secures a patent for a car run on gasoline

1896: John Ford produces his first motor car

1898: The Rothschild brothers launch the first oil tanker, which plies the Caspian Sea

1900: · Worldwide demand for oil reaches 500,000 bpd

1901: Azerbaijan, which outpaces the United States in annual oil output by 11.5 million tons to 9.1 million tons, is producing more than half of the global supply. A gusher at Spindletop, Texas, starts a boom in the American oil industry. Muzaffar al Din Shah Qajar of Iran gives an oil concession to British entrepreneur William Knox D'Arcy

1905:   Henry Ford markets the Model T car in the United States. The gasoline-powered car has defeated its rivals run by steam or electricity

1907:   The first successful oil well in China is drilled near the north-western city of Yunan

1908:   The first continuously flowing oil well is drilled in the Middle East at Masjid-e Suleiman in Iran. With reserves of more than one billion barrels, it becomes the fourth such field in the world. Cargo ship owners in the United States switch from coal to oil

1910:   German and American corporations pioneer commercial petrochemical products by using as feedstock a tar produced as a by-product from the chemical treatment of coal

1910:   Ordered by Kaiser Wilhelm II, the German Navy starts switching to oil to power its warships

1911:   The U.S. antitrust laws break up John Davison Rockefeller's Standard Oil into thirty-seven independent companies, while the Rockefeller interests retain substantial shareholding in all of them

1912:   As the first lord of the British admiralty, Winston Churchill orders the building of a fleet of oil-fueled warships

1913:   One million gasoline-powered vehicles are on the road in the United States and Europe

1914:   World War I breaks out

1915:   The process of lifting oil with injected gas is tested successfully when deep pumps are submerged in an oil field in the Baku region. Global oil demand reaches 1.25 million bpd

1917:   With the United States' entry into World War I, its output of 920,000 bpd amounts to two-thirds of the global total

1918:   World War I ends with the defeat of Germany, Austria-Hungary, and the Ottoman Empire

1923:   German scientists Franz Fischer and Hans Tropsch patent a process to transform coal into liquid fuel

1927:   Oil is struck in Iraq near Kirkuk

1929:   The global oil demand is 4 million bpd

1931:   Due to the Depression, the oil price collapses. In the United States, the governor of Oklahoma sends state troops to shut down oil wells and the governor of Texas closes the eastern Texas oil fields

1932:   Oil is found in Bahrain

1933:   U.S. president Franklin D. Roosevelt appoints Harold Ickes as interior secretary with a mandate to bring order to the oil industry. He decides to reduce national output by 300,000 bpd

1935:   The United States produces 64 percent of global oil needs, with six other countries jointly producing half as much

1938:   Oil is struck at Burgan in Kuwait, with the field turning out to be the largest so far in the world. Oil is found in Saudi Arabia's Dammam region. Mexico nationalizes its oil industry. German scientists Otto Hahn, Lise Meitner, and Fritz Strassman conduct the first successful experiment with nuclear fission

1939:   World War II starts

1941:   Russell Ohl, a scientist at Bell Telephone laboratory, invents a silicon solar cell

1942: Enrico Fermi achieves a self-sustaining nuclear chain reaction at the University of Chicago
1943: President Roosevelt declares that Saudi Arabia is vital to U.S. security and provides it with financial aid
1945: In February, Saudi king Ibn Saud meets Roosevelt aboard an American cruiser in the Suez Canal. In August, World War II ends with the defeat of the Axis Powers. Global oil demand hits 6 million bpd
1946: The United States consumes more oil than it produces. U.S. president Harry Truman establishes the United States Atomic Energy Commission to foster and control peacetime development of atomic energy
1947: Venezuela's new law requires the oil companies to pay half of their profits as tax. Middle Eastern oil-producing countries follow suit
1948–50: The fully discovered Ghawar oil field in Saudi Arabia is the largest in the world, with reserves of eighty-seven billion barrels
1949: Defeating their nationalist opponents, the Chinese Communists establish the People's Republic of China. Oil and gas produce only 1 percent of energy
1950: The world oil output is 10.4 million bpd
1951: The National Reactor Testing Station in Idaho produces usable electricity from nuclear fission
1951–53: The Iranian oil nationalization crisis results in the flight of the shah of Iran and his restitution following a coup engineered by the CIA
1953: In his "Atoms for Peace" speech, U.S. president Dwight Eisenhower proposes international cooperation to develop peaceful applications of nuclear energy
1954: The Soviet Union builds the first nuclear power plant at Obillioninsk
Mid-1950s: West Texas Intermediate (WTI)—intermediate between light and heavy oil—becomes the accepted international benchmark
1955: The seven-year-old apartheid regime in South Africa establishes South Africa Synthetic Oil Ltd (Sasol) in 1955 to use synfuel technology to convert coal into petroleum products, including diesel
1956: When the troika of Britain-France-Israel invades Egypt in October 1956, the Egyptians block the Suez Canal, thus cutting off oil supplies to western Europe from the Persian Gulf
1957: Egyptian president Gamal Abdul Nasser convenes a conclave of Arab oil experts in Cairo. The United Nations establishes the International Atomic Energy Agency (IAEA) to encourage the peaceful use of atomic energy. The first industrial accident occurs at Britain's Windscale (later renamed Sellafield) nuclear reactor, when its graphite core catches fire and spills radiation into the environment
1958: The Soviet Union enters the international petroleum market by supplying oil at low prices
1959: Egypt convenes the Arab Petroleum Congress in Cairo
1960: OPEC is founded in Baghdad with five members. The global oil demand is 21 million bpd, with the United States accounting for a third
1962: A Proton Exchange Membrane (PEM) cell is produced by Willard Grubb and Leonard Niedrach of General Electric Corporation for the Gemini space program

1967:   In surprise attacks, Israel inflicts a quick, humiliating defeat on Egypt, Syria, and Jordan, and occupies territories in all three countries in a six-day war in June. An Arab oil embargo against the United States, Britain, and West Germany for helping Israel fails to hurt these countries since the United States has a spare capacity to supply Britain and West Germany. The Arabs end the boycott in August

1968:   The Kuwaiti ruler convenes a meeting of the rulers of Algeria, Iraq, Libya, and Saudi Arabia to form OAPEC. The seven leading Western oil corporations control 78 percent of the world's oil production, 61 percent of refining, and 56 percent of marketing facilities

1969:   Following the overthrow of monarchy in Libya, the republican regime slashes oil production

1960s: Two-thirds of the increased demand of 21 million bpd during the decade is met by the growth in oil output in the Middle East and North Africa

1970:   In the past two decades, oil output has grown 4.5 times, to 45 million bpd, and living standards in the United States and Western Europe have risen sharply. Conventional oil production in the Lower 48 reaches a peak at 11.3 million bpd

1972:   Iraq nationalizes its oil industry

1973:   The five leading Persian Gulf producers supply 36 percent of the world's oil demand

1973:   The Arab-Israeli War lasts from October 6 to 25. OAPEC imposes an embargo on oil sales to the United States and the Netherlands for helping Israel militarily. In November, Algeria raises the price of its crude from $4.80 to $9.25 a barrel; three weeks later the oil ministers of the eight Persian Gulf countries, including Iran under the shah, push the figure to $11.65 a barrel

1975:   The recession caused by the oil-price explosion lasts until the end of 1976. U.S. president Gerald Ford implements the Corporate Average Fuel Economy (CAFE) standards as required by a congressional law to improve vehicle mileage per gallon used. Kuwait completes the nationalization of its oil industry

1976:   OPEC produces more than half of the global output and provides seven-eighths of the exports. Qatar completes the nationalization of its petroleum industry

1979:   Following the overthrow of the Iranian shah, an Islamic regime is established in Iran. U.S. president Jimmy Carter sets up a Rapid Deployment Force to protect the sea lanes in the Persian Gulf used by oil tankers. Petroleum prices rise to $38 a barrel. There is a partial core meltdown at Three Mile Island nuclear plant in Pennsylvania. The U.S. administration stops authorizing new nuclear reactors

1980:   Carter declares: "An attempt by any outside force to gain control of the Persian Gulf region will be regarded as an assault on the vital interests of the United States, and will be repelled by the use of any means necessary, including military force." Saudi Arabia completes the nationalization of its oil industry. In September Iraq invades Iran

1979–81: The Second Oil Shock causes a recession. The price of natural gas jumps from 5 cents to $3 per 1,000 cubic feet

1981: The contribution of the nuclear-fueled power plants to the national grid in the United States has risen from 4.5 percent to 20 percent

1982: Non-OPEC outpaces OPEC's output of 19 million bpd, about a third of global production

1985: The share of the five leading Gulf producers falls to 16 percent of world demand. Much of the new non-OPEC production comes from offshore and remote areas that incur high front-end investment

1986: Oil prices fall below $10 a barrel in spring, causing a virtual collapse of the oil industry in the United States and severely damaging Iran's ability to finance its war with Iraq. In April, an explosion at the Chernobyl nuclear plant in Soviet Ukraine produces a mile-high plume of radioactive particles, which drifts over 40 percent of Europe and as far away as Japan and the East Coast of the United States. In Western Europe the accelerating construction of nuclear power plants comes to a virtual halt. The Soviet Union follows Western Europe's lead

1988: The United Nations appoints the Intergovernmental Panel on Climate Change (IPCC) to study the subject. The Iran-Iraq War ends in August

1990: Iraq invades Kuwait in August. The subsequent United Nations sanctions on Iraq result in the loss of Iraqi and Kuwaiti oil to the market, spiking prices. The IPCC report warns that if greenhouse gases are not curtailed drastically over the next few decades, global temperatures will rise between 1.5 and 5.8 degrees Celsius by 2100, causing worldwide havoc

1991: The U.S.-led coalition expels the Iraqis from Kuwait. In December the Soviet Union disintegrates into its constituent republics. An experimental fusion reactor, called the Joint European Torus, built at Culham near Oxford, Britain, is ready to use fusion fuel

1992: The recession caused by the hike in oil prices results in the defeat of U.S. president George H. W. Bush. The UN Framework Convention on Climate Change at the Earth Summit requires every signatory to the convention to reduce greenhouse emissions, without specifying figures

1993: Moscow and Washington sign a twenty-year program to eliminate 500 tonnes of Russian nuclear warhead material by diluting it into nuclear fuel and selling it to utility companies in the United States. A similar program is to be implemented later in the United States

1995: Toyota introduces a "concept" automobile, powered by a hybrid engine—part gasoline, part electric. Car ownership reaches ten million in China

1997: Toyota markets its hybrid cars in Japan. In China, oil and gas produce 20 percent of all energy. In December, the UN Framework Convention on Climate Change in Kyoto, Japan, agrees that the buildup of greenhouse gases in the atmosphere over the past two centuries is almost entirely caused by the industrialized nations. It specifies a collective 4.8 percent reduction in greenhouse gas emissions by 2012 for 38 industrialized countries out of the 156 signatories

1998: The U.S. Senate refuses to ratify the Kyoto Protocol

1999: Following the bust of the "tiger" economies in East and Southeast Asia in mid-1998, the oil price collapses to below $10 a barrel in early 1999 and leads to megamergers of Western oil companies

2000: On the fortieth anniversary of its founding, OPEC is pumping 42 percent of global oil output. But its spare capacity has declined from 25 percent of the global demand in 1985 to 2 percent. In September, the oil price hits $37 a barrel. U.S. president Bill Clinton releases 1 million bpd for thirty days from the U.S. Strategic Petroleum Reserve, an unprecedented step to take in peacetime to lower prices. In Germany, the coalition government of Social Democrats and the Greens reaches an agreement with energy companies on the phased closure of nineteen nuclear power plants, producing 25 percent of electricity, by 2020

2001: Coal provides 28 percent of electric power worldwide, marginally less than the 1970s figure, the percentages varying between 20 percent in the United States and 80 percent in China. The Gas Exporting Countries Forum (GECF) is established in Doha

2002: The greenhouse emissions in tonnes per capita are the United States, 5.5; Canada, 4.5; Russia, 2.8; Britain, 2.7; Japan, 2.6; Germany, 2.5; China 0.7; and India, 0.25. Annual oil consumption in barrels per capita is the United States, 65; Canada, 59; Japan, 46; Britain, 30; Germany, 29; Russia, 16; China 4; and India, 2

2003: Of the 750 million vehicles in a world of 6.1 billion people, 231 million are in the United States, with a population of nearly 300 million. Since 1984, the number of air conditioners in China has grown fiftyfold, refrigerators tenfold, and televisions fivefold. In March the Anglo-American alliance invades and occupies Iraq, alleging that the Iraqi regime possesses weapons of mass destruction—which are not found. There are 370,000 U.S. Army troops deployed in 120 countries, including some 150,000 in Iraq, out of a total active duty force of 491,000

2004: Vauxhall puts its hydrogen cell car, Zafira, through a test run of six thousand miles. China becomes the second-largest consumer of oil in the world after the United States, producing only about a half at home. China burns a third of the world's consumption of 4.1 billion tonnes of coal. Studies show that between 1912 and 2004 alone, carbon emissions jumped sevenfold, from 1 billion tonnes a year to 7 billion tonnes

2005: In February the Kyoto Protocol becomes international law. Research shows that CO_2 has increased from 280 parts per million (ppm) to 380 ppm in two centuries, and will rise to 550 ppm by 2050 at the current rate of fossil fuel use, and that there is more CO_2 in the atmosphere now than at any time in the past 650,000 years. In India car sales reach 1 million, a fivefold increase in just over a decade, but are only 6 percent of the American figure. Article 109 of Iraq's new constitution states that hydrocarbons are "national Iraqi property"

2006: In April the oil price hits $75 a barrel. The distribution of the world's oil reserves in percentages: Persian Gulf region, 62; former Soviet Union, 10; Latin America, 10; Africa, 10; North America, 4; Asia Pacific, 4. OPEC members possess 75 percent of the total reserves, and non-OPEC 25 percent. The latest research shows that greenhouse gases not only lead to higher temperatures but are themselves increased by higher temperatures, and that global warming may be up to 78 percent worse than previously predicted

2006: California passes two laws—one requiring the greenhouse gases emission to be reduced to 1990 levels by 2020, and the other barring out-of-state utilities that fail to meet the state's standards for pollution.

Select Bibliography

BP Statistical Review of World Energy 1994 to *BP Statistical Review of World Energy 1997*.

BPAmoco Statistical Review of World Energy June 1998 to *BPAmoco Statistical Review of World Energy June 2000*.

BP Statistical Review of World Energy June 2001 to *BP Statistical Review of World Energy June 2006*.

Campbell, Colin J. *The Coming Oil Crisis*. Brentwood, UK: Multi-Science Publishing Company and Petroconsultants S.A., 1998.

Deffeyes, Kenneth S. *Hubbert's Peak: The Impending World Oil Shortage*. Princeton, NJ and Oxford, UK: Princeton University Press, 2001.

Downs, Erica. *China's Quest for Energy Security*. Santa Monica, CA: Rand Corporation, 2000.

Emerson, Steven. *The American House of Saud*. New York: Franklin Watts, 1985.

Everest, Larry. *Oil, Power and Empire*. Monroe, ME: Common Courage Press, 2004.

Freese, Barbara. *Coal: A Human History*. London: Arrow Books, 2005.

Geller, Howard. *Energy Revolution: Policies for a Sustainable Future*. Washington, D.C.: Island Press, 2003.

Goodstein, David. *Out of Gas: The End of the Age of Oil*. New York and London: W. W. Norton, 2004.

Henson, Bob. *Rough Guide to Climate Change*. London and New York: Rough Guides, 2006.

Hiro, Dilip. *Inside the Middle East*. London: Routledge & Kegan Paul, 1982/New York: McGraw Hill, 1982.

———. *Desert Shield to Desert Storm: The Second Gulf War*. London: Harper-Collins, 1991/New York: Routledge, 1992.

———. *Neighbors, Not Friends: Iraq and Iran after the Gulf Wars*. London and New York: Routledge, 2001.

———. *The Essential Middle East: A Comprehensive Guide*. New York: Carroll & Graf, 2003.

———. *Secrets and Lies: Operation "Iraqi Freedom" and After*. New York: Nation Books, 2004/*Secrets and Lies: The True Story of the Iraq War*. London: Politico's Publishing, 2005.

———. *The Iranian Labyrinth: Journeys through Theocratic Iran and Its Furies*. New York: Nation Books, 2005/*Iran Today*. London: Politico's Publishing, 2006.

Holden, David, and Richard Johns. *The House of Saud*, London: Sidgwick and Jackson, 1981.

Keating, Aileen. *Mirage: Power, Politics and the Hidden History of Arabian Oil*. Amherst, New York: Prometheus Books, 2005.

Klare, Michael. *Blood and Oil: The Dangers and Consequences of America's Growing Petroleum Dependency*. New York: Metropolitan Books, 2004/ London: Penguin Books, 2004.

Lacey, Robert. *The Kingdom*. London: Hutchinson, 1981.

Leggett, Jeremy. *Half Gone: Oil, Gas, Hot Air and the Global Energy Crisis*. London: Portobello Books, 2006.

Olien, Roger. *Black Gold: The Story of Texas Oil and Gas*. San Antonio, TX: Historical Publishing Network, 2004.

Roberts, Paul. *The End of Oil: On the Edge of a Perilous World*. New York: Houghton Mifflin, 2004/London: Bloomsbury, 2004.

Smil, Vaclav. *Energy at the Crossroads: Global Perspectives and Uncertainties*. Cambridge, MA: MIT Press, 2003.

Unger, Craig. *House of Bush, House of Saud: The Secret Relationship between the World's Two Most Powerful Dynasties*. New York: Scribner, 2003/ London: Gibson Square Books, 2004.

Woodward, Bob. *The Commanders*. New York and London: Simon & Schuster, 1991.

———. *Plan of Attack*. New York and London: Simon & Schuster, 2004.

Yeomans, Matthew. *Oil: Anatomy of an Industry*. New York and London: The New Press, 2004.

Yergin, Daniel. *The Prize: The Epic Quest for Oil, Money and Power*. New York and London: Simon and Schuster, 1991.

Index

For a name starting with Al, El, or The, see its second part. A person's religious or secular title has been omitted. For a monarch, see his first name; for other hereditary rulers, see the family name.

bedouin, 28
Beijing, 198, 202, 327
Bekran, Muhammad, 6
Belarus, 245, 255, 256
Belgium, 258
Bennett, Robin, 160, 161
Benz, Otto, 332
benzene, 49
Berenger, Henry G., xiv, 78
Berlin, 1991, 246, 253
BG, 251
Bharat Petroleum, 216, 219, 224
Bharatiya Janata Party, 218
Bible, xiii, 4
Bibi Heybat Bay, 6, 7
Big Oil, 211, 304, 344, *see also* Oil majors
Al Bilad (Company), 113
Bilkadi, Z., 4
bin Laden, Osama, 129, 140
bin Sulayem, Sultan Ahmad, 186
biofuels, xvii, xli, 306, 324
biogas plants, 326
Bishkek, 207, 210
bitumen, xlii, 4, 46, 49, 332
Black City, 12
Black Sea, 11, 39, 43
Blessit, Arthur, xxxviii
Blix, Hans, 135
BMW (Company), 287
Bodman, Samuel, xli, 263, 314
Boiling Point: How Politics, Big Coal, Big Oil, Journalists and Activists Have Fueled the Climate Crisis, 301
Bolivar, Simon, 181
Bolivarianism, 181
Bolivia, 175, 181, 243, 351
Bolshevik Revolution, 7, 12, 151
Bombay, 228, 229, 230
Bombay High oil and gas field, 215–16, 218, 220, 250
Book of Daniel, 4
Bosporus, 158
Bow Valley Company, 133
Bowen, Stuart, 147
Boykoff, Jules, 301
Boykoff, Maxwell, 301
BP, 33, 62, 99, 133–34, 160, 161, 239, 245, 252, 285, 304, 305–06, 313
BPAmoco, 133, 157, 166
BP Solar, 305
Bradford, Peter, 264
Brady, Bruce, xviii, xxviii–xxix, 66, 67, 242

Brando, Marlon, xxiii
Brazil, 67, 156, 175, 314, 318, 344
Bremer, Paul, 145, 146
Brent oil, 115, 222, 291
Britain and British, xviii, xxx, xxxi, 31, 75, 228, 323, 331; and climate change, 258, 296; coal in, 268, 269, 324; electricity generation in, 249, 250, 251, 259,324; and France, 75, 76, 79, 98; and Germany, 75–76; as imperialist power, 213, 335; Indian Empire of, 213, 335; and Iran, 72–73, 76, 83–84, 85, 91, 93–94, 97–98; and Iraq, 75–76, 85; and Israel, 98; and Mexico, 81; and natural gas, 250–51; and nuclear power, 253, 254, 258–63, 324; oil and gas industry of, 54, 123, 125; and oil lobby, 334–35; and renewable energy, 321–24, 356; and Saudi Arabia, 28–29, 84–85, 87–88, 111; and wind power, 321–22; and United States, 24, 26, 76, 84–85, 87, 93–96, 98, 120, 142
British Asia Company, 187
British National Oil Company, 123
British Nuclear Fuel Limited, 261
British Petroleum, 45, 154, 338
Bromley, Carl, xviii
Brower, David, 38
Brown, Gordon, 295
Brown, Lester, 294
Browne, John, 243
Brush, Charles Francis, 318
BTC pipeline, *see* Baku-Tbilisi- CEyhan pipeline
al Buainain, Juma Ali, xviii, xxxi–xxxii, 65
Bulgaria, 245
Bundnis, 90, 257
Burgan oil field, 25–27, 43, 44, 57, 67
Burma, 213, 214, *see also* Myanmar
Burmah Oil Company (BOC), 18–19, 20, 74–75, 213–14
Burmah Shell Refineries, 216
Bush, Barbara, xx, xxii
Bush, George Herbert Walker, xix, xx, 143; biography of, xxi–xxiii, xxxv–xxxvi, 16; links with Arab Gulf super-rich, xxxix, 114; and Kuwait Crisis and 1991 Gulf War, 127–28, 130, 342; as President, xxxviii, 127–28, 129, 209; as Vice President, xxxvii, xxxviii, 125–26
Bush, George Walker, xiv, xxi, xxiii, 53, 125, 146, 275, 292, 300, 351; as an alcoholic,

199–201, 203, 247, 248, 347–48; and Iraq, 131–32, 197; and Japan, 206; and Kazakhstan, 165, 166, 201–03, 348; and NATO, 192; and Myanmar, 205–06, 221, 227; and natural gas, 187, 190, 191, 196, 198, 200, 205; oil imports and consumption, 190–92, 195–96, 207, 331, 342; oil industry in, 5, 65, 186, 187–91, 193–94, 195–96, 303; and Nigeria, 175, 203, 205; nuclear power in, 254, 262, 266; and pollution, 326–28; and Persian Gulf region, 184, 185–86, 196–98, 203, 204; and renewable energy, 329; and Russia, 170, 194, 205, 207–08, 348, 352; and Saudi Arabia, 197–99, 203, 224; and Shanghai Cooperation Organization, 201, 207, 210; and Soviet Union, 187–88, 207; student protest in, 190; and Sudan, 191, 203, 204; and synfuel, 272; and United States, 192, 207, 208–11, 226; and Uzbekistan, 210–11; and Venezuela, 182

China Council for International Cooperation on the Environment and Development, 328

China National Offshore Oil Company (Cnooc), 189, 190, 205, 208–09

China National Petrochemical Corporation (Sinopec), *see* Sinopec

China National Petroleum Corporation (CNPC), 131–32, 166, 182, 189–91, 200, 201, 203, 204, 205, 342, 348

The China Syndrome, 254

Chirac, Jacques, 264, 265

Chivers, C. J., 163–64

Chula Vista, 64

Churchill, Winston, 22, 37, 71, 72, 75, 76, 87, 89

Citgo, 180

Citigroup, 333

Clean Development Mechanism. (CDM) 296

cleaning agents, 47

climate change, xvii, 258–59, 260, 269, 288, 289, 293–94, 296, 301–302, 306, 309–10, 313, 356;

Clinton, Bill, 129, 136, 152, 154, 155, 192, 209, 247, 274, 285, 295, 298, 342–43

coal, xiii, xvi–xvii, 251, 267–69; chemical composition of, 267; and climate change, 269; decarbonizing of, 270–71, 314; economics of, 45; history of,

31–32, 44, 268–69; in Western Europe, 44–45, 103, 333; electricity generation by, 268, 324, 354;

coal tar, 35, 47

Cold War (1946–91), 131

Collins, John M., 117

Colombia, 156, 175–76, 181, 344

The Coming Oil Crisis, 31, 55

Comité Generale du Pétrole, xiv, 78

Committee on International Petroleum Policy (U.S.), 86

Communist Party of China (CPC), 187, 188, 193, 203, 326

Compagnie, Française des Pétroles, 21, 79, 97, 335

Competitive Enterprise Institute (U.S.), 301

Concession Syndicate, 19, 20, 74, 76

Congo, 203

Congress Party (India), 216, 217, 221

Congress (I) Party (India), 215

Conheeney, John, 109

Connaughton, James, 310

Conservative Party (U.K.), 274

Contras, 120

Cooney, Phil, 301

Corsicana, 13

Corley, T. A. B., 74

Cornplanter, 8

Corporate Average Fuel Economy (CAFE) standards, 112–13, 126, 275, 276, 278

Cotte, Edouard, 18

Courbevoie, 134

Crawford, xix, xxxx, xxxvi, 142

Cretaceous Age, 43

Cuba, 135, 179, 180, 227

Culham, 355

Curzon (British Lord), 78

Czech Republic, 245

D

Dahan, Rene, 316

Daimler cars, 285

Daimler-Benz, 285

Daimler-Chrysler, 275, 286

Dallas, xxxvii, 125

Dammam, 30,

Dammam Number 7 oil well, 30, 31

Daqing oil field, 188, 196, 206

D'Arcy, William Knox, 17, 18, 19, 71, 72, 73, 74, 334–35

Darfur, 204

Defense Intelligence Agency (U.S.), 119, 137

About the Author

Born in the Indian subcontinent, DILIP HIRO was educated in India, Britain, and the United States, where he received his Master's degree at Virginia Polytechnic Institute and State University. He then settled in London in the mid-1960s, and became a full-time writer, journalist and commentator. His articles have appeared in the *New York Times, Washington Post, Los Angeles Times, Wall Street Journal, Boston Globe, Toronto Star, International Herald Tribune, The Nation, Economist, Guardian, Observer, Sunday Times, Independent, Independent on Sunday, Times Literary Supplement, New Statesman,* and *Spectator.*

He is a frequent commentator on Middle Eastern, Central Asian, and Islamic Affairs on such British and North American broadcasting channels as CNN, Fox News, NBC TV, ABC TV, C-SPAN, CBC (Canada), BBC News, BBC World, News-24, Sky News, National Public Radio (U.S.), Pacifica Radio Network (U.S.), Democracy Now!, BBC World Service Radio, and BBC Radios Four and Five.